# La Raza Unida Party

*A Chicano Challenge to the U.S. Two-Party Dictatorship*

# La Raza Unida Party

A Chicano Challenge to the
U.S. Two-Party Dictatorship

Armando Navarro

TEMPLE UNIVERSITY PRESS

PHILADELPHIA

Temple University Press, Philadelphia 19122
Copyright © 2000 by Temple University
All rights reserved
Published 2000
Printed in the United States of America

⊗ The paper used in this publication meets the requirements of
the American National Standard for Information Sciences—Permanence of
Paper for Printed Library Materials, ANSI z39.48–1984

Library of Congress Cataloging-in-Publication Data

Navarro, Armando, 1941–
La Raza Unida Party: a Chicano challenge to the U.S. two-party dictatorship /
 Armando Navarro.
     p. cm.
   Includes bibliographical references (p. ) and index.
   ISBN 1–56639-770–7 (cloth : alk.paper) —ISBN 1–56639-771–5 (paper : alk. paper)
   1. Raza Unida Party (U.S.)   2. Mexican Americans—Politics and government.
   I. Title.
 JK2391.R39 N38   2000
 324.273'8—dc21

                                                          99–054861

I dedicate this book to my daughter Marie Antonette and sons Armando III, Miguel Antonio, Orlando, and Xavier as a token of my gratitude and love for their support and understanding. *Gracias por Todo y Que Dios Me Los Bendiga.*

# Contents

Photographs follow page 172

# Preface

From the womb of the Chicano Movement's militancy and protest, a Chicano third-party movement was conceived. After four years of struggles over land grants, farm worker rights, education, police brutality, and the Vietnam War, Chicano activists broadened their social-change agenda to include the people's political empowerment. In 1970, two major leaders of the Chicano Movement, José Angel Gutiérrez in Texas and Rodolfo "Corky" Gonzales in Colorado, led the crusade to organize the first Chicano political party—La Raza Unida. Believing the Democrat and Republican Parties did not represent the interests of Méxicanos, activists inspired by RUP's early successes in Texas and by Gonzales's call for a *partido* (party) joined in the partido experiment, which lasted eleven years. Thus, from 1970 to 1981, from California to Texas to the Midwest, RUP was a defiant third party struggling against the country's two-party dictatorship.

This book is a comprehensive examination of the political history of RUP's rise and decline throughout the Southwest and Midwest. It is part of a four-volume series on the Chicano Movement and on the building of a new movement, a "quadrilogy" of interrelated books. The first, *Mexican American Youth Organization: Avant-Garde of the Chicano Movement in Texas* (1995), is an in-depth case study of the rise and demise of the Mexican American Youth Organization from 1967 to 1972. The second, *The Cristal Experiment: A Chicano Struggle for Community Control* (1998) is an in-depth case study of the first (1963) and particularly the second (1970) Méxicano electoral takeovers, or revolts, in Crystal City, Texas. The third is this one. The fourth, whose working title is *What Needs To Be Done: The Building of a New Movement,* is a theoretical work on the strategic options of building a new movement that includes a new partido in the twenty-first century.

This case study is the most comprehensive political history of RUP to date, from its emergence in 1970 to its demise in 1981. The existing literature specifically on RUP is extremely limited. Two early works are Richard Santillan's *La Raza Unida* (1973) and John Staples Shockley's *Chicano Revolt in a Texas Town* (1974). The former provides a cursory examination of RUP in the Southwest, while the latter is a case study of the first three years (1970–1973) of RUP's political takeover of Crystal City, Texas. A few other works on the Chicano Movement include a chapter or two on RUP: Tony Castro, *Chicano Power: The Emergence of Mexican America* (1974); Carlos Muñoz, *Youth, Identity, Power: The Chicano Movement* (1989); and F. Arturo Rosales, *Chicano! The History of the Mexican American Civil Rights Movement* (1996). Méxicano historians such as Rodolfo Acuña, Juan Gómez Quinoñez, John Chavez, Matt S. Meier, and Feliciano Ribera provide terse accounts of RUP's rise and fall. Historian Ignacio Garcia, in his work *United We Win: The Rise and Fall of the Raza Unida Party* (1989), was the first scholar to provide a more complete historical account of RUP's development.

The introduction to this book provides a theoretical and historical framework for third parties. Over the next ten chapters, I examine the events, leaders, ideology, structure, strategy and tactics, changes effected, organizing problems, issues, and electoral campaigns that shaped RUP's genesis and demise in California, Texas, Colorado, New Mexico, Arizona, Utah, and the Midwest. In the last two chapters, I look at RUP's national and international politics and its profile as a political party. In the epilogue, I offer several arguments as to why Latinos need to struggle to effect change within the liberal capitalist system, four strategic partido options, and make the call for the creation of a New Movement.

## Research Methods

I have relied on both primary and secondary sources. Specifically, I used three methods: in-depth interviews, document content analysis, and participant-observations. My main source was 56 in-depth interviews conducted with the RUP leaders and organizers. Although the research began in 1974 while I was a professor at the University of Utah, the divisions and power struggles within RUP caused me to suspend my research, although at the time I had secured 10 in-depth interviews with various RUP leaders from California and Texas.

Specifically for this study, I conducted 56 additional interviews during 1996 and 1997, which complemented the 10 collected during 1974 and 1975. The 95 in-depth interviews conducted for my previous two books brought the total to 171 interviews that covered various aspects of the Mexican American Youth Organization's RUP development. For the 1996 and 1997 interviews, to identify the RUP's influential persons and leaders, I used a combination of the "positional" (which identifies influential individuals by the position they hold) and "reputational" (which identifies influential individuals according to their reputation) methods used by social scientists in conducting power structure research. My purpose was to secure not a scientific sample but a cross section of RUP's main leaders.

Since I was one of the major organizers of RUP in California and was generally cognizant of who held what leadership positions within the partido, I used the positional method first. RUP's two past national chairpersons, several state chairpersons, state candidates, and several county chairs were interviewed. Then, using the reputational method, I asked each positional leader to identify five others who were important RUP leaders in their respective areas and states. I ranked the leaders identified from one to five. The top five for the state (or area, as was the case with the Midwest) were interviewed. Most of the interviews were conducted on site, although I conducted several extensive interviews by phone, especially those of leaders from the Midwest. Because of the extensive RUP organizing activity in Texas, California, and Colorado, in those states I interviewed several more than the five leaders identified by positional leaders, but I did not interview all the county or local leaders.

Money and time determined who I interviewed and the number of interviews per state, region, and community. Although I traveled to Colorado with the specific intent of interviewing Rodolfo "Corky" Gonzales, I was unable to do so because he was ill. I did, however, interview José Angel Gutiérrez at length, since he graciously gave me many hours of interview time. Even though I was not able to interview others who also played important leadership roles, I feel comfortable in saying that I interviewed a good cross-section of RUP's main leadership. Each of the interviews I conducted lasted a minimum of two hours.

My second research method was the content analysis of other primary sources (e.g., documents, letters, minutes, diaries, position papers) and of secondary sources (e.g., newspaper and magazine articles, campaign literature, books, journal articles). I conducted archival research in Crystal City, Texas, in 1973 at the local library, where I had access to José Angel Gutiérrez's personal files. Between 1994 and 1997, I continued my archival research at the University of Texas, Austin and San Antonio; University of Arizona, Tucson; University of New Mexico, Albuquerque; University of California, Los Angeles, Berkeley, and Riverside; as well as at local libraries in the cities I visited. I also consulted my own archives.

Third, I relied on participant observation as well as on my own experiences as a RUP organizer in San Bernardino and Riverside Counties. In addition, I was a participant observer while I lived for four months, from March to June 1973, in Crystal City, Texas. There, I had the opportunity to experience RUP's peaceful revolution firsthand. I also made several trips to Crystal City between 1974 and 1975 and again in 1995 for two weeks of additional research. From 1971 to 1973, I participated in numerous RUP meetings and conferences, including the El Paso, Texas, national convention. From 1970 to 1972, I was one of RUP's main organizers in Southern California (see Chapter Five). My role within the partido gave me access to many of its leaders and contributed significantly to the analyses and conclusions that appear in this book.

# Acknowledgments

This work is a cumulative project of years of research and personal activism; therefore, I am indebted to a number of people for their inspiration and assistance, invaluable to the completion of this study. I want to acknowledge specifically all those who participated in the organizing of the Raza Unida Party. Without their leadership, commitment, sacrifice, courage, and determination to extricate our people from what I call in this book the tyranny of the Democratic and Republican Parties, this book and others as well would have never been written. To José Angel Gutiérrez and Rodolfo Corky Gonzales, I want to say *gracias* for the leadership you provided both Raza Unida Party and El Movimiento Chicano and for being an inspiration to me and countless other activists.

To the fifty-six RUP leaders I interviewed extensively, I want to extend my most gracious thanks for their time, cooperation, and assistance. In particular, I would like to thank José Angel Gutiérrez, Juan José Peña, Mario Compean, Viviana Santiago, Fred Aguilar, Luz Gutiérrez, Alberto Luera, Xenaro Ayala, Ernesto Vigil, Herman Baca, Ernesto Chacon, and Salomon Baldenegro for their guidance and insights, which were helpful in conducting and completing my research. My gratitude also goes to the ninety-five persons I interviewed for my two earlier books.

I would like to acknowledge and thank those individuals who directly assisted in the preparation of the book manuscript and in the conduct of my research. I want to extend my most indebted thanks to Maria Anna Gonzales for assisting in the archival research as well as her arduous and meticulous editing, which greatly strengthened the quality of both the analysis and content of the book. I also want to acknowledge Bobbe Needham for the superb job she did in editing the final draft. Also, my thanks to Marcella Ruiz for transcribing the interviews, Pam Norman for assisting in the editing of the first draft manuscript, and my research assistants, Rina Gonzales and José Perez, who assisted in the archival research. It is important that I also recognize the following students, who did research on some aspect of the Raza Unida Party: Laura Araujo, Steven Benavides, Lilia Garcia, Waunetah Goins, Andrea Henson, Kate Lee, Katricia Lee, Jayne Liera, Corina McGraw, Roberto Tijerina, Damien Tryon, Brandon Woods, and Jorge Avila. I would be remiss if I did not also thank Jean Middleton who did the indexing.

In addition, I want to thank Professor Rodolfo Acuña and scholar Ernesto Vigil for reviewing the manuscript and making important and incisive recommendations that greatly improved the book's scholarship quality and content. My thanks also to political scientists Carlos Muñoz and Mario Barrera for having taken time from their busy schedules to edit and make suggestions on the introduction. At the University of California, Riverside, I thank for their moral support Dean Carlos Velez-Ibañez of the College of Humanities, Arts, and Social Sciences. I also want to thank the University of California, Riverside, Ernesto Galarza Public Policy and Humanities Research Bureau and the Academic Senate for the grants that allowed me to conduct my research.

Last but not least, I want to acknowledge the love, support, and guidance given to me by my parents, Silvestre and Altagracia Navarro. I want to also thank for their support my brother, Alfonso, and sisters Gloria, Delia, and Lydia; my children, to whom I have dedicated this book; my grandchildren Anthony, Marcella, Cynthia, Alyssa, Brittany, and Alejandra; and my nieces and nephews. To my fellow activists and scholars, I extend my most gracious appreciation for inspiring me to try to make a difference in bettering the lives of our people during this short journey called life. *Gracias!*

# Introduction

---

# Third-Party Movements:
# A Theoretical and Historical
# Framework

Third parties have colored the political landscape of the United States since the 1820s. Their raison d'être has been rooted in their disenchantment with the politics of the dominant two parties. Although political scientists debate their impact and efficacy, few disagree that third parties have acted as safety valves for the discontent of some alienated constituencies of the electorate at both the state and federal levels. Third parties have always been the David battling the Goliath of the nation's monolithic two-party system. Unlike David, third parties have usually lost the battle, at least at the ballot box.

The reality is that since the emergence of the present two-party system in 1856, no third party, with the exception of Theodore Roosevelt's Bull Moose Party in 1912, has ever posed a serious threat to the hegemony of the Democratic and Republican Parties. Nonetheless, third parties have played a significant role in the nation's political marketplace. They have struggled to democratize a political system that purports to be democratic, but that in practice has always been a two-party monopoly.

Until Chicanos founded the Raza Unida Party in 1970, no ethnic group had ever broken out of the system to form its own political third party. This introduction provides a framework for examining that party, which is the primary focus of this bookcase study.[1]

### Political Parties in the United States:
### Origins, Definitions, and Variations

Political parties are relatively young institutions. They are products of the seventeenth and eighteenth centuries, a consequence of the political changes in the West. The collapse of aristocratic society, the emergence of struggles for social and political egalitarianism, and the development of political ideologies, especially classical liberalism, all contributed to a political climate propitious for the development of political parties. Yet they did not emerge without a struggle. For some time after the first stirrings of egalitarianism in the seventeenth century, philosophers and politicians had difficulty with the idea of political parties having a legitimate role. To English political theorist and leader Henry St. John, Viscount Bolingbroke, parties were "a political evil."[2] He equated them with special interests, whose endless squabbles would threaten national welfare and the common good.[3]

Before the nineteenth century, only one political theorist had defended political parties as intrinsic to the development of representative government: English politician and philosopher Edmund Burke (1729–1797). Burke believed that political parties would help organize the nation's diverse interests for purposes of developing public policy: ."[A] party is a body of men united, for promoting by their joint endeavors the national interests, upon some particular principle in which they all agree."[4] In short, he viewed parties as the connection between the governed and the government. The debate on the vices and virtues of parties resulted in the emergence of a quasi-two-party system made up of the Tories and the Whigs.[5] However, it was in the United States that political parties matured.

Governance in the thirteen colonies was a product of individuals who predicated their authority on their royal birth, military position, religious position, wealth, or specialized knowledge or training. With power thus vested in the hands of the few, the occasional transient oligarchy, faction, or group looked something like a political party.

Yet political parties are not mentioned in the Constitution. In fact, many of the nation's founders perceived them to be dangerous. James Madison, in Federalist Paper No.10, wrote on the need to control the potential effects of what he deemed the "violence of faction." To Madison, the most common and durable cause of factions was the unequal distribution of property.[6] President George Washington in his farewell address to Congress in 1796 warned the young nation "of the baneful effects of the spirit of party." His vice president, John Adams, concurred: "There is nothing I dread so much as the division of the Republic into two great parties, each under its own leader." Thomas Jefferson, often referred to as the father of the nation's political party system, vowed: "If I could not go to heaven but with a party, I would not go there at all."[7]

Yet, while the founders considered a party system, as Frank Sorauf explains, "an extra-constitutional excrescence not to be dignified by mention in the constitutional document," parties began to take shape. For the first century of the country's existence, competing groups clashed over economic and foreign policy issues and over the proper role of the federal government.[8] With the emergence of the Federalists and Anti-Federalists in the 1790s, the mold was cast for the nation's present two-party system, which has persevered despite several party realignments and many challenges.

Today, most traditional political scientists concur that political parties are indispensable to the maintenance of the U.S. liberal capitalist system. Political scientist E. E. Schattschneider states their case: "Political parties created democracy . . . and democracy is unthinkable save in terms of the parties."[9] To Marxists, however, political parties are weapons for revolutionary change via class struggle. For some two hundred years, and particularly during the twentieth century, political parties impelled by a myriad of ideologies have colored the political landscape not only in the United States but in most of the nations of the world.

What is a political party? The definitions in political science are plentiful and diverse, as Sorauf suggests: "As there are many roads to Rome and many ways to skin a cat there are also many ways to look at a political party."[10] Charles Chambers defined a party in the United States as multidimensional—a symbol or a name on a ballot; a psychological attachment, a national convention; a legislative caucus; a national office with staff; a loose coalition of interests, and a legal entity that selects and runs candidates.[11]

However, most political scientists concur that political parties are groups in the electoral arena that compete for control of government. Anthony Downs, for example, defines a political party as a "team of men [and women] seeking to control the governing apparatus by gaining office in a duly constituted election."[12] Dan Nimmo and Thomas D. Ungs focus on what a party does: It is "a coalition of fairly stable, enduring, and frequently conflicting interests, organized to mobilize support in competitive elections in order to control public policy."[13] Political parties can be differentiated from interest groups and other types of political entities by their functions: Parties run candidates, provide financial assistance to their candidates, organize campaigns, bring about political socialization, and formulate and advocate public policy. Most are stabilizing forces that preserve the social order.

Unlike parties, interest groups seek merely to influence, not to control, government. David Truman in his landmark work *The Governmental Process* defined an interest group as "a shared-attitude group that makes certain claims upon other groups" by acting through the institutions of government. Interest groups, sometimes called pressure groups, come in various forms. Some political scientists describe them as lobbies, which try to influence public policy using conventional tactics that include contributing money, writing letters, circulating petitions, and endorsing politicians. Other interest groups seek to influence policy via less conventional routes, usually protest tactics such as marches, sit-ins, picket lines, and boycotts.

Political parties in the United States are not as formally structured and centralized as their Western European counterparts. In Great Britain, for example, people pay dues to join the Labor or Conservative Party. In some European countries, parties issue membership cards. In the United States, people join parties by registering or re-registering to vote. U.S. political parties are actually coalitions of individuals and diverse interests that—every two years or so—come together in their quest for electoral power and control.

In the United States, a third party—what some political scientists call a "minor" party—is any political party other than the Democratic and Republican Parties. Although third parties perform many of the same functions as these two governing parties, they seldom win elections, and so they do not control the institutions of power.

More specifically, Joseph M. Hazllett defines a third party as "any group of individuals, other than Democrats and Republicans, that are united by some common interest, who raise money, offer candidates, and actively campaign for some office or offices under a party label, regardless of their rate of success."[14] J. David Gillespie describes a third party as "an organized aggregate of leaders, members, and supporters that (1) designates itself a party, (2) articulates perceived interests of its devotees, (3) presses these interests upon or in contradistinction to the American political and party systems using electoral and/or other political methods, and (4) either never attains or is unable to sustain the primary or the secondary share of loyalties of people making up the national body politic."[15]

As a rule, U.S. third parties want to be major parties and thus to pose a challenge to the two major governing parties. Both Republicans and Democrats point to them as proof that the country is predicated on the notion of democratic pluralism, an erroneous idea.

## Third Parties: Intrinsic to the U.S. Political Fabric

The formation of the Anti-Masonic Party in 1826 marked the genesis of the country's third-party system. Nelson W. Polsby explains that, historically, "third parties have come in several flavors."[16] More than 900 local, state, and national groups have sought to become alternatives to the nation's two major parties.[17] During what can be described as the golden age of third-party movements, 1826–1900, scores of third parties emerged, then faded from the political scene. Some that played politically significant roles include the Liberty Party (1840–1848), Free Soil Party (1848–1852), American Party (the Know-Nothings) (1856), Constitutional Union and Southern Democrat Parties (1860), Liberal Republican and Prohibition Parties (1870), Greenback Party (1876–1884), Socialist Labor Party (1876), and Populist Party (1892–1908).[18]

In the twentieth century, numerous third parties also emerged at the regional and national levels. Out of the ashes of the Populist Party rose Teddy Roosevelt's Progressive (Bull Moose) Party in 1912, reconfigured under the leadership of Robert LaFollette in 1924. Concomitantly, a number of sectarian socialist and Marxist-oriented parties emerged: Socialist Party (1901), Communist Party (1919), Socialist Workers' Party (1938), and New Party (1992). Other third parties to spring up include Henry Wallace's Progressive Party and the Dixiecrats (1948), George Wallace's American Independent Party (1968), Libertarian Party (1971), and the environmentally activist Green Party (1989). By the 2000 presidential elections, Ross Perot's Reform Party (1996), the nation's most viable third party, was visibly shaken by internal leadership schisms.[19]

## Third Parties: Agents of Protest and Change

Some third parties in the United States have impacted the political system; others have not. Some have been transient expressions of minor discontent related to a specific issue. Still others have been ideological parties committed to the transformation of the liberal capitalist system. Splinter parties have momentarily left one of the major parties over some disagreement, only to eventually return to it. A few others have functioned as "satellite" parties that revolve around one of the two major parties. In addition, some have sought to affect the balance of power by impacting election results. Regardless of the role third parties play, the great majority have been change oriented. Where they differ is in the scope or type of change they advocate.

Many third parties set on minimal change, for example, resemble interest groups rather than true political parties. For this reason, some scholars make the argument that third parties are not real political parties but agitating associations, debating societies, or educational organizations.[20] Like interest groups, third parties tend to be more effective at articulating interests than at interest aggregation. Particularly at the local level, in most cases, they fail to meet the definition of a party. Schattschneider, who echoes these sentiments, finds that third parties use elections only as points of departure for other forms of agitation; that most tend to develop around specific, focused, and well-defined issues or sets of principles; and that they tend to be too intransigent in their politics, unwilling to compromise so as to foster a spirit of reconciliation among divergent interests.[21] "For some third parties, the focus or the array of primary interests is in fact as narrow as that of a single-issue interest group."[22] Hesseltine explains that as change agents, third parties have made distinct contributions: "In general, third parties have performed the function of calling attention to serious problems and pointing a way to their solution. They have stimulated—sometimes by frightening them—the lethargic or timid politicians of the major parties. They have advocated reforms, which the older parties have adopted and enacted into law. And sometimes they have trained leaders for the major parties."[23]

Besides acting as gadflies to drive the dominant two parties to alter their policies and politics, most third parties also seek to mobilize voters and represent them, just as do the two major parties. They provide policy alternatives to the usual Republican-Democrat dichotomy and offer a range of issue choices not normally found in the two major parties.[24] In addition, third parties act as electoral safety valves that allow alienated voters to ventilate their discontent.

The foremost function of some third parties is to purvey new ideas to the electorate, government, and major parties.[25] Historically, some third parties have proposed innovative ideas, later adopted, that at the time of their introduction were deemed controversial, unpopular, and even radical. Some have proven intellectually ahead of the two major parties as public policy innovators. Clinton Rossiter explains that third parties, by agitating for reform, have significantly impacted the development of the U.S. Constitution's various amendments, particularly the twelfth, sixteenth, seventeenth, eighteenth, and nineteenth.[26] According to Charles Merriam and Harold Gosnell, "as formulators of issues, the minor parties have often been more successful than the major parties; and as advance guards of new issues, these newcomers have been bolder than the established organizations."[27] Thus, third parties may lose the political battles but win the conceptual war via the cooptation of their issues and ideas by one of the major parties.

Third parties have managed to capture over 5 percent of the popular vote in a third of the presidential elections since 1840. They have won over 10 percent of the vote in one out of five contests, and fourteen of the last thirty-six presidents (40 percent) have won the presidency without a popular vote majority. This means that, theoretically, third parties have controlled enough votes in the right states to swing the results in one-third of the electoral college figures. On several occasions (e.g., 1856, 1860, and 1912), over a fifth of the electorate left the major parties. Yet in other presidential elections (e.g., 1868, 1940, and 1960), third parties were not able to garner even one-half of 1 percent of the vote.[28] Unlike their counterparts in European nations such as Italy, Germany, Norway, and Switzerland, U.S. third parties have not become powerful competitors.

Not all scholars perceive third parties as making a positive political contribution. Judson James believes that "the very existence of third parties is evidence that they are outside the political consensus that rewards pragmatic two-party politics."[29] V. O. Key propounded that third parties persist outside this consensus without seriously challenging it.[30]

## The Etiology of Third Parties: Products of Discontent

Third parties, like some political movements, are the products of discontent with the two major parties.[31] They give people frustrated and alienated from those parties an outlet by which they can voice their anger and disapproval over issues or deliver an ideological rebuke to the two-party system. Sometimes they are triggered by a polarizing crisis situation, if we define a crisis as an episode of extraordinary division that fosters a level of conflict and polarization within society over one or more salient issues. This is Daniel Mazmanian's position.

> The leading precondition for a significant third-party vote is severe political crisis. Only in times of extraordinary stress do the division of public opinion, the positions taken by the major parties, and the energies of third-party entrepreneurs take on importance. . . . No significant third party has appeared at a time other than one of crisis. And only in periods of crisis following the Civil War and during the Great Depression have third parties failed to appear.[32]

Frederick Hayes suggests that "social and economic problems are the real forces behind third parties."[33] Such third parties as the Liberty, Free Soil, Greenback, Populist, and, more recently, American Independent were all products of national crises.

Third parties emerge only when a portion of the electorate is dissatisfied, angry, or alienated from the two major parties. Rosenstone, Behr, and Lazarus found in 1996 that voter estrangement caused voters to support and vote for third parties, and that third-party voting occurs when there is a substantial distance between the voters and major-party candidates.[34] Thus, one could argue that third parties are the result of relative deprivation and unmet rising expectations.[35]

Moreover, several third parties have been led by alienated politicians who have deserted from the Democratic or Republican Party. Most third-party movements, especially those that made an impact in the twentieth century, have been driven by the power of personalities.[36] The examples are many, including: David Deleon, Socialist Labor; William Jennings Bryan, Populist; Eugene Debs and Norman Thomas, Socialist; Theodore Roosevelt, Progressive; Robert LaFollette, Progressive; Henry Wallace, People's Progressive; Strom Thurmond, Dixiecrat; George Wallace, American Independent; Ross Perot and Jesse Ventura, Reform. Personality-driven third parties draw much higher vote totals than other third parties, but most have lacked staying power.[37]

Party factionalism has also contributed to the formation of third parties. Some political scientists allude to the major parties as huge tents or umbrellas that house divergent factions that come together every two and four years to wage a state or national election. At times, irreconcilable differences develop in one of them, and a faction will bolt to form its own party. The Liberal Republicans of 1872, the Gold Democrats of 1896, the Progressives of 1912, and the Dixiecrats of 1948 are four examples. The reality is, however, that in most cases, this is nothing more than a temporary political separation, quickly mended. Third parties themselves are not immune to factionalism and splintering. This was very much the case with the Socialist Labor Party, which splintered by 1901, with its more moderate members exiting to form the Socialist Party.

## Third Party Models: A Dichotomy

Political scientists readily admit that trying to classify third parties as to their functions and roles is difficult and risky, but some have taken a chance. Clinton Rossiter breaks down third parties into six distinguishable types: (1) "left-wing splinter" (e.g., Socialist.); (2) "one-issue obsessionists" (e.g., Prohibition Party); (3) "one-state" (Progressives of Wisconsin); (4) "personal following of the dissident hero" (Bull Moose Party); (5) "dissident wing of the major party" (Dixiecrats of 1948); and (6) "true minor Party" (Populists).[38]

Third parties generally fall into two theoretical types: Issue Reformist (IR) and Sectarian Doctrinaire (SD). IR parties have been the most prolific and commonplace. Although the issues and circumstances that precipitate their formation sometimes differ, most IR parties tend to be (1) issue driven, (2) reform oriented, (3) mostly transient, (4) regional or state in scope, and (5) mass-appeal oriented. IR parties can be broken down into subtypes: single issue, economic protest, secessionist, and satellite. Examples of Issue Reformist parties include the Prohibition, Populist, Progressive, Dixiecrat, Conservative, and the Liberal Party of New York. During the 1990s a new crop of IR parties emerged, among them the Green Party, U.S. Taxpayers Party, and Labor Party.

Sectarian Doctrinaire parties are less common and electorally less competitive than IR parties. Their discontent, however, is ideologically more anti–liberal capitalist. Their "sectarianism" is manifested in their strong adherence to a politics predicated on morality, ethics, ideas, and beliefs that are hypercritical of the liberal capitalist system. They strategically manipulate issues in order to raise the consciousness of and organize their constituencies, for example, masses, working class, or Whites. SD parties span the ideological spectrum, from the Right of unbridled liberal capitalism to the Left of some form of socialism.

No SD third party has ever mounted a credible electoral challenge to either of the two major parties. Rather than focus on electoral politics, these parties tend to act more like pressure groups; their tactics include direct action, propaganda, agitation, and political consciousness building. Six characteristics differentiate the SD third party model. They are (1) ideological, (2) major-change oriented, (3) propaganda educationalist, (4) permanent, (5) regional to national in scope, and (6) cadre or vanguard in structure. It is the power of their doctrine or ideology—or simply put, their ideas or beliefs—that impels their politics.

Left-oriented SD parties range from the Socialist Labor Party of the late 1800s to the centrist New Party of the 1990s. Hugh Bone explains that Marxist-oriented SD parties "are strongly ideological oriented, so much that there are several different Marxist groups, each purporting to be the 'true' one. . . . Spokesmen for each faction and splinter acclaim themselves as the apostles of Marx and denounce each other as traitors to the master."[39] During the twentieth century, some of the most resilient and viable SD parties were the Socialist Party (1901), Communist Party of the United States (1919), Socialist Worker's Party (1938),[40] and Progressive Labor Party (1962). However, with the decline of the Soviet Union by 1991, some Left-oriented SD parties such as the Peace and Freedom Party (1968) and New Party (1992) have considerably toned down their sectarianism. The New Party, for example, proposes the peaceful transformation of liberal capitalism. It advocates the establishment of a society where the wealth of the nation is equitably distributed and the manifold needs of the people are met. Its lexicon is more social democratic than openly Marxist.[41]

George Lincoln Rockwell's American Nazi Party (late 1940s–1960s) is one example of an SD party on the extreme Right. The less doctrinaire American Independent, Libertarian, and Reform Parties represent the more center-right wing of the model. Mark Paul explains the doctrinaire posture of the Libertarian Party:

> Libertarians, unlike the major parties, are more than a sum of their programs, which to most voters look like an unlikely amalgam of left and right. A vote for the libertarians is a vote for an ideology that is both unusually consistent and rigidly unwavering. Their ideology dictates that they support civil liberties and an end to militarism; it also leads them to the defense of a laissez-faire capitalism purer than it has ever existed in American history.[42]

The differences separating an IR from an SD party are sometimes blurred; for example, a third party can be a splinter party with a doctrinaire orientation. But regardless of the general type, none have posed a serious challenge to the Democratic and Republican Parties' monopoly of power and hegemony.

## The U.S. Party System: A Two-Party Dictatorship

For more than two hundred years, the United States has sought to convince the world that its two-party system is representative democracy incarnate. Most people in the United States and some people elsewhere believe this misinformation and propaganda. Nothing could be further from the truth. As a political scientist, I posit the argument that the United States has been and is today governed by what is tantamount to a two-party dictatorship. While it is true that the electorate has the power to elect their representatives, which theoretically validates the principle of popular sovereignty and the country's claim to being a representative democracy, the people's choices are limited. According to Gordon S. Black and Benjamin D. Black, "a democracy is a political system in which citizens have *both the right and opportunity to choose between candidates*" and political parties. They further write that "take away choice and you have taken away the essence of what it means to be democratic. After all, elections are regularly held in countries with dictatorships, but there is no choice except to vote for the party in power."[43]

The bottom line is that citizens in the United States, as in other totalitarian states, by design have no real party alternatives. The symbolic choices are two, Democrats and Republicans, which offer no ideological alternatives. The Democratic and Republican Parties, due to the monopoly of power they exercise, have unlimited control over the electoral and policy processes that govern the nation. So pervasive is their power that for the last 138 years, no third party has posed a serious threat to them—and none will in the future, unless major reforms are enacted. Kay Lawson writes, "The United States does not have a two-party system, but rather a 'bi-hegemonic' one, where control of almost all the elective posts rests in the hands of the elected representatives of the two major parties."[44]

Few political scientists have suggested that a two-party dictatorship governs the country's state and federal institutions. Clinton Rossiter in his classic book, *Parties and Politics in America*, came close. He recognized the important role political parties play in politics:

> No America without democracy, no democracy without politics, no politics without parties, no parties without compromise and moderation. So runs the string of assumptions on which hangs this exposition of the politics of American democracy. . . . The most momentous fact about the pattern of American Politics is that we live under a persistent, obdurate, one might almost say "tyrannical," two-party system. We have the Republicans and we have the Democrats, and we have almost no one else, any other political aggregate that amounts to a corporal's guard in the struggle for power. The extent of this tyranny of the two parties is most dramatically revealed in the sorry condition of third parties in the United States today . . . whose present situation is almost hopeless.[45]

Two other scholars, Gordon S. Black and Benjamin D. Black, in their book, *The Politics of American Discontent*, get more specific:

Money and power now completely rule the political marketplace, real political choice has died, and perhaps democracy has died along with it. We are ruled by a tyranny more dangerous than a dictatorship. . . . It is a tyranny that spends a fortune each year to persuade us that its intent is benign, all the while stealing our future. . . . Without a gun being fired, the politicians have almost entirely eliminated democratic choice in . . . state and national elections.[46]

The nation's two-party system is in fact tyrannical; both the Democratic and Republican Parties exert oppressive power over most aspects of government and public policy. One of the most important characteristics of a democratic system of government is the freedom of individuals, factions, or political parties to compete. A democratic government rests on the right to organize and vie for control of the government by peacefully appealing to the electorate, combining these varied interests into a legitimate majority, and then offering candidates for decision-making positions through reliable and legitimate processes that reflect the electorate's issue preferences.[47]

Yet the political reality is that third-party challenges have been symbolic at best. Political scientist Judson James writes, "The very existence of third parties is evidence that they are outside the political consensus that rewards pragmatic two-party politics."[48] V. O. Key suggests that third parties that are sectarian persist outside this consensus without seriously challenging it.[49] In short, third parties, according to Daniel A. Mazmanian, "rarely provide serious competition for the two major parties in American presidential elections."[50]

Very few political scientists have taken the view that the nation is governed by a two-party system that is not just tyrannical, but totalitarian and a two-party dictatorship as well. More specifically, the two-party system is tyrannical because it denotes "the cruel and unjust exercise of power of any sort" by the two major parties against third parties. In addition, it is dictatorial because of its totalitarian underpinnings: The Democratic and Republican Parties have deliberately relegated third parties to a "subordinate and powerless" political status. Their totalitarianism is evident in both major parties' exercise of "strict control of all aspects of the life and productive capacity of the nation," especially by the use of multiple constitutional and institutional methods or constraints.[51] These intertwined concepts help explain why power is in the hands only of Democrats and Republicans.

I reject the notion that the United States has in place a pluralist democracy. To the contrary, I contend that the nation's political system, while democratic in theory, is in actuality a plutocracy governed by an omnipotent power elite. Through their pervasive control of government, this elite uses such socialization agents as the mass media and educational institutions to exercise power and control over the most perfect party dictatorship ever conceived.

*Dictatorship* aptly describes a two-party system that is oppressive of or contemptuously overbearing toward third parties. The justification for using this term is that third-parties are not outlawed but merely contained, controlled, and allowed to freely express their views, and to participate symbolically in politics to legitimize the so-called democratic nature of the nation's liberal capitalist system. Especially dictatorial is the elite's absolute power in the federal, state, and even local legislative, executive, and judicial branches of government. Because the Constitution does not mention political parties, they come under the aegis of state laws that have been drafted by both major parties, including the laws that govern third-party activity. Thus, the nation's two-party dictatorship at the federal and state levels is both constitutionally and legally condoned.

The Democratic and Republican Parties have been politically invincible since 1860. While they compete with each other for control, it is customary for each party to solicit support for the passage of legislation from the other. Historically, with few exceptions, power sharing occurs only among the two major parties, which means they exercise a monopoly of power."[52] In addition, all public policy passed by either or both parties lies within the ideological perimeters of the liberal capitalist system.

Furthermore, both parties profess themselves ideological adherents of liberal capitalism. Democrats and Republicans not only control the nation's superstructure; but both are purveyors of the belief system that is grounded politically on classical liberalism and economically on capitalism.[53] (Classical liberalism as a political theory has its roots in Europe and was brought into the colonies by early settlers during the seventeenth and eighteenth centuries. Politically, it became the theoretical foundation upon which this nation's superstructure was developed.)

At the political core of liberalism are six intrinsic concepts: individualism, freedom, equality, popular sovereignty, limited government, and private property—all of which both major parties embrace. While all six are important, politically it is individualism that is the very essence of liberalism. This is manifested in the nation's popular dictum of "life, liberty, and the pursuit of happiness" (property). So pronounced is this belief within liberalism that the Declaration of Independence further states, "Whenever any form of government becomes destructive of these ends, it is the right of the people to alter or to abolish it, and to institute new government, laying its foundations on such principles, and organizing its power in such form as to them shall seem most likely to effect their safety and happiness."[54] The individual's right to self-fulfillment is the ultimate goal of the state. This complements classical liberalism's adherence to a belief in freedom, meaning that the individual has the right to make choices with a minimum of governmental constraint. A belief in equality is important to classical liberalism because it rejects, categorically, systems of hereditary privilege. As a result, classical liberalism embraces popular sovereignty—the concept that government should reflect the general will of the people. The belief in limited government enhances all of this, since it accentuates the need to circumscribe the power of government. Last, a belief in private property denotes that individuals must control their material possessions in order to define themselves, as well as to find a niche for themselves in society.[55]

The Democratic and Republican Parties are zealots regarding capitalist economics. Particularly with its adherence to individualism and private property, liberalism was a catalytic force behind the development of capitalism, an economic system in which individuals and corporations own and control the means of production and the distribution of profits and wealth. The central features of the capitalist system in its classical form are the dominance of private property, the dynamics of the profit motive, the existence of a free market, and the presence of competition. Capitalism assumes that private ownership and control of property maximizes the people's interest and productive potential. It also assumes that the profit motive provides the most viable incentive to economic activity, efficiency, and progress.[56]

But capitalism is inherently exploitive, as Howard L. Reiter explains: "Capitalism is intensely individualistic, based as it is on the assumption that the people share no fundamental interest and that the economic system functions best as 'every person for himself or herself.' At the base of capitalism therefore, is a social system in which inequalities are not only tolerated, but also essential. . . . This is one of the most important contradictions between American capitalism and democracy."[57] While the two major parties differ significantly in their opinion of the degree to which a government should intervene in the economy and the public welfare, both claim to be strong proponents of the free enterprise system.

Yet, some political scientists allege that the nation's politics are nonideological, given that ideological conflicts over displacing the liberal capitalist system have been rare. At no time has there been a serious threat that socialism, fascism, or some other "-ism" might replace liberal capitalism. This is not say that the parties are homogeneous or the same. Differences do exist as to some beliefs about the role, power, and utility of government. Today, Democrats tend to be politically more moderate and Republicans more conservative. In contemporary political parlance, liberals favor the federal government having an expansive role in the management of the economy as well as in the promotion of equality of opportunity, civil rights, and social justice. Conversely, conservatives show a preference for individual liberty, oppose excessive government intervention on most economic and social issues, and favor government deregulation. Only momentarily, from Roosevelt to McGovern (1932–1972), did Democrats espouse what can be described as a "liberal" political agenda.

The truth of the matter is, neither party offers the electorate a real choice. As Helen Keller wrote, "Our democracy is but a name. We vote. What does that mean? It means that we choose between two . . . bodies of autocrats. We choose between Twiddledee and Twiddledum."[58] Similarly, James Bryce once charged that "the two major parties are like two bottles, identical in size, shape, color, bearing different labels, but both empty." During his presidential campaign in 1968, George Wallace said, "There's not a dime's difference between the Democrats and Republicans."[59] In the words of Chicano Movement leader Rodolfo "Corky" Gonzales, "the two-party system is one animal with two heads eating out of the same trough."[60] The fact is, this nation's political party system is governed by a two-party dictatorship that functions more like a *one-party dictatorship* governed by two ideologically compatible parties—Democrats and Republicans. Michael Parenti underscores their compatibility:

> Both the Democratic and Republican Parties are committed to the preservation of the private corporate economy; huge military budgets; the use of subsidies, . . . and tax allowances to bolster business profits; the funneling of public resources through private

conduits, including whole new industries developed at public expense; the use of repression against opponents of the existing class structure; the defense of the multinational corporate empire and intervention against social-revolutionary elements abroad. In short, most Republican and Democrat politicians are dedicated to strikingly similar definitions of the public interest, at great cost to the life chances of underprivileged people at home and abroad.[61]

Today, Democrats and Republicans appear to be more similar than ever. Both parties have embraced a more right-of-center posture.[62] On foreign policy matters, there is no real distinction. Both major parties adhere to the Manifest Destiny–driven policy of Pax Americana and the idea of creating a world order (monopoly capitalism). Domestically, both parties have moved on downsizing the federal government, balancing the budget, cutting taxes, promoting trade agreements, and so on. Neither is willing to venture into what is perceived as the Left or Right extremes of the political spectrum. This is particularly evident among the Democrats, who since the McGovern presidential debacle of 1972 have turned their backs on the liberalism of Roosevelt, Kennedy, and Johnson and moved toward a moderate to conservative posture, as illustrated by Bill Clinton's administration. Each major party seeks pragmatically to appeal to as many constituencies as possible in order to win elections. Kevin Phillips points out that "Washington's self proclaimed 'vital center' is really a 'venal center,' molded by campaign contributors, not the public, which gives independents and third parties the political equivalent of a Goodyear blimp to shoot at."[63]

Moreover, today, neither party, especially the Democrats, has what can be considered a viable liberal wing. In fact, in the lexicon of both parties, the word "liberal" has pejorative connotations. It conjures up images of big government–government intervention into the lives of the individual, government as a big spender—and of associations with religious, ethnic, racial, labor, and gender special interests that espouse the view that government must be more proactive in advancing their respective policy agendas. Hence, party politics in the 1990s moved to a place where the people have fewer and fewer choices and viable alternatives. While the nation's social problems increase to the crisis point, neither party cares to effectively address their resolution. Instead, they are immersed in such issues as tax cuts, which advance the powerful economic interests of the plutocrats and corporations rather those of the increasingly alienated middle and lower classes. By the year 2000, however, former Democratic senator Bill Bradley in his unsuccessful quest for the Democratic Party's nomination sought to rekindle the spirit of the liberal agenda with his stance on such issues as health care, racism, and corporate loopholes in the tax code.[64]

## The Workings of the Two-Party Dictatorship: Constraints on Third Parties

Why is it that other liberal capitalist nations such as France, Italy, Israel, and Holland have a multiparty system that allows the viable participation of third parties?

The answer to this question lies in the multifarious controlling mechanisms both major parties use to perpetuate their two-party dynasty. Paradoxically, most political scientists concur that numerous factors or constraints obviate a serious third-party threat to either major party. (However, most also posit the view that the nation's political system is democratic, pluralistic, and competitive.) The nation's two-party dictatorship is maintained by seven major constitutional and institutional constraints.

The first major constraint is the nation's political culture, which embodies the beliefs of liberal capitalism. Political culture, according to Gabriel A. Almond and G. Bingham Powell Jr. "consists of attitudes, beliefs, values, and skills which are current in an entire population, as well as those special propensities and patterns which may be found within separate parts of that population."[65] From birth to death, all of us undergo a well-systematized and orchestrated socialization and conditioning process in which certain agents (e.g., schools, media, etc.) transmit particular values, beliefs, attitudes, and symbols to us (and to society in general). According to Gillespie, "Third parties are beset by a political socialization process that (1) signals to each generation that multiparty deviations from national two-party patterns are 'un-American' and (2) normally engenders either loyalty for the GOP or Democrats or a nonpartisan disposition ('vote for the person, not the party')."[66]

People are programed to believe the big lie via multiple socialization agents, such as the two major parties, parents, schools, media, peer groups, family, churches, organizations, and the military. These agents work hand in hand to propagate a value system that scorns and deprecates other political parties, especially those that embrace a platform antithetical to liberal capitalism. Consequently, the average voter grows up programed to believe that third parties are peripheral and inconsequential political entities.[67] The nation's core values, predicated on liberal capitalism, have engendered a political culture that is impervious to other "-isms." It acts as a powerful deterrent or constraint for third-party formation. Thus, as Everett Carll Ladd explains, "the dominance in the United States of a distinct political ideology has precluded certain political solutions and ordained others."[68]

The existence of single-member districts is the second major constraint. Mandated by the Constitution, elections in single-member districts are predicated on the "winner takes all" system, which means that only one candidate can win.[69] In order for a party or candidate to win, they must win a plurality, meaning the most votes. Based on the notion "winner takes all," this constitutional mechanism has substantially contributed to the preservation of the two-party system. Regardless of the number of votes garnered by a third-party candidate, a major party candidate who gets a plurality wins. This has discouraged voters from voting for third parties, since they do not want to waste their vote. Most voters are cognizant that third parties have only a slim chance of winning.[70]

By contrast, most European countries use "proportional representation" to elect their representatives, which is conducive to a multiparty system. In this system, a political party is allocated legislative seats according to the percentage of the votes it wins. If, for example, in a state entitled to ten congressional seats, a third party wins 30 percent of the vote, it would get three seats. Under this much more equitable electoral system, third parties could accumulate enough votes in any partisan election to gain representation in the Congress, state legislatures, and so on. Some political scientists and journalists argue that proportional representation is extraneous to the nation's political culture and so overly complex that it would increase the number of third parties. Furthermore, they contend that it would be so chaotic it would foster legislative instability, encourage divisions, and encourage unrestrained competition.[71] Thus, the impact of the single-member-district plurality system on third parties has been devastating, since it makes them unable to effectively compete against the two major parties. It has served to perpetuate the hegemony of the Democratic and Republican Parties and has contributed to the transitory nature of third parties, for it stifles their longevity and growth.

The third constraint is the use of overly stringent ballot-access laws. Because of the nation's federalist system, states are the principal overseers of elections. State control of elections translates to Democratic and Republican hegemony over the legislative and executive process. Both parties have sought to insulate themselves from any serious challenge by passing election laws that have impeded the access of third parties and independent candidates to the ballot. Writing in 1957, Hesseltine pointed out that "in many states, the two old parties are as firmly entrenched in the laws as the Communist Party is in Russia."[72] Whereas candidates from the two major parties automatically appear on the ballot, third parties must petition state election officials to be placed on the ballot. This can be difficult, because every state has its own legal requirements. Some defenders of the two-party system claim that severe legal restrictions are necessary to keep hordes of "frivolous" candidates from clogging ballots.[73]

This was not always the case. Before about 1890, political parties, not states, prepared and distributed their own election ballots. With the introduction of the "Australian ballot" during the 1890s, this changed. The state became responsible for preparing the official ballot listing all candidates, and voters would mark it secretly. With Democrats and Republicans in control, the state legislatures passed laws that made it difficult for third parties to qualify for placement on the ballot, deterring the successful development of any third party perceived to be a threat to their hegemony.

For third parties, the struggle to gain access to the ballot and thus become official political parties has been arduous, even for those that were well financed. The cardinal reason for this is that for a third party to get on the ballot, in most cases, it must register a given number of voters or gather petition signatures within a prescribed time frame. Using the former method, for example, to get on the ballot in California requires that a third party register a minimum of 89,007 people. Implicit in such requirements is the assumption that the prospective new party should have the organization, leadership, volunteers, and finances to effectively mount the organizing effort called for.

The petition method is also problematic in most cases, because of the high number of signatures required, cumbersome procedures, rather short filing deadlines, and bewildering array of laws governing third-party access to the ballot. For instance, the number of signatures required to get a third party on the ballot varies from state to state. In the seven southwestern states, California requires 890,064 petition signatures by October 24; Texas, 43,963 signatures by May 23; New Mexico, 2,339 signatures by July 9; Arizona, 15,062 signatures by May 21; Nevada, 3,761 signatures by July 11; and Utah, 500 signatures. Colorado has no petition procedure;. Outside the Southwest, states such as New York, Illinois, and Washington also supposedly have no procedures. Florida, in 1998, required 196,788 petition signatures by July 16. Kansas required 16,417 signatures by April 11.[74] According to Parenti, in a national election, it takes 750,000 signatures for an independent or minor-party candidate to get on the ballot in all fifty states—but only 25,000 signatures for a Democratic or Republican candidate to do the same.[75] The petition requirement is further complicated by limitations on where and when petitions may be circulated, who may circulate them, and who may sign them. In some states, the time to collect signatures has been cut to one week, an almost impossible organizing task.

Filing fees have been yet another ballot-access problem for third parties. In Louisiana, a candidate must pay a $5,000 filing fee to get on the ballot.[76] As Rosenstone states, "This lack of a uniform petition period or filing deadline means that a third-party or independent candidate cannot mount a nationwide effort; instead, he must hold fifty-one different drives at different times during the campaign."[77] Thus, filing fees are also used by the major parties to make it difficult for third-party candidates to join the political fray. Most of the states in which some victories have been secured by third parties have had no filing fees at all.[78]

The fourth constraint is the electoral college, which is a constitutional variation on the single-member district/plurality system. It too embraces the "winner takes all" principle—in this case in the election of the president of the United States. Although the nation's founders preached the virtues of representative democracy, they adhered to only a limited form of it that excluded women, the propertyless poor, and enslaved Blacks (who were considered to be only three-fifths of a person). As the ruling elite, they did not put their trust directly in the people to elect the president. Instead, they created the electoral college. The president is elected by a slate of electors in each state equal to the number of U.S. senators and representatives from that state. California, for example, as a result of the 1990 census, has 54 electoral votes (two U.S. senators and fifty-two congressmen). It takes a minimum of 270 electoral votes to win the presidency. There have been a few instances in which no candidate got the required number of electoral votes or a candidate had the majority of the popular vote but not of the electoral vote. Two such cases have occurred, when Thomas Jefferson tied with Aaron Burr in 1800, and in 1824 when John Quincy Adams, Andrew Jackson, and William H. Crawford failed to get a majority in the electoral college; the House of Representatives decided the results. Rutherford Hayes in 1876 and Benjamin Harrison in 1888 won the presidency via the electoral college, even though they lost in the popular vote.[79] Thus, the electoral college has effectively served to obviate the rise of any serious presidential challenge by third parties.

The fifth constraint is the nation's federal election campaign laws. Although originally designed to limit the influence of big money in the electoral process, the 1974

Federal Election Campaign Act (FECA) in particular has become a major impediment to third parties. Rosenstone and other political scientists consider it "a major party protection act." As Rosenstone writes, this act "is the most recent instance of the major parties adopting a 'reform' that freezes out third-party challengers."[80] In addition to setting limits on the amounts individuals and political action committees can contribute to congressional and presidential candidates, FECA also guarantees each of the two major party presidential candidates access to millions of dollars in federal campaign funds. For example, the two major parties each automatically receive funds to pay for their conventions, which in 1996 was more than $12 million apiece.

A third party can also qualify for convention subsidies, but with the provision that its last presidential candidate must have received at least 5 percent of the popular vote— about four million votes.[81] Very few third parties have managed this. One of them is the Reform Party, which qualified for $12.6 million in federal campaign funds, available to its nominee in the 2000 presidential elections.[82] This feat is almost impossible without sufficient funding and media access.[83] Even if a third party succeeds in getting 5 percent of the vote, it is not eligible to receive the money until after the election. Although third parties do not receive public funds from the Federal Election Commission (FEC), they are still required to observe all federal recordkeeping and reporting requirements, which are complex. To add insult to injury, they are also subject to limitations on contributions and expenditures.

During the 1996 presidential elections, each of the two major party presidential candidates received some $100 million from the FEC. This deep-pocket principle has served as the weapon used by both parties to ensure the financial exclusion of third parties. According to journalist James P. Pinkerton in 1995, the FEC "exists now mostly to serve its powerful constituency, the Democratic and Republican Parties. In the next year, the FEC will shove more than 100 million in the direction of the two parties and its presidential candidates."[84] The control of the FEC by the two major parties provides them with enough public funds to finance their national conventions, primaries, and presidential campaigns.

In 1996, the *Los Angeles Times* reported that in spite of the avowed commitment of the Democratic and Republican Parties to campaign finance reform, each received millions of dollars from corporations, labor, and wealthy individuals.

> More than two months before the November election, the Republicans and Democrats have taken in far more so-called soft money than they garnered in the entire 1992 campaign. . . . The total of such contributions for the Republican National Committee and various committees is $75.2 million; for the Democrats, 67.4. In 1991–92, the GOP collected 36.9 million; the Democrats, 51.5 million. . . . Both parties have benefited from the largess of Wall Street, health care interests, real estate developers, and telecommunications companies.[85]

The dictatorial power exercised by both major parties becomes self-evident if one examines the governance of the FEC. As stipulated by law, each of the two parties appoints three commissioners, who are charged with looking into campaign finances. However, they spend a great deal of their time looking into the accounts of third parties and filing suits against them and against other independent candidates.

The sixth constraint is the two major parties' control of state and federal courts. Both state and federal judicial appointments come from the Democratic and Republican ranks, and the Supreme Court is made up of justices appointed by the president and approved by Congress. Since 1860, Republicans and Democrats have always controlled both the executive and legislative branches of government, including the judicial appointment process. The courts, through their rulings, seldom make decisions that would endanger or weaken the hegemony of the two major parties.

In 1996, for example, a seven-to-two Supreme Court decision lifted restrictions on the amount of money state parties could spend. In each election cycle, the FEC establishes state-by-state limits on party spending, figured from a formula based on population. To complicate matters even more, the state parties can turn over their allotments to the national party.[86] In 1997, the Supreme Court in a six-to-three ruling placed new limits on third parties: States could prevent candidates from appearing more than once on a ballot, even if a third party and a major party both nominated them. The decision bans fusion, an electoral process that allows the nomination of a candidate by two separate and legal political parties, with the votes of each party counting toward the candidate's total. This approach has been used in New York. In the nineteenth century, such progressive parties as Grangers, Greenbackers, and Populists were able to gain strength by nominating candidates who were also the favorites of the major parties.[87]

The seventh constraint is the presence of a mass media biased in favor of the two major parties. No third party can expect to do well politically without access to the media, often described as the fourth estate, the fourth branch of government. Mass media coverage is indispensable to any viable political campaign. The power of the mass media is such that it has the capacity to create or destroy a third-party or independent movement or candidate. It is the principal medium by which candidates generate name recognition and a base of support. Third parties have rarely been befriended by the mass media. In fact, in most cases, third parties have been victims of what can be described as the politics of exclusion.

When the mass media do give coverage to third parties, it tends to be negative, if not hostile. This is evident from the exclusion of third-party candidates from televised debates. Two exceptions were John Anderson in 1980, when he debated only Ronald Reagan, and Ross Perot and his vice-presidential candidate in 1992. In 1996, even though Perot was on every state ballot and had almost $30 million in federal campaign funds, he was excluded from participating in the presidential debate by the Commission on Presidential Debates, a private entity funded by large corporations.[88] The same scenario applies for third-party candidates running for lesser offices.

Years ago, under the guise of the fairness doctrine, third parties were given greater access to radio and later to television. The Communications Act of 1934 required broadcasters to provide equal access to all legally qualified candidates. In 1949, the Federal Communications Commission compelled broadcasters to cover issues of public importance and to reflect the range of differing views on these issues; but by 1998, after much pressure from the two major parties, the 1934 law was repealed.[89]

The Supreme Court in a six-to-three decision ruled in 1998 that third-party candidates have no First Amendment right to participate in debates sponsored by public radio and television stations.[90]

Third parties do not have enough money to buy airtime on either television or radio or to run political advertisements in newspapers. This is not the case with most candidates of both major parties. According to Rosenstone, Behr, and Lazarus, "The primary reason third-party candidates receive so little coverage is that broadcasters and publishers do not think they warrant attention."[91] The mass media, like the overwhelming majority of the electorate, do not perceive most third parties in a positive or credible lights.

The mass media's bias toward the two parties becomes evident with the commitment of the major television networks—NBC, CBS, ABC, and CNN—and their coverage of Democratic and Republican conventions. No third party, not even Perot's Reform Party, is given millions of dollars of free exposure and access to the nation's millions of voters. This media bias is contagious—hundreds of other television and radio stations across the nation, not to mention newspapers, join in the two-party-orchestrated media blitz. The same applies to the exposure given to them during and after elections. While major party candidates are deemed newsworthy, most third-party candidates are perceived as a bunch of kooks and extremists who are unworthy of coverage. Thus, because third parties are generally perceived as inconsequential, without viable or serious candidates, and as having little chance of winning an election; the electronic media does not give them the same attention or coverage given to Democratic and Republican Party candidates.[92]

The politics of exclusion for third parties also applies to newspapers and magazines. Third parties are denied equitable press coverage. As the two-party ethos permeates the electronic media, so it affects the press, a stance reflected by James M. Perry of the *Wall Street Journal*: "We base [our decision] on the simple proposition that readers don't want to waste time on someone who won't have a role in the campaign. We're not going to run a page-one spread on a fringe candidate. We don't have a multiparty system. Until we do, nobody's going to cover these candidates."[93]

For mass media, it is simply good business to support the two-party system, since it can be financially lucrative. Whereas the two major parties spend hundreds of millions of dollars on their presidential, congressional, and state races, third parties spend only a few hundred thousand dollars, if they are lucky. Only when a third-party presidential candidate emerges with enough money to buy airtime and press coverage does the mass media open up somewhat. Such was the case with Independent candidate John Anderson in 1980 and Independent and Reform Party candidate Ross Perot in 1992 and 1996, respectively. Thus, the mass media are biased against third parties and on a daily basis reinforce the socialization of the people to accept the hegemony of the two major parties and liberal capitalism.

All of these constitutional, institutional, and legislative constraints have significantly contributed to the emergence of the nation's two-party dictatorship. Third parties have also faced a multiplicity of other internally induced constraints, especially a lack of finances. Without access to the financial lubricant that oils the machinery of politics and with their limited fund-raising capabilities, third parties, in most cases, are barely able to mount even symbolic campaigns. Unless a third party has a leader like Ross Perot who can finance most of the campaign costs, its electoral constituency is comprised only of the most alienated voters who identify with its issue(s) or beliefs. Activities such as getting on the ballot, running candidates, holding conventions, campaigning, buying access to the media, and printing campaign materials become insurmountable obstacles for most third parties. Financially, third parties are like islands of protest in a huge two-party ocean full of powerful currents of special interests, all committed to the perpetuation of the liberal capitalist system.

Because most third parties are financially weak, they are organizationally weak as well. Most third parties lack the requisite infrastructure and mass of volunteers to mobilize the electorate. This hampers dramatically their capacity to disseminate their program and platform, recruit members and supporters, and raise funds. Their small budgets preclude most from having adequate offices, full-time paid staff, office equipment, literature, television and radio spots and newspaper ads, and election surveys. The result is that most third-party campaigns are dependent on a small core of true-believer volunteers, which is insufficient for mounting a serious electoral challenge.

Yet in spite of this political reality, Chicanos in 1970 revolted against what they perceived was an oppressive two-party monopoly by forming their own political party, El Partido de la Raza Unida (the United Peoples Party).

*Chapter One*

---

# Catalyst for Empowerment:
# The Rise of RUP in Texas, 1970

As a third-party movement, the Raza Unida Party (RUP) made its greatest impact in Texas. There, the Méxicano[1] electoral revolt against the hegemony of the nation's two major parties and internal colonialism was at its most intense and intractable.[2] Nowhere else in the country was the RUP perceived as a real threat to the Democratic and Republican monopoly—particularly in Texas, since the Democratic Party controlled state politics. The emergence of the RUP in 1970 and its electoral victories in Crystal City, Cotulla, and Carrizo Springs set off thunderous roars heard throughout Aztlán and beyond.[3]

## The Chicano Movement: Precursor of RUP

In spite of the harsh political realities that third-party movements face, impelled by the dynamism and fervor of the Chicano Movement (CM)—a result of external and internal antagonisms—in 1970, RUP was born.[4] Driven by years of neglect, alienation, and powerlessness, activists in Texas and Colorado revolted against the traditional two-party system by opting to form their own political party. The activism and militancy that permeated the CM era (1966–1974), particularly in the first four years, contributed to the political conditions or climate of change that made RUP's rise possible.[5]

From its emergence in 1966, the CM's change agenda was multi-issue oriented— land grants, farm workers' rights, education, ending police brutality, and so on. Throughout Aztlán (the Southwest) and even the Midwest, activism was epidemic in the barrios and increasingly in universities and colleges. Reies Lopez Tijerina's Alianza Federal de Mercedes, Cesar Chavez's United Farm Workers (UFW), and Rodolfo "Corky" Gonzales's Crusade for Justice became the three organizations whose leaders most impacted the emergence of the CM.[6]

From 1966 to 1970, these leaders and organizations were at the forefront of the CM. All three were major contributors and catalysts to the growing dynamism and activism of the CM. Tijerina and his Alianza sought the return to Chicanos of millions of acres of New Mexico land originally owned by Méxicanos. Their occupation of Kit Carson National Park in 1966 and the Tierra Amarrilla raid in 1967, along with Tijerina's incarceration in 1969, contributed to the CM's radicalization. Chavez's UFW, in its struggle to unionize farm workers, from 1966 to 1970 mounted an effective national grape boycott that further fostered a climate of change. The boycott was so successful that in 1970 several grape growers signed contracts with the UFW. Gonzales's Crusade, initially a civil rights organization, transformed itself by 1969 into a militant nationalist separatist organization that by 1970 advocated the establishment of a Chicano nation—Aztlán.

During the late 1960s, the emerging CM engendered an "organizational renaissance." Scores of change-oriented organizations were formed that joined in the struggle of La Causa. Disenchanted with several of the existing traditional organizations, such as the League of United Latin American Citizens, G.I. Forum, and Mexican American Political Association for being too conservative and prosystem in their politics, many of these new groups adopted a more militant and political protest posture. In particular, the Chicano student and youth movement, led by such advocacy organizations as the Brown Berets, Black Berets, United Mexican American Students, Movimiento Estudiantil Chicano de Aztlán, and many others, categorically rejected integration and assimilation and, impelled by cultural nationalism and an unprecedented militancy, sought to effect educational change.

From 1967 to 1970, student and youth groups were involved in numerous school walkouts and protest mobilizations. Their educational agenda, inspired by the growing CM and Chicanismo, called for the establishment of Chicano Studies programs, bilingual/bicultural education, student recruitment/retention programs, and the hiring of Chicano faculty, staff, and administrators. The universities and colleges as well as some high schools became bastions of Chicano activism. Numerous student activists reached out into the community and supported, and in some cases led, numerous social change struggles in the barrios.

Influenced by Rodolfo "Corky" Gonzales's poem "Yo Soy Joaquin" (1968), "El Plan Espiritual de Aztlán" (1969–1970), and "El Plan de Santa Barbara" (1969), Chicano activists became ardent proponents of what evolved into the CM's quasi-ideology, Chicanismo. They embraced a new nationalism predicated on rediscovered pride in the Méxicano culture, history, heritage, and language, in both the Southwest and Mexico. By 1970, Chicanismo, which had begun as a form of cultural pluralism, had become increasingly anti–liberal capitalist.

The most ardent nationalists among the Chicano activists were now hypercritical of the nation's political institutions and capitalist economy; some adopted a separatist political posture. To these activists, the ideology of Chicanismo was grounded in the belief that the new CM agenda should call for self-determination—the creation of a Chicano nation, Aztlán. Rudolfo "Corky" Gonzales, the Crusade for Justice, and the Brown Berets were its main and most passionate supporters. Yet at no point did Chicanismo provide the CM with a unified vision or belief system, a common direction, or a strategic and tactical plan of action, either for the present or the future.

Still, the nationalism that was fostered by Chicanismo gave the CM a semblance of an ideology that was increasingly critical of the nation's White-dominated society and liberal capitalism. In turn, the CM was instrumental in fostering a climate of change that proved propitious for the emergence of RUP. This climate was furthered by the radical activism and politics of other social movements, particularly the Civil Rights, Black Power and Anti–Vietnam War Movements.

Two groups that emerged out of the CM would prove to be RUP's predecessors: the Mexican American Youth Organization (MAYO) in Texas, founded in 1967, and the Crusade for Justice in Colorado, formed in 1966. Both contributed significantly to the CM's shift to a more political agenda. By 1970, political cries for "Chicano Power" rang out at all levels of the CM's activist ranks. That year both MAYO and the Crusade for Justice moved almost in sync in their struggle to politically empower La Raza by organizing RUP.

## Gutiérrez: The Organic Intellectual

In the 1960s, Méxicanos in Texas became increasingly active in their struggle to end their political powerlessness. This was evident in 1963 when Méxicanos orchestrated the first political takeover of the Crystal City Council in Crystal City, Texas (Cristal, to Chicanos). A coalition comprised of the Political Association of Spanish Speaking Organizations (PASO) and the local Teamster's Union mounted the successful effort to elect five Méxicanos, led by Juan Cornejo, to the city council, ousting the five-member gringo council. It was through this first electoral revolt in Texas that a young Méxicano, Jóse Angel Gutiérrez, was raised to prominence as a political leader.[7]

Gutierrez was born on October 25, 1944, in Crystal City, Texas. His father was a physician, who during the Mexican revolution (1910), served as a medical officer in Pancho Villa's army. During the 1920s, the senior Gutiérrez moved to Cristal, where he married and set up practice. Because of his family status, unlike other Méxicano children, who were poor and lived under the specter of segregation, for many years during his childhood, Gutiérrez lived a comfortable middle-class life. His family did not suffer from the indignities fostered by segregation. In fact, as Gutierrez many years later said, both the White and Méxicano communities treated his family with respect. This was evident in his being one of a few Méxicanos allowed to attend White schools.

For José Angel, who was twelve at the time, and his mother, the situation dramatically changed when his father died. All of a sudden, he learned what it was to be Mexican. His father left them without a sound economic base. Whites now treated him and his mother, Concepción, like the rest of the Méxicanos. Their credit at the bank, drugstore, and local department store was cut off. His mother, who had only an eighth-grade education, could not find work. The ensuing years proved difficult for them both. His mother toiled in the fields to make ends meet. José Angel also worked in the fields after school and during the summer months. The traumatic rejection coupled with the social degradation fueled in Gutiérrez an anger and frustration that intensified as he matured.

In spite of his hard life, Jóse Angel did very well in school. While in high school he was a champion debater, maintained excellent grades, and served as president of his junior and senior class. As a student at Uvalde Junior College in 1963, he began his career as an activist by participating in the Cristal revolt, handling much of the media coordination and giving numerous speeches during the campaign. In 1966 he graduated from Texas A and M University at Kingsville, where he had been active in student politics. After a brief try at law school at the University of Houston, he enrolled at Saint Mary's College graduate school, where in 1968 he obtained a master's degree in political science. It was during these years at Saint Mary's, and later at the University of Texas, Austin, while working on his Ph.D. in government that his leadership as an activist flourished, first with MAYO and then RUP.

## MAYO: Predecessor of the RUP

Third parties, like social movements, are products of antagonisms that produce a climate of change, impelled by the discontent of an alienated segment of society. This was very much the case with the emergence of RUP in Texas. Its genesis as a third party can be traced to MAYO, from 1967 to 1972 the most assertive and militant Méxicano organization in Texas.[8] MAYO took on the "gringo" power structure with unprecedented ferocity, impelled by the belief that it controlled Méxicanos though an oppressive, internal colonial system.[9] No organization in the state was as despised by the gringos in power.

MAYO grew out of the epoch of protest in general and the nascent CM in particular. The organization was born in March 1967 in San Antonio, where Méxicanos, who constituted some 40 percent of the population, were powerless and impoverished. It was the brainchild of five young Chicano student activists—José Angel Gutiérrez, Mario Compean, William "Willie" Velasquez, Ignacio Perez, and Juan Patlan. All were graduate or undergraduate students at Saint Mary's, a small liberal arts college in San Antonio.[10] At the Fountain Room, a bar several blocks from Saint Mary's, Los Cinco (as they became known), over the course of several weeks, met on a regular basis and held a number of study sessions, which culminated in MAYO. José Angel Gutiérrez explains: "All of us were the products of the traditional Mexican American organizations . . . of a changing mood in the community . . . [and had] spent time working on one issue or another. All of us were very frustrated at the lack of political efficacy, at the lack of any broad-based movement, and at the lack of expertise."[11]

The crux of their collective concern was that existing traditional Méxicano organizations in Texas were ineffective as agents of social change. These included the League of United Latin-American Citizens, the G.I. Forum, and the Political

Association of Spanish-Speaking Organizations. Los Cinco perceived them as too conservative, middle-class oriented, and unable to effect substantive change for the impoverished, powerless Méxicanos in Texas. The students were critical of the conventional approach—passing innocuous resolutions, holding social activities, conferencing, petitioning, and conducting voter registration drives.[12] Los Cinco felt that the times were auspicious for the formation of a new, activist, youth- and change-oriented organization that could take on issues in a much more assertive and forceful manner.[13]

Los Cinco examined a myriad of topics related to organizational development, ideology, strategy and tactics, and other aspects of building a movement. They followed carefully the media accounts of the New Left, Anti–Vietnam War, and Black Power Movements. They also monitored the activities of emerging Méxicano leaders such as Reies Lopez Tijerina, Cesar Chavez, and Rodolfo "Corky" Gonzales.[14] They went through an eclectic and in-depth internal organizing process and made trips to the South and throughout the Southwest to study the various non-Méxicano and Méxicano organizations.

For the next two years, MAYO with its cultural nationalist orientation and its student and barrio youth constituency would become an organization of organizers. Educational and social issues, not the building of a Chicano political party, were the cardinal catalytic forces that energized and directed its development. MAYO, relying heavily on nonconventional types of protest such as marches, boycotts, picketing, and sit-ins, chose educational change as its paramount focus. No other organization within the context of the CM matched MAYO's attack on educational institutions it perceived as racist. MAYO's call for educational reform included support for bilingual and bicultural education, the hiring of Méxicano teachers and administrators, the introduction of Chicano studies courses into the curriculum, and an end to punishing children for speaking Spanish in school. It conducted thirty-nine school walkouts in 1968 and 1969 in which hundreds of Méxicano students participated, some lasting for weeks. The number of walkouts was indicative of MAYO's militant organizing posture.[15] Not until its thirty-ninth walkout, staged in Cristal, however, did MAYO succeed. (The first thirty-eight walkouts failed mainly because they lacked strong parental and Méxicano community support. In other words, MAYO did not have the numbers, pressure, and stamina needed to overpower the recalcitrant administrators, who were increasing their intimidation of students and parents supportive of the boycott.)

MAYO carried out its mission of bringing about social change for Méxicanos. It used its barrio- and university-based chapters to initiate direct action on a number of social issues. For example, in 1967, it played significant leadership and organizational roles at the Raza Unida Conference held in El Paso, Texas. Scheduled by the Lyndon B. Johnson administration, the conference was organized to protest the cabinet hearings on Mexican American affairs. A week earlier, Reies Lopez Tijerina's Alianza held its annual meeting in Albuquerque, New Mexico, at which time the hearings were discussed. MAYO's leadership was instrumental in convincing those in attendance to endorse the Raza Unida Conference. Ernesto Galarza, a prominent scholar and former union organizer, was the conference's first chairperson. In 1968, at subsequent conferences held in San Antonio and Laredo, MAYO played a significant role in developing policy recommendations on issues affecting the community.[16]

Inherent in MAYO's social change strategy was the establishment of nonprofit social service and social justice entities, which were used to supply the resources needed to sustain and advance its own organizing capability. In the social service area, MAYO formed two nonprofit, tax-exempt corporations: the Mexican American Unity Council (MAUC) and the Texas Institute for Educational Development (TIED).[17]

MAUC was formed in 1968 by Willie Velasquez and José Angel Gutierrez as a nonprofit confederation of various community groups. It was at first funded by a large grant from the Southwest Council of La Raza. Velasquez, who wrote the initial proposal, became its first director. Although its primary focus was on economic development, MAUC also facilitated the formation of various badly needed youth, educational, housing, and civic participation programs and services by way of its various member organizations. TIED was organized in 1969 by MAYO leader Ignacio Perez. A recipient of both state and federal funds, TIED focused on developing health care services for farm workers and other disadvantaged groups in South Texas.

MAYO also used such programs and services to gain entry into the barrios and to provide jobs for some of the group's organizers and supporters. As Luz Gutiérrez, former wife of José Angel, explained: "We were thinking of setting up funds so we could . . . have something to work from. In other words, we had to have an organization to provide jobs for the people doing the organizing. So this is why we organized the MAUC."[18]

To control resources, MAYO also relied on infiltrating existing programs, including Volunteers in Service to America's (VISTA) Minority Mobilization Programs (MMP) in South Texas. MAYO leader Mario Compean, who was hired as a VISTA recruiter and trainer, later said he "went to recruit people to be VISTA volunteers and many members of MAYO became volunteers."[19] By 1969, however, MAYO began to come under the scrutiny of political officials in the Del Rio area for allegedly using the VISTA MMP to organize communities. As a result, MMP was terminated, but not before MAYO organized a combination of direct actions that culminated in the famous Del Rio March, attended by more than 3,000 people from throughout Texas. MAYO presented its long list of grievances as the Del Rio Manifesto. As a result of the earlier allegations, MAYO also came under heavy attack from federal, state, and local officials.[20]

MAYO also forged a working alliance with the Mexican American Legal Defense and Educational Fund (MALDEF). Formed in 1968 in Texas, with its main office in San Antonio, MALDEF's cadre of attorneys became an important legal asset for MAYO. For nearly two years, it provided MAYO with free legal assistance in dealing with a variety of issues. The relationship was so amicable that MAYO leader José Angel Gutiérrez was hired by MALDEF as a field researcher and troubleshooter.[21] Indicative of the close collaboration between the two groups is an excerpt from a letter sent by MALDEF director Pete Tijerina to then MAYO chairperson José Angel Gutiérrez: "Since the MAYO objectives emphasize the need for social changes and to provide equal opportunities for Chicanos in employment, education, and the administration of justice, please be assured that MALDEF's legal staff will be available to provide legal defense in all those cases arising out of arrest as a result of confrontations on the issues which involve violations of civil rights."[22]

As a result of MAYO's perceived radical social and educational activism from 1969 to 1971, Congressman Henry B. Gonzalez mounted what was tantamount to a personal crusade against MAYO and its leadership. He viewed MAYO as a racist, militant organization that was polarizing Texas. MAYO's relationship with the VISTA MMP, MAUC, and MALDEF were particularly scrutinized. In April 1969, José Angel Gutiérrez at a press conference in San Antonio made his infamous "kill the gringo" statement—essentially, that unless social change came to Méxicanos in Texas, it would be necessary to eliminate gringos by killing them.[23] The statement angered many Whites and conservative Méxicanos throughout Texas. A few days earlier, before the House of Representatives, Gonzalez had accused MAYO and its leadership of propagating hatred: "MAYO styles itself the embodiment of Good and the Anglo-American as the incarnation of evil. That is not merely ridiculous, it is drawing fire from the deepest wellsprings of hate."[24] He and others now used Gutiérrez's statement to go after MAYO and its front organizations and allies.

By the end of the year, MAYO had lost most of the resources that it needed for its front and allied organizations. Its organizers were purged from the VISTA MMP. MAUC's funding also came under attack, limiting MAYO's access to MAUC's resources and programs. MALDEF came under so much political fire that it moved its main headquarters from San Antonio to San Francisco, California, and substantially decreased its working relationship with MAYO.

As MAYO came under siege from powerful Democratic political forces, it began developing a much more political agenda. Up until 1969, its political agenda had not been well defined and had taken a backseat to education and social change issues.[25] After two years of indecisiveness on the issue of the Vietnam War, MAYO in 1969 became involved in organizing antiwar marches and demonstrations.

Until 1968, forming a Chicano political party had been a nonissue. Then, with the exception of Willie Velasquez, who opposed the idea on grounds that third parties were not viable political entities, the MAYO cofounders basically supported the Chicano party idea. They felt strongly that neither of the two major parties had been sensitive or responsive to the manifold needs of the Méxicano and poor communities.[26] In 1968, Gutiérrez began researching the legal requirements for forming a political party in Texas.

Upon completing his research, he drafted a report and circulated it among the various MAYO leaders and members, soliciting their input. He continued his research on third parties while on active duty in the U.S. Army Reserve, with a particular focus on Governor George Wallace's American Independent Party.[27] In a position paper titled "La Raza and Political Action," he examined various problems he felt impeded Méxicanos' political empowerment—from the prevalent fear, distrust, and ignorance of the political system to the pervasive parochialism among Chicanos. He concluded:

"A partial solution to our current dilemma in the political area lies in our developing parties for the promotion and protection of our interests. There are no reasons why we should not be masters of our destiny. All we have to do is look around us and within us to see why we must."[28]

When interviewed in 1973, Gutiérrez said initial response to the idea within MAYO had been poor: "No one really wanted to do it. It hurt a little, that people thought it was not a good idea." Later that year, Gutiérrez reintroduced his Chicano party scheme at a MAYO statewide executive committee meeting, but once again the reaction was negative. Gutiérrez explains, "They thought I was crazy and that it would never happen."[29]

In December 1968, at MAYO's annual board meeting, while not ready to support Gutiérrez's Chicano party scheme, the group's leadership did decide to become involved politically—they would run candidates for San Antonio's city elections scheduled for April 1969. Although Gutiérrez warned them that conditions were not propitious for MAYO to run candidates, Compean and others disagreed. They felt that after nearly three years of intensive organizing in the various barrios of San Antonio, conditions were auspicious.[30] As was customary in MAYO's adherence to a form of democratic centralism, Gutiérrez joined their ranks and supported the idea.

Under the guise of the Committee for Barrio Betterment (CBB), MAYO in 1969 made its political debut in San Antonio. It ran two candidates for the city council and mayorship, challenging the power of the Good Government League (GGL), a political machine that had dominated the city's politics for more than two decades.[31] Central to the campaign's strategy was testing bloc voting as an electoral tactic, the premise being that if it worked in San Antonio, it could work elsewhere, especially in South Texas.[32] MAYO's two candidates for the city council, C. H. "Candy" Alejo and Diario Chapa, and its mayoral candidate, Mario Compean, ran on a Chicano platform that stresssed Chicanismo and community control of the city's institutions, and that addressed the issues plaguing the barrios. According to Ignacio Garcia in *United We Win*: "Compean . . . expounded the concept of La Raza Unida and even placed the slogan in all his campaign literature. He talked of Chicano self-determination and called for the development of alternative political models to the Republican and Democratic parties even though the elections were non-partisan."[33]

The CBB candidates limited their campaigning to the city's west-side barrios. In the end, after an acrimonious electoral fight, the GGL triumphed over the CBB. Alejo and Chapa respectively received 13,787 and 17,877 votes. Compean, who ran against Mayor Walter McCallister, received 11,838 votes and ran third in a six-person race.

The results did not foster great momentum for the Chicano party idea. Outside of Gutiérrez and Compean, most of the MAYO leaders and membership were still skeptical. While becoming more politicized, some still saw the whole idea of forming a Chicano party as ludicrous and infeasible. Most supported community control of local nonpartisan institutions rather than continued use of militant confrontations and protests. The nonpartisan nature of local elections allowed them to have electoral designs without considering the need for a new party.[34]

At a MAYO statewide meeting held at Uvalde in May, once again Gutiérrez introduced his proposal for a Chicano political party. Using organizational charts and maps, he delineated strategies on how a Chicano partido could be organized. Of the group's lukewarm response, he commented, "Its just one of those things that when it's new, it demands a lot of work and people don't want to get into it."[35]

Instead, MAYO opted for the Winter Garden Project (WGP), which was oriented toward community control and committed to the decolonization of South Texas.[36] Its cardinal thrust was to have the Méxicano control the area's local political, educational, and economic institutions. MAYO, particularly Gutiérrez, took the position that there were some twenty-six counties in South Texas where Méxicanos constituted a majority of the population and were living under the yoke of internal colonialism. MAYO selected three counties, Zavala, La Salle, and Dimmit, for the implementation of its WGP. Gutierrez in a speech he delivered in 1970, provided statistics for two of the three counties to buttress his internal colonialism argument:

> You got a median educational level among mexicanos in Zavala County of 2.3 grades. In La Salle it's just a little worse—about 1.5 grades. The median family income in La Salle is $1, 574 a year. In Zavala it's about $1, 754. The ratio of doctors, the number of newspapers, the health, housing, hunger, malnutrition, illiteracy, poverty, lack of political representation—all these things put together spell out one word: colonialism. You've got a handful of gringos controlling the lives of *muchos* [many] mexicanos. And it's been that way for a long time.[37]

Moreover, the idea of Chicano self-determination buttressed by Chicanismo made it a unique plan within the context of the Chicano Movement. Compean, who had just been elected MAYO state chairperson, appointed Gutiérrez to implement the WGP. Gutiérrez pragmatically accepted Compean's assignment, believing that this could give him the opportunity to actualize both the WGP and his Chicano party idea.[38]

### The Cristal School Walkouts:
### Antagonism for RUP's Emergence

The approval of the Winter Garden Project could not have been timelier. During a trip to his native Cristal, in the spring of 1969, Gutiérrez found himself in the midst of a controversy over the selection of cheerleaders. The White high school administrators were using de facto quotas in the selection.[39] Traditionally, the students selected the cheerleaders, but with Méxicanos comprising some 90 percent of the students, the White administrators implemented a highly discriminatory unofficial system, which resulted in the selection of three Whites and one Mexicana. A faculty committee appointed by the White principal was in charge of the selection process. The committee moved to fill the vacancies by selecting two White students, even though Diana Palacios, a Méxicana, had formally applied. She was rejected on the grounds that the Méxicano quota had already been met in Diana Perez.

The rejection set off a protest by students. Severita Lara, one of the three main student leaders, explains the response: "We asked why. We started questioning the system." The protesting students circulated petitions demanding equitable representation and delivered them to the principal. After the principal refused to move on their requests, the students took their demands to the district's superintendent, John Billings.[40] The students broadened their protest to include other issues related to discrimination. Billings acquiesced to the student's demands, which included the selection of three Mexicanas and three Whites as cheerleaders; the election of twirlers and student favorites to be resolved either through a quota system or by the administration; and the establishment of a bilingual/bicultural program.[41]

The students considered initiating a school walkout that spring, but Gutiérrez convinced them to wait.[42] His reasoning was that the timing was not propitious since the school year was almost over and it would therefore be difficult to sustain a walkout. He did, however, recommend that they continue to pressure the administration and seek as many concessions as possible.[43] Despite the students' efforts, in June, the White-controlled school board reneged on Billings's earlier concessions to the students' demands.

That same June, Gutiérrez and his family moved to Cristal to implement the WGP and his Chicano political party idea. Years later he would write that he returned to "begin the process to recapture our Chicano homeland."[44] For the next few months he, his wife, Luz, and VISTA volunteers Bill and Linda Richey would spend long and laborious hours organizing throughout the targeted three-county area. By November 1969, Gutiérrez had organized Cuidadanos Unidos (United Citizens, or CU) in Cristal, which ultimately became the most powerful Méxicano grass-roots political organization in Texas.

After spending months building a power base, under the direction of Gutiérrez, in November the students carried out the only successful school walkout initiated by MAYO—the Cristal Boycott. Gutiérrez used the boycott as the "organizing catalyst" for the implementation of both the WGP and the formation of the Raza Unida Party (United Peoples Party, or RUP).

Gutiérrez, in October, used the school queen coronation issue to kick off the WGP. The students seized on a request by the White Ex-Student Association to use the football field for their queen's coronation, which had excluded Mexicanos, as an opportunity to resubmit their grievances. The pressure exerted by the Méxicano students was so intense that the school board denied the Ex-Student Association's request. In protest, the Ex-Student Association held an "all-White" queen coronation not at the high school, but at a local packinghouse.[45] The board, in an effort to defuse the escalating conflict, tabled all action on the remaining grievances until December.

Aware that the board had reacted to their pressure, the Méxicano students continued with their protest and mobilization strategy. In December, the students, supported by CU, augmented their original grievances to eighteen demands. Some of the most important demands stated that all student elections be conducted by students and not the administration; that all administrators, teachers, and staff become bilingual and bicultural; that the district develop a bilingual/bicultural program; and that the district hire a Méxicano counselor. The administration rebuffed their demands.[46]

On December 9, the students carried out the walkout that catapulted them into the national media limelight. At the peak of the walkout, some 1,600 students boycotted the elementary, junior high, and high schools. For weeks, Cristal was a battleground of protest marches, demonstrations, community meetings, and attempts to mediate the growing boycott.[47] Never before had Méxicanos been so united in their determination to break the template of White racism and prejudice. Méxicanos were so unified and organized that by early January the board caved into most of the students' demands. It was during these tumultuous weeks of protest that Gutiérrez wove the issue of the walkout and that of forming a Mexicano political party.

## The Genesis of RUP: Vehicle for the Second Revolt

In late December 1969, in the midst of the Cristal walkout, Gutiérrez finally won open support for his Chicano party idea at MAYO's first national conference, held in Mission, Texas, at La Lomita (an abandoned Catholic seminary). The conference agenda focused on the future of the Chicano Movement in Texas. Gutiérrez seized the opportunity to reintroduce his third-party scheme. In an attack on the reigning parties, he said: "Democrats and the Republicans are all alike. They are all Gringos . . . neither party has ever delivered for the Chicano . . . both parties have promised a hell of a lot, but neither has delivered. Now we as Chicanos are calling their bluff. . . . As far as we in MAYO are concerned, the only viable alternative is to look into political strategies which will yield maximum benefits for la Raza."[48]

Gutiérrez's scheme, however, still met with resistance among some MAYO members who wished to continue to prioritize education and cultural issues. A compromise was reached in which two significant resolutions were passed. One, led by Narciso Aleman, called for the promotion of alternative education systems through the establishment of Colégio Jacinto Treviño, a university without walls. The second resolution, pushed by Gutiérrez, called for MAYO to form a Chicano political party, conduct voter registration drives, develop a party platform, and raise funds for political campaigns.[49] According to Viviana Santiago, not a MAYO member at the time: "The emphasis was on winning elections and taking control. It wasn't enough to just do walkouts and marches, it was time to take hold of the political system and start winning elections and running the show."[50] Gutiérrez's resolution prevailed. Eager to accelerate the WGP and his party scheme, he solicited volunteers from the 600 delegates at the conference.[51] Despite his passionate appeal, Gutiérrez returned to Cristal with only three volunteers: Viviana Santiago, Alberto Luera, and Ruben Barrera. They became the embryo for Los Voluntarios de Aztlán, RUP's version of the VISTA MMP.[52]

Filled with enthusiasm, in January 1970, Gutiérrez next moved to launch the RUP. The walkout victory had prepared the political climate for its emergence. Gutiérrez did not allow the situation to defuse itself, instead he began to advocate for the formation of a political entity that would take over where the student strikers had left off. He convinced them that only by controlling the school board and the city council would Méxicanos in Cristal be successful in enacting major change.[53]

For months Gutiérrez spoke out against the evils of the two-party system—against the Méxicano being socialized into believing that Democrats were the party of the poor and Republicans the party of the rich. A Chicano political party was a reminder to both major parties that Méxicanos were determined to make democracy and community control a reality in their pursuit for self-determination. When interviewed, Luz Gutiérrez explained that to her and many RUP supporters, there was no difference between the two parties: "Whether you were Democrat or Republican, we were getting screwed. So, the fact that we set up the Raza Unida allowed us to have some influence in being a balance of power and we proved it."[54] Alberto Luera said that "it was very obvious to us that if we were going to create the maximum amount of change in our communities we could not do it within the confines of the two established political parties."[55] John Staples Shockley further elucidates why RUP was formed: "There were ideological as well as practical reasons for forming a third party. The Raza Unida Party leadership had little love for the Democratic Party. The party had, after all, been the dominant party throughout South Texas and thus to them it had been the main instrument of repression in the area. And the Republicans had been a nearly totally Anglo party in the community from the beginning. Gutiérrez argued that by forming a third party, Raza Unida supporters could participate in their own institution, one that valued rather than exploited them."[56]

On January 17, some 150 people attended a meeting for the specific purpose of forming a Chicano party in Zavala County. By accentuating local issues, Gutiérrez succeeded in garnering their support.[57] Interim officers were elected and goals were set. Gutiérrez's wife, Luz, was elected chairperson, four precinct committee persons were elected, and the name of the party was approved. The name "La Raza Unida Party" was selected before the meeting by a handful of people that included Gutiérrez, Bill Richey, and Viviana Santiago. Initially, Gutiérrez pushed for the name "Mexican American Democratic Party"; however, attorney Warren Bennet, who had been assisting Gutiérrez in troubleshooting the legal aspects of party formation, advised him that under Texas electoral laws, the word "democratic" could not be used because it was already the name of the Democratic Party.[58] The selection of "La Raza Unida" was a strategic choice, since the term was in vogue among the activists of the CM. Gutiérrez continued to stress that the creation of RUP was an answer to the unresponsiveness of the two controlling major parties and that it was oriented toward making politics more effective for Méxicanos.[59] Since the Texas Election Code allowed for the formation of political parties at the county level, that is where he worked to get RUP on the ballot.

On January 23, Gutiérrez filed a petition signed by eighty-nine persons for party status in Zavala County. Similar petitions were filed in Dimmit, La Salle, and Hidalgo Counties. Three percent of the voters from each county who had voted in the last general election had to sign the petition. In Zavala County, for example, 2,261 persons who voted in the November 1968 election translated to 88 voters having to sign the petition.[60] Gutiérrez announced that, as required by Texas election laws, RUP would hold conventions on May 2 in each of the four counties for the purpose of nominating candidates for the November county elections. Reaction to the announcement was mixed. Many Chicano activists applauded it as being necessary for the Méxicanos' political empowerment. Conversely, gringos judged it un-American, nationalistic, racist, and segregationist.[61] By February, the embryonic RUP was moving aggressively to implement MAYO's Winter Garden Project.

## The Winter Garden Revolt: Impetus for RUP

The struggle to organize RUP was dramatically advanced as a result of the electoral successes of the Winter Garden revolt.[62] Upon his arrival in Cristal during the summer of 1969, Gutiérrez concomitantly moved to implement the WGP in the neighboring counties of Dimmit and La Salle. In Dimmit County, he secured assistance from Juan Patlan and David Ojeda, who became a WGP staff member. In La Salle County, he was able to get the assistance of Bill and Linda Richey, both of whom were VISTA MMP volunteers. While propounding the virtues of the WGP, he sought to convince people of the merits of forming a Chicano political party. He found it easier, however, to sell people on the WGP's notion of community control than on the idea of abandoning the Democratic Party. In his diary, Gutiérrez wrote: "I think Juan [Patlan] is sold on it as I am, but I find it difficult to sell it to our people because of their traditional orientations toward the Democratic Party."

As a result of the Cristal school walkout victory, many Méxicanos supported the movement to organize the RUP. By late January 1970, all three county seat communities, Cristal, Cotulla, and Carrizo Springs, were in motion to run candidates not only for the county offices, but also for the school board and city council. RUP's cardinal political agenda was to win control of these local political structures. Finding qualified, eligible, and willing candidates who would toe the RUP political line proved, however, to be difficult. In the past, Méxicano candidates who opposed the interests of the local gringo power holders were harassed or intimidated and faced possible loss of employment. In the three-county region, jobs were scarce. With the economics very much controlled by the gringo minority, as John Staples Shockley explains, "If the Mexicans got out of line and tried to limit the economically powerful, the Anglo would, and did, first try to fire them and prevent them from getting any other jobs."[63]

In all three counties, the emerging RUP ran an unprecedented political mobilization targeting Méxicanos. Candidates were selected to run in four communities. In Cristal, three candidates ran for the school board and two for the city council; in Carrizo Springs, two ran for the city council and two for the school board; in Cotulla, four ran for the city council and two for the school board; and in Robstown, located in Hidalgo County, one ran for the city council. In Cristal, with Méxicanos comprising 85 percent of the community, RUP ran an aggressive grass roots–oriented campaign under the aegis of Cuidadanos Unidos. In neighboring Dimmit and La Salle Counties, where Méxicanos comprised the majority with 82 and 57 percent respectively, the campaigns were not as organized as in Cristal.[64] Still, thousands of Méxicanos were registered by RUP. In Cotulla, for example, under the leadership of Juan Ortiz, Arseño Garcia, and Raul Martinez, some 2,000 were registered.

For its political education and get-out-the-vote efforts, RUP relied on community meetings, rallies, social and cultural events, and door-to-door and telephone canvassing of the heavily Chicano precincts. RUP's newspaper, *La Verdad,* staffed by Voluntarios de Aztlán, a volunteer group of young people from throughout the Southwest, carried information on the campaigns as well as on RUP.[65] RUP also recruited voters through radio spots; mobile vehicles equipped with sound systems that saturated the Chicano precincts; and the distribution of a large array of campaign literature, buttons, bumper stickers, posters, and house signs. In order to ensure clean and fair elections, Gutiérrez secured federal marshals from the Texas Advisory Committee to the U.S. Civil Rights Commission to act as observers.[66]

Gringos in the three counties did not feel politically threatened. Many remembered how Méxicanos in Cristal politically self-destructed during the first electoral revolt, in 1963–1965. Some perceived Méxicanos as incapable of successfully coordinating and executing a community control–oriented plan like the WGP. But a few weeks before the elections, the gringos realized that they were facing a serious threat to their political hegemony and in response mounted a political counteroffensive. In Cristal, for example, Pablo Puente was temporarily disqualified from running for office as a result of the court's ruling that he was not a property owner, a requirement for running for the city council. A few days before the election, with legal assistance from MALDEF, Puente was reinstated on condition that he forfeit any absentee votes received before the election.[67]

An anti-RUP coalition of conservative Méxicanos and Whites resurrected Citizens Association Serving All Americans (CASAA), the group that had orchestrated the electoral counterrevolt in 1965 against the Political Association of Spanish-Speaking Organizations (PASSO). They selected Méxicano candidates who did not pose a threat to the gringo's political and economic interests. The gringo power holders had learned from the first revolt that with Méxicanos constituting an overwhelming majority of the city's population, it was by far politically more expedient to run Méxicanos that they could influence and control rather than to run themselves. CASAA's strategy against RUP was basically threefold: (1) Attack Gutiérrez as a militant radical who had no credibility as a candidate; (2) characterize RUP's candidates as unqualified to hold public office; and (3) threaten economic reprisals against Méxicanos who voted for RUP.

Gutiérrez countered by attacking CASAA ferociously. He cast himself as the defender of the poor and exploited, who fought against those who wished to continue the subjugation of the Méxicano. Paradoxically, to build up his image as a credible leader and candidate at rallies and meetings, he showed off his autographed pictures of Ted Kennedy and George McGovern and his invitation to the 1969 Nixon-Agnew inauguration.[68]

In Carrizo Springs, Cotulla, and Robstown, the gringo power holders responded similarly to those in Cristal. In Carrizo Springs, the campaign became bitter and divisive. Ultimately the two RUP candidates refused to be part of RUP's partisan slate; nevertheless, RUP continued to support them.[69] In Cotulla, it was a different story since RUP was better organized. As was the case in Cristal, the campaigns in both communities were intense. In Robstown, separated by great distance and without benefit of Gutiérrez's leadership or the WGP, RUP activists were not as well organized as in the Winter Garden region.

In early April, the budding RUP movement emerged triumphant. It was victorious in Cristal, Cotulla, and Carrizo Springs. In Cristal, it won all its races for the school board and city council. The voter turnout was higher than in the 1968 presidential campaign. Of the 3,100 people registered to vote, 2,544 went to the polls for the school board elections. RUP got 56 percent of the total vote. Three days later RUP's city council candidates garnered an impressive 60 percent of the vote. In Cotulla, RUP won three of the four seats for the city council, including the mayor's seat and the two school board seats. RUP's two candidates for the city council in Carrizo Springs won, but in Robstown, RUP's candidate for the city council lost.[70]

## RUP's Peaceful Revolution in Cristal

Of all the electoral victories, it was the effort in Cristal that had the most impact. From 1970 to 1975, RUP's victory in Cristal fostered what I have described as the "peaceful revolution" and the "Cristal Experiment." During those five years, Cristal became a laboratory for political, educational, economic, and social change. For Gutiérrez, the architect and social engineer of the WGP and the second revolt, the electoral victories were but the beginning of a movement toward empowerment, community control, and change that spread like a prairie fire throughout South Texas, the state, and ultimately the rest of Aztlán. The "political" takeover gave added impetus to the fledgling RUP that in turn fostered an organizing contagion.

For many activists, Cristal became the political matrix or locus of the CM. To some it was, metaphorically speaking, an emerging island of Méxicano self-determination in the midst of a sea of White-controlled internal colonialism. The magnitude of the change enacted in Cristal during those five years was unprecedented. No other community in the nation underwent as much change in such a short period of time. For many Méxicanos, Cristal was a model to be emulated; conversely, to the gringo, it was a flame of radicalism that needed to be quenched.

RUP's electoral victories in Cristal did not, however, produce immediate control of the school board and city council. Lacking a working majority in both, RUP won control as a result of the defection of school board member Eddie Treviño, who initially had been appointed by the White-controlled board, and Francisco Benavides, a local businessman. The two defections gave RUP a critical four to three majority on the school board and a three to two majority on the city council.

RUP's takeover kicked off the "browning" of Cristal's city administration. Whereas before the takeover few Méxicanos had held high-ranking administrative positions, within the next two years they would occupy every single one. A systematic purge of Whites occurred. So much pressure was exerted by RUP that most Whites resigned— some in protest—rather than be fired.[71] RUP's leadership required absolute loyalty in return for city employment. It was not just Whites who felt the impact of the changing of the guard. The new rules also applied to Méxicanos who were not supportive. RUP moved with impunity, since the people's seal of approval was evident in their participation at city council meetings and in their willingness to serve on the city's various commissions and ad hoc committees.

In Cristal, Cuidadanos Unidos became the mass-based organizational backbone of RUP in the Winter Garden area. What began as a political organization of a few male community leaders in 1969 by 1975 claimed a membership of nearly 500 families. By 1973, it had evolved into a political machine directed by political boss José Angel Gutiérrez. No other political organization that emerged during the course of the CM was as effective in mobilizing its membership and supporters for elections and direct actions. CU's influence was so great that RUP's leadership came from its ranks.

Still, it was in the arena of educational change that RUP's peaceful revolution scored its most impressive victories. With Méxicanos comprising some 87 percent of the district's students in 1970, and historically subjected to de facto segregation and discrimination, RUP school officials, from the outset, made educational change their priority. As was the case with the city council, RUP began the swift browning of the school's personnel. The old-guard school superintendent, John Briggs, was replaced in August with Angel Noe Gonzalez. What ensued was a systematic, orchestrated purge of White administrators, teachers, and staff, and of Méxicanos who were not supportive of RUP. By 1975, all the school board members and most of the school district's students, administrators, and staff were Méxicanos.

RUP's takeover of Cristal's school board and city council was met with contempt by the gringo. The Whites pulled their children out of Cristal's schools and their businesses out of Cristal. Many of them relocated their businesses and children to such adjacent communities as Carrizo Springs and Uvalde. The few gringo families that remained in Cristal established a private school for their children, as well as for the children of those Méxicanos who opposed RUP which they perceived was a Communist-inspired movement led by Gutiérrez the despot.

The new RUP administration produced unprecedented educational change. Led by Gutiérrez, who was elected board chairperson, the school board moved aggressively to ensure that all of the student demands approved by the previous White-controlled board were implemented. During the next five years, new schools were built and existing ones were refurbished. A plethora of federally funded programs were developed and implemented, all directed toward improving the quality of education. Inspired by Chicanismo, bilingual/bicultural education became the cornerstone of RUP's educational change efforts. Implemented initially in 1970, by 1975 it was offered in kindergarten through twelfth grade. Other improvements occurred in the areas of student tutorial programs, teacher and administrator development and training, adult education, student retention, and encouragement of students to go to a four-year college or university.[72]

The district's curriculum was changed to reflect the importance of the "Chicano experience." Courses in Chicano history, literature, and arts were introduced. The fundamental intent was to instill in the students the importance of pride and of retaining their Méxicano culture, heritage, and Spanish language. Assimilation was rejected and a form of cultural pluralism was enacted. This was reflected in the district's celebration of México's Independence Day (September 16) as a legal holiday. Other holidays such as Dia de la Raza (October 12) and Cinco de Mayo (May 5) were also celebrated, but not as legal holidays.

Many of the high school students were so politicized that they participated in local elections and direct actions in support of RUP candidates and issues. The students' high level of politicization and adherence to Chicanismo was also reflected in the district's music program. The high school marching band's musical repertoire was oriented less toward John Phillip Sousa marches and more toward Méxicano pieces such as "Guadalajara," "Jalisco," "Marcha Zacatecas," and "La Negra." It became one of South Texas's most award-winning marching bands. Its half-time shows, however, became an issue of controversy due to their political nature. As part of the kickoff, both the band and the athletes used the clenched fist symbolizing "brown power" as the official salute. At times this situation created conflict and altercations between Méxicanos and Whites.[73]

The White ownership of 99.7 percent of all county property coupled with the prevalence of poverty among Méxicanos led RUP's peaceful revolution to promote the people's economic empowerment by way of such nonprofit organizations as Industrias Mexicanas, Constructora Aztlán, and such for-profit corporations as Winter Garden Development Corporation. Most of the ventures were unsuccessful due to a lack of capital, technical assistance, and trained personnel. Individually, however, some Méxicanos during RUP's five golden years of community control established businesses, for example, grocery stores, bars, restaurants, gas stations, and automotive repair shops. This was in part ascribable to the White business exodus that started right after the takeover in 1970. The void was filled in part by Méxicanos; however, some businesses were never reopened.

RUP's peaceful revolution also sought to deal with Cristal's manifold social problems. During the first five years of its community control, such city services as trash collection and street maintenance were dramatically improved. In Cristal's various barrios, streets were paved, sidewalks, curb, and gutters were built, sewer and water pipes were installed, and through Urban Renewal scores of homes and public housing units were built. Health care, mental health programs, legal aid programs, and a credit union were created by RUP in the form of nonprofit corporations, such as the Zavala County Health Association, Inc., Zavala County Mental Health Outreach Program, and Oficina de la Gente (Office of the People).[74]

Cristal became a paragon of civic participation. Contributing to the participation renaissance was the formation of various organizations, such as CU (RUP's political machine), Obreros Unidos Independientes (Independent United Workers—RUP's local union at the Del Monte plant); and Barrio Club (RUP's security entity). Moreover, several existing organizations were also strengthened and brought into the CU's network. Women played a key role in enhancing RUP's social change agenda. It was through the participation of women such as Virginia Musquiz, Luz Gutiérrez, and Viviana Santiago that the peaceful revolution bore fruit.[75]

## RUP's Four County Elections

The electoral successes of the Winter Garden Revolt coupled with the emergence of RUP fostered a RUP organizing contagion in Texas and beyond. For MAYO, in particular, the electoral successes in Cristal and Cotulla proved the value and credibility of its Winter Garden Project. The victories were used effectively to demonstrate to Méxicanos that they were capable of politically organizing, governing, and wielding the power to control their own destiny. In addition, the rise of RUP was indicative of the direction the Chicano Movement needed to take. The rise of RUP demonstrated the willingness of some Méxicanos to shift their loyalty from the Democratic Party to RUP. This was an important achievement, since for decades, the loyalty of many Méxicanos to the Democratic Party had been unshakable.

In May 1970, RUP held countywide conventions in four counties—Hidalgo, Dimmit, LaSalle, and Zavala. A total of sixteen RUP candidates filed for November's elections. RUP was confident that its candidates could win all of the contested elections, since they were running in districts that were heavily Méxicano. RUP conducted voter education and registration drives. Only in Hidalgo County was RUP organizationally weak.

Fearing the RUP challenge, the White-controlled Democratic Party mounted a counterattack in all four counties. Their strategy was to keep RUP off the ballot. By the summer, the issue became so political that it resulted in litigation. County officials had refused to place RUP candidates on the November ballots. As Gutiérrez explains: "We definitely had to fight this thing out in the courts to decide just what exactly we had to do to qualify for the ballot."[76] He denounced the Democrats for deliberately maneuvering to preclude RUP from getting on the ballot for fear of losing control.

The struggle to get RUP on the ballot became a political and legal nightmare due to Texas's cumbersome election code regarding third parties. In both the electoral and court arenas, the decision to give RUP access to the ballot at the county level was decided by Democrats. Their rationale for denial was based on a laundry list of alleged technical errors. County Democratic Party officials contended that information given on county forms contained serious errors. For example, in Zavala County, the date said 1969 instead of 1970. In La Salle County, the alleged discrepancy was holding precinct conventions in improper locations and at the wrong time of day. In Dimmit

County, they alleged that RUP had allowed people who voted as Democrats in the county primary to sign RUP's petition to be on the ballot.[77] And in Hidalgo County, it was charged that RUP had filed its application on January 19, too early to be within the voting year, which began on March 1.[78] Despite intense protests by Méxicanos, only in Hidalgo County did White county officials back down and allow RUP to get on the ballot.[79]

In the courts, RUP attorneys litigated unsuccessfully in both the Fourth Court of Appeals and the Texas Supreme Court that RUP be placed on the ballot. Associate Judge Fred Klingman, in explaining the ruling of the state's highest court, said "there had not been substantial compliance with the provisions of Article 13:54 concerning holding conventions." RUP attorney Richard J. Clarkson argued that the secretary of state recognized the petitions as having fulfilled all election requirements and that the Texas attorney general had concurred. He further pointed out the contradictory legal opinions and stressed that if ballot status were not given to RUP, substantial numbers of Méxicanos would be disenfranchised in the November election.[80]

RUP attorneys argued that its candidates' civil rights had been violated because county officials had placed stricter requirements on RUP than on the Democratic and Republican Parties.[81] Facing a political dilemma, RUP's leadership decided in October to go ahead with the campaigns using a write-in voting strategy. But, as Shockley has pointed out, "Owing to the nature of the procedures for write-in votes under Texas law, such a campaign had little chance of success. Stickers could not be used; names had to be written in. In a community where many of the Méxicanos were functional illiterates, getting them to write their names correctly and in the proper place became an insuperable task. Although the courts did rule that election officials could help illiterates vote if they requested, the Anglo election officials refused to do so since they were not required to do so."[82]

In all four counties, RUP mounted grass-roots campaigns to educate Méxicanos on the procedures of voting via the write-in. RUP's newspaper, *La Verdad*, carried numerous articles explaining in detail the write-in procedures. Huge rallies and town hall meetings were held, and classes were offered for the purpose of teaching the voters how to write in the names of RUP candidates. This was an extremely difficult task, since the median education of Méxicanos in Cristal and Cotulla, for example, in 1960 was 1.3 years; by 1970, the median level in Cristal had increased to a mere 2.3 years.[83] Luz Gutiérrez, when interviewed, explained RUP's message to the people: "If all of us do our humble effort, we can create a triumph for the Raza Unida Party against those who seek to destroy it. We have a great opportunity to put an end to the political training that gringos here in Texas call democracy."[84]

The elections became vicious; the Democrats resorted to red-baiting tactics, alleging that RUP was a radical party that propagated "hate" and "separatism." Gringos relied on fear, polarization, and confusion to mobilize the conservative Méxicano and White voters. In their media blitzes and literature, they depicted RUP candidates as unqualified. They alleged that they would be detrimental to the area's business economy because RUP's "spend" policies would cause their taxes to be raised. In their mailers, the Democrats also listed their various community accomplishments, claiming that if RUP won, chaos would surely follow.

RUP countered with its grass-roots, get-out-the-vote mobilization.[85] It repudiated the Democrats allegations and claims of accomplishment. In Zavala County, RUP used the refusal of Democratic county officials to issue food stamps to Méxicanos as a polarizing issue. Throughout the four counties, RUP accentuated the importance of Méxicanos winning control from Whites and of extending the changes being made in Cristal to the county level. On Election Day, RUP's machinery was in full operation; however, throughout the targeted counties, incidents of harassment of Méxicano voters by White judges, election officials, and police were commonplace.

RUP's first bid to become a certified four-county party ended in failure. Within the Winter Garden area, of the sixteen seats its candidates ran for, RUP was able to win only one. The only RUP victory came in La Salle County with the election of Raul Rodríguez, who was elected county commissioner for Precinct Three. Yet, in spite of all the obstacles, RUP candidates averaged nearly 40 percent of the vote. In Hidalgo County, despite being on the ballot, RUP candidates garnered only 10 percent of the vote.[86] Illiteracy among Méxicanos coupled with the difficulties of organizing a write-in campaign proved insurmountable obstacles. White judges disqualified many of the votes that spelled the names of RUP's candidates incorrectly. Regardless of the negative results, RUP's leadership was optimistic about its political future. *La Verdad*, in an editorial, noted that RUP had won the election but lost on technicalities, proving that the idea of a Chicano political party was viable. In response to the election results, Gutiérrez declared: "We proved our point. The party is something visible, meaningful, and attractive to the Chicano voter. We'll go statewide in 1972. We start work in January 1971. The party has got nowhere to go but up."[87]

## Chapter Two

# RUP's Expansion Statewide:
# The Beginning of the End, 1971–1974

The November defeats did not impede the Raza Unida Party's expansion to other parts of Texas, especially to South Texas. At the core of its expansion was the Mexican American Youth Organization's (MAYO) commitment to build RUP into a viable political party. During 1971, much of RUP's expansion beyond the four-county area was attributable to MAYO. For the next two years, MAYO became the primary force statewide in organizing RUP. Many of RUP's top leaders came from MAYO's leadership ranks, among them José Angel Gutiérrez, Luz Gutiérrez, Mario Compean, Ramsey Muñiz, Carlos Guerra, Alberto Luera, and Lupe Youngblood. Moreover, MAYO chapters in the universities and communities shifted their priorities from taking on other issues to building RUP. They used the major changes being enacted in Cristal and Cotulla to market RUP to Méxicanos throughout the state. With the spirit of the CM still strong, other Méxicano activists joined MAYO in the organizing of RUP.

### RUP's Development: Rural vs. Urban Strategy

While most MAYO members were very supportive of RUP, there were a few who still opposed it. One such person was MAYO cofounder Willie Velasquez, who left MAYO because he opposed forming a Chicano third party and MAYO's increasing militancy.[1] As Luz Gutiérrez says," I don't think he was sold on us hook, line, and sinker."[2] Armando Gutiérrez, who was a MAYO member and RUP state vice chairperson in 1974, told me: "It was a mixed bag. Not everybody was totally supportive of the idea of creating a Chicano third party. . . . I don't think anybody had the idea of what it would eventually evolve to. It was virgin territory none of us had ever been involved in and there wasn't much history of third parties in our community. . . . Some people felt that we should use it [RUP] more as leverage in terms of opening up the Democratic Party. It was interesting because . . . in some ways . . . that is where you separated the people who for lack of a better term were truly 'radical' and those that were simply looking for an avenue to move into more middle-class positions."[3]

With growing support to expand RUP, some 300 activists from throughout Texas gathered at the Salon Tella, a dance hall in San Antonio, on October 31, 1971, to hold the first statewide RUP convention to discuss and plan RUP's future. Of those present, 42 were official delegates from eight counties and some 250 were observers and other county delegates who did not meet the strict legal requirements to be seated. Most were young people, and of them at least 25 percent were women. Many of them were members and supporters of MAYO.[4] After heated debate, the decision was made to expand RUP statewide.

At the crux of the debate were strategic differences between the two MAYO co-founders, José Angel Gutiérrez and Mario Compean, over how to develop RUP. Gutiérrez represented a much more "rural" perspective, and Compean opted for what became known as the "urban" perspective.[5] Gutiérrez's rural position at this time was different from the one he had enunciated less than a year before, when he publicly proclaimed that RUP would become a statewide party by the 1972 national/state elections. Before the convention, he shared with some of his close associates that he felt it was important to keep RUP at the county level. He felt that going statewide was a major political mistake. The requisite organizing ingredients such as money, a trained cadre of experienced and knowledgeable organizers, viable candidates, and a statewide infrastructure were virtually nonexistent. He believed that MAYO was not ready to take on such an arduous political endeavor.[6]

At the convention, Gutiérrez contended that before going statewide, RUP needed to develop a strong community power base, especially in the twenty-six South Texas counties where Méxicanos were a majority. He told the delegates that RUP should first be organized regionally on a county-by-county basis before expanding statewide. He cautioned that there would be strong opposition from the Mexican American Democrats because they would perceive RUP's statewide development as a threat to their political interests. Alberto Luera, who was elected RUP state secretary, when interviewed years later explained: "He [José Angel] said that we couldn't do it, because we were trying to run before we knew how to walk. But most people wanted to run. . . . Some people made accusations that he was being selfish in not wanting the partido to go statewide, just because he had the partido in Cristal. . . . Nevertheless, he wanted to build a regional party first, then, after solidifying the power, expand."[7]

Compean, strongly supported by Jesus Rameriz and Efrain Fernandez from Hidalgo County, led the fight for a statewide party. They were the chief proponents of the "urban" perspective. Unfortunately for Gutiérrez, the 1970 school board and city council elections in the Winter Garden area coupled with the major changes underway in Cristal contributed to the rising expectations among some Méxicanos throughout Texas. Compean was resolute that RUP should become a statewide party by the 1972 elections. He felt that many Méxicanos throughout the state would support RUP.[8] According to Luera, Compean argued: "If we go back and evaluate the position of both parties, we will see that they have never done anything for us. We have always had to grab from them, pressure them to be able to get something." He further reminded the delegates that politically, as Méxicanos, "we have nothing." He felt the CM was in trouble and that time was running out. By going statewide, he believed, RUP would help "reenergize" it.[9]

Furthermore, since there were 254 counties in Texas, it was far more practical and expeditious to get RUP on the ballot via the petition drive than to go on a county-by-county basis. The resources were just not there to accomplish such an impossible feat. In addition, many delegates were aware that the Socialist Workers Party was litigating to get on the ballot. Some felt that RUP could piggyback.[10]

With delegations present from twenty-one counties, forty-seven voting delegates from eight counties were certified. Compean declared, "We must go ahead. We can't just rely on Cristal for the rest of our lives."[11] The vote on the issue was twenty-one to fifteen for expanding RUP statewide. The convention's delegates then approved the decision by acclamation, demonstrating their unity of action.[12] Armando Gutiérrez, who supported Compean's position, explained why Compean prevailed: "Hey, we have got Chicanos in Lubbock, in Houston, and all kinds of places who want to be part of this movement and struggle."[13] Also, according to Carlos Guerra, "the reality was that we were having a hard time getting RUP on the ballot at the county level."[14] Martha Cotera, who supported Gutiérrez's rural position, explained that she was torn because "I knew that if we went statewide it was going to be very difficult. I felt we were going to lose a lot of the focus on those areas where the [Méxicano] population was very great and where we needed to do a lot of development and had a lot of support."[15]

The convention delegates elected RUP's provisional state officers. Compean nominated Gutiérrez as state chairperson, but Gutiérrez refused on the grounds that he was lawfully barred because he was president of Cristal's school board. Compean was then elected. Other officers elected were Efrain Fernandez of Pharr, cochair; Alberto Luera of San Antonio, secretary; José Gonzalez of Fort Worth, treasurer; Roberto Villarreal of Kingsville, committeeman; and Alma Canales of Austin, committeewoman.

Some discussion also concerned possible statewide candidates for the 1972 elections. Names recommended for governor included state senator Joe Bernal, Bexar county commissioner Albert Peña, and Roman Catholic bishop Patrick Flores, all of San Antonio. Also suggested were state representative Carlos Truan and Dr. Hector Garcia of Corpus Christi. Interestingly, none of these individuals were present.[16] Gutiérrez was considered for governor but declined because he did not meet the minimum age requirements.

For a brief moment, some delegates proposed supporting candidates from other racial and ethnic groups for purposes of expanding RUP's base. The names of two Black women from Houston were unsuccessfully suggested for the U.S. Senate: state senator Barbara Jordan and P.T. Bonner of Operation Breadbasket. Former U.S. senator Ralph Yarborough's name was also mentioned.[17] This was an interesting development, since many of the delegates were also members of MAYO and thus supposedly were ultranationalist and supportive of MAYO's Winter Garden Project.

The delegates adopted a left of center progressive posture. This was evident in the forty or so resolutions that were passed and became the basis for its platform. Essentially, the platform was populist and reformist in nature, and very much within the ideological parameters of the nation's liberal capitalist system. It advocated strong planks on public ownership of all natural resources, national medical and preventive care, immediate withdrawal from Vietnam, bilingual/bicultural education, abolition of capital punishment, abolition of state sales tax, implementation of a corporate profits tax, and abolition of state personal income tax. The resolution, however, that drew the most thunderous applause was the one that called for the "abolition" of the Texas Rangers. The convention closed with Compean explaining that what had transpired was truly historical, because the major parties "had ceased to be relevant to our people."[18]

After the convention, a great deal of planning went into developing the process that would get RUP on the ballot in time for the 1972 presidential and state elections. Throughout much of the early part of 1972, RUP leaders spent considerable time seeking qualified candidates for local and state offices.[19] As is the case with most third parties, this became a formidable task. Gutiérrez along with Compean contacted those who were mentioned at the convention as possible candidates; however, no one was successful in convincing them to run as RUP candidates. They were all Democrats, and they were not willing to go up against the party. This compelled RUP's leadership to search within its ranks for candidates, but none of MAYO's main cadre leaders were interested in running for the statewide offices, especially for governor. Garcia explains the circumstances that led to the selection of Ramsey Muñiz as RUP's gubernatorial candidate: "The next choice was Ernesto Garcia, a war veteran from Waco who was contemplating joining the Raza Unida Party but was still an active participant in local Democratic circles. He said no but suggested a young lawyer from Waco who was an administrator in the Model Cities Program. He was Ramsey Muñiz, an active local member of MAYO."[20]

Initially, Muñiz contemplated running for the state board of education. In fact, he filed for both board and governor positions, only to withdraw from the state board of education race. This was a result of a closed meeting that involved only a handful of MAYO leaders at which the decision was made to go with Muñiz for governor. This created conflict, since Compean had indicated an interest in running for the post.[21]

Through a coordinated recruitment effort, candidates were selected for the other races. On February 9, 1972, MAYO's leaders held a press conference at which Muñiz and a list of fifty-two other RUP candidates were presented. Joining Muñiz at the press conference were Alma Gonzales, candidate for lieutenant governor; Flores Anaya, candidate for the U.S. Senate; Ruben Solis, candidate for state treasurer; Fred Garza, candidate for state railroad commissioner; and Robert Gómez, candidate for land commissioner. Also, present was Compean, who informed the press that RUP was fielding candidates for numerous other state and county offices in Hidalgo, Zavala, La Salle, Starr, Nueces, Victoria, Mclennan, Tassant, and Bexar Counties.[22]

With candidates selected, the energies of the RUP activists turned to getting the party on the ballot via a petition drive, difficult to mount in the time frame of May 7 to

June 30 for securing the required signatures. Most of the responsibility to get RUP on the ballot fell on MAYO. It was at that point that a political metamorphosis took place: MAYO became RUP. Luera commented that the petition drive to get RUP on the ballot gave many MAYO members an opportunity to change their image from "South Texas radicals and militants" to a "community-oriented" group.[23] While MAYO's leaders, including RUP's candidates and supporters, played significant roles in the movement to secure the required 22,365 signatures, Luera and Compean, operating out of a small MAYO office in San Antonio, were the main coordinators statewide.

As Gutiérrez later wrote, "Getting the signatures . . . was a nightmare ordeal."[24] Guerra explains that the time factor was the most difficult aspect to overcome. "You had a thirty-day period after the primary during which you had to find the signatures of some 23,000 people who had not voted in the primary . . . and their signatures had to be notarized."[25] Luera explains that, as RUP's state secretary, it was his responsibility to stay on top of coordinating countless meetings at both the county and state levels in order to ensure all was being done according to the Texas Election Code. In order to secure the required signatures, RUP relied on a quota system devised by Gutiérrez in which each of the twenty-six or so targeted counties, all with heavy concentrations of Méxicanos, would produce a given number of signatures.

The petition drive from beginning to end was plagued by problems, especially by acute shortages of volunteers and money. One of the most difficult tasks was explaining to the people why they should leave the Democratic Party and register with RUP. Martha Cotera said they were being asked "to leave the party and come into a wild adventure."[26] The situation by June looked rather gloomy. According to Muñiz, "People really didn't know what was going to happen. We didn't know if we were going to be on the ballot or not. People had already given up and they were saying we are not going to make it."[27]

In June, about 500 delegates and observers met at the second RUP statewide convention held in San Antonio. Gutiérrez announced in a speech that the party had successfully gathered some 23,000 signatures, enough to qualify RUP as an official statewide party. But, he told them, in order to play it safe, they needed to go beyond the required amount and secure some 40,000 signatures. He also tongue-lashed both the Democrats and the Republicans: "You can't tell what comes out of the mouth of one Democrat from what comes out of the mouth of a Republican."[28] He accused both parties of being liars, hypocrites, and fools. He reminded them that RUP in Texas could sway the "balance of power" in the coming presidential election by controlling 40,000 votes.[29] By holding the convention, the second legal requirement for third-party status was fulfilled. Compean was elected state chair for a second term, numerous candidates were nominated for state office, and a platform was ratified.

Inspired by the convention, RUP supporters went after additional signatures by running a few ads in some newspapers, such as the *San Antonio Express*, soliciting support for the petition drive. This was particularly important, since the White-controlled press had depicted RUP, especially its leader Gutiérrez, as radical. A RUP political ad titled "Raza Unida Party Needs Your Help" read: "We need contributions from the little people who are tired of paying high taxes just to make politicians rich."[30]

In spite of some difficulties encountered in submitting the petitions, by June RUP had secured some 25,000 signatures, enough to get RUP on the state ballot.[31] When Gutiérrez and Compean went to deliver the final petitions to Secretary of State Bob Bullock, they were forced to wait for hours. Moreover, a contentious debate occurred with Bullock over the usage of "Raza Unida" as a party name. Finally, after a lengthy discussion that began caustically and ended in a humorous fashion, Gutiérrez succeeded in getting Bullock to certify RUP as an official party.[32]

## The 1972 Elections: David and Goliath

By the summer of 1972, RUP had expanded its organizing base to various counties in which, demographically, Méxicanos had a strong presence. In April, RUP strengthened its control of Cristal's city council and school board. In Cotulla, it gained control of the city council, and Arceñio Garcia at the age of twenty-four was elected mayor, one of the nation's youngest. As for the school board, only one of the three RUP candidates won in 1972. Of major significance was the third takeover by RUP, this time in the small South Texas town of San Juan. MAYO activists led by Jesus Ramirez and Edgar Ramirez orchestrated the area's first electoral revolt, which produced Méxicano control of San Juan's five-person commission (comparable to a city council)—two RUP candidates were elected to the town's commission, and one as mayor.

Under the auspices of Familias Unidas (United Families), a mass-based political organization similar to the CU in Cristal, RUP won a seat on the Robstown city council. In nearby Kingsville, after a hard, bitter electoral struggle, RUP succeeded in electing a Méxicano to the city council. In San Marcos, two of the three candidates endorsed by RUP won school board seats. This was not the case, however, in Hondo and Uvalde, where RUP supported for both the school board and city council candidates who lost. Thus, before the November elections, RUP enjoyed majorities on three city councils.[33]

From August to November, Texas politics witnessed the emergence of RUP, the first Chicano political party in Texas history. Ramsey Muñiz's campaign for governor provided the main surge of energy for RUP's electoral struggle against the Democratic Party's monopoly .[34] Muñiz was catapulted from political unknown to political star. Nothing in his background suggested that he was political superstar material. He was twenty-nine, married with one child, and a former football star from Baylor University where he got his B.A. and law degrees. In 1972, he was director of the Urban Development Corporation of Waco. Muñiz had been involved with MAYO since 1968, in a somewhat undistinguished way.

In no time, Muñiz became one of the most prominent Méxicano leaders in Texas. Political scientist Armando Gutiérrez describes him as a phenomenon. "He was a very handsome guy, well-built ex–football player, extremely charismatic, very articulate, wonderful speaker. . . . There was not an ounce of doubt in his body that he could run at the statewide level."[35] Historian Ignacio Garcia described Ramsey as having a very quick mind. "He would come into a community and say, 'What are the issues here?' And you would tell him on the way to the platform. He could then speak for forty-five minutes."[36] Luz Gutiérrez describes him as projecting "a Mister Clean image."[37] By election time, Muñiz, in many political circles, was perceived as the state's most prominent RUP leader.

The other RUP state candidates failed to foster the electricity and following among Méxicanos or the media that Muñiz did. Alma Canales from Austin, for example, according to Garcia, "was radical, poorly dressed, married to a MAYO activist, and the less articulate candidate. Her name on the ballot was the result of the women's strength in the party caucuses. She remained on the ballot, despite efforts to remove her by the Waco chapter, due to Compean being her strongest supporter."[38] Compean's support of Canales was an indicator of the emerging rift between him and Muñiz.

Other RUP candidates besides Muñiz had kicked off their campaigns before RUP's June convention. Their focus was on getting RUP on the ballot and also developing name recognition as candidates with the electorate, especially among Méxicanos. All the candidates, however, particularly Muñiz, faced a multiplicity of obstacles and challenges in getting their campaigns off the ground: scarce money, weak campaign organization, little political know-how, and almost no staff, just to name a few. José Angel Gutiérrez, in August, became Muñiz's campaign manager, which in itself turned into a campaign issue. Regardless of the flack, Muñiz defended Gutiérrez: "You can't find any person more sincere about the needs and problems of the state of Texas. If people really believed what the press thought about his actions, we wouldn't be making the impact we are."[39]

By 1972, most of MAYO's leaders had become RUP's main leaders, including Gutiérrez, Compean, Luera, Guerra, Youngblood, and Muñiz. Compean, for example, became RUP's state chairperson and Luera RUP's state secretary. However, due to the changeover in many counties, MAYO was doomed. Few MAYO chapters continued to organize, although in Uvalde during the spring of 1972, MAYO initiated a series of protest activities against the White-controlled school district. However, most MAYO chapters by 1972 were absorbed by RUP, bringing about the demise of MAYO.[40] Former national MAYO chairperson Carlos Guerra explains that with RUP on the ballot, "there was no practical point in keeping MAYO alive."[42] MAYO member Maria Elena Martinez from Austin said that MAYO disappeared because Raza Unida "required all our energy, time, and thought."[42]

Even though RUP candidates and leaders did not really believe that they could beat the Democrats, they made numerous public statements that suggested otherwise. At the June convention, Gutiérrez stressed that Muñiz had a chance of winning if RUP were to convince Anglos, Blacks, some of the labor unions, teachers, and professionals that there would be no benefit to the state if another "millionaire, backward rancher, such as Dolph Briscoe (Democratic candidate for governor) were elected."[43] RUP had to garner a minimum of 2 percent of the vote to ensure ballot status for the 1974 elections. After the convention, RUP attorney Jesse Gamez went to court and addressed a federal panel of three judges, arguing against the Texas Election Code's 2 percent ballot qualification requirement. Gamez told the court: "I guess we're just shell-shocked, your honor. We have been in positions before where we were on the ballot and at the last minute we were taken off." He argued that the process was unfair and extremely costly. He noted that RUP had spent around $100,000 to secure ballot status. RUP was joined by other third parties, among them the Socialist Workers Party, American Party, and New Party, in challenging various aspects of the Texas Election Code.[44]

RUP's strategy also focused on consolidating support from within the Méxicano community. A number of prominent moderate to conservative Méxicanos, some of them members of the League of United Latin American Citizens (LULAC), endorsed Muñiz's candidacy. Tony Bonilla, state director of LULAC, for instance, not only endorsed Muñiz and the entire RUP slate but also contributed $1,000. At a banquet honoring Muñiz, Bonilla said: "I am here as a Chicano and a *carnal* [barrio slang for brother] to Ramsey Muñiz. There is no question as to who should get the vote. One of his opponents has become rich by using Mexican Americans and Mexicans and the other has ideas that run along with the John Birch Society. Briscoe and Grover are not different."[45] State representative and Democrat Paul Moreno endorsed him. A great deal of support came from Chicano students from various universities.

Some effort also went into securing support from non-Méxicanos. In June, Muñiz unsuccessfully solicited support from defeated Democratic gubernatorial candidate Francis Farenthold. Moreover, in his appeal to Democratic liberal voters, he said: "Liberals have always talked about helping the minorities. How much more can they help us than by voting for us." He further noted, "What we are saying to Texas liberals is how liberal are you?"[46] Some liberals responded by accusing RUP of being responsible for Farenthold's loss to Briscoe. In an apparent act of political expediency, Muñiz asked for the votes of voters who were supportive of George Wallace. He felt he needed votes regardless of where they came from.

Muñiz and RUP assembly candidates Albert Peña III, Hector Rodriguez, and Ruben Sandoval were all able to garner some union support. On October 8, the AFL-CIO Local 180, Radio Electricians and Machine Workers Union of San Antonio, endorsed them. Just before the election, Muñiz and other RUP candidates got the endorsement of the International Paper Mill Workers Union, AFL-CIO.[47] Muñiz was also able to get some support from the black community. In August, his campaign got a shot in the arm when Rev. Ralph Abernathy, head of the Southern Christian Leadership Conference, and Corretta King, widow of civil rights leader Rev. Martin Luther King, showed their support.[48]

RUP's primary strategy, however, was to focus on securing the Méxicano vote. RUP candidates spent most of their time and limited resources reaching out to the Méxicano electorate. Muñiz and his wife, Albina, with their two-year-old daughter, Delinda, were constantly on the campaign trail, canvassing the state. They attended forums at universities, rallies, picnics, and press conferences in countless Méxicano communities. His trekking included visits to other states where there were large numbers of Méxicano migrant workers from Texas. According to Guerra, "Ramsey was tireless. I mean, once Ramsey took it on, he took it on with a vengeance."[49] Most of those I interviewed marveled at the stamina, energy, and zeal he drew on to promote RUP's political gospel of empowerment and change.

Muñiz's commitment to the Chicano Movement showed through his support for RUP at the national convention held in September in El Paso. Although he was not allowed to address the 3,000 or so RUP delegates and supporters, he openly supported Gutiérrez's bid for the national chairmanship of the party. Gutiérrez's winning the chairmanship, however, produced negative consequences for the Muñiz campaign. A major power struggle developed between Gutiérrez and Rodolfo "Corky" Gonzales. For Gutiérrez, the rift was time consuming and a major political distraction before and after the convention. Instead of concentrating on consolidating RUP in Texas, scarce resources and time were directed toward organizing the convention. After the convention, the situation only got worse for Gutiérrez. He found himself fending off attacks, traveling out of state, and essentially being consumed by RUP's supposed "national" agenda. Overextended, Gutiérrez could not be a "hands-on" campaign manager.[50]

In spite of the rift between the two titans, the national convention did produce some important results for RUP in Texas. First, Muñiz's gubernatorial candidacy was strongly endorsed by the convention's delegates, catapulting him into a much brighter limelight. Second, the delegates voted to boycott the presidential election by exhorting Latino voters not to cast their votes for either Nixon or McGovern, and instead to concentrate on local and state efforts. And third, the media coverage of the convention in Texas was extensive, which assisted RUP's efforts to reach the Méxicano voters.

Inherent in its strategy was the polarization of the electorate so that there would be no doubt as to where the underrepresented voters should place their primary loyalty and commitment. Muñiz's campaign exemplified this. The campaign had two recurrent themes—"unity" and "determination."[51] He always addressed issues that primarily affected Méxicanos. In the area of education, he was critical of what it considered Texas's racist educational system. He propounded the need for bilingual and bicultural education, an end to corporal punishment, and community control of barrio schools, among other reforms. Muñiz also spoke out against the busing only of Méxicanos and Blacks. He was articulate on the theme of cultural pride, which was also an intrinsic part of RUP's cultural nationalist posture.

On the campaign trail, Muñiz rebuked allegations that RUP had taken money from Republicans, even though Gutiérrez did have some contact with Republican operatives for the purpose of securing financial support for RUP's campaigns and support for its programs in Cristal.[52] Moreover, although unsuccessful most of the time, RUP took issue with newspapers it felt were racist in their reporting. For example, it filed a suit against the *San Antonio Express* and lost.

In spite of limited finances, RUP was able to distribute some 120,000 buttons and over a half million pieces of literature, flyers, and bumper stickers, mostly in the barrios.[53] On Election Day, numerous barrios across Texas were involved in RUP's get-out-the-vote drives. Earlier in the campaign, Muñiz had predicted that he would get at least a million votes.[54] The final count was much lower. Muñiz got only 219,127 votes, 6.43 percent of the vote, to Democrat Dolph Briscoe's 1,632,287, 48.90 percent; Republican Henry Grover's 1,532,075, 44.96 percent; and Socialist Worker Party Debby Leonard's 24,072, less than 1 percent. Of the 254 counties in Texas, Briscoe carried 229, whereas Graves won 23, and Muñiz 2. Muñiz won only in Zavala and Brooks Counties. The highest number of votes, however, came from the two heavily Méxicano populated counties of Bexar and Travis, where he got 28,424 and 21,964, respectively.[55]

Muñiz did not meet his goal of one million votes nor did he carry the twenty-six majority Méxicano counties. RUP failed to fulfill its promised "balance of power" role. Yet Muñiz won a partial victory in that he garnered enough votes to ensure RUP official party status for the 1974 elections. Election night, Muñiz commented to the media: "The people here tonight have experienced true democracy for the first time, a democracy never experienced under the Republican and Democratic parties. In this sense, it's been a tremendous victory and I'll guarantee you, we will be back."[56]

As for the other forty-nine RUP candidates, they went down in disastrous defeat. For the U.S Senate, RUP candidate Flores Amaya got 64,819 votes to Republican John Tower's 1,850,983; Democrat "Barefoot" Sanders got 1,512, 065; and Socialist Worker Tom Leonard received 11,009 votes. The other RUP candidates fared a little better: Lieutenant governor candidate Alma Canales received 131,627 votes; state treasurer candidate Ruben Solis Jr. garnered 123,135 votes; and railroad commissioner candidate Fred Garza secured 159,623 votes.[57] In eleven legislative races, RUP failed to seat one candidate and did not generally impact the results at all. In the race for the state house of representatives, in District 57-J, which covered parts of San Antonio, RUP candidate Albert Peña III received some 3,000 votes, nearly 35 percent of the total.

RUP ran candidates in eight county races, yet it seated only seven candidates in two counties. Five candidates, including county attorney, sheriff, one commissioner, and two constables, were elected in Zavala County, RUP's birthplace. In neighboring La Salle County, RUP elected one commissioner and one constable.[58]

For RUP's leaders, the fact that the party had won a place on the ballot for the 1974 state elections meant that this was only the beginning of bigger things to come. RUP indeed had concentrated on consolidating its power base at the local level, where that year it scored several victories. In Cristal, it handily won three seats for the city council and three for the school board. On May 18, *The Militant* reported a summary of the RUP victories from 1971 to 1973. Others, such as the *San Antonio Express*, while it reported the election results, played down the RUP victory. On November 10, the paper's editorial headline read, "Raza Unida's True Power Is in Local Elections." The editorial writer concluded that "Raza Unida's true strength is not statewide but in local elections. . . . This is as it should be, for Mexican-Americans are in a majority and should determine their local affairs."

RUP won a majority on the school board and city council in Edcouch-Elsa, two seats on the city council in Kyle, one city council seat in Lockhart, one school board seat in Hebbronville, one city council seat in Robstown, and two city council seats in Beeville.

In Carrizo Springs, the party won one seat on the city council, which it had lost in 1971, and it won back control of the city council and the mayor's seat in Asherton, which it had also lost in 1971. The party for the first time had won control of the Marathon city council and regained control of the city council in Anthony, which is near El Paso, and increased its seats on the Anthony school board from two to five. In La Joya, the party picked up three seats on the school board. In San Marcos, two candidates backed by the Raza Unida were elected to the school board. In Eagel Pass, Raza Unida backed a successful incumbent who was running as an Independent. While Raza Unida lost control of the San Juan city council, for the first time the party won control of the Juan-Alamo school board. In Pearsall, in 1972, two Méxicanos were elected to the city council and two to the school board. After failing to forge a coalition with Whites and getting defeated by them in 1973, those Méxicanos who were a part of CU opted for becoming part of the RUP—with them came the two Méxicanos on the city council and the two on the school board.[59]

While the party had gone statewide, it ostensibly practiced Gutiérrez's 1971 "rural" strategy. All of its 1973 local victories were won in small rural communities. RUP did not run candidates in any of Texas's larger cities, many of which had big Méxicano populations. According to Gutiérrez, one reason was lack of money. Another was that in the traditional political machinery in many of the big cities there were schisms involving Méxicano Democratic candidates. He said: "We did not want to be on the ballot and be baited by having the accusation that there was one Mexican running against the other."[60] Numerous other RUP leaders from various urban areas strongly disagreed with Gutiérrez. Albert Peña III, who got the highest percentage of the vote for the state house of representatives, said that running RUP candidates in the large cities would have been the best way to maintain the political momentum created as a result of the 1972 elections.

Statewide, the Democrats stiffened their resistance against RUP. That year, Congressman Henry Gonzalez escalated his attacks on RUP, particularly on its leadership. At a conference, he said that RUP suffered from a common third-party weakness: lack of staying power. For political parties, "essentially the goal is power—its acquisition and its use. Once acquired, the problem is how to use it and how to keep it." Moreover, he said, dissidence was a good means by which to awaken the people to the political potential of their vote; however, he strongly defended the view that the two-party system still offered the people the best vehicle for exercising political clout.[61]

Not threatened by the acrimonious attacks by Democrats, RUP too functioned as a political pressure group, organizing demonstrations and lobbying against legislation, especially that which would further thwart third parties in Texas.[62] RUP in Cristal succeeded in organizing its own Chicano-based union, Los Obreros Unidos Independientes (the United Independent Workers), which ultimately was certified at the local Del Monte plant. RUP's leaders and supporters always found time to participate in direct-action protest activities. In fact, RUP in Cristal, via CU, at times functioned as a rapid deployment force willing to travel to support issues the party was backing.

In October, RUP held a statewide conference in Harlingen for the purpose of gearing up for the upcoming 1974 state and county elections. The conference drew some 200 delegates, most from about twenty-five counties from Central and South Texas. Compean said, "This meeting informally signifies the beginning of the '74 campaign. It will let the party members around the state know that we are all ready to go."[63]

After the conference, RUP's executive committee faced the dilemma of whether to use the primary or the state and local convention method to select its candidates. Those opposed to the primary method argued that it would create unnecessary expenses due to filing fees and that there would be a dissipation of energies that would lessen the number of candidates. After much heated debate, at the exhortation of Compean, the committee opted for the primary elections method.[64] The decision was based on these rationales: RUP would be eligible for state reimbursement of expenses incurred during the primary; the primary was the most efficacious method of confronting, head-on, the Mexican American Democrats; and the use of the primary would further develop RUP's party structure and enhance its organizing activities.

Several strategy meetings were held in late 1973 and early 1974 by RUP's leaders. Of major concern was new state legislation that affected the certification of third parties. The legislation in the Texas Code in 1973 now required that a political party secure at least 20 percent of the vote in order to stay on the ballot as a full-fledged political party. The party would still be recognized if it received more than 2 percent of the vote but would not be eligible to receive funds for its subsequent primaries.[65] The pressure was now on RUP's leadership to come up with a strategy that would yield, at the minimum, 2 percent of the vote.

Mexicanas from the very start of RUP's formation in 1970 had played a significant leadership role. In 1971, RUP's platform included a plank on La Mujer (women). By the end of 1972, 36 percent of the county chairs and 20 percent of the precinct chairs were women. In January 1973, some of RUP's women leaders met in Cristal and organized Mujeres por La Raza Unida, and by the summer of 1974, led by Evey Chapa, Martha Cotera, Chelo Avila, Juana Bustamante, and Irma Mireles, held several meetings. Their culmination was a statewide conference in the fall of 1974 of Mujeres por la Raza Unida.[66]

In January, RUP officially kicked off its 1974 campaigns when Muñiz formally announced that he would again seek his party's nomination for governor. At a press conference in Corpus Christi, Muñiz lashed out at both Democrats and Republicans: "Hardly a day passes that I am not approached with a familiar story: 'I have been a Democrat or Republican all my life, and I have nothing to show for it.' " During the press conference, he also mentioned that RUP's campaign would focus on Watergate, taxes, education, mass transportation, medical care, and the oil monopoly, and that RUP would have candidates in at least ten counties.[67]

Democrats attacked Muñiz's candidacy by accusing him of taking illegal payoffs from the Committee to Re-Elect the President (CREP). Several newspapers, such as the *Fort Worth Star Telegram* and the *Houston Post*, carried articles charging that RUP had made a deal in 1972 with CREP to withhold support from McGovern. Gutiérrez and Muñiz denied the charges and demanded that the Senate Watergate Committee allow them to testify. Throughout much of its 1974 statewide campaign, RUP was plagued by serious power struggles between the Muñiz and Compean forces. When I interviewed Compean, he said that "the conflict reached an explosive stage to where Ramsey Muñiz and I had a falling out."[68] The two personalities polarized party factions.[69]

The growing conflict between the two leaders stemmed from serious differences over campaign strategy as well as clashing egos.[70] One area of disagreement was Muñiz's major shift from a campaign that in 1972 had targeted essentially the Méxicano poor and middle class to one in 1974 that was more broad based and inclusive of the middle- and upper-class Méxicanos and non-Méxicanos. According to Guerra, who was Muñiz's campaign manager in 1974, "Muñiz figured he had a good shot at securing much more than the 20 percent of the vote needed to keep RUP in the ballot. In fact, he was optimistic that he could win, providing Republicans fared better than they did in 1972. In order to do this, he felt the campaign had to produce a broad-based coalition that included White liberals, Blacks, unions, et cetera."[71] This change in focus and image was exemplified by Tarrant County RUP chairperson Carlos Puente's comments to the press: "We're trying to dilute the image that it's solely a Chicano party, especially in the North Texas area." He further stated, "In this area, as well as other urban areas, its always been stressed that the party is for Blacks, Anglos, Chicanos and those who are disenchanted with the other two parties."[72]

Muñiz's new mainstream strategy was also evident in his effort to change the name of the party. According to Guerra in our interview, Muñiz said, "We are a party of people—people together, or as we say in Spanish, Raza Unida." Rather than Raza Unida being emphasized, the new campaign slogan was in English, "People Together." In addition, in an attempt to purge his campaign of the "Chicano nationalist" underpinnings that had characterized the 1972 campaign, all of Muñiz's campaign literature was a "patriotic" red, white, blue. Much of the campaign literature, including posters and bumper stickers, did not carry the party logo. The literature highlighted Muñiz's name, not that of the party. Some journalists alleged that Muñiz was "out gringoing the gringo." In short, the campaign's intent was to mainstream RUP, giving it a more inclusive and less radical image. This change brought on a negative reaction from RUP's state chairperson, Compean, who accused both Muñiz and Guerra of abandoning the Méxicano grass-roots community by opting for the Méxicano middle class and of altering RUP's focus on including everyone.[73]

The signs of division within RUP's state leadership became more apparent as the campaign unfolded. When I interviewed Compean, he said that "the campaign alienated a good part of the cadre element that had been the backbone of the '72 campaign."[74] Martha Cotera, in explaining Muñiz's and Guerra's position on the matter, said that "Ramsey got a taste for success. He wanted to win. So they wanted to broaden the base. They wanted to cut deals with . . . all the constituencies of the liberal democratic infrastructure. Mario, being much more of a nationalist, much more doctrinaire, says 'Wait a minute, this is not the Raza Unida.' Ramsey wants to take us into a vehicle that's just for him, not for the people, and not for the movement of what the Raza Unida is all about."[75]

To Lupe Youngblood, a former MAYO leader, the conflict stemmed from differences over methodology and not petty leadership jealousies. Mario Compean represented the "purist "school of thought and Ramsey Muñiz the "realist." The former propounded sticking to mobilizing the grass-roots people in the barrios; whereas the latter wanted to go after the middle- and upper-class Méxicanos who supposedly had the money.[76]

Compean became increasingly critical of Muñiz and Carlos Guerra. The conflict between Compean and Guerra actually went back to the days of MAYO and stemmed from personal as well as political differences. According to Youngblood, by Muñiz's second gubernatorial try, Compean had concluded "that Ramsey was doing it for Ramsey and not for the Raza. He was into self-promotion."[77] Rumor also had it that Compean wanted RUP's nomination for governor in 1972 and again in 1974. According to Guerra, when the 1974 nomination was not his, he got "pissed."[78]

The conflict between the two leaders culminated at RUP's state convention in Houston, September 21–22. Attended by some 200 delegates and observers at the Whitehall Hotel, the convention dealt with various aspects of RUP's program and the election of statewide party officers. The fact that the convention was held in Houston suggested that RUP's support in the urban areas was growing. However, instead of the convention being a manifestation of growing party unity, it became one of rifts between the two warring political camps as well as between urban and rural delegates.[9]

Indicative of the growing internal rifts, before the convention, two RUP Houston-based factions became engaged in a contentious power struggle over RUP's leadership in that city. One faction, led by Daniel Bustamente, claimed to be community based. The other claimed to be university based and was led by Tatcho Mindiola, who had recently taken a faculty position at the University of Houston. The first major struggle developed at a countywide intraparty election for the leadership, when Mindiola won by a mere two votes. The second struggle concerned where the convention would be held. The Bustamante faction wanted it at Jeff Davis High School in northern Houston, where it would be more accessible to the Méxicano community; Mindiola's faction wanted it at a place where it would attract the media and project a much more mainstream image. Muñiz agreed with Mindiola's position. With the backing of Muñiz, the Whitehall Hotel was selected as the convention site.[80]

At the convention itself, the discord between the Muñiz and Compean forces came to a head. The election of a new RUP state chairperson also became a point of contention. Compean, who had served as RUP's first state chair, vacillated about whether to run. José Angel Gutiérrez called a private meeting for the purpose of mediating the conflict. The meeting, which included Compean, Muñiz, and a few other RUP leaders, ended in an altercation between Compean and Muñiz. According to Lupe Youngblood, who was present, Compean threw a drink in Muñiz's face.[81] Muñiz responded by attempting to strike Compean.[82] They were separated, and the incident was not made public.

As a result of the meeting, however, Youngblood of Robstown, originally considered a dark-horse candidate, eventually became RUP's state chairperson. Compean was nominated but withdrew after it was apparent that he did not have the votes to win.[83] Ignacio Garcia provides a further explanation for his withdrawal: Compean was "distraught over his divorce," and he did not want to divide the party even more. Mindiola, who had been Muñiz's preferred candidate, also withdrew his name from nomination. Lupe Youngbood emerged as the compromise candidate. With the Youngblood victory, Compean's influence within RUP and the campaign diminished substantially.[84]

When Compean withdrew, some of the women delegates nominated Maria Elena Martinez from Austin. She had been a former MAYO member and was José Angel Gutiérrez's first choice. Led by Martha Cotera, Alma Canales, Rosie Castro, Evey Chapa, and Virginia Muzquiz—women who had been involved in Mujeras por La Raza Unida, a women's caucus in RUP—the women announced that they were no longer willing to take a secondary leadership role. Martinez explained when interviewed, "I challenged, Why can't a woman run for chairperson?" Some women spoke out against her candidacy on the grounds that women should be in supportive roles, that is, working in the kitchen, cooking, and so on. Martinez said of that response, "It floored me, that it was not appropriate for a woman to run for the chairmanship."[84]

When the final vote was taken, Youngblood was elected RUP's state chairperson and Martinez the vice chairperson. In his address, Youngblood promised more party communication at the statewide level. Moreover, he informed the convention delegates, he intended to revitalize "the old MAYO structures" in order to expand the party. This was important, since many of RUP's leaders were former leaders and members of MAYO.

One of the convention's major orations was by Imamu Amiri Baraka, secretary general of the National Black Political Assembly and chairperson of the Congress of African People, whose Houston chapter endorsed the Muñiz campaign. Baraka called for capitalism's elimination. "We are in the era of the final elimination of imperialism, monopoly capitalism, and racism. . . . We must first decide whether our goal is to get into the American system or to eliminate it."[86] This speech did nothing to advance Muñiz's desire to give RUP a much more "populist" and "liberal-reform" image and ideological posture. Instead it reinforced, if not validated, the gringos' and Mexican Americans' image of RUP as radical if not Communist.

Muñiz's speech denounced both major parties, but his primary attack was directed at the Democrats. "Democratic Party, keep your flunkies and hacks," he said. "We will not have yes men or people waiting for orders in our party. If you are wondering when are we going to return to the old parties . . . we will not go back to your crooked poker game party. In order to defeat you, we are dedicated to bringing down the kind of politics that the old parties represent."[87] He also addressed the various aspects of RUP's continued populist and reformist liberal democratic platform. He called for the abolishment of the sales tax, equitable school financing, free day care, free tuition to community colleges and vocational schools, lowering the retirement age to sixty, bilingualism in every aspect of life, and a constitutional provision that would allow the state to take over the public utility companies. He went on to point out that "to finance them [such programs] the state could replace the income tax with a tax on corporation profits and tax all petroleum produced in Texas, not just gasoline sold at the pump."[88] There was nothing in the platform that buttressed allegations that RUP was "communistic." At best, it continued to be more populist and militant integrationist in its orientation.

Unlike 1972 when RUP ran four candidates for statewide office, in 1974 it ran only two: Muñiz for governor and Fred Garza for railroad commissioner. It fielded candidates for thirty-five local offices, for sixteen state representative seats, and for various county offices. At the local level, RUP ran three candidates for constable and ten for justice of the peace.[89]

RUP's get-out-the-vote efforts were impeded by limited financial and people-power resources. Consequently, it was not able to run a well-organized voter drive in all of the twenty-six majority Méxicano counties. The reality was that RUP was running as a state party without the necessary infrastructure to be competitive against the major parties. For instance, it ran a semblance of an effective campaign for the state legislature in only four urban areas. In Houston, it ran Maria Jimenez; in Austin, Dr. Armando Gutiérrez; in San Antonio, Daniel Meza; and in the Corpus Christi–Robstown area, Dr. Jorge Treviño. Some door-to-door canvassing was done; some literature was distributed. Meza was believed by some to have the best chance of actually winning. He had a campaign headquarters and had secured some union support. When interviewed by a reporter from *The Militant*, Gutiérrez suggested that the races were oriented more toward political education than winning. He said that RUP's responsibility was to educate the Chicano and others as to the basic reasons for their conditions—"why we are powerless, what the nature of the system, the society is."[90]

The election produced very few victories for RUP. Even after all the talk about mainstreaming the party, the Muñiz campaign did not fare well. Muñiz was able to garner only190,000 votes, 5.6 percent, about half a percentage point less than in 1972.[91] The sad reality was that of the twenty-six counties in which Méxicanos comprised more than 50 percent of the population, Muñiz carried only one: Zavala County, with 52 percent of the vote. Table 1 lists the ten counties with the highest Méxicano populations and pertinent voting data on the Muñiz campaign.

Why did Muñiz do so poorly? There are several reasons. First, Democratic governor Dolph Briscoe succeeded in consolidating his power base with conservatives in particular. Second, Briscoe was successful in winning back some of the Méxicano voters who had voted for Muñiz in 1972. Third, Republican candidate Jim Granberry did not mount a strong campaign against Briscoe. Fourth, liberals either voted for Briscoe or simply stayed at home.[92] Muniz's defeat may also be ascribed to the presence of many "endogenous antagonisms," including declining financial and volunteer resources, a growing disillusionment among RUP's small voter constituence, RUP defections to the Democratic Party, interparty squabbles and schisms, and a declining CM.

TABLE 1.   Results of the Ramsey Muñiz Gubernatorial Campaign

| County | Votes for Muñiz | % of Total Votes | % Méxicano |
|--------|-----------------|------------------|------------|
| Starr | 992 | 18.04 | 97.87 |
| La Salle | 738 | 36.53 | 92.16 |
| Jim Hogg | 707 | 31.00 | 91.86 |
| Zapata | 387 | 28.71 | 91.54 |
| Maverick | 156 | 37.00 | 90.35 |
| Webb | 3,855 | 27.62 | 85.62 |
| Duval | 308 | 9.90 | 84.00 |
| Dimmit | 731 | 31.00 | 82.00 |
| Zavala | 2,035 | 52.18 | 81.57 |
| Brooks | 1,369 | 51.00 | 80.00 |

*Source:* RUP Research Committee, n.d.

The other RUP state representative races also ended in defeat. No RUP candidate even came close to winning. RUP's only major victory came in Zavala County, in the race for county judge (the most powerful position in county government, since it has both executive and judicial powers). Against an incumbent White Democrat, Gutiérrez won by some 266 votes. RUP won an additional seat on the county's court of commissioners, giving it a three to two majority for the first time. In addition, it won the races for county clerk, district clerk, and county treasurer. RUP now had total community control of the county and of Cristal's school board and city council.[93] In neighboring La Salle County, according to Leodoro Martinez, RUP won "two constables and one justice of the peace." He added, "We'd never won a countywide race as Raza Unida."[94] In Bexar County, Ciro D. Rodriguez, now a congressman, was elected to the Harlandale school board. His victory was a first for RUP in that county.[95]

The resounding defeat of RUP by the Democratic Party served to remind political aficionados of the realities that face third parties who challenge the hegemony of the two-party system—in the case of Texas, at that time, winning was next to impossible. Without adequate financial resources, experienced leadership, viable candidates, organizational infrastructure, and access to the media, and in a political climate that was very conservative, RUP found it difficult to compete effectively. Journalist Tony Castro of the *Houston Post*, the author of *Chicano Power*, somewhat prophetically wrote that year: "Perhaps an obituary on Raza Unida is premature. But it is not too much to suggest that Raza Unida has no future as a statewide party—or, for that matter, as a dominant political force outside a few strongholds in South Texas. By their nature in the American political system, third parties come along every so often to make a point on behalf of a dissatisfied or disenfranchised minority, and then they fade into oblivion."[96]

Right after the election, as RUP's leadership licked its wounds and wondered about its political future, the *Texas Observer* editorialized: "The hard political fact is that the Raza Unida has to run legislative campaigns in brown communities if it is to run legislative campaigns at all—and given the electoral success of José Angel Gutiérrez as opposed to Ramsey Muñiz, a small-electorate campaigns seem to be more promising."[97]

Thus, the 1972 and 1974 gubernatorial elections would be the pinnacle events of RUP's development. The party's defeat in 1974 marked the beginning of its decline as a third party in Texas.

# Chapter Three

## Victim of the Politics of Self-Destruction: The Decline of RUP in Texas, 1975–1978

The years 1970 to 1974 were the golden era of the Raza Unida Party's organizing in Texas. These were history-making years, when thousands of Méxicanos repudiated the Democratic Party's dictatorship. Of the RUP organizing efforts in the Southwest and Midwest, that in Texas was the strongest. In four years as a third party there, RUP had shaken up the party power structure by winning several local races, getting on the ballot, becoming a certified political party, and running candidates in two statewide elections. But after the 1974 state elections, RUP began to lose its organizing momentum. Declining effectiveness brought its demise in 1978..

### Texas's Changing Political Climate: A New Ethos

With the Chicano Movement (CM) all but dead by 1975, RUP also entered a state of decline.[1] At the same time, the epoch of protest ended, and the epoch of the Viva Yo generation began. The end of U.S. military involvement in the Vietnam War by 1974 brought an end to the Antiwar Movement. The demise of other antagonisms such as the Civil Rights, New Left, and Black Power Movements also contributed to the emergence of the increasingly conservative, materialist, and "me-oriented" epoch. With the end of these protest movements, an ideological shift occurred; the new ideology rebuked protest and militancy and embraced a return to the normalcy of the status quo. This new ethos, with its emphasis on individualism and political accommodation, reembraced the basic tenets of the liberal capitalist system.[2]

The scores of MAYO and RUP leaders who were interviewed for this study agreed that the CM's decline contributed to RUP's becoming a casualty of a changing political climate and ethos. Alberto Luera made reference to the emergence of a "me" generation and acknowledged that a change in attitude had occurred by the midseventies. "We were all getting older and tired of having to struggle just to keep jobs. Not necessarily burned out, but our priorities changed. . . . No one before us had had the perceptions we had and nobody after us came with perceptions of our reality."[3] Luz Gutiérrez added: "We got tired and burned out. We grew up."[4] While some protest and change activity continued well into the late 1970s, it lacked the ingredients requisite to any viable social movement—a climate propitious for change, dynamic leadership, multiple strong organizations, a well-defined ideology, a strategic and tactical plan of action, and the ability to exercise power.[5]

The poor results of the November state elections foreshadowed RUP's decline in Texas. Moreover, with the collapse of the CM, Méxicanos in Texas witnessed a dramatic decrease in RUP's organizing activities and electoral victories. By 1975, Méxicanos had begun to join a move toward the old political status quo. Former RUP leaders and supporters left RUP and returned to the Democratic Party. The years 1975–1977 were disastrous for RUP. During this time, the partido failed to win any significant political victories or conversions. Instead, it began to decline rapidly after 1975,[6] even though a few local RUP chapters managed to consolidate power and made some organizing headway.[7]

## The Aftermath of the 1974 State Elections

The losses in the 1974 state races did not mean that RUP stopped organizing. After the elections, RUP's leadership sought to make the best of a bad political situation. Meetings were held in order to evaluate the election results as well as to determine the next steps that needed be taken if they were going to succeed at consolidating the party. Compean continued to be critical of Muñiz's efforts to transform RUP into a populist multiethnic party. From his perspective, Muñiz had been a dismal failure and had "turned off" a lot of people from the barrio who also happened to be the backbone of RUP's support.[8] As political scientist Richard Santillan wrote, "The results of the 1974 elections were a major disappointment to La Raza Unida Party and for those who advocated state and national elections."[9]

Former 1972 RUP state representative candidate Albert Peña III told the press that "the party is what we should be pushing, not personalities." He felt the party needed independent thinkers. "Even within the party that we've set up to be an alternative, we'd better have our own voice within the party or we're not doing much." He was critical of RUP because it had yet to define itself clearly as an alternative to the two major parties. Without providing the people with a viable alternative, he said, "We're just setting up another party like the Democrats and Republicans." He warned that RUP was at a critical juncture.[10] Jesus "Chuy" Rameriz, one of RUP's top organizers in South Texas, explained why he and others left RUP in 1975 and began returning to the ranks of the Democratic Party: "I suspect that maybe a lot of it had to do with just running the numbers. I've always been a numbers person in terms of politics and very practical. I think if you were to run the numbers in '74 and say, 'If we're pulling 35 to 40 percent of the votes in some Democratic precincts on the Raza Unida ticket, can you imagine what we can do as Democrats? Can we go into the party and in effect . . . replace those folks that had been in the party for all these years and haven't been doing a damned thing?' I think the motivation was 'Let's go out there and kick 'em in the ass as Democrats. Let's go out there and surprise them.' "[11]

Other RUP leaders held opinions that differed with these assessments. In an article in *The Militant*, a few weeks after the election, José Angel Gutiérrez made no apologies for the campaign RUP had executed. "We weren't so confident of making the 20 percent. We decided that Ramsey ought to go out and appeal to everybody—in his rhetoric, in his campaigning, and so on. We realized full well there was going to be some criticism about the position."[12] Carlos Guerra, Muñiz's campaign manager, took a more optimistic view. He called the 1972 showing the "protest vote" and the 1974 total "our vote."[13] He reaffirmed this view when interviewed twenty-three years later: "Actually, we were fairly happy that we were able to maintain the percentage."[14] Martha Cotera concurred; she found the campaign "very exciting and energizing."[15] Lupe Youngblood commented that "the 1974 campaign was a lot better organized than the 1972 campaign." In Robstown, he added, " by the time 1974 came around we were much more established. The local chapters of the *partido* were very well organized. . . . Locally, the '74 campaign was a tremendous campaign here because we had a lot of support."[16]

The diehard RUP zealots agreed that in order for RUP to continue, it would have to concentrate on campaigns that it had a chance of winning—in the local rural areas where Méxicanos were concentrated.[17] This strategic decision, however, was not made until November 1975, one year after the election, at a meeting of the party's executive committee. It was also agreed that RUP would not run candidates for any statewide office in the 1976 elections. In addition, RUP activists in urban areas would lend their efforts and resources to RUP candidates in small towns and rural areas. Political scientist Armando Gutiérrez pointed out that "one of the problems with running in urban areas is if you constantly get beat, and get beat bad—and the Democrats are now putting an effort into beating us—there's always the danger the people won't take you seriously anymore."[18]

## RUP's Political Downward Spiral, 1975–1976

RUP would never again hold the stature or have the support of as many Méxicanos as during its first four years of existence. In spite of Muñiz's dismal 6 percent electoral showing in 1972, the final vote count was enough to rattle the cage of the entrenched and omnipotent Democratic Party leadership. As journalist Harry Boesch of the *Corpus Christi Caller-Times* observed, "Raza Unida accomplished in just a few years what many third parties never achieve—enough influence to affect the outcome of the governor's race and a guaranteed spot on the 1974 general ballot."[19] In an effort to thwart RUP's challenge, the Democrat-controlled state legislature, supported by the Democratic governor, passed legislation in 1975 that made it even more difficult for any third party to achieve full legal status as a certified political party. Passed under the guise of election reform, the legislation required that a political party obtain 20 percent instead of the previous 2 percent of the vote in gubernatorial elections in order to qualify for state-funded primaries.[20] Another law was passed that changed the governor's term of office from two to four years, which meant that the next gubernatorial election would be held in 1978. The Democrats had made it virtually impossible for RUP or any other third party to maintain or gain ballot status.

Despite the obstacles, in 1975 RUP sought to consolidate and expand its power base in the small and rural communities, especially in South Texas. It was at this time that RUP was at its strongest in the rural communities of Cristal, Robstown, and Cotulla. On the other hand, several communities that had previously elected RUP local candidates, such as San Juan, had broken their ties with RUP and either rejoined the Democrats or were now independent in their politics.

RUP's organizing contagion impacted other communities in Texas positively. Even though some Méxicanos refused to support RUP, they became increasingly politicized. Communities such as Alamo, Donna, Edinburg, Pharr, San Juan, and Weslaco carried on the empowerment struggle independent of RUP. As Michael Miller explains, "Although not running under the banner of La Raza Unida, primarily because of its radical connotations and the fear of alienating a portion of the voters; the new [Mexicano] officials [elected in those communities] appear to be oriented to reform."[21]

RUP continued its political activity in some of the state's urban areas. In cities such as San Antonio, Houston, Corpus Christi, El Paso, and Dallas, RUP chapters or better-defined county organizing committees continued their organizing efforts, keeping RUP tenuously alive. In Austin, Dallas, and Houston, RUP's main organizing cadre came from the universities, with little or no base in the barrios. Regardless of the gains RUP had made, even after four years it had failed to effectively penetrate the urban areas of Texas and truly become a countervailing power to the Democrats. Without money and large numbers of volunteers, RUP activists found it difficult, if not impossible, to compete with the Democrats' machine. Even in San Antonio, which had a sizable Méxicano population, the Democratic Party had a monopoly on the political marketplace.

Part of the problem was that RUP activists had not been able to develop a viable party superstructure. The party's state and county structures were not adequate for maintaining RUP's organizational drive. For example, it never established an organizational presence in all of Texas's 254 counties. At best, RUP had a presence in 26 counties that had large Méxicano concentrations. Only a few of the communities had popular-based political organizations, such as Cuidadanos Unidos (CU) in Cristal and Familias Unidas (FU) in Robstown. They were structured, well led, grass roots in membership, and able to mobilize voters.

Another problem RUP faced was that the traditional Texas-based Méxicano organizations, such as the League of Latin American Citizens (LULAC), American G.I.

Forum, and unions, including the United Farm Workers (UFW), did not support RUP's agenda. They chose unofficially to remain loyal to the Democratic Party. Even UFW leader Cesar Chavez, when visiting Cristal, applauded the changes that were being implemented by RUP but chose to stay zealously loyal to the Democratic Party. By 1975, RUP had failed to consolidate the support of Méxicanos statewide. Its main base of support continued to come from the blue-collar worker, farm worker, student, and only a small segment of the middle class. Although RUP's state leadership was for the most part middle class, most of its county and local leaders came from the lower class. From a class perspective, RUP was a predominantly working-class political party.

Initially, the Mexican American Youth Organization (MAYO) was the major organizing buttress for RUP. By 1972, however, in some urban areas, the party became dependent on student groups that called themselves RUP Clubs.[22] According to Youngblood, in some cases this presented a major organizing problem, since often students "wouldn't go out to the community. They didn't have anything to do with [the people in the barrios]."[23] While some clubs did do community outreach, most did not. They suffered from what can be described as an "infantile disorder," meaning that they sought to organize the partido from the sanctuary of academia without involving the people directly in the process. Too many times, they expected barrio residents to attend meetings and conferences at the university, not understanding that most of them felt like strangers there.

This problem was compounded by still another factor. With the absence of a CM, and in particular its progeny the Chicano Youth Movement, the student activists who in the past had provided a lot of the manpower and even leadership in organizing RUP by 1975 were joining the ranks of the nascent Viva Yo generation, which rebuked much of the CM ethos. As a result, some Chicano student organizations had lost their movimiento posture and were becoming more mainstream in their orientation.[24] In the poor rural areas of South Texas, RUP had greater success in developing the semblance of a power base and was able to show some political resistance.

Yet, in the 1975 local elections managed to produce victories in only two communities, Cristal and Robstown. In Cristal, RUP continued to vanquish its opposition by the power of its political machine, Cuidadanos Unidos. For four years, CU in Cristal succeeded in fending off efforts to seize from it community control of Cristal's city council and school board. In 1974, RUP wrested political control from the Democrats of the Zavala County Court of Commissioners, with Gutiérrez serving in the dual role of county judge and political boss. By this time, CU had evolved into the political machine headed by political "boss" José Angel Gutiérrez, who between the years 1970 and 1975 used both material and nonmaterial inducements, namely patronage, to consolidate and hold on to power.[25]

Cristal's elections for the school board and city council in 1975 produced another decisive victory for RUP. With three seats in contention for the city council and two for the school board, CU's powerful grass-roots machine of nearly 500 families overwhelmingly defeated its La Raza Libre opposition by a three to one vote ratio. Before the election, the media made it seem as if La Raza Libre was an RUP offshoot comprised of former RUP supporters, alleging that RUP was coming apart. The fact was, La Raza Libre was comprised of RUP adversaries who were a political minority. Using their economic power, the local gringo power holders backed La Raza Libre and in most cases pulled the party's political strings. However, once again CU proved to be politically invincible—RUP won three of the five open seats on the Zavala County Board of Education. The victory was unprecedented for two reasons: It was the first time that RUP had elected anyone to the county school board; and RUP's candidates won by an impressive ten to one vote margin.

RUP in 1975 also made significant political inroads in Robstown. Near the city of Corpus Christi, Robstown was a small town of some 11,200 people, of whom 92 percent were Méxicanos—96 percent, when the three contiguous unincorporated areas were added. As in Cristal, RUP's political success in Robstown was ascribable to two major factors: the presence of a well-organized grass-roots political organization, Familias Unidas, and the adroitness of Lupe Youngblood as an organizer. Familias Unidas (FU) was formed in 1972, as a consequence of the school boycott that produced some educational reforms. During the course of the protest, busloads of students from Cristal came to Robstown to support the picketing. In order to protect some of the reforms, a combination of students and parents formed FU (on a pattern similar to that in Cristal).[26] During and after the school issue, several meetings were held to define FU's direction and purpose. Some members dropped out as a direct result of the decision to support RUP over the Democrats. The majority, explains Youngblood, "took a vote and it was unanimously voted that we're Raza Unida." At its high point in 1975 as a political organization, FU claimed some 200 families as members.[27]

As RUP consolidated its political gains after the elections, it became embroiled in a controversial issue that would ultimately impact negatively on the party. After the April local elections, a national delegation of RUP leaders, headed by then national chairman José Angel Gutiérrez, traveled to Cuba on a fact-finding mission. In explaining the purpose of the delegation's trip, Gutiérrez informed the press that they would be gathering valuable information in Cuba that could, in turn, be helpful to RUP in its development of programs in education, housing, health care, and farming. He was particularly interested in learning more about Cuba's collective farms, since a cooperative farm was being proposed for Zavala County.[28]

The initial invitation by the Cuban government to RUP was made in January. After several delays, the delegation, comprised of RUP leaders from various states, traveled to Cuba through México; circumventing the U.S. embargo that banned air travel to Cuba from the United States. During the delegation's ten-day stay, the RUP leaders met with high-ranking government officials on various aspects of the Cuban revolution. Upon its return, the delegation held a press conference in San Antonio at which Gutiérrez praised various aspects of the Cuban revolution; his admiring comments proved to be incendiary. The headlines reporting his remarks read: "Raza Chief Would Try Socialism in Zavala" (San Antonio Express); "Socialism a Better Way of Life than Capitalism" (Corpus Christi Caller-Times); "Raza Unida Wants To Create Little Cuba in South Texas" (Alice Echo News). One of Gutiérrez's assertions was that Cuba was in some instances more advanced than the United States: "There's no crime, no illiteracy and few health problems." He made a semiqualified but quasi-provocative statement interpreted by the media to mean that Gutiérrez wanted to bring socialism to South Texas: "The specific applicability [of socialism] to South Texas or any place would depend first of all on local initiative—the people wanting to change their own situation by whatever means necessary, ballots or bullets or whatever. . . . I really don't think there's going to be a revolution any time soon in the United States. So, leaving that out, it reduces the options one has to ballots for peaceful change."[29]

Gutiérrez's controversial comments set off a firestorm of criticism from a number of Democratic politicians, particularly Governor Dolph Briscoe, as well as some from within RUP. Understanding the conservative nature of Texas's political culture, Democrats used the opportunity to cast aspersions on Gutiérrez and the party. José Mata, one of Gutiérrez's trusted lieutenants in Cristal, explains the negative impact of the comments: "Yes, it affected us because of the negative national publicity. Even the president of the United States spoke on national TV against Cristal. . . . Governor Briscoe labeled us as a little Cuba. It affected us badly even though we were a movement and free to exercise our rights. But because we were Chicanos and we were a new movement that was growing rapidly, well, the government didn't like it."[30]

The impact was such that even within RUP's ranks, discord occurred. In Cristal, for instance, some of the RUP loyalists expressed disapproval of the trip as well as of the subsequent statements made by Guiterrez, aggravating the schisms developing within RUP's ranks. According to Rev. Sherrill Smith, a longtime activist priest and the local pastor, Gutiérrez's "trip to Cuba made a lot of people nervous."[31]

For the next three years, the power of the media was used to neutralize any serious challenge from RUP. RUP's adversaries knew all too well that Méxicanos tend to be conservative on some issues; thus the trip to Cuba would not play well with them. The media blitz served to reinforce RUP's radical if not Communist image among some Méxicanos, especially members of the middle class.

## Cristal's Rupture: The End of the Peaceful Revolution

By August 1975, after almost five years of unprecedented change, RUP's peaceful revolution in Cristal came to an abrupt and disastrous end.[32] For the first four years, there were few schisms within CU and no challenges to Gutiérrez's power and authority as Cristal's political boss. By 1974, however, more and more disagreements began to surface within CU. Its meetings became increasingly contentious as the various emerging factions vied for Gutiérrez's influence.

A dramatic change in the ethos of some RUP leaders and supporters occurred. MAYO's Winter Garden Project tenets of community control, empowerment, and a "de-colonization political movement" gave way to greed, avarice, and hunger to control the material inducements and perks of patronage. The sense of "we" that had permeated and impelled the peaceful revolution, buttressed by the emotional trappings of Chicanismo, became secondary. The power of the "I" (blatant self-interest) replaced the collective spirit.

In addition to the trip to Cuba, several other issues surfaced between April and August that also fostered conflict: CU's progressive income tax; the establishment of the secretariat; the Chief Garza controversy; the Ruiz and Casares defections; and the firing of School Superintendent Cantu.[33]

Upon Gutiérrez's return from Cuba, he convinced CU to impose a progressive income tax—in some cases, 10 percent—on each member. The monies were used to finance RUP's local political activities. That spring he created a "super committee," a nine-person "secretariat," for purposes of streamlining CU's policy-making process. Who could serve on the secretariat became an issue that intensified the power struggle.[34]

By July, three major factions had developed within CU: the Gutierristas (those loyal to Gutiérrez), the Barrioisatas (Barrio Club members who originally had served as Gutiérrez's security force), and the technocrats (disgruntled teachers and administrators).[35] This factionalism led to the dismantling of the secretariat by the Barrioistas, who had taken it over. Shortly afterward came a power realignment—an alliance between the Barrioistas and technocrats, forming what I call the "New Guard."

By August, the New Guard had politically outmaneuvered the Gutierristas. With the defection of councilperson Gene Ruiz and school board member Mercedes "Chachi" Casarez, the New Guard held a three to two majority on the city council and a four to three majority on the school board. This left the Gutierrista faction with only tenuous control of the county government. Despite the stiff resistance of the Gutierristas, the New Guard exercised its newly gained power by appointing Ramon Garza as Cristal's chief of police. By mid-August, the New Guard—controlled school board had fired Gutierrista superintendent Adan Cantu, which precipitated the political rupture. The media went into a reporting frenzy induced by the newsworthiness of RUP's "politics of self-destruction."

What followed over the next three years was reminiscent of Cristal's "first revolt" (1963–1965): the emergence of a politic that was self-destructive in nature. Lawsuits, altercations, internecine power struggles, greed, and grabs for power consumed what was left of RUP in Cristal. From 1975 to 1978, a political game of seat swapping ensued between the three RUP power factions. Yet even when RUP was split, its traditional local adversaries failed to successfully challenge the factions electorally.

Some Méxicanos who claimed to be Raza Unida continued to govern the city, schools, and county by applying the "politica del movimiento"(the politics of the movement) rather than the "politica de movidas"(the politics of underhandedness) and personal agendas. But there was little left of RUP's populist/progressive agenda; thus, Cristal's politics returned to a mode oriented much more toward accommodation and preserving the status quo. This resulted in the dismantling of many of the changes effected in the schools, city, and county.

In 1978, there was a brief interlude of unity among the divergent RUP factions. They came together and regained control of the city and school board; however, within a few months, they reverted to their old self-destructive mode of politics. By the 1978 gubernatorial elections, Cristal was no longer the beacon of movimiento politics or a citadel of progressive activism.

## RUP's 1976 Politics: The Decline Accelerates

The political rupture in Cristal only expedited RUP's decline and negatively impacted RUP's statewide efforts. Some Méxicanos who had been strong supporters and activist participants of RUP became disillusioned and left the party to return to the Democratic Party. Sociologist Tatacho Mindiola reminded them in a news article that the "Raza Unida exists because of the deprivation which Méxicanos historically have had to endure and the Democratic party's failure to do anything about it."[36]

In early 1976, RUP was handed a major legal victory. Judge Jack Roberts ordered that RUP be allowed to hold primary elections May 1 without requiring its candidates to pay filing fees. In addition, the costs for holding a primary election would be picked up by the state. The court ruling was based on the U.S. Justice Department's objection to a 1975 Texas statute that prevented RUP from holding a primary because it had not garnered 20 percent of the vote in the 1974 gubernatorial election.[37]

The ruling, however, did not benefit RUP, since its leaders had decided not to contest the upcoming state election, but rather to concentrate on preparing for the 1978 gubernatorial elections. That year RUP ran half as many candidates as it had run in 1974, in less than half the counties—thirty-five candidates in only 9 counties. Of the 254 counties in Texas, it held primaries in only 12. The only statewide candidate to run that year was Fred Garza, who ran for railroad commissioner.[38] This sparsity was indicative of RUP's rapid decline.

While RUP in Cristal was caught up in conflict, in 1976 two other South Texas communities, Robstown and Cotulla, scored impressive political victories. In Robstown, from 1972 to 1976, Familias Unidas was at the forefront of organizing RUP in the area. After several unsuccessful campaigns for the local school board, city council, and county offices, in 1976 it successfully ran three candidates for the city council and two for the school board.

RUP's candidates were opposed by two slates of candidates: the Unity Party, which represented the old-guard gringo establishment and was nothing more than a front for the Democratic Party, and Amigos for Progress, a mostly middle-class, Mexican American independent group, whose sole purpose was to siphon away votes from RUP. But in spite of the stiff opposition, FU prevailed, because it focused on wedge issues that were important to the Méxicano community. Two such issues were police brutality, which had dramatically increased during the previous eighteen months, and utility rates, which had skyrocketed in Texas.[39]

Between 1975 and 1976, Robstown was a hotbed of controversy and political conflict as FU aggressively pushed its change agenda. It relied on a multiplicity of issues and social services to maintain its organizing fervor and power base. FU controlled three of the seven seats on the school board, two of the seven on the city council (including the mayor's seat), and two of the five on the utilities board. As a result of the significant gains made by FU, the Unity Party and Amigos for Progress joined forces to thwart RUP's political advances, especially in the areas of bilingual education and the formation of a farm cooperative.

FU was successful in boycotting four businesses owned by Mexican American city councilman Arnold Hinojosa, a member of the Unity Party. It alleged that the boycott was a consequence of Hinojosa's reneging on promises to support certain FU proposals. The boycott proved to be successful; in less than a year, Hinojosa was out of business. When interviewed by the *Corpus Christi Caller-Times*, he expressed concern over FU's new political clout and referred to its "communist leanings": "I'm more concerned about the Cuban influence that is taking place. I don't know what to make of it. As a businessman and a Vietnam veteran I would oppose any effort to superimpose a veneer of home-grown Marxism on the community's political or economic life. I am not in agreement with any of the socialist or communist ideas at all."[40]

Periodically, FU's leaders included Ramsey Muñiz and Carlos Guerra in their organizing activities. The former had a law practice in nearby Corpus Christi and the latter lived in Robstown. FU was always optimistic that it would win control of both the city council and school board, as Youngblood stated in an interview before the election, because of the success of the boycott.

The initial results of the local elections were impressive. RUP had won two of the three seats open for the city council by a margin of some 500 votes. In addition, it won the two open seats on the seven-member school board by a margin of more than 250 votes, as well as one position on the utility board.

The local Democratic powers, however, contested the results of the elections. The vote recount gave the White mayoral incumbent, B. D. Berryman, the victory by a margin of 164 votes, electing him to his ninth term. Berryman garnered a total of 1,802 votes to FU candidate Ricardo Gutiérrez's 1,638 votes. Only one FU candidate won, Juan Barrera, who was elected to the school board. The others on the slate lost by margins of between 107 and 405 votes. FU challenged the election results, alleging fraud. It claimed it had won the elections but had been cheated out of the victories.[41] At that point, explains Youngblood, FU "starts falling apart."[42]

Another RUP stronghold, Cotulla, located near Cristal, was struggling to regain control of both the city council and the school board. A community of 5,000, with Méxicanos comprising some 72 percent of the population, Cotulla was one of the few communities that until 1976 remained strongly supportive and committed to RUP. In 1970, the Winter Garden revolt had produced major electoral victories in Cristal, Cotulla, and Carrizo Springs. Next to Cristal, Cotulla was the strongest base of support for building the all-Chicano political party. That year it had won control of the city council.

However, after two years of political struggles with the old gringo guard, RUP lost control of the city council due to three defections, leaving it with only one member on the city council. Notwithstanding, in 1974, RUP candidates Arseño Garcia, Rosalinda Rodriguez, and Leodoro Martinez were all elected to the city council, once again giving RUP control. But the control was short-lived, due to a successful challenge of the election results in the courts by the local gringo power holders. A judge ruled in favor of the gringos, thus disqualifying the newly elected mayor on what *The Militant* called "a trumped-up 'non-residency' point."[43]

After two years of intensive reorganizing, RUP regained community control of Cotulla's city council in 1976 by winning three seats, with 53 percent of the vote. With two members already on the city council, RUP now had total control of the governing body.[44] Leodoro Martinez, who was elected mayor, explained that in order to broaden their appeal and gain support the candidates had to tone down their partisan RUP rhetoric: "It was an inclusive operation . . . we got a lot of support from the middle group that had not supported us in the past. We became politically very viable."[45] At a time when political problems were increasing for RUP, Gutiérrez used the victories in Cotulla to remind RUP skeptics that RUP could win in communities other than Cristal.[46]

This was, however, not the case with the Cotulla school board. Although Méxicanos constituted a demographic majority in 1976, RUP was not able to win a majority on the school board. In 1970 it won two seats, and subsequently others were elected; but it never was able to foster the educational changes that RUP had instituted in Cristal. Martinez notes that "the school system was always the hardest to establish total control. . . . For whatever reason, it never gelled." Regardless of their minority status, the RUP school board members were successful in fending off the gringo resistance and pushing through various educational changes such as bilingual/bicultural education and the desegregation of the schools.[47]

While RUP's state leadership celebrated the victory in Cotulla, it was keenly aware that RUP had entered a state of decline. In an article in *The Militant,* Gutiérrez projected a somewhat bleak picture of RUP's organizing efforts since 1974: "It's been a dull two years. Kind of anticlimactic, nothing spectacular happening. I don't know why. I guess it's the mood of the country. It's everywhere. . . . I can't put my finger on it. The activists aren't dropping out. They're all there. They're working very hard, but it just doesn't seem to gel."[48] While Gutiérrez expressed some gloom over the lack of progress in organizing RUP, he never indicated that he was willing to quit.

By 1976, RUP's loss of political appeal had become apparent. In San Antonio, Pablo Escamilla Jr., a well-known RUP activist and member of the Edgewood school board, chose to run on an independent slate known as CARE (Committee for an Alternative and Relevant Education), rather than on a RUP slate. The school district was 94 percent Méxicano and 6 percent Black. Escamilla won, and the opposing slate comprised of Democrats won the other two seats on the board.[49]

On September 18 and 19, 1976, RUP held a statewide convention in Seguin. Maria Elena Martinez, a veteran activist and a schoolteacher originally from Wylie, a small farming community near Dallas, was elected state chairperson. Once again there was heated debate on whether to use an urban strategy or a rural strategy for further developing RUP. Martinez made it clear that she would support broadening RUP's appeal in both areas in preparation for the 1978 gubernatorial elections. She also stressed that RUP would strengthen its urban base by organizing service centers, such as the Centros de Aztlán in Laredo and Houston.[50]

At the convention, José Angel Gutiérrez and others alleged that RUP was being spied on by the FBI and the CIA with the intent of destroying the party. He told the delegates that by using the Freedom of Information Act, the leadership had secured about a hundred pages from files that the CIA had been keeping on them. The files documented government surveillance of RUP nationally and in Texas. Convention delegates voted unanimously to file suit. A number of resolutions were also passed that day. One of the most notable was the approval of a resolution presented by Mujeres por La Raza Unidas in support of the Equal Rights Amendment.[51]

The 1976 November election returns proved dismal for RUP. The Democrats had soundly defeated the RUP candidates running for state or congressional office. For example, Fred Garza, who ran for Texas railroad commissioner, received only 64,000 votes. Ramon Carrillo, candidate for the Twenty-first Congressional District, located near San Antonio, reportedly won only 5 percent of the vote. In the northern part of Texas, the Lubbock area by 1976 had developed into one of the strongest RUP support bases. The absence of a large concentration of Méxicanos, however, limited the area's capacity to elect candidates who ran on RUP's pro-Méxicano nationalist platform. That year, RUP's candidate there for county commissioner, Trinidad Zepeda, lost to a Democrat.[52] In Zavala County, however, RUP did score five victories. In reaction to the election results, RUP state chair Martinez said: "It's no longer the Chicano against the Anglo. Many Chicanos do not understand the difference between the Raza Unida Party and the Democratic party. We have a big education job to do."[53]

## Muñiz Incarcerated on Drug Charges

Further impeding RUP's organizing efforts was the arrest of 1972 and 1974 RUP gubernatorial candidate Ramsey Muñiz on drug charges in 1976. After his unsuccessful gubernatorial bid in 1974, Muñiz established residence and a law practice in Corpus Christi. By early 1976, he was enjoying a lavish life-style. When approached by community activists to either sign petitions or join a protest event, he turned them down. According to journalist Evan Moore from the *Houston Chronicle*, after the 1974 election, "he became distant from old contacts." "Muñiz had apparently cultivated new friends. Among the new connections was Fred Brulloths Jr.," who was known to local narcotics officials as a major drug dealer from Brownsville.[54]

Brulloth was arrested in late 1975 by the Drug Enforcement Administration. He began trading information for a reduced sentence. In late July, federal prosecutors used Brulloth's testimony to indict Muñiz, his brother Roberto, and four others for conducting a marijuana-smuggling ring that planned to move 6,500 pounds of marijuana from México to Alabama by plane.[55]

News of the indictment made the front pages of many of Texas's newspapers. On July 31, 1976, the *Corpus Christi Caller-Times* carried a front-page story under the headline "Ramsey Muñiz Sought for Drug Trafficking." The next day, Ramsey and his brother Roberto surrendered to Nueces County sheriff's authorities. The eleven-count indictment was the result of an eighteen-month investigation. The investigation revealed that between June 15 and December 7, 1975, Muñiz, his brother, and two RUP supporters were involved in the transportation of large amounts of marijuana—485 pounds on one occasion, 1,100 and 1,380 on two others—with plans for moving 1,500 more pounds.[56] Muñiz was released on a $7,500 bond and his attorney worked out a plea bargain for three years' probation.[57]

Four months later, on November 26, the situation got even worse for Muñiz. A San Antonio grand jury indicted him on four new counts of trafficking marijuana. Muñiz, however, scheduled to appear at a Corpus Christi courthouse, jumped bail and went into hiding in México. He was a fugitive for about a month, until Mexican police arrested him in Reynosa. According to Moore, Ramsey "was beaten soundly and dumped in the middle of the International Bridge in Laredo on Christmas Eve. His bond was raised to $2 million and courtroom wags quickly dubbed him 'The Two Million [Dollar] Chicano.' " Muñiz pleaded guilty in both cases. He was given a five-year prison sentence with ten years' probation upon his release.[58]

For RUP, Muñiz's arrest and subsequent imprisonment carried serious political ramifications. Some of RUP's leaders and supporters reacted with disbelief and shock, while others reacted with anger and a sense of betrayal. Ignacio Garcia describes the reaction: "Throughout the state, activists scrambled to explain to their constituents either that Muñiz had been framed for political purposes or that he did not represent the party. The urban chapters declared the former, and the rural the latter. Both groups believed Muñiz had been singled out because of his party activities, but although some in the urban chapters wanted to avoid any fallout if he proved to be guilty, few in the party hierarchy ever believed that he had been framed. Most had been privy to rumors that Muñiz had become involved in drug trafficking."[59]

While in jail in San Antonio, however, Muñiz was visited by José Angel Gutiérrez, Mario Compean, and other RUP leaders. Muñiz's wife, Abbie, and Gutiérrez, among others, made an unsuccessful attempt to form a legal defense committee to finance the trial as well as the appeal.

When interviewed twenty years later, some of the RUP leaders were more critical of Muñiz. Armando Gutiérrez said, "The only conclusion that I have come to in the many years since, is that Ramsey was not patient enough to achieve wealth and riches by being an attorney. He wanted to shortcut through it."[60] Mario Compean explained that many within RUP's leadership ranks were cognizant of Muñiz's dealings with drugs: "The grapevine was busy. There was a sense of resignation that it was going to blow, so we tried to minimize it."[61] Maria Elena Martinez explained that at first she believed that Muñiz had been set up. She was not that surprised when he was arrested, since "we had our marijuana smokers in the party. It was part of our culture too."[62] Lupe Youngblood, on the other hand, rejected the idea that Muñiz was framed.

He said, "You don't get your hand trapped in a cookie jar if you don't put it in there, do you understand? They caught him because he was in it up to his head."[63]

The Muñiz incident proved to be extremely damaging to RUP's image and organizing efforts. Jesus "Chuy" Rameriz from nearby McAllen said that Ramsey's arrest and conviction gave some Méxicanos an excuse to defect from RUP and join or rejoin the Democratic Party. Others felt that RUP was plagued by too many problems. He said some reacted by saying, "God, . . . there is only so much a person can take."[64] From Laredo, Alberto Luera said that the "Muñiz incident" got "the biggest media play. It was the biggest gig happening." In explaining his and the others' reactions, Luera added that "a lot of us walked away."[65]

Muñiz's incarceration had compromised RUP's credibility, left it wide open to attack by Democrats, and made it the target of negative media exposure that tainted its image, especially among many traditional Méxicanos, who tended to be socially conservative. (This was not the first time that a major RUP leader was indicted on narcotics charges. In 1975, Flores Anaya, former senatorial candidate of the party, in spite of his denials was convicted of possession of heroin.)[66] With the incarceration of Muñiz, RUP's leadership was weakened. Although RUP had other leaders, such as Gutiérrez, Compean, and Martinez, Ramsey Muñiz, was by far the most powerful, effective, and energizing leadership force statewide.

## RUP Comes under Siege

In the midst of the Muñiz incident, RUP was also under attack by Democrats, particularly Governor Dolph Briscoe. For the rest of the year, Briscoe and other Democrats continued to denigrate the character of RUP and its leadership. Briscoe's point of attack was the establishment of a thousand-acre farm cooperative in Cristal that was being proposed by the Zavala County Economic Development Corporation (ZCEDC) established in 1975 by Gutiérrez. The communal farm was depicted as being a Communist effort. By August, when the ZCEDC received a $1.5 million grant, the attacks had become more frequent and more acrimonious. In September, Briscoe alleged that RUP was seeking to develop a "little Cuba on Texas soil."[67] Furthermore, in October, at a press conference, he was quoted as saying, "In practical terms there is no room in Texas for Raza Unida. . . . The severe economic decline in Zavala County is the result of La Raza Unida dominance." One White-controlled newspaper, the *Austin American-Statesman*, in an editorial took issue with the governor's anti-RUP inflammatory remarks: "The fact that Briscoe thinks there is no room in great big Texas for a political party he doesn't agree with is outrageous." The editorial also reminded readers that the state of Texas, for all intents and purposes "had been a one-party state since reconstruction."[68]

RUP also came under attack by Georgia Democratic congressman Larry McDonald for holding a meeting with México's Partido Revolucionario Institucional presidential candidate José Lopez Portillo in Hermosillo, México, on May 21. Headed by Gutiérrez, the delegation included RUP leaders and scholars (including myself) from throughout the Southwest. Gutiérrez stressed that the government of México should create "politically inclusive" programs that would link Chicanos to México. Coming from an extreme right-wing perspective, McDonald inserted his comments in the form of a letter in the *Congressional Record*. In the letter he described the meeting as one "between Marxist Chicano leaders and a Mexican presidential candidate." He alleged that it was all part of an effort to create a separate Chicano nation, "Aztlán." Even though RUP was in a state of decline, there were still elements within the Democratic Party that perceived it as a real threat to the nation's politics.[69]

By the end of 1976, the demise of RUP was inevitable. According to Ignacio Garcia, Martinez "inherited a party in financial chaos, suffering from a steady desertion of activists and low morale. There were few mid-level organizers or activists left who seemed willing or financially able to carry on the struggle."[70] In October, Martinez admitted to the press that RUP faced problems of survival due to its negative media image. She said that the party's image problem centered on its association with drugs, radicalism, and Communism, and that fair media coverage would help combat the problem.[71]

The effects of a changing political climate coupled with RUP's position as a third party in a political system controlled by a one-party dictatorship had become insurmountable obstacles. Yet paradoxically, more Méxicanos were being elected to public local office. Many were former RUP supporters, who in many cases had become "reborn Democrats." Believing that RUP was too radical in its politics, and not a viable party option, Méxicanos in increasing numbers opted for the Democratic Party.

In early December, RUP functioned as a political pressure group by organizing a march against Governor Briscoe in Dallas to protest his attacks on RUP and its leadership.[72] That same month, the Democratic Party as part of its political offensive to neutralize RUP announced the formation of Mexican American Democrats (MAD). It was organized as a Méxicano political force to be used to further combat RUP. Ignacio Garcia described it as "a conglomeration of numerous activists, trade unionists, bureaucrats, young professionals, and old time liberals who sought to take over the 'progressive wing' of the Democratic Party."[73]

Former RUP leader Chuy Rameriz became one of the major MAD leaders. When interviewed, he explained that after years of struggling, he was frustrated and felt "this isn't worth it," there was "no cohesiveness, no structure, no rules." His frustration was also, in part, a result of the problems the RUP local elected officials encountered in San Juan when trying to implement RUP reforms. Rameriz's defection left RUP without a capable leader and organization in the Rio Grande area of Texas. In no time, MAD absorbed several former RUP leaders who had become disillusioned with RUP and some who were simply looking for new political opportunities.

## RUP's 1977 Politics: The Struggle for Survival

During 1977, RUP's development as a political party continued in a downward spiral. The attacks from Democrats intensified. Governor Briscoe, as well, continued his personal crusade against RUP, particularly against the federal government's funding of RUP's cooperative farm in Cristal. In a speech at the University of Texas at San Antonio, Gutiérrez reacted by accusing the governor of deliberately trying to destroy RUP. He defended the cooperative farm projects and alleged that the governor's opposition was a conflict of interest. He said that Briscoe owned some 13,000 acres (the *Texas Observer* claimed the figure was 22,000) in Zavala County, that only twenty-six individuals owned 87 percent of the land in Zavala County, and that a cooperative farm owned by Méxicanos presented an economic threat to them.[74] Even though the ZCEDC got a $67,000 federal grant for the farm, as the Carter administration settled in, the resistance to funding the project increased in the ensuing months. The Democrats' attacks now also came from the direction of the federal government.[75] Thus, only while a Republican administration was in power did RUP withstand the Democrats' attack on the project.

Between 1975 and 1978, RUP's electoral record at the local level was virtually zero. The few victories that were scored were in Cristal, where RUP's two major factions continued to do battle with each other. In April, the New Guard won over the Gutierristas, winning three seats on the city council and two on the school board. The political situation in Cristal became more precarious after the local gas company, Lo-Vaca, shut off the town's gas supply on September 23, which compelled residents to use either propane, which was very costly, or wood-burning stoves. Governor Briscoe accused RUP officials of being responsible for the fuel crisis in Cristal.

By now, Familias Unidas in Robstown had also cut its ties with RUP. The same occurred in Cotulla. The RUP supporters in both communities had lost faith in RUP and rejoined the Democratic Party. As for the rural areas of Texas, even though some political activity continued in Lubbock, San Antonio, Houston, and Austin, there were no new victories to speak of.

As a result of RUP's declining electoral base, by 1977 it resembled a pressure group more than a political party. During that year immigration became its main focus of concern. In March, Gutiérrez took issue with the Carter administration's proposed crackdown on undocumented immigrants. Gutiérrez charged that Méxicanos were under attack and said, "We are taking steps backward, to the epoch of Hitler."[76] When the Carter administration intensified its anti-immigrant policies, RUP called for a national conference. In May, RUP leader Compean, Cecilio Garcia, publisher of *Caracol* magazine, and MAYO cofounder Ignacio "Nacho" Perez convened a meeting in San Antonio. Addressing some fifty persons representing various organizations, Gutiérrez made a "call for action" against the anti-immigrant policies. The meeting produced a broad-based coalition that agreed to follow up by holding an antideportation conference.

In December, RUP held a statewide conference in Austin to develop a political strategy for the upcoming 1978 elections. The conference was part of RUP's compliance with the Texas Election Code, required to maintain its status as an official party. (Over the course of six years, RUP held numerous county and state conventions to discuss how to maintain its party status.) RUP state chairperson Martinez in her address mentioned that the elections were crucial to RUP's viability as a party. She said that despite the efforts by many to eliminate the party, "we have only grown stronger.[77]

## The 1978 Elections: RUP's Last Hurrah

The 1978 gubernatorial elections proved to be RUP's last political act of defiance against the Democrat and Republican Parties. RUP had to face some insurmountable problems: a meager local community power base; defections within its ranks to the Democratic Party; a growing conservative political climate impelled by a Viva Yo mind-set; the relentless attacks by media and Democratic demagoguery; schisms within its ranks; and the absence of financial and people-power resources.

Before Muñiz's incarceration, RUP's leaders had discussed having both Gutiérrez and Muñiz act as organizers for the 1978 gubernatorial election. As 1978 arrived, however, Gutiérrez was besieged with political problems in Cristal as well as at the national level, and Muñiz was doing time in prison. Of the original main MAYO and RUP leaders, only Mario Compean remained. Early on, he had indicated his desire to run for governor, and in 1977 he made it official that he would be running. When I interviewed him years later, he explained that he had wanted to run because he honestly believed that his candidacy could help stop RUP's decline.[78] He said he was cognizant of the manifold difficulties his campaign faced, but that he "wanted to bring the party back." He just did not want RUP's legacy to be "Muñiz in jail." Furthermore, he understood that the campaign had to produce a minimum of 2 percent of the vote if RUP was going to maintain its official party status.

Reaction to Compean's candidacy was mixed. For months he traveled throughout Texas seeking to ascertain the feasibility of his making a run for the governor's seat. Ignacio Garcia has assessed Compean's problems: "The new leadership, with the exception of Maria Elena Martinez, did not see him as a good candidate. Even among his close associates, Compean found loyalty and enthusiasm in short supply. Compean's problems in inspiring confidence stemmed from two factors, one personal and the other external. Raza Unida followers used to the charismatic, good looking, and physically imposing Muñiz, did not see Compean as a better alternative. He seemed too fragile physically to withstand a vigorous campaign and his speaking ability paled in comparison to the former candidate."[79]

There were also serious external problems. For many so-called Mexican Americans, Compean's credentials as a candidate were weak. They said he lacked charisma, sophistication, and the experience to run a credible campaign. Those from the Left saw him as a reactionary "nationalist" who disliked Whites, even the radical ones. Still others saw Compean as a lackey for Gutiérrez. RUP supporters felt that the timing was not propitious, and that some of Compean's ideas were antiquated. Many were just plain tired of running what they felt were symbolic races. The lack of adequate financial resources added to the skepticism about Compean's candidacy.[80] Nineteen years later, when interviewed, he admitted, "We had no money or manpower."[81]

Compean first expressed a serious interest in running for governor in 1976 at a RUP state convention.[82] When RUP leaders were asked why he ran, Youngloed, for instance, replied, "It was the last hurrah. He wanted to see if we could rally the troops."[83] Jesus "Chuy" Rameriz said, "I was surprised because Mario Compean, I felt, was always good not in the big picture, but in the small picture." Carlos Guerra explained that he was concerned because Compean was not an aggressive campaigner, yet he said, "There was a concerted effort in Robstown to support him."[84] According to Luz Gutiérrez, "Mario [didn't] have the charisma, the ability to generate that same kind of following" that Muñiz had.[85]

When the initial discussion was held on the 1978 elections, Gutiérrez too expressed an interest in running for office. A scenario was discussed in which he would run for Congress and Compean would run for governor. Compean, particularly, felt this could have a catalytic organizing impact on RUP. However, when Gutiérrez announced that he would not run, it psychologically deflated the cadre of RUP activists who were still left in the party. Thus, concerned about RUP's legacy, Compean decided to run.[86]

The number of candidates that ran under the aegis of RUP was small. RUP candidates ran for seven state and congressional seats and several local ones. Compean and Luis de Leon, who ran for U.S. senator, were RUP's only statewide candidates. Augustin Mata ran against incumbent Chick Kazen in the Twenty-third Congressional District. Abelardo Marquez from Cristal ran for the state board of education from that district. Juan S. Hernandez ran for the state senate and Daniel Bustamante and Josue Faz ran for state house seats.[87] In the primary, RUP participated in only 20 counties but was on the ballot in all 254. RUP's liberal populist platform had changed very little from the previous two elections. Some of the more salient planks spoke to property tax reform; replacement of the regressive sales tax with a corporate income tax; public ownership of natural resources; abolition of the Texas Rangers; decriminalization of personal marijuana use; unconditional amnesty for illegal aliens, including equal access to all social services; an increase in the minimum wage to $3.50; and an end to police brutality.[88]

As was the case with the two earlier party platforms, there was little to suggest that RUP was Marxist and revolutionary. The fact was that even with its strong liberal reform posture and its cultural nationalism, it was only militant integrationist in its politics. While its leadership was often perceived as radical, the reality was that in Texas, most who supported RUP, including its leadership, did not preach about restructuring the liberal capitalist system but rather about reforming it. Most really only wanted to ensure that Méxicanos got into the political system so as to effect needed changes.

Compean's campaign theme and issues complemented RUP's populist liberal platform. His theme for the campaign was "change." A campaign piece described his stance: "Mario Compean is a candidate because he feels that the voters of Texas are asking for a change in Texas politics." As to issues, he focused on energy, education, and the elderly. A content analysis of the campaign's literature and newspaper clippings clearly illustrates that he ran a moderate Left campaign designed to appeal to all ethnic and racial groups. In other words, like Muñiz in 1974, he did not run a campaign exclusively oriented to the Méxicano. Likewise, he denied any accusation that RUP was a radical party and that he was just as another Méxicano running for Méxicanos.

With a budget of no more than $20,000, Compean's campaign had only a limited capacity to reach voters.[89] And with only a semblance of organization in no more than twenty counties, its organizational capability was limited as well. Although a campaign headquarters was established in San Antonio, all staff members were volunteers. Compean's effort to organize a state steering committee, Amigos de Mario Compean, failed. Moreover, he did not succeed in gaining the support of established traditional organizations, such as the League of United Latin American Citizens (LULAC) and the American G.I. Forum. Gutiérrez was essentially not present; he did little to assist Compean's campaign.[90] There were even those within the partido's ranks who refused to support Compean. Their unwillingness to cooperate was based on the fear that the campaign could bring on too much of a backlash and cause them to lose funding.[91]

With only the semblance of a constituency, the partido's infrastructure had all but disappeared. Even in Cristal, the combination of Democratic attacks on both RUP and José Angel Gutiérrez and the three years of the politics of self-destruction made RUP's demise almost inevitable. Without Gutiérrez's strong support, Mario Compean, however determined to keep RUP alive, was left without financial or volunteer support. There were exceptions around the state, however. Lubbock, for instance, until 1978 was still a viable RUP stronghold. Armed with the *El Editor* newspaper, RUP candidates there for years ran for the school board, state senate, and county commission.[92]

After months of intensive campaigning, Compean and the rest of RUP's candidates went down to disastrous defeat. Compean garnered only slightly more than one-half of 1 percent of 2.3 million votes cast, which translated to some 15,000 votes. The significance of the election was that the combined total vote of RUP and the Socialist Workers Party of some 19,886 created a "spoiler" impact. Republican candidate William Clements upset Democrat Dolph Briscoe by a mere 18,000 votes.[93]

Trying to salvage something from the campaign, Compean declared that RUP had made the difference in Clements's victory over Briscoe: "I was considered the spoiler, but as far as I am concerned, we won."[94] In the race for the U.S. Senate, DeLeon received 18,478 votes. In the Senate race, Republican John Tower defeated Democrat Bob Krueger by 13,689 votes.[95] RUP's candidates in the congressional, state senate, and state house races were all decisively defeated. The election of a Republican governor ended the Democratic Party's hegemony of Texas politics; the one-party dictatorship became a two-party dictatorship.

## RUP's Demise: The End of an Era

The results of the election tolled the death knell for RUP. The one-half of 1 percent that Compean got was nowhere near the required 2 percent needed to preserve RUP's official party status and its eligibility for state funds for its primary. Regardless of the fact that it had failed to secure the required vote percentage, according to the Texas Election Code, the party could remain on the ballot by collecting signatures totaling 1 percent of the total vote cast for governor in the last election.[96]

Yet RUP's defeat was so decisive, the few RUP zealots who remained were not willing to mount a petition drive. As the RUP advocates became involved in fighting issues rather than running candidates, RUP was transformed into an advocacy-oriented interest group instead of a viable political party. Compean was overwhelmed with frustration and grief over his poor showing at the polls. Even though the Republican governor-elect offered him a major position in his administration, after giving it some consideration, Compean turned the offer down.[97]

For months after the election, no formal meetings were held to discuss what could be done to resurrect RUP. LULAC president Ruben Bonilla told the press that "La Raza Unida Party is in the political cemetery where it belongs."[98] According to Compean in our 1997 interview, neither he nor anyone else, including Gutiérrez or Martinez, sought to do anything to salvage what was left of RUP.[99] It was as if everyone had given up. Bitter and disillusioned, in April of 1979, Compean left for Wisconsin to go to graduate school.

Over the next two years, there was a dismantling of what little was left of RUP. By 1978, the ZCEDC in Cristal had lost its $1.5 million federal grant due to Democratic political pressure and the Lo-Vaca energy issue. Politically, Cristal's various RUP factions came together briefly and won seats on both the city and school boards. However, this union did not last long. For the next two years, the politics of self-destruction again prevailed. Gutiérrez lost control of both the schools and the city, and in 1979 he lost control of the county.[100] Little was left of the reforms made by RUP's peaceful revolution. By 1980, most RUP supporters had returned to the Democratic Party. Gutiérrez in early 1981 was pressured into resigning as county judge by the Democrat-controlled court of commissioners. A few months before his resignation, Gutiérrez had moved his family to Oregon, where he had been residing periodically since 1979.[101]

Beyond Cristal, after the election what few RUP structures did exist quickly succumbed. Maria Elena Martinez continued to communicate with other RUP efforts outside Texas, namely in California and New Mexico. She became involved in a much more progressive political agenda that included a trip to Cuba and meetings in México with that country's Socialist Workers Party.[102] Gutiérrez did likewise. When dealing with foreign governments, he continued through 1979 to sell himself as RUP's national chairperson. He then resigned and transferred what was left of the RUP leadership mantle to Juan José Peña of New Mexico.

RUP's decline in Texas was ascribable to both exogenous and endogenous antagonisms. As a third party, RUP was no different than any other third party. In the case of Texas, it was subjected to the dictatorship of the Democratic Party, since at the time the Republican Party was not a real political threat. RUP's rise was thwarted by a number of the obstacles mentioned in the introduction: (1) stringent election and finance laws;

(2) single-member, winner-take-all plurality elections; (3) a gringo-controlled mass media that was often relentless in its attacks against both RUP and its primary leader, José Angel Gutiérrez; (4) characterizations by both media and Democrats that RUP was a radical if not communist party; (5) a conservative political culture that rebuked RUP's cultural nationalist politics; and, most important, (6) the omnipotent power exercised by Democrats at all levels of politics.

The political war waged by RUP from 1970 to 1978 against the Democrats epitomized the David versus Goliath metaphor. RUP's rise as a third party was a product, first, of MAYO's Winter Garden Project and Gutiérrez's brilliant ability to organize around issues and, second, of a political climate induced by the CM. After five years of progress, RUP began declining in late 1974. The salient endogenous factors in its demise by 1978 included: (1) insufficient finances, staff, and equipment; (2) lack of qualified and prepared candidates; (3) lack of support from the Méxicano middle and lower classes; (4) organizational problems owing to Texas's enormous size; (5) inability to develop a power base in Texas's 26 Méxicano majority counties; (6) the high numbers of leadership defections, schisms, and power struggles; (7) the failure to elect RUP candidates at the state level; (8) the scandals associated with the party, especially the arrest of Muñiz on drug charges; and (9) Gutiérrez's loss of power, resignation as county judge, and departure to Oregon.

Yet for eight years, RUP in Texas had accomplished what no other RUP organizing effort had been able to . It won several local elections, controlled some local governments, and became an official political party on the ballot.

## Chapter Four

# A Cadre Party of Ultranationalism: The Rise and Fall of RUP in Colorado, 1970–1976

As the Raza Unida Party (RUP) was emerging in Texas in 1970, almost simultaneously it emerged in Colorado as well. Next to the experience in Texas, no other organizing effort impacted RUP's expansion as greatly as that in Colorado. Headed by the charismatic leader of the Crusade for Justice, Rodolfo "Corky" Gonzales, it became in many respects a coequal catalytic organizing force to that of José Angel Gutiérrez's Texas RUP. While in Texas the Mexican American Youth Organization was RUP's predecessor, in Colorado it was Corky Gonzales's Crusade for Justice.

## The Founder of the Crusade for Justice and RUP

Organizations, like political movements, are products of people. Equally important, however, is that both are induced and invigorated by the presence of leaders. In some cases there are several leaders involved, and in others it is the dynamism and charisma of one that stands out above the rest. This was very much the case with both the Crusade for Justice and RUP in Colorado. Although several leaders contributed significantly to the development of both entities, the charismatic leadership of Corky Gonzales set the standard.

Corky Gonzales was born one year before the Great Depression, June 18, 1928, at a Denver hospital. His poor migrant parents, with a family of eight, worked the sugar beet fields north of Denver.[1] As a young man, he worked as a stoop laborer in Colorado's agricultural fields. While living in the barrios of Denver, he attended various schools and while in high school worked in a slaughterhouse at night and on weekends.[2] He graduated from high school in 1946 and attended the University of Denver for one semester. Determined to break out of the cycle of poverty, Gonzales relied on his talent in the boxing ring. He was good enough to be the third-ranking contender for the world featherweight title. In boxing circles he was known as the "king of the little men."[3]

Gonzales's fame in the boxing ring catapulted him into the business and political arenas. From 1952 to the early 1960s, he became a successful businessman. During those years, he had a bar, a bail bond business, an auto insurance agency, and several other investments. He prospered both with his fists and his business acumen. Some would say he had made it.[4]

Gonzales's political career began in 1955 when he ran unsuccessfully for Denver's city council. He received much of his political training in the Democratic Party. In 1957, at the age of twenty-nine, he was appointed Denver's first Mèxicano Democratic Party district captain. During the 1960 presidential election, he became the state coordinator of the Viva Kennedy campaign. His political success put him in the role of a Mexicano political broker who delivered the vote for those who were supportive of his agenda. In 1964, he unsuccessfully ran for the state's house of representatives seat in District Seven. He was disqualified on the grounds that he was ineligible to run for the seat, as he was not a resident of the district. Gonzales appealed but in the end lost the court decision.[5] The year 1964 would be the last year he would campaign for a Democrat.

Gonzales was also active in various organizations. In the 1950s he was a founding board member of the Latin American Educational Fund, the Colorado G.I. Forum, and the Latin American Research and Service Agency. He also served on the National Board of Jobs for Progress (SER, a major funding group for the barrios) and on the board of directors for the Job Opportunity Center. In addition, he was the president of the National Citizens Committee for Community Relations and a member of the steering committee of the Anti-Poverty Program for the Southwest.[6]

Drawing on his political and organizational experience, in 1963 Gonzales founded Los Voluntarios as a result of a case involving a young Mexicano who was beaten by a Denver police officer. With its newspaper, *Viva: The Battle Cry for Truth*, the fledgling organization with some support from business and political leaders led the battle over the issue. As an advocacy organization for the Méxicanos of Colorado, Los Voluntarios became the predecessor of the Crusade for Justice. During the next three years, Los Voluntarios addressed a variety of issues, but it was the issue of police brutality that served to gradually radicalize Gonzales's politics.[7]

Despite a growing disenchantment with the status quo, in 1965, Gonzales, then thirty-seven years of age, was appointed by Denver's mayor to head the Denver War on Poverty's Neighborhood Youth Corps. When the story broke, one of the newspapers carried a photo of Gonzales with President Lyndon Baines Johnson and his family. Yet his volatile political personality and his determination to establish that he was not a rubber stamp for anyone became evident when he accepted the position and told the press: "I'm an agitator and trouble-maker. That's my reputation and that's what I'm going to be. They didn't buy me when they put me in this job."[8] His increasingly rebellious attitude became apparent with his participation in a walkout by some fifty Méxicanos at an Equal Employment Opportunity Commission meeting held in Albuquerque, New Mexico, in 1966 over employment issues affecting Méxicanos.[9]

By 1966, as a War on Poverty administrator, Gonzales came under heavy fire and criticism. Despite the attacks, he continued to increase his activism, which brought him into conflict with the Democratic Party's leadership over his efforts to politically empower Méxicanos by forging them into a powerful voting bloc. His evolving radicalism became more apparent as a result of attacks on his running of the Neighborhood Youth Corps. In spite of Gonzales's increasing activism, in 1966 he refused to support the formation of a Méxicano third party, the New Hispano Party. Although his relations with Democrats were increasingly poor, at an organizing convention he urged the New Hispano Party not to go the third-party route and to continue with the regular parties. Without Gonzales's support, the fledgling New Hispano Party did poorly. Their candidate for governor, Levi Martinez of Pueblo, collected only 16, 201 votes— some 50, 000 votes short of the 10 percent required to be an official party.[10]

That year Gonzales came under fire from the *Rocky Mountain News*, which alleged that the Neighborhood Youth Corps was disorganized and mismanaged, and that it practiced discriminatory hiring against Whites and Blacks.[11] Washington, D.C., War on Poverty officials supported him, but local city officials remained quiet. Gonzales responded by having Los Voluntarios picket the newspaper. As a result of the picket, on April 24 Denver mayor Thomas Guida Currigan, whom Gonzales had helped elect, fired him as director of the Neighborhood Youth Corps.[12] Gonzales retaliated by accusing the mayor of lacking courage and being susceptible to pressure. This incident marked Gonzales's passage from conventional to unconventional politics and a growing militancy. Angry about the way he was treated, Gonzales organized a huge rally attended by some 1,200 people at Denver's Civic Center. At this rally he said, "This meeting is only the spark of a crusade for justice we are going to carry into every city in Colorado."[13] This rhetorical statement carried the name of his new grass-roots organization that was to lead a movement for social change.

## The Rise of the Crusade for Justice

With schisms becoming more frequent in Los Voluntarios, Gonzales moved expeditiously in November 1966 to transform the informal group into a civil rights–oriented action organization. Naming it the Crusade for Justice (CJ), Gonzales designed the organization to be grass-roots based, very political, and change-oriented.[14] "Originally," according to writer Juan Gómez Quiñonez, "the Crusade's social base was comprised of approximately thirty working-class families and was directed by an executive board concentrating on civil rights activity, discrimination in the schools, police brutality, and cultural programs."[15] Furthermore, according to historian Ignacio Garcia, "Gonzales sought an organization that extolled the virtues of the 'comunidad' by sponsoring theater productions, cultural dances, and fiestas to foster unity, as well as political discussions that promoted a self-help approach to solving problems."[16]

Like so many other Chicano Movement–oriented organizations, CJ's development was leader driven. From beginning to end, Gonzales was CJ and CJ was an extension of its *jefe*, or leader. As the leader became more militant, so did the organization. With Gonzales's power base in Denver, CJ remained in that city, with no infrastructure at either the state or national level. By design, CJ never sought to form chapters. Gonzales chose to keep CJ a local organization with linkages to numerous other organizations that operated at different levels. Gonzales felt that for reasons of security, management, and individual development, it was not necessary for CJ to have an elaborate structure that included chapters. CJ's main constituency was comprised of the barrio youth, students, *pintos* (former inmates), and some adults from Denver's barrios. To barrio youth, CJ was attractive because it was bold rather than apologetic, and it put them in the vanguard of a developing Chicano Movement (CM).[17] As did the Brown Berets, CJ gave a *causa* (cause) to young Chicanos who had none.

From the outset, CJ's development was guided by an evolving cultural nationalism, or Chicanismo, that with time became more pronounced. Although it never developed a well-defined ideology of its own, CJ's nationalist posture was imbued with a socialist rhetoric that viewed liberal capitalism critically. This became evident in the many pronouncements and speeches delivered by Gonzales and others. Yet Ernesto Vigil, another of CJ's secondary tier of leaders, described him as a "nationalist" who was "critical of capitalism, but was very cautious about never opting for an open leftist political stance. I don't think he understood leftist ideas."[18] As the epoch of protest became more radicalized, so did Gonzales's nationalism and activism. The leader became increasingly critical of the local, state, and national power structures. In 1966, he had spoken to a liberal coalition about a new sense of Méxicano solidarity and the importance of urban organizing. He voiced apprehension over coalitions and electoral strategies as untrustworthy and unworkable. Yet that same year, the CJ worked with the Congress on Racial Equality (CORE), Student Nonviolent Coordinating Committee (SNCC), and Denver Stop the War Committee, among others.

While few if any CM organizations had protested against the Vietnam War, the CJ did so in August 1967. It participated with other anti–Vietnam War groups in a rally and march in downtown Denver. As one of the speakers, Gonzales charged that U.S. society was run for and by "the ruthless financial lords of Wall Street" and by "great and powerful corporations."[19] His comments against the war were important, in that no other CM leader had spoken out so vociferously. Almost from the outset to the war's end in 1974, unlike other Chicano Movement groups, CJ maintained a consistent stand against the war, embracing the view of other New Left groups that it was an unjust and imperialist war of aggression by the United States against the struggling peoples of Vietnam. Gonzales's and CJ's emerging politics were influenced by an epoch of protest that was imbued with a militant ethos for dramatic change. This cross-fertilization effect was a product of Gonzales's close working activist relationship with other leaders from antiwar, Black power, and Native American power groups. This strategic pattern would continue to characterize CJ's politics well into the seventies.

The change in the CJ's political ethos was reflected in Gonzales's break with the Democratic Party by 1967. In a letter of resignation addressed to Democratic county chairperson Dale R. Tooley, Gonzales wrote: "The individual who makes his way through the political muck of today's world, and more so the minority representatives, suffers from such an immense loss of soul and dignity that the end results are as rewarding as a heart attack, castration, or cancer! . . . You and your cohorts have been accomplices to the destruction of moral man in this society. I can only visualize your goal as complete emasculation of manhood, sterilization of human dignity, and that you not only consciously but also purposely are creating a world of lackeys, political boot-lickers, and prostitutes."[20]

By this time, Gonzales had figured out that major social change would be easier to accomplish outside the established two-party system. To him, CJ was the very much needed independent force that would not play by anybody's rules but its own.[21] His frustration and anger toward what he described as the "establishment" became so exacerbated that he resigned from all boards and councils, and most organizations. It was part of the political catharsis he went through in his transition to a more radical politic. CJ politics did not allow for "wheeling and dealing." It embraced principle and conviction above compromise. A doctrinaire purity permeated Gonzales's thinking as well as that of CJ's secondary leadership and membership.

During CJ's first two years, Gonzales became increasingly involved in issues and causes outside Colorado. The CJ was very supportive of Reies Lopez Tijerina and his Alianza Federal de Mercedes's land grant struggle in New Mexico. In great part this was ascribable to the historical linkages between the Méxicanos of Colorado and New Mexico. Also, the struggle to recoup millions of acres lost by Méxicanos was a righteous one, from CJ's perspective.

Gonzales attended the Alianza's convention in 1966. The result was an informal alliance forged between the Alianza and CJ. For example, when the Alianza's Tierra Amarilla Courthouse raid occurred in 1967, the CJ responded with a large rally in support of the Alianza and a national call for solidarity. Two days later, Gonzales led a caravan of CJ members into New Mexico to support the Alianza and to assist it during the incarceration of Tijerina. Throughout 1967, CJ continued to support and monitor developments involving Tijerina and the Alianza.[22]

By the latter part of 1967, CJ had accelerated its networking and outreach efforts beyond Colorado. Gonzales's published poem "Yo Soy Joaquin," which was a powerful portrayal of the historical evolution of the Chicano experience, served to enhance his image as not only an emerging leader, but a poet and playwright. (In 1966 he had written the play The Revolutionist, which was performed in several church halls throughout Denver.)[23] The poem along with his growing leadership stature fostered a growing demand for him to make public appearances.

Due to Gonzales's eloquent antiestablishment and growing nationalist posture, many groups, from students to community people, were eager to hear him speak. For example, in October 1967 he and Tijerina both spoke at California State College's Los Angeles colloquium. Attended by some 200 people, it was organized by the newly formed chapter of the United Mexican American Students. A few days later, Gonzales spoke at a peace rally, also in Los Angeles.

In October 1967, the CJ participated in the Raza Unida Conference held in El Paso, Texas. The conference was organized to protest the Johnson administration's three days of cabinet committee hearings on Mexican American Affairs. The hearings were designed to cover such areas as agricultural labor, health, poverty, education and welfare, housing and urban development; and economic and social development. The hearings came about because in 1966, Méxicanos had walked out of a meeting of the State of New Mexico Equal Opportunity Commission in Albuquerque, because it was failing to address the problems confronting Méxicanos.

While President Johnson had agreed to hold a conference, after months of delays he reneged, opting instead for interagency committee hearings. Organizational leaders such as Gonzales, Tijerina, and Chavez were not invited. Gonzales, along with Tijerina and student leaders representing the Mexican American Youth Organization (MAYO), United Mexican American Students (UMAS), and others, boycotted the interagency hearings and instead held their own conference in the barrios of El Paso.[24]

The theme for the conference, "La Raza Unida," was selected at a planning session that same weekend. It became the rallying cry not only for the conference, but also subsequently for the emerging CM and ultimately for RUP. Moreover, as a result of the conference, an eight-point preamble entitled "Plan de La Raza Unida" was drafted. With its call to organize the Méxicano communities, it proposed effecting changes in education, job creation and training, housing, political representation; putting an end to police harassment; and enforcing the Treaty of Guadalupe Hidalgo. Also, the Southwest Council of La Raza (the predecessor of today's National Council of La Raza) was formed in 1968.

The conference gave Gonzales national exposure as an emerging Chicano leader and demonstrated his determination to oppose what he perceived as the national establishment, which in his view was not serving the interests of the Chicano. Throughout much of 1967, CJ was on the move as an emerging power within the growing Chicano Movement. That year, much of CJ's organizing effort in Denver was in response to cases involving police brutality. With its newly established iconoclastic newspaper, *El Gallo,* CJ used the power of its own press to propagate its positions on a variety of issues. As the CM accelerated its protest activities, so also did CJ.

During 1968, Gonzales continued to escalate his attacks on the White-controlled establishment. In January at a panel discussion held by the G.I. Forum in Denver on the topic "Will the Mexican American riot?" members and supporters of CJ demanded that Gonzales be allowed to speak. Though Gonzales did not predict that Méxicanos would riot, he did suggest that there could be "guerrilla warfare in the Southwest." In February, Gonzales traveled to California to the Los Angeles Sports Arena, where before some 5,000 people he shared the podium with Black Power advocates Stokely Carmichael and Rap Brown. While in Los Angeles, joined by Tijerina, he spoke at the New Left School, where he vehemently attacked U.S. involvement in the Vietnam

War, declaring that the battles that needed to be fought were not in Vietnam but in the United States.[25]

## The CJ's Participation in the Poor People's Campaign

Late in 1967, Gonzales and Tijerina were invited by Martin Luther King to attend a meeting in Chicago to join him in organizing the Poor People's Campaign in Washington, D.C., scheduled for 1968. Gonzales viewed the Poor People's Campaign with enthusiasm, for it gave him an opportunity to further catapult himself and CJ into the national limelight. The campaign's strategy was to pressure the federal government on behalf of poor people and to bring the capital to a standstill via the use of militant civil disobedience if the government did not respond positively.[26]

Gonzales and Tijerina led the Southwest contingent of some 400 people. While the group included Native Americans and Blacks, it was mostly made up of Méxicanos. Ultimately, division set in among the various participants over issues of leadership, allocation of resources, and strategy. Following the assassination of the Reverend Martin Luther King earlier that year, Reverend Ralph Abernathy assumed leadership of the Poor People's Campaign. Both Gonzales and Tijerina had disagreements with Ralph Abernathy and between themselves as well. The differences between the two leaders were primarily over strategy. Former CJ leader Ernesto Vigil writes, "Gonzales's opinion, as well as the Crusade's was that Tijerina's style was marked (or marred) by personal flamboyance at the expense of sound organizing."[27]

Not willing to depart from his movimiento agenda, Gonzales adjusted to the situation by promulgating "El Plan del Barrio." It called for housing that would meet Chicano cultural needs; for education, basically in Spanish, that would be based on the concept of community; for barrio businesses that would be owned within the community; and for reforms in landholding, with emphasis on restitution of pueblo lands."[28] But although increasingly critical of liberal capitalism, Gonzales had not yet advocated separatism. His politics were those of a militant reformer.

The Poor People's Campaign culminated with a Solidarity Day rally held on June 19, with the campaign's temporary Washington living quarters, Resurrection City, closing on June 24, 1968. Gonzales returned to Denver to hold a press conference to announce that a Poor People's Embassy was to be established in Washington. Its function was to offer leadership training, provide lodging for lobbying groups, and serve as a communication entity for the groups that had participated in the campaign. Gonzales served as the board's temporary chairperson. Unable to raise the needed resources, the board failed in its attempts to keep the campaign's various groups working together. However, for Gonzales the campaign paid off handsomely in CJ's success in networking with various progressive groups. In addition, it served to raise his growing leadership stature within the emerging CM. This was illustrated by his demanding speaking schedule in 1968, which included numerous universities and organizations throughout the Southwest and Midwest. Increasingly, he appeared as an apostle of nationalism propagating the faith of his developing Chicanismo. In Denver, CJ became more involved in issues of police brutality and in organizing the barrio youth. Dances were held every week for fund-raising and for promoting barrio unity. Gonzales continued his travels, networking with emerging CM-oriented groups and speaking out against the war and the issues impacting the nation's barrios.

The CJ in 1968 purchased the Calvary Baptist Church, located on Downing Street near downtown Denver, for $76,000. The money for the down payment came from CJ's board members.[29] Even though CJ's membership was still small, Gonzales had plans to develop the facility into the group's multipurpose headquarters. That summer, a program called the Freedom School was organized in which the youth were taught various aspects of Chicanismo. Also instituted were Fishermen's Meetings, held every Wednesday at the CJ complex. They were used by CJ to raise the consciousness of, proselytize, and organize the residents of Denver's various barrios.[30]

The CJ's newspaper, *El Gallo,* was more widely distributed. It had become a viable propaganda weapon in the CJ's organizing arsenal. Numerous issues, from local to international, were addressed and commented on from an anti–liberal capitalist perspective. Increasingly, it manifested CJ's growing nationalist posture. By the end of 1968, the CJ had embarked upon organizing the first Chicano Youth Liberation Conference.[31]

## The Crusade's Youth Liberation Conferences, 1969–1970

In late 1967, Gonzales had called for a national youth conference, but because of CJ's involvement in the Poor People's Campaign it did not materialize until two years later. On March 23–27, 1969, the CJ held the first national Chicano Youth Liberation Conference (CYLC) at its new headquarters complex in Denver. Two days before the conference began, CJ became immersed in organizing a walkout that began with West High School and spread to other high schools throughout Denver. What started with 75 students ultimately involved some 1,500 students.

Sparked by the racist remarks made by a White high school principal, the walkout turned into a riot, with windows of police cars broken and several students, as well as Gonzales, arrested. (Gonzales was subsequently acquitted of the charges against him.) CJ leaders met with the governor and mayor, and as a result the police were ordered to pull back from Denver's barrios.[32] In order to calm the conflict, school officials granted amnesty to the students and in principle agreed to look into the students' demands for including the Chicano experience in the school curriculum.

In the midst of all the turmoil, the CYLC was held. The conference proved to be a historical milestone for the CM. Some 1,500 youth representing more than 100 organizations from all over the nation attended. As historians Elizabeth Martinez and Enriqueta Vasquez write, "Because so many Crusade people had been arrested, the conference was not tightly planned—which in the end worked out for the best."

The youth spontaneously organized their own discussion groups and workshops and put forth their own topics.[33]

The conference's greatest achievement was the drafting of "El Plan Espiritual de Aztlán" (the spiritual plan of Aztlán), which became the CM's most important document. Inspired by Gonzales, it was an extremely cultural nationalist and separatist manifesto that sought to provide some ideological definition to a CM that was in need of direction and purpose. The call was made for the creation of Aztlán (the legendary Aztec homeland—the Southwest). At the heart of the plan was the idea that Chicanos needed to liberate themselves by forming their own separate nation. Excerpts illustrate the radical nature of the document: "In the spirit of a new people . . . we, the Chicano inhabitants . . . of Aztlán declare that . . . we are free and sovereign to determine those tasks which are justly called . . . by our hearts. Aztlán belongs to those who plant the seeds, water the fields, and gather the crops, and not to foreign Europeans. . . . We declare the independence of our Mestizo Nation. We are a Bronze People with a Bronze Culture. . . . We are a union of free pueblos, we are Aztlán."[34]

The plan was much more a poetic, romantic, and nationalist proclamation than a strategic and tactical agenda for how a separate Chicano nation was to be established. It buttressed Gonzales's view that nationalism was the common denominator that would bring about the mobilization and organization of La Raza and Aztlán. As Garcia further explains: "Gonzales may have been romanticizing the abilities of Chicano people to free themselves, his views were consistent with the premises of most national liberation movements that required class collaboration until the final victory was achieved. Gonzales, in essence, wanted a unity based on culture and national origin rather than on class interests, though he believed that the dominant ideals were generated from the experience of the working class."[35]

The conference did much to enhance the images of both Gonzales the leader and CJ the organization, especially among Chicano activists. Gonzales gained further credibility and legitimacy as one of the major leaders and theorists of the CM. As for CJ, historian Carlos Muñoz describes its growing importance to the Chicano Movement: "Corky Gonzales and his followers . . . had developed the image of the Crusade for Justice as the 'vanguard' of the rapidly growing Chicano Power movement. The Crusade . . . came to symbolize Chicano self–determination and espoused a strong nationalist ideology that the youth found extremely attractive."[36]

The impact of Gonzales and CJ was obvious. Hundreds of young activists who participated in the historic conference returned to their universities, colleges, and barrios infused with a newfound nationalism predicated on self-determination.[37] "Chicano" as a term came into vogue and began to displace "Mexican American." The Chicano's affinity to cultural nationalism became embodied in the concept of Chicanismo. As historian F. Arturo Rosales wrote, "The conference was more a celebration than a strategic planning meeting, but no other event had so energized Chicanos for continued commitment."[38]

This activist contagion became evident in California, where another conference was held just a few weeks later at the University of California, Santa Barbara. Inspired by the CJ Liberation Conference and "El Plan Espiritual de Aztlán," activists drafted "El Plan de Santa Barbara," which addressed changes that were needed in Chicano higher education. In addition, it propounded the formation of a new student umbrella organization, Movimiento Estudiantil Chicano de Aztlán.[39]

Throughout the rest of 1969, two salient issues dominated CJ activism and organizing: the nationalization or takeover of Westside Park by CJ and the celebration of Chicano Liberation Day, or Mexican Independence Day, which led to another school walkout.[40] Once again, CJ was involved in student walkouts in Denver, engaged in run-ins with the police, and accelerating its defiance of the war. With Tijerina incarcerated in a federal penitentiary from 1969 to 1971 on charges of destroying federal property, Gonzales's leadership stock went up dramatically among many CM activists.

In 1970, the CJ hosted the Second Youth Liberation Conference, once again in Denver at its headquarters. Attended by some 2,500 activists from fifteen states, including Puerto Ricans and Dominicans from New York and Chicago, this conference endorsed the call for forming a national Chicano political party.[41] Four major sections were added to "El Plan Espiritual de Aztlán" drafted in 1969. Section Three, item number six, called for the formation of an independent local, regional, and national political party.[42] Furthermore, the conference called for the creation of a national congress, the Congreso de Aztlán, of which the party would be a part. Various other resolutions were passed, including one that supported the National Chicano Moratorium Committee's antiwar march, scheduled for August 29 in Los Angeles. The conference's call for a Chicano political party precipitated RUP's rise in Colorado.[43]

## The Genesis of RUP in Colorado

Changing conditions within the expanding Chicano Movement fostered the political climate that was propitious for activists to push for RUP's emergence. RUP's rise officially began in January 1970 in Texas with José Angel Gutiérrez's announcement that efforts to organize it had begun. Cognizant of the developments in Texas, Gonzales by March 1970 considered himself the "unchallenged movimiento trailblazer for the formation of a national Chicano party."[44] While Gutiérrez was busy orchestrating the electoral revolts in the Winter Garden area and building RUP in Texas, Gonzales at the second CYLC, held in March 1970, was supported on his call for RUP's formation throughout Aztlán. On March 30, the CJ held a press conference at its headquarters to formally announce that efforts to form RUP had begun in Colorado. He exhorted Méxicanos to come together and support its organizing effort. In explaining why RUP was being formed, Gonzales said: "We are setting up a new party to use the same methods that they use to try to brainwash us, to start to educate and clear up the minds of our people who have been brainwashed and have had their cultural feelings, cultural traditions, completely raped and destroyed by the society of mass media and capitalism."[45]

Right after the conference, a letter signed by several Chicano leaders was sent to Democratic Party chairman Hugh Burns announcing their resignation from the Democratic Party: "The reason is that we, the Chicanos, have decided that it is now time that we control ourselves economically, socially, but most important, politically. . . . The present two party system does not represent and does not want to represent the Chicano."[46] On April 17, 1970, the CJ held a political caucus at its headquarters to officially initiate the organizing of RUP. Two weeks earlier, RUP in Texas had won several local victories, including gaining control of Crystal City's school board and city council. RUP's victories in Texas gave Gonzales's organizing efforts further impetus. Aspiring to be the CM's most powerful leader, Gonzales used RUP as his vehicle for moving up.

The barrios of Colorado had never experienced the intensity of the political mobilization that followed, led by CJ. As the Mexican American Youth Organization was in the forefront of organizing RUP in Texas, so was CJ in Colorado. Throughout RUP's six-year existence, the primary loyalty of Gonzales and other CJ leaders was to CJ. Ernesto Vigil, who became one of the most prominent leaders of both CJ and RUP, said in our 1997 interview, "I always considered the Crusade my primary loyalty and the party just as an electoral vehicle for the Crusade and for our state movement."[47]

By 1970, CJ had so grown in stature, membership, and resources that its headquarters had been developed into a multipurpose complex that included its own alternative school, La Escuela Tlatelolco.[48] The complex also housed CJ administration, an art gallery, a library, a gym, a nursery, a community center, and a community cafeteria—all offering Chicanos a variety of social services.[49] In 1970 CJ reached the apogee of its success and influence.

From April to August a number of RUP regional and state conventions were held in Colorado. On May 16, the first statewide RUP convention was held in the city of Pueblo at Southern Colorado State College.[50] With some eighty-eight people in attendance, Gonzales was elected state RUP chairperson. He delivered a speech that became a template for explanations of why Chicanos needed to form their own political party: "The truth is that both parties, the elite Republicans and the party of promises, the Democrats, operate for their own selfish interests. They are both ruled and controlled by money and racism. . . . The two-party system is one animal with two heads eating out of the same trough."[51]

A slate of RUP candidates for statewide office was selected that included Albert Gurule for governor, age twenty-seven, a former social worker with a master's degree; George Garcia for lieutenant governor, age twenty-nine, a consultant to the Denver Commission on Community Relations; Patricia Gómez, a housewife, for state representative; and Mark Saiz, age thirty-four, for regent of the University of Colorado.[52] When asked by the press why he was running for governor, Gurule said: "I have the interest of the Chicano and the poor at heart and I'll be addressing myself to the needs of these people. I'm perhaps the more qualified than any other candidates because I'm untarnished. I don't owe anybody anything and I don't have to worry about losing votes if I take a stand on an issue."[53]

The convention delegates also adopted a platform that was ultranationalist, reform, and communitarian oriented. It called for major changes in a number of areas.

In *education* it called for a free education from kindergarten to college; bilingual/bicultural education from kindergarten through college; Spanish as the first language; the rewriting of textbooks to reflect the contributions of Méxicanos; and creation of neighborhood schools governed by their own school boards.

In *economics,* it called for Méxicano-owned businesses and industries in the barrio; low interest loans to be provided for the Méxicano-owned businesses; establishment of co-op industries and businesses that engendered profits that stay in the community; restitution to the pueblos of mineral and natural resources, grazing and timber; subsidies in taxes and payoffs to corporations to revert to the people; and a redistribution of wealth by instituting economic reforms that would provide for all the people.

In the *social arena,* it propounded the need for job training programs controlled by the people themselves; formation of unions and the ending of existing discriminatory practices of unions; suspension of officers suspected of police brutality until a full hearing is held in the neighborhood where the beating occurred; suspension of the citywide juvenile court system and creation of neighborhood community courts; replacement of the prowl car precinct systems with neighborhood systems in which residents are hired to assist in policing; and the establishment of farm worker programs. Lastly, an anti–Vietnam War plank was included in the platform, calling for a major overhaul of the draft system and strong condemnation of the U.S. involvement in the Vietnam War.[54]

From the outset, CJ's inseparable relationship with RUP was evident in the omnipresent leadership of Gonzales and RUP's platform and strategy, although there was a division of labor between the two entities.[55] CJ was the everyday and functional advocacy and change-oriented pressure group. RUP was the electoral entity designed to carry forward CJ's agenda of self-determination. Throughout the campaign, the CJ pursued at an accelerated pace its advocacy activities in the areas of police brutality and education. CJ was not concerned that its actions could negatively impact RUP's electoral efforts.

RUP's organizing agenda from the start was interwoven with the CJ's agenda. During the summer of 1970, young political activists took over a swimming pool in the north side's Columbus Park. One year later, CJ symbolically proclaimed Alma Park, Mestizo Park, and La Raza Park as liberated territory. This meant that, without the sanction of city officials, CJ activists essentially ran and maintained the parks for organizing purposes. The parks were policed by CJ and cleared of drug dealers, but overall, the police continued to view Gonzales and CJ as dangerous radical forces.[56]

This was illustrated in the events surrounding CJ's strong support for the August 29 National Chicano Moratorium Anti–Vietnam War march held in 1970 in East Los Angeles, California. Attended by some 25,000 people from throughout the nation, the event was the largest Chicano protest against the Vietnam War. Some 100 Colorado activists attended. Gonzales and RUP gubernatorial candidate Albert Gurule, who were scheduled to speak, never reached the march. They, along with twenty-seven other activists traveling on a flatbed truck, were stopped by police and detained on charges of "suspicion of robbery" because Gonzales had $370 in his possession and of carrying concealed weapons.

Among those detained, according to Vigil, were five of RUP's first slate of candidates: Gurule, George Garcia, Carlos Santistevan, Martin Serna, and José Gonzales, who were running for governor, lieutenant governor, state senator, U.S. congressman, and state representative, respectively.[57] José Gonzales and Gurule were singled out, arrested, and jailed.[58] Their trial in Los Angeles began in November and ended in December with the jury acquitting Gurule and split on José Gonzales. Meanwhile, rioting broke out at Laguna Park and in the streets of East Los Angeles. More than a hundred people were injured and three killed, including reporter Ruben Salazar.

The arrests and trial came at a time when RUP's campaigns were intensifying. From June to August, six regional and state conventions were held throughout the state. Their purpose was to recruit RUP candidates for other local and state offices. Since RUP was not an officially certified political party, all its candidates had to circulate petitions in order to run as independents.[59] The petition requirements were not excessive in Colorado. Only 300 signatures were required to run as an independent for governor or lieutenant governor, and candidates for lesser office required only 100 signatures. The filing deadline for the petitions was forty-five days before the general election.[60] In order for RUP to become an official party, one of its statewide candidates had to garner at least 10 percent of the total vote.[61]

RUP in late September was successful in defeating a challenge against seven of its candidate-nominating petitions. Colorado secretary of state Byron A. Anderson turned down a challenge filed by John Lopez of the Colorado Labor Council against seven of RUP's candidates. Lopez had alleged that the RUP candidates did not meet the age requirement, thirty years of age. He alluded to Gurule, twenty-seven, and Garcia, twenty-nine, as being too young to appear on the ballot. The RUP candidate for treasurer interpreted Lopez's allegation "as no more than an action to suppress competition by the Democratic Party."[62] Anderson in part based his decision on the opinions of Colorado deputy attorney general John P. Moore and assistant attorney general Eugene C. Cavalier, who said that despite the age provision in the state constitution the requirement could not prevent the men from running for office.[63] Only if any of the candidates won could their qualifications be challenged. RUP's leadership viewed Anderson's decision as a major victory.[64]

RUP's candidates knew that the possibilities of victory were remote, since Méxicanos in Colorado constituted only 10 percent of the population.[65] In neither the rural nor urban areas did they have a substantial demographic base or concentrations sufficient to win elections, as Méxicanos had in Texas.[66] The highest number of Méxicanos was in Pueblo, where they comprised about 40 percent of the city's population; in Denver, they comprised only 20 percent. This demographic reality impacted RUP's development, strategy, and mission.

In essence, RUP candidates ran not because they believed they could win, but because they had a nationalist *causa* to advance.[67] RUP candidates deliberately targeted only Méxicanos.[68] They pushed RUP's progressive nationalist platform. Historian F. Arturo Rosales writes that at one of the RUP conventions, many of the "candidates for office mainly delivered speeches on liberation or spoke out against the war, rather than address issues that would attract rank-and-file voters to their cause."[69] Their purpose in running was not necessarily to win, but to raise the people's consciousness, to organize, and to unify the state's Méxicano communities.[70] When interviewed, Vigil further amplified this point: "We thought we could use the partido as a platform to address the issues at election time when there'd be a lot of media coverage, when the part of our community who do participate . . . would be paying attention to the issues and looking at what candidates were saying. So we used it as a platform to propagandize movement issues in general."[71]

Yet there were a few RUP candidates who did believe they had a chance of winning. Salvador Carpio, RUP candidate for Denver's First Congressional District, said the main purpose of running RUP candidates was to build power for the future and believed that RUP could win some offices.[72]

RUP's structure of regions and chapters provided the campaign organization. Colorado was broken down into four regions: northern, Denver, western slopes, and southern. Each region was comprised of several chapters. The chapters provided the campaign organization at the local level for the candidates. They were loosely structured and were generally composed of a few hard-core barrio activists supportive of CJ, with a sprinkling of white-collar workers and professionals. The better-organized chapters were those from Denver, Pueblo, and Boulder. Many of the chapters, however, had a large barrio youth constituency. Not many barrio adults participated in the chapters. Some were skeptical of RUP and thought its politics in general were too radical and that its campaign was an exercise in futility.[73]

However, several CM-oriented groups did get behind RUP. These included the Brown and Black Berets and student organizations from various universities and colleges, for instance, UMAS and MEChA. By and large, the older and more traditional organizations, such as the G.I. Forum and the League of United Latin American Citizens, were not supportive of RUP. RUP's espousal of nationalism excited many young Chicano activists and some barrio resident adults. However, it turned off many of the middle-class Méxicanos, who were not swayed by Corky Gonzales's incessant discourses on self-determination, Chicano liberation, and the evils of the establishment. But RUP's candidates all the way up to Election Day remained zealous. At community meetings and media appearances, in press releases, literature, and the canvassing of barrios, they ran on RUP's progressive platform. Vigil has written that Corky Gonzales "positively portrayed La Raza Unida effort as an act of dignity, not as a campaign for a loosing cause."[74]

Their commitment to the people's dignity was evident when in late October RUP candidates and CJ initiated an emergency assistance program for some 200 migrant families. RUP candidates, especially in the Pueblo area, collected money, clothing, and food.[75] This overture was indicative of RUP's service role as a third party. The action was not typical of either of the two major parties or of other third parties in the state.

On Election Day, RUP's chapters, strongly supported by the financial and manpower resources of the CJ, conducted their get-out-the-vote drives. Only those precincts with large numbers of Méxicanos were targeted. This became the strategic template for RUP's subsequent elections. However, even after months of campaigning, none of RUP's candidates were elected, and the group failed to garner the 10 percent required to gain official party status. RUP candidates for governor and lieutenant governor, Gurule and Garcia, both received only 1.8 percent of the vote, or 12, 296 votes. In Denver, congressional candidate Salvador Carpio garnered a mere 5,257 votes, 3.2 percent of the total. Third Congressional District RUP candidate Martin Serna received 1, 739 votes, 1.3 percent of the total vote. RUP candidate for University of Colorado regent Marcella Trujillo had the most votes of any candidate from within the party, 221,644. State treasurer candidate Leo Valdez had more than 18,700 votes, and the other RUP candidate, Marcos Saiz, received 17, 139 votes.[76] RUP also fielded twenty-three other candidates, including some for the state board of education, state senate and house, and several county offices. RUP candidates for sheriff and county assessor polled some 2,000 votes each in Pueblo County, which translated to about 7.5 percent of the total vote in each race.[77] In none of the races did RUP candidates pose a serious political threat. According to an article in *The Militant*, however, RUP's leadership did not interpret the election results as a major defeat. They believed that RUP had succeeded in making the argument that Colorado's traditional two party politics had short changed the poor, especially Méxicanos. Corky Gonzales in an interview with Antonio Camejo provided an assessment of RUP's campaign efforts:

> "We won the biggest number of votes that's ever been given to an independent party in the state of Colorado, and we've put on the line every social problem that impacts the Méxicano. We were able to become a pressure group just by creating the party alone. Both opposition parties came out with more Chicano candidates than they've ever had in the history of the state."[78]

In reference to the low percentage of votes received by RUP candidates, Corky Gonzales said, "We can still get on the ballot by petition. It's probably easier that way. We feel that this was the first step, an experiment."[79]

The climax of the RUP's election efforts actually came before the election. On election eve, Denver police conducted a raid on CJ's headquarters, under the pretext of searching for illegal weapons. They said there had been a report that someone from the office had fired a weapon. Armed with a search warrant, the police forced open the doors to the headquarters. They found only one shotgun, which was supposedly stolen, and arrested only one person. Corky Gonzales alleged that the police had stolen $850 in RUP funds and caused some $5,000 in damages to CJ's headquarters.[80] The police raid was an omen of things to come for both CJ and RUP. The incident dramatized the "state of siege" CJ would soon be under by law enforcement agencies.

## The Second Year of RUP"s Struggle, 1971

During 1971, CJ continued to press hard for the building of the RUP into a viable political third force. In March, at a RUP state meeting, elections for state party officers were held. Corky Gonzales was reelected state chair; Albert Gurule, vice chairperson; Amelia Alvarado, secretary; and Denise Lovato and John Haro, cotreasurers. Concurrently, RUP prepared for its next electoral battle, Denver's municipal elections, which were scheduled for May 18. At a press conference, Corky Gonzales introduced RUP's two candidates for Denver's city council and three for the school board.

Interestingly, outside of community control issues, none of the RUP candidates had proposals that could be considered radical or revolutionary. The two city council candidates called for better recreational programs for Denver's youth and more and improved employment opportunities for minorities. As for the school board candidates, their main issues were community control of schools, improvement of facilities, changes in the schools' curriculum, and opposition to forced busing.[81]

John Haro announced his candidacy for mayor of Denver. He was RUP's co–state treasurer and vice president of CJ. At a press conference held at CJ headquarters, Haro delineated a thirteen-point program that was the basis of his campaign platform. Six of the most controversial planks were: (1) "equitable" income tax to halt spiraling property taxes; (2) abolition of the head tax for Denver residents; (3) requiring persons who lived outside Denver but worked in the city to pay the head tax; (4) requiring all police and firefighters to live in Denver; (5) establishing neighborhood citizen councils to investigate charges of police brutality against the poor; and (6) free public transportation for persons on welfare, social security, and old age pensions. Asked how he planned to secure the needed resources to implement his progressive agenda, Haro said, "I plan to cut the fat from the city administration. There's quite a bit of fat."[82]

In spite of a comprehensive "get out the vote drive" in Denver's various barrios, none of RUP's candidates even came close to winning. Still, Corky Gonzales and other CJ and RUP leaders did not perceive RUP's losses as a detriment to RUP's development. For them, these elections were strategically conducive not only to politicizing the community, but also to organizing it.

CJ hosted the third annual Chicano Youth Liberation Conference in June in Denver. Although the conference was not as well attended as the previous two, Corky Gonzales used it to further enhance "El Plan Espiritual de Aztlán" as the basis for forming RUP into a national party movement. Gutiérrez was the conference's keynote speaker. Although the Texas RUP stalwart was now beginning to rival Gonzales in national stature within the "movimiento," the two seemed to agree on the need for a Chicano political entity that would never make compromises with traditional parties.[83] The conference became an organizing catalyst for a RUP national and international convention.

In November, in an attempt to transform the RUP into a national political force, RUP in Colorado hosted a three-day convention at Southern Colorado State College in Pueblo, which was attended by some 500 delegates. José Angel Gutiérrez, leader of RUP in Texas, was unable to attend. In his place, Texas RUP state chair Mario Compean attended and spoke to what was billed by RUP in Colorado as a "historical" meeting. The convention's two other major speakers were Corky Gonzales and Gurule. Gonzales called for a national RUP convention to be held sometime in 1972, before the presidential elections. Gurule exhorted delegates to establish linkages and alliances with elements who sympathized with RUP in Cuba, Mexico, and other South American countries. He reminded the delegates that "the white man is our enemy, he is continually going to be our enemy and he is never going to help us out."[84]

At the end of the three-day session, Corky Gonzales's and CJ's influence was evident with the passage of various planks that included: (1) the beginning of the building of the nation of Aztlán; (2) the establishment of an independent national RUP with "El Plan Espiritual de Aztlán" as its initial platform; (3) the establishment of the Congreso of Aztlán as the governing body for the party, to handle all political questions concerning the nation of Aztlán; (4) the decision that Congreso and RUP first and foremost maintain their activities within the United States and set an example for the rest of the world; (5) the intention of RUP to support only RUP candidates and under no conditions to support Democrats or Republicans; (6) and the opposition of RUP to all wars of oppression.[85]

However, the convention was not without debate and controversy. The opening shot in what subsequently became a political war between Gutiérrez and Corky Gonzales was fired by Compean. He took issue with the emphasis on building a Chicano nation, declaring that the idea of Chicanos forming their own country was not realistic. He said that Aztlán was a "nation in spirit," and he expounded on the need for Chicanos to unify.[86] The convention revealed major differences between the two main RUP organizing forces. While RUP in Colorado was much more ultranationalist, committed to nation building,[87] RUP in Texas was more reform oriented, interested in winning elections and in community control.

## The Third Year of RUP's Struggle, 1972

After being retried and found guilty in 1971 in Los Angeles, Corky Gonzales in January 1972 began serving a forty-day sentence on what he alleged was a trumped-up charge of possession of an illegal weapon.[88] That April, RUP officials formally announced the party's election plans. Carpio urged all RUP supporters not to vote in the major two-party primaries, since by doing so they would be disqualified from signing RUP's candidate petitions.[89] On May 5, the RUP launched a four-month voter registration drive for the November elections. It also opened five storefront campaign offices in Denver's barrios, staffed by young party activists. *El Gallo*, the CJ newspaper, was reoriented to provide political emphasis on RUP and the antiwar struggle.[90] By this time, it had become apparent that leaders of Colorado's Democratic Party were concerned about the RUP's potential impact on the election. Dan Lynch, state chairperson of the Democratic Party, alluded to RUP as "racist" in its attempt to organize Méxicanos.[91]

Ignoring the accusations, RUP held a weekend conference in Denver in June for the purpose of accelerating its voter registration drive. Before the conference, Corky Gonzales, José Gonzales, and Arturo Vasquez held a press conference. They explained that the intent of the conference was to enhance RUP's efforts to attain the needed 10 percent to become an official party and to begin the candidate-selection process.[92] The conference, chaired by Sal Carpio, drew some 100 persons from throughout Colorado. Some RUP protagonists took issue with organizers from Cesar Chavez's United Farm Workers Union (UFW). José Calderon of Greeley reported that UFW officials had said to him that if he wanted to continue to organize farm workers, he would have to stop attending antiwar demonstrations and cut all ties with the RUP. He informed the body he could not accept their conditions and would instead focus on organizing RUP.[93] This incident illustrates the precarious relationship that developed between the UFW and CJ because of RUP's formation.

That summer, the Crusade for Justice was again embroiled in confrontations with the police over CJ's control of La Raza Park, one of four parks it had "nationalized." During the ensuing weeks, several incidents occurred between the police and Chicano youth involving the use of the park. *El Gallo* reported: "Since La Raza Park opened around June 9th, the police have been breaking heads, arresting park-users, and otherwise harassing our community for the benefit of the Northside Mafia."[94] This was rather typical of the political climate the RUP was organized in—one of perpetual conflict with the police.[95]

In August, RUP held a state convention in Greeley at which Corky Gonzales was the keynote speaker. He described the Democrats and Republicans as "one monster with two heads," condemning their capitalist policies and actions and stressing the need to organize independently of both parties. RUP's platform was reapproved and in its introduction asserted: "It is the right, responsibility, and obligation of Chicanos, urban and rural, to seek and gain control of their lives and communities—politically, economically, educationally, and socially." The platform called specifically for an end to U.S. involvement in the Vietnam War; for a free and independent Puerto Rico; and for the end to all U.S. military and economic intervention in Latin America.[96]

At the convention, RUP announced most of its candidates: José Calderon and Maria Arellano for Weld County commissioners; José Muñiz for state house in District 3 (Denver); Emilia Alvarado for state house in District 8 (Denver); Tina Sanchez for state house in District 48 (Greeley); Carlos Gonzales for state house in District 50 (Weld County); Ron Martinez for state senate in District 50 (Greeley); and Florencio Granado for University of Colorado Board of Regents.[97] A total of seventeen state and local RUP candidates ran in 1972.

After months of squabbling between Gutiérrez and Corky Gonzales, at RUP's first national convention, held in El Paso, Texas, September 1–4, the power struggle between the two escalated into a full-fledged war over the issue of who was to be RUP's national chair. With some 3,000 activists in attendance representing eighteen states, the meeting ended in a confrontation between two very powerful charismatic *caudillos* (leaders). Their differences were over questions of organization, strategy, and ideology. In the end, Gutiérrez prevailed; he was elected national chairperson of RUP's Congreso de Aztlán.[98]

As if Corky Gonzales's defeat was not enough, before the convention, both CJ and Colorado's RUP suffered a major tragedy with the death of Richard Falcon.[99] While en route to the convention, he stopped at a gas station in Orogrande, New Mexico, to put water in his vehicle's radiator. He engaged in an altercation with a White station attendant, Perry Brunson, who was a member of George Wallace's American Independent Party. When Brunson refused to allow Falcon access to water to cool off the radiator, a struggle ensued between the two. Brunson pulled out a gun and shot and killed Falcon. His death was a major loss for both CJ and RUP, since he was not only a key leader but also an excellent organizer in the northern Colorado area. He was described by RUP officials as "a humanitarian and a man dedicated to fighting injustice."[100] Falcon's death created a "gap in the CM in Colorado," said José Calderon, but the gap would "be filled by little Chicanitos who will rise throughout the Southwest."[101] Brunson was charged with voluntary manslaughter and in December went to trial and was found not guilty.[102]

Determined not be deterred by the death of Falcon and the convention defeat, CJ and Colorado's RUP, joined by various other organizations, held a massive march and rally on September 16 in downtown Denver commemorating Mexican independence. The combined parade and rally drew some 5,000 people. All along the parade route, shouts of "Viva Ricardo Falcon!" "Chicano power!" and "Que viva La Raza!" were heard. At the rally, Corky Gonzales spoke on the connection of the Chicano struggle for self-determination with those of other oppressed peoples in Puerto Rico and Southeast Asia. José Gonzales, RUP candidate for the state house, blasted the Democrats and Republicans as being controlled by the nation's rich, declaring that for Méxicanos to support either one of the two parties would be to betray the Chicano Movement.[103]

On October 21, RUP filed a lawsuit over the placement of state house candidate José Gonzales's name, which appeared on the ballot next to those of Communist Party candidates. RUP's legal counsel, Ken Padilla, argued that the placement of Gonzales's name on a horizontal line with that of the Communist Party candidates was detrimental to his election chances.[104] RUP officials also complained about their party not having its own line on the ballot and appealed for "parity," to be "brought up to equality."[105] Just a few days before the election, the Denver District Court ordered that Gonzales's name placement on the ballot be changed. However, RUP failed in finding relief for the rest of its candidates. At a press conference, Corky Gonzales called the placement of the RUP candidates next to Communist Party candidates "a deliberate attempt to 'red-bait' us and label us. No other party has had the trouble we have."[106]

RUP's electoral impact on the 1972 November general election was minimal. Once again, it failed to secure the required 10 percent for official party status and none of its candidates fared well. Secundino Salazar, who ran for the U.S. Senate, out of a total of 212,123 votes cast received a mere 4,079 votes, or about 1.5 percent of the vote. For the University of Colorado Board of Regents race, out of a total of 417,358 votes, RUP candidate Florencia Granados received 22,903 votes, or 5.5 percent. José Gonzales, RUP candidate for the state house, District 9, garnered 1,586 votes out of a total of 8,573.[107] Corky Gonzales's showing turned out to be the most impressive of all the RUP candidates'. His 1,586 votes translated to 18.4 percent of the total vote. Michael Montoya, who ran for the State Board of Education, received 6,499 votes, nearly 4 percent. And José Calderon, who ran for Weld County commissioner, received 6 percent.[108]

Clearly, the results reflected that RUP's exclusive appeal to the small percentage of Méxicanos in Colorado was not enough to achieve official party status. Moreover, RUP's perceived radical image and association with CJ did not help to garner votes among the moderate to conservative Méxicanos or from other ethnic groups. This was further exacerbated by the fact that there were few, if any, crossover votes from non-Méxicano voters.[109]

Even though RUP's leadership had not expected to be victorious against the two-party monopoly, it had hoped for a better showing. Corky Gonzales's political stock vis-à-vis his ongoing power struggle with Gutiérrez had taken a dip as a result of RUP's poor results. After three years of organizing, RUP had failed to elect a single candidate in Colorado.

## The Fourth Year of RUP's Struggle, 1973

Undeterred by the losses, throughout 1973 CJ continued its efforts to organize RUP. The Gonzales versus Gutiérrez power struggle continued to be a major distraction for RUP in Colorado. The acrimonious power struggle preoccupied Gonzales. The Congreso meetings held late in 1972 and 1973 continued to be sessions of conflict and division, a political chess game in which neither faction won. Not only was the power struggle a distraction, but also the CJ's constant battles with the Denver police became more consuming.

On March 17, 1973, in what the CJ's leadership would describe as an unprovoked police attack, an incident developed as a result of the detainment of a youth who was attending a party at the CJ complex. With CJ members protesting the youth's detainment, scores of police arrived to quell the so-called disturbance. The incident turned into a full-fledged confrontation, with shots fired by both police and CJ supporters. Two units owned by the CJ in an adjacent apartment complex were destroyed as a consequence of an explosion set off due to police fire.[110] The incident produced casualties: Luis "Junior" Martinez, a CJ member and dance teacher at La Escuela Tlatelolco, was killed; three others were wounded; and four police were wounded in the melee. In addition, the Denver police arrested thirty-six youths. CJ alleged that Martinez had been executed by the police in "cold blood." The incident further exacerbated CJ and police relations, and for several weeks the CJ became more occupied with organizing antipolice protests and rallies than with organizing RUP.[111]

On April 28, 1973, CJ held an antipolice rally in Denver that drew some 1,200 people in support of CJ defendants Ernest Vigil, Mario Vasquez, and Luis Rameriz, who as a result of the incident had been arrested and indicted on such charges as first-degree assault and possession of a firearm. In response to their arrests, CJ formed the Denver Chicano Liberation Defense Committee in support of "Los Tres," as the three defendants were designated. Numerous CM-oriented organizations participated, such as Bert Corona's Centro de Accíon Social Autonoma (Center for Autonomous Social Action, or CASA).

The rally took on a multiethnic dimension in that it drew the participation and support of such speakers as former Black Panther Party activist Angela Davis, Clyde Bellecourt and Russell Means of the American Indian Movement, activist and Catholic priest James Groppi, and several others who represented non-Chicano struggles. The agenda reflected a broadening of CJ's nationalism to one that was becoming increasingly oriented toward Third World struggles. Corky Gonzales reminded the activists that the CJ was "locked in a struggle for survival." He said, "We are witnessing the work of a conspiracy, a conspiracy to crush the Crusade and render it ineffective." Angela Davis told the crowd that "the spirit and legacy of Luis Martinez will live on."[112]

In late July, another rally was held by the CJ at Mestizo Park in Denver. Corky Gonzales delivered "El Grito de Denver." He called for the release of all political prisoners, specifically Los Tres.[113] That July, the police harassment of CJ's leadership increased. RUP leader José Calderon was arrested by police at the University of Colorado for impeding traffic and questioned by the FBI regarding two bombings.[114] On August 20, Luis Rameriz of Los Tres was found not guilty. Corky Gonzales told the press that "Luis being found innocent is proof of other political prisoners."[115] In late September, CJ picketed the United States Court House in protest of U.S. involvement in the overthrow of Chile's socialist President Salvador Allende. For the rest of 1973, the CJ came under increasing police pressure with several of its leaders and members arrested on a variety of charges.

In the midst of the attacks and all the distractions, CJ continued its efforts to build a strong RUP in Colorado.[116] It also persisted in its struggle to neutralize Gutiérrez's leadership. Moreover, that year, the RUP was successful in thwarting an effort by the Democrats to increase the required number of petition signatures for independent candidates from 300 to 10,000. It was an obvious attempt by Democrats to disenfranchise RUP in Colorado.[117] However, the proposed legislation was defeated; the Republican Party was not about to vote for a bill that would strengthen or help the Democrats.[118]

In May, RUP unsuccessfully ran three candidates for the school board in Denver: Nita Aleman (daughter of Corky Gonzales), Madeline Navarro, and Antonio Archuleta. Their campaigns focused on three issues: the lack of teacher training to deal with the Méxicano students; the unequal financial expenditures in barrio schools; and the lack of relevant materials for Méxicano students.[119] The campaign was difficult, in that the CJ was simultaneously organizing protests and fending off police harassment.

The political climate in Denver became polarized to the degree that RUP's candidates were depicted by the opposition as being part of the CJ, a radical and antisystem organization.[120]

Not deterred by the election losses, RUP in June held a statewide convention in Denver where it reaffirmed its commitment to the nationalist and change ideas stated in its 1970 and 1972 platforms. In addition, it reaffirmed its adherence to "El Plan Espiritual de Aztlán." Elections were held for RUP's Colorado officers for the 1973–1975 term. Elected were: José Calderon, state chair; Corky Gonzales, cochair; Felicitas Alfaro, treasurer; Gloria Montes Keller, secretary; Salvador Carpio Jr., coordinator. Also elected were several state county coordinators: José Gonzales, Denver; Eddie Montour, Pueblo; Maria Arellano, Weld; Francisco Coca, Las Animas; and Dora Esquivel, Boulder. A call was also made for a RUP national Congreso conference to be held at the CJ complex that August to promote the Chicanos' solidarity with other oppressed nations, particularly in Latin America.[121]

That August, the three-day national and international RUP conference fell short of its goal of attracting 1,500 delegates from throughout the nation and Latin America, yet it did manage to bring together some 800 delegates from Colorado, Illinois, New Mexico, Texas, and Oklahoma.[122] A report in *El Gallo* stated, "The purpose of this conference was the exchange of solidarity commitments and support among oppressed nations and Liberation Movement Organizations throughout La Nacion de Aztlán and Latin America." The resolutions passed reflected an ardent anticapitalist posture that called for freeing all political prisoners and rekindled its commitment to support struggles of liberation. It was also resolved that the development of RUP would be predicated on "no compromise" and it would "become a mass party based on nationalism." The theme, "nationalism, a tool to educate towards internationalism," was emphasized. A call was made for RUP's Congreso to meet in Albuquerque before November.[123]

The conference discourse also focused on an issue that was part of the Gonzales-Gutiérrez power struggle—the role of RUP. Corky Gonzales was critical of Gutiérrez's reform, electoral orientation, and willingness to compromise. His perception of RUP was that it should be not just an electoral party, but one that functioned day to day in the communities, confronting their issues.[124] While not strategically clear as to how it would be achieved, Gonzales perceived RUP as the political arm or "vanguard" in the struggle to create Aztlán.[125]

At the conference, delegates were openly critical of RUP national chairman Gutiérrez's politics. They accused Gutiérrez of shaping the RUP into just another party replete with compromise and corrupted idealism.[126] Colorado RUP state chairman Calderon said, "Major changes have never come about through the electoral process but through organizing the masses." He further added that the party should be "revolutionary," "not a part of the system but fighting against the system." Calderon told the delegates that if RUP became just another party, the Colorado RUP would withdraw.[127]

This shift to a much more socialist and internationalist posture caused the defection of some of RUP's leaders and supporters. One such leader was Sal Carpio, who left both the RUP and CJ that year. When interviewed, Carpio explained that he had left the party because it was starting to dissipate and because, thanks to RUP, the Democrats were becoming more concerned about Chicanos' issues. He further explained that RUP and CJ "were just too radical for people to understand. It might have been good for discussion within the four walls of the Crusade and people there could understand, but to take the message to the rank-and-file Chicano out in the street, they could never understand."[128]

RUP closed the year 1973 with two other conferences. In late November, RUP held a state conference in Pueblo, the Youth Awareness Conference. The agenda focused on ways of strengthening RUP and on preparations for the 1974 elections. A state steering committee was formed to screen potential RUP candidates. RUP chapters were directed to move to create alternative educational systems and to use barrio art as a way to educate the people. A resolution critical of Chicano professionals was approved; it read that all Chicano professionals should "quit selling out the community" and become involved in the struggle for liberation. The White press was accused of deliberately trying to destroy the Chicano Movement.[129]

In December, another RUP Youth Awareness Conference was held in Greenley. Organized by José Calderon, the conference focused on the necessity for Chicanos in Weld County to challenge the political and economic power of the White ranchers and sugar beet farmers who ruled the county via the Democratic and Republican parties. Calderon explained that RUP was concerned with striking a balance between running election campaigns and being involved in day-to-day struggles. He reported that RUP in Weld County had organized a labor committee to help support the boycotts against Coors and Farah pants, and UFW's grape and lettuce boycotts.[130] The support for the UFW's boycott was something of a paradox, because of the UFW's continued support for Democrats.

As 1973 came to a close, RUP in Colorado had entered a state of decline. With the Crusade for Justice overwhelmed by the attacks by law enforcement agencies and with RUP's failures to produce any electoral successes, defections began to occur within its leadership and supportive ranks. RUP began a transition toward becoming a vanguard and more issue-oriented political party.

## RUP's Fifth Year of Struggle, 1974

The law enforcement siege of the CJ had debilitated its organizing of RUP. Limited in finances, constantly in a defensive organizing posture, immersed in a no-win power struggle with Gutiérrez, and a victim of negative publicity, CJ in 1974 held on for dear life. In spite of all these difficulties, RUP organizing activity continued, but at a reduced level. RUP's leadership continued its shift to a more "internationalist" political posture. Increasingly, it identified with various struggles of liberation, especially in Latin America. Pronouncements of support were made for the guerrilla struggles in Mexico led by Lucio Cabañas and Genaro Vasquez. RUP remained steadfast in its anti–Vietnam War position.

While RUP prepared to select its candidates in April, in March CJ won a major legal victory in its struggle against Denver's police with the acquittal of Ernesto Vigil.[131] At a RUP conference held on April 20, the delegates nominated Vigil to run for the First Congressional District against Democrat Pat Schroeder. Another six candidates were nominated: two for the University of Colorado Board of Regents, three for state house races; and one for county sheriff. By the summer, the number of RUP candidates increased to eight; some of the original seven were replaced by others, and Vigil changed from a congressional bid to one for the state senate. RUP suffered another blow with the resignation of Corky Gonzales as RUP's state cochairperson. He relegated himself to an advisory role, and in his place José Gonzales, who headed CJ's La Escuela Tlatelolco, was elected.[132]

Before the November elections, CJ was immersed in a number of issues related to police harassment. In January 1974, CJ member Gary Garrison was arrested and charged with attempted bombing. Three months later, six young people died in two explosions that left a sole survivor burned and maimed. Vigil writes, "The Crusade's most sympathetic supporters were now confronted with supporting an organization whose members and teachers were portrayed as bomb-throwers and terrorists."[133] Throughout most of the year, CJ was occupied with organizing protest activities. In July, some 200 activists protested the grand jury probe of the two bombings. A Méxicano Independence Day March was held on September 16 protesting police repression. With some 5,000 people in attendance, CJ used the march and rally to gather support for its defense of Gary Garrison, who faced arson and bombing charges.[134]

## RUP's Sixth Year of Struggle, 1975

With the Crusade for Justice overextended and struggling for survival, RUP organizing activities in 1975 greatly diminished. Content analysis of *El Gallo* for 1975 shows very few articles devoted to the RUP. The focus of many of the articles was the ongoing struggle with the police and other security agencies. Ernesto Vigil, the only candidate to run for one of Denver's council seats, ran against a former RUP leader, Sal Carpio, who had left the party in 1973 and become a Democrat in 1974. Vigil ran to prevent Carpio from winning.[135] Both men lost the election, but Carpio by 1976 was elected to the city council.

Hence, in 1975, CJ was in a state of dissaray.[136] The Gary Garrison controversy continued to be a focus of organizing. Corky Gonzales was arrested in February on charges of "interference." Subsequently, the charges were dismissed and Gonzales filed an unsuccessful suit for $1,100,000 for eleven claims of false arrests, false imprisonment, deprivation of civil rights, and conspiracy.[137] La Escuela Tlatelolco also felt the ill effects of the siege on CJ. Several of its foundation grants were not renewed, causing financial hardships to the school, and some of the parents removed their children from the school due to fear of police attack. In May, CJ went to court as a result of a $20 million lawsuit against the *Rocky Mountain News*, alleging slander against CJ and its leadership.[138] In September, CJ kept the pressure on law enforcement agencies by holding its annual September 16 march and rally. By then, however, the CJ had become engaged in a conflict with conservative Méxicanos over who was going to control the festivities.

The exodus of RUP leaders continued with the resignation of José Calderon as RUP's state chairperson. In 1975, he was working with a number of other groups and causes. He had developed a center in Greeley that housed RUP, the Welfare Rights Organization, a legal defense committee, and an immigration advocacy organization, Centro Autonomo de Social Accion (Center for Autonomous Social Action, or CASA). By this time, CASA, under the leadership of Antonio Rodriguez from Los Angeles, was vying for the organizational leadership of what was left of the Chicano Movement. Differences over finances and turf had developed between CASA and the Crusade for Justice. When CASA held a national meeting in Greeley in November attended by some fifty persons, the CJ responded in a quasi-bellicose manner.[139] Calderon had facilitated the meeting with the understanding that the focus of the agenda was to troubleshoot CASA's newspaper, *Sin Fronteras*, not realizing that the real intent was to discuss CASA's political agenda. As a result of the meeting, tensions increased between the two groups. Feeling caught between the two, Calderon submitted his resignation as RUP's state chairperson to the CJ.[140] His resignation left a leadership vacuum within RUP that further contributed to the group's decline.

## RUP's Demise in Colorado, 1976

By 1976, RUP was no longer the organizing priority for CJ that it had been.[141] The resignation of Calderon opened a can of worms for RUP in Colorado. Divisions over ideology and RUP's role as a party became apparent at a conference held in Alamosa on January 16 and 17. Attended by some 400 activists from Colorado and New Mexico, the conference, organized by United Mexican American Students from Adams State University, debated the topic of developing a strategy for Chicano political action.[142]

The conference's debate focused on the role of the RUP. Panelist Calderon, who by this time had declared himself a Marxist-Leninist, and Rudy Garcia from Denver both argued that Chicanos needed to construct a "multinational revolutionary vanguard party, guided by the principles of Marxism-Leninism Mao-Tse-Tung thought." In an obvious jab at CJ and RUP in Colorado and Texas, both speakers belittled nationalist struggles for Chicanos and alleged that they had failed. They further argued that Chicano struggles to control the political, social, and economic institutions in their communities, such as those in Texas, had failed to advance the struggle for Chicano liberation.

While Colorado's RUP had no one on the panel, from the floor Eddie Montour, who had replaced Calderon as RUP state cochairperson, defended the group's adherence to Chicano nationalism as an organizing tool.[143] The one point of consensus was the vehement attack on Gutiérrez. Calderon and Garcia as well as Montour attacked Gutiérrez for having allegedly "compromised" and "sold out." The conference illustrated the growing divisions and fragmentation that plagued what was left of the RUP and were omens of its decline. Neither Montour nor the other Colorado RUP activists had put forth their views nor had RUP announced any candidates for the 1976 elections.[144]

The Colorado RUP contingent at the conference released a statement dated January 16 that essentially reaffirmed RUP's role as a nationalist-oriented revolutionary party committed to the liberation of the Chicano. RUP's direction, it read was "a political direction that was from the beginning projected as a Revolutionary Party for Chicanos, an alternative Party that would educate, organize, and struggle against racism, injustice, exploitation, and colonization of Chicanos in Aztlán, and that will seek our total liberation."[145]

Throughout 1976, RUP remained a low organizing priority for the CJ, which continued in its preoccupation with simply surviving the siege. Little attention was given to RUP and to preparing for the oncoming elections.[146] RUP's dependence on CJ became a growing liability. Juan Haro, vice chairperson of CJ, was convicted in January on charges of violating federal firearm laws, specifically, possession of hand grenades. CJ alleged that Haro had been a victim of a set-up by an undercover agent and an informer. At a press conference, CJ leader Ernesto Vigil commented, "We will not be intimidated by law enforcement officials, their huge financial budgets, or their political witch-haunts, because justice is on our side."[147]

That February, Haro was sentenced to six years in prison. He and the CJ alleged that he was a victim of a frame-up. Further exacerbating CJ's precarious existence was the allegation made by police that Corky Gonzales and the CJ were plotting to murder Denver police. Gonzales denied the accusations and charged that they may have originated with the FBI or the Central Intelligence Agency.[148]

RUP's last electoral struggle in Colorado came in September, when it was announced that it would field Joséph Eddy Montour for county commissioner in Pueblo's First District and Alfredo Archer for the Third Congressional District. Neither candidate espoused what could be considered a radical platform. Montour addressed the importance of improving health care and defended Méxicano professionals who were under attack.[149] Archer's campaign issues included providing financial aid for poor students; prison reform, with an emphasis on rehabilitation, training, and educational programs; health care based on need; and job creation.

While the two RUP candidates campaigned, an incident occurred in October involving CJ leaders and two members of the Socialist Workers' Party (SWP). While tensions between the two entities had been growing over political turf issues, an altercation occurred at the CJ headquarters that further divided RUP's thinning ranks both within and outside Colorado. When two SWP members and Vigil exchanged words and accusations, the SWP members were told to leave; in the process of leaving, they made a threat against Vigil. At that point an assault occurred: the two SWP members were beaten and ejected from the Crusade building by CJ members. Vigil was arrested on charges of gun possession and spent two days in jail. The attack became the basis of a major controversy that engulfed both organizations and other Chicano activists throughout the nation. A petition was circulated condemning the CJ for "using intimidation tactics and using physical violence against other activists."[150] The issue further contributed to the schism between Corky Gonzales and Gutiérrez, since Gutiérrez sided with the SWP. For months, charges and countercharges were made by both entities.

In the November elections, RUP's two candidates were defeated. Montour received 3,894 votes, or 9 percent of the vote, while Archer received a mere 719 votes to the Democrat victor's 24,796. This became RUP's last electoral act in the drama of building a Chicano political party in Colorado.[151]

RUP's decline in Colorado was due to various endogenous and exogenous antagonisms. The most salient were Colorado's two-party hegemony, stringent election laws, winner-take-all plurality elections, and hostile, white-controlled communications media that depicted RUP as a radical separatist party. The endogenous antagonisms were: (1) Colorado's small Méxicano population; (2) lack of concentrated Méxicano populations; (3) RUP's failure to become an official party on the ballot; (4) extremely limited resources, both financial and manpower; (5) RUP's rather weak organizational infrastructure; (6) RUP's inability to draw mass Méxicano support from both lower and middle classes; and (7) RUP's dependency on and affiliation with CJ politics and struggles.

The latter antagonism, in particular, accelerated both the rise and fall of RUP in Colorado. After all, RUP was CJ, and CJ was RUP. But because CJ was a nonprofit advocacy organization, RUP was created; therefore, RUP was the political vehicle. It took CJ's politics and nationalist agenda into the political marketplace. CJ used RUP for three functions: as an instrument of political education or "conscientization" on CJ's nationalist agenda and ideas; as the political arm in the struggle for change and nation building; and as the political medium by which to catapult Corky Gonzales into the position of the CM's most powerful national caudillo. RUP in Colorado was a third party built on the charisma of a personality. Unfortunately, as is the case with other third parties built around a personality, when the leader leaves, the party eventually dies.

This relationship was the overriding factor in RUP's demise in Colorado. As the CJ came under siege by 1972 by law enforcement agencies, RUP's electoral agenda diminished in importance. CJ's leaders became increasingly preoccupied with trying to survive. Plagued by internal problems (limited resources, too little time, and increasing confrontations with the police that resulted in members being jailed and even killed by police), CJ was not able to continue building RUP statewide. These internal problems were further exacerbated by the power struggle for RUP's national leadership between two competing CM titans, Gonzales and Gutiérrez. The division eventually disillusioned RUP activists and supporters to the point that the electoral agenda was no longer a priority. Instead, some wanted RUP to become a revolutionary vanguard partido in the struggle to build Aztlán. The result was that, after 1974, there was little interest in running candidates or keeping RUP alive.

By 1976, after six years of struggle, the RUP experiment in Colorado ended and CJ continued under a state of siege. The battles with law enforcement agencies continued. This took its toll; CJ as well began to decline. Moreover, it became harder to maintain CJ in the changing conservative political climate. With CJ's base of support all but gone and with no resources, Gonzales was forced to close its doors. With its dismantling in 1982, an important Méxicano political chapter ended.

*Chapter Five*

---

# The Cucamonga Experiment:
# The Precursor of RUP in California,
# 1968–1973

Impelled by the electoral successes of the Raza Unida Party (RUP) in Texas, particularly in Crystal City, and encouraged by its emergence in Colorado, Méxicanos in California's San Bernardino and Riverside Counties leapt on the bandwagon. After two years of intensive work under the aegis of the Mexican American Political Association (MAPA), emphasis shifted in October 1970 from education and other social justice issues to political empowerment and building a political party, RUP. This became part of what I call the Cucamonga Experiment in community control. I was its main organizer, from 1968 to 1973.

## The Historical Setting for RUP's Emergence in California

By the late sixties, the nation was alive with the radical spirit of militancy.[1] Out of this milieu, the Chicano Movement (CM) emerged in California by 1966. Cesar Chavez's United Farm Workers' (UFW) Delano strike with its grape boycott and direct action mobilizations, such as the march on Sacramento, and the promulgation of "El Plan de Delano" in 1966, as well as the frequent visits to California of Chicano leaders Reies Lopez Tijerina of New Mexico and Rodolfo "Corky"Gonzales of Colorado, added impetus to the CM in the state.

From 1967 to 1970, the emergence of the Chicano student and youth movements further energized California's CM. Such organizations as the Brown Berets, United Mexican Student Association (UMAS), Moviemiento Estudiantil Chicano de Aztlán (MEChA), and their growing activism both in the universities and barrios, added to the growing CM contagion. The East Los Angeles school walkouts in 1968, the

Catholic Church issue of Catolicos Por La Raza and the drafting of "El Plan de Santa Barbara" in 1969, and the National Chicano Moratorium Committee's antiwar march in Los Angeles in 1970 were but a few of the events essentially organized by young Chicano activists that helped impel the CM.[2]

Chicano activists in California by 1970 repudiated assimilation and espoused the quasi-ideology of cultural nationalism of Chicanismo.[3] The barrios were alive with the spirit of "El Movimiento." The activists' cries of "Viva La Raza!" "Viva La Causa!" and "Chicano Power!" were indicative of a community that was restless and determined to improve its overall condition. The activism was driven by unmet rising expectations, a corollary of relative deprivation. Frustrated, angry, and impatient, activists protested against what they perceived as inequities that needed to be corrected. The fury of marches, school walkouts, demonstrations, and picket lines colored the state's political landscape. From the vineyards of Delano and the lettuce fields of Salinas to the barrios, Chicanos were on the march.

The political climate in California by the latter part of 1970 was propitious for RUP's emergence. Chicano activists had become increasingly critical of the nation's liberal capitalist system. Some realized that the barrios' colonial status was very much a result of a liberalism that fostered a two-party system that was not serving their interests and that kept Méxicanos powerless.[4] As historian Juan Gómez Quiñonez notes: "Neither of the traditional parties was interested in increasing the political voice of the Chicano community through dialogue. . . . The failure of California state politicians to open government to Chicano representation served to disillusion some of the activists within the community and to cause them to consider other options for gaining political leverage."[5]

By 1970, Méxicanos comprised 19 percent of California's population—close to 2.25 million people.[6] Their population growth, however, was not commensurate with Méxicanos' level of political representation. In 1967, the California legislature had not one Méxicano in either the assembly or senate. Furthermore, with some one million Méxicanos residing in Los Angeles County, neither the Los Angeles City Council (fifteen members) nor the Los Angeles Board of Supervisors (five members) had a Méxicano serving. Edward Roybal was the only Méxicano congressman from California. Out of 15,650 elected and appointed officials throughout the state, only 310, slightly less than two percent, were Méxicanos.[7] None of the top 40 state officials, the governor's top 28 advisors, or the 132 top state court positions were filled by Méxicanos. At the state level, Méxicanos comprised only 1.98 percent of California's appointed and elected officials.

Hence, among some Chicano activists, there was a growing political alienation toward the state's two major parties. Activists looked at the nation's political system and found that after almost 120 years, the Méxicano was a victim of gerrymandering, disenfranchised and powerless.[8] The Chicano had sought to work within the two-party system, but it had failed him.[9] There was a sense of betrayal, especially with the Democratic Party, which was erroneously perceived by many Méxicanos as the "party of the poor." Republicans were depicted by some as the "party of the rich."

Furthermore, the perception was that Democrats took Méxicanos for granted (as voters in their hip pocket) and that Republicans were simply too racist to care.

Not only the political system had failed the Méxicano, but also the economic system. The capitalist system with its emphasis on private ownership of the means of production had relegated barrios (Chicano enclaves) to an impoverished and internal colonial status. As sociologist Joan Moore has pointed out, Méxicanos suffered from chronic poverty, and no other group in the Southwest was so "severely pinched economically." By 1970, California had the largest Méxicano population in the nation, some 2.5 million. Most Méxicanos, however, lived in barrios that were plagued by a "poverty syndrome" that manifested in such social problems as high unemployment, inadequate housing, crime, drug and alcoholic abuse, gang violence, and inferior education.[10] The prevalence of racism, prejudice, and discrimination further exacerbated the barrios' internal colonial status.

The political crisis for Méxicanos was compounded by the absence of a powerful political organization with roots in the barrio. Although the MAPA had existed since 1959 and was bipartisan in theory, in practice it was in the hip pocket of the Democrats.[11] Although some of the chapters were well organized and activist oriented and some MAPA state leaders, such as Bert Corona and Abe Tapia, were progressive, too many of the chapters were middle class and traditional, meaning they were not barrio based. They did not identify with the militant and protest aspects of the Chicano Movement. Too many of the chapter leaders and members were "cocktail activists" who were more concerned about attending conferences, conventions, and social and cultural events than about taking on the barrios' issues. Thus, there was no barrio political muscle beneath MAPA's thin political armor.

Other political parties in 1970 sought unsuccessfully to garner support from Méxicanos. In 1968, the Peace and Freedom Party was formed as a progressive left-of-center party. In 1970, Ricardo Romo ran as its gubernatorial candidate. His candidacy was important for two reasons: He was the first Méxicano to run for governor in some hundred years, and he was endorsed by MAPA over Democrat Jesse Unruh. The Congress of Mexican American Unity, comprised of some 250 organizations in Los Angeles, had a history of being a rubber stamp for the Democrats; it endorsed Romo. Although he garnered only some 67,000 votes, his campaign served as a warning to the Democrats of a growing dissatisfaction among some Méxicanos.[12]

The Socialist Workers Party also that year ran several Chicano candidates for statewide office. Froben Lozada ran for attorney general and Antonio Camejo for superintendent of schools. Both candidates targeted the barrios with a message that the major parties were puppets of the ruling class and were responsible for the deplorable and wretched conditions in the barrios.[13] RUP's emergence in Texas and Colorado fostered the feeling among activists that California needed to join the crusade for a Chicano partido.[14] However, unlike those in Texas and Colorado, efforts to organize RUP in California, underway by late 1970, were not led by any one organization or person, but by several. The Cucamonga Experiment was one such effort.

## The Cucamonga Experiment: Template for RUP's Rise

The RUP in San Bernardino and Riverside Counties emerged as a result of the Cucamonga Experiment.[15] In 1969, in what was then a small and unincorporated community in Southern California, Méxicanos orchestrated the CM's first political takeover of a school board in Aztlán (the Southwest). After one year of intensive organizing, Méxicanos wrested political control from the local gringo elite by winning three seats, giving them a majority on the Cucamonga School District's board of trustees. This unprecedented political event preceded the successful electoral revolts orchestrated by the RUP in the Winter Garden area of Texas in 1970. The takeover was an intrinsic part of what I call the Cucamonga Experiment in community control and social change.[16] It would give rise to RUP in San Bernardino and Riverside Counties.

The Cucamonga Experiment began in the barrios of Cucamonga and Upland on March 12, 1968, with the formation of a chapter of MAPA.[17] The germination of the idea to form a political organization, however, began several months before at Turi's (Arthur's) barbershop, located in "el barrio de El Dipo" (the neighborhood of the train depot), today known as Rancho Cucamonga. Almost every Saturday, I and others from the community would gather at the barbershop and engage in discussions on a variety of topics—from music, since I was a musician, to politics.[18]

By January 1968, with the Chicano Movement picking up momentum, the discussions increasingly revolved around the social problems and issues plaguing the community's barrios.[19] Cucamonga's barrios were no different than others throughout the nation, particularly those of Aztlán—reflections of internal colonialism.[20] Poverty, subordination, powerlessness, and racism characterized them all. The most salient social problems and issues were poverty; substandard housing; cantinas (bars) situated within residential areas; unemployment; some unpaved streets; no curbs or gutters; schools with high push-out rates and functional illiteracy; growing crime, gangs, alcoholism, and drug abuse; a vacuum of individual and organizational leadership; and political disenfranchisement.[21] The barrios of Cucamonga were cauldrons of alienation and discontent.

During the next two months, three preliminary meetings were held in the barrios of Cucamonga. The objectives were several: first, to introduce the idea of forming a community political organization; second, to ascertain if the barrio residents were interested in forming such an organization; and third, to conduct a form of power structure research using the "reputation" method.[22] People were asked to identify those they perceived to be community leaders and influential, and the community's major issues. The idea was to identify those who could be supportive of the organizing effort. Personal visits and telephone calls were made inviting those who were identified to attend the meetings.

Even though the meetings drew only a handful of people, a core group of seven persons solidified—three were from Upland, including myself. The decision was made that a political organization was to be formed and that the focus of the organizing should be in Cucamonga, since it had three contiguous barrios—El Norte, El Dipo, and Dog-Patch—and Upland's two barrios were small and not contiguous.

Before the group was formed, considerable time was spent conducting research on various existing organizations: the League of United Latin American Citizens, G.I. Forum, and Community Service Organization. A consensus was reached that none of the three organizations was sufficiently political or advocacy oriented. At the third meeting, held in late February, Arturo Ayala, who had contacts with MAPA, suggested to the group that MAPA be considered. Some felt it was too militant and expressed concerns about allegations made by some White politicians that it was Communist infiltrated. Some of the student activists expressed concern over MAPA's lack of a barrio political power base and its bourgeois nature. Various MAPA officials—among them, Southern California MAPA regional coordinator Chris Carlos, Colton MAPA chapter chair Marina Vidarri, and Ruben Gonzales of the Pomona MAPA chapter—came to meet with core leaders. After much deliberation, the decision was made to opt for MAPA, even though it had its share of problems.

With a requisite start-up membership of fifteen members, the Cucamonga/Upland MAPA chapter was formed. Elections were held, and I was elected chair; Delfino Segovia, vice chair; Carmen Betancourt, secretary; and Larry Zambrano, treasurer. The small membership immediately moved to win over the barrio residents. In order to do this, the chapter quickly took on the form of a structured organization: Recruitment and scholarship committees were formed, dues collected, and a checking account opened.

Before undertaking any major project or issue, the leaders spent time exploring the members' diverse interests and views by continuing to hold individual and group discussions on a variety of topics. This was done with two organizing objectives in mind: to engender a feeling of being a unified *familia* (family) imbued with a spirit of *carnalismo* (brotherhood); and to formulate the chapter's philosophy and goals and objectives.

From the outset, the leadership, which included the officers and committee chairs, sought to create a MAPA chapter that was political-action, movimiento, and reformist oriented.[23] Its five cardinal objectives were: (1) the creation of a nonpartisan organization for the social, economic, cultural, and civic betterment of the Mexican American through political action; (2) the election and appointment to public office of Mexican American and other persons sympathetic to our aims; (3) the taking on of political issues, and the running and endorsement of candidates for public office; (4) the launching of voter registration drives; and (5) the carrying on of a program of political education.[24]

A pamphlet entitled "M.A.P.A." contained the chapter's movimiento mission statement, which complemented its objectives:

> The Cucamonga-Upland Chapter of the Mexican American Political Association was organized because we (the Chicano) can no longer be the passive element in our society, because of the necessity of social and political reform, because the education of our

children has suffered for the last 122 years, because of the great amount of discrimination in employment against the Mexican/American and because we have no government representation.

M.A.P.A. members believe the "Mexican cause" is every American's cause. An injustice to one, is an injustice to all Americans. Chicanos are distinctly signifying their participation and involvement in movements such as M.A.P.A. attempting to achieve the realization of the true principles stated in the United States Constitution. Join M.A.P.A. today and start contributing your ideas—become part of the movement. Be involved! Despierten! [Wake up!] Viva La Raza![25]

The chapter's leadership embraced the Chicano Movement's victimization thrust and rhetoric as well as its adherence to a strong cultural nationalist posture, which encouraged ethnic pride in being Chicano or Méxicano. Arnold Urtiaga, a barber who worked with barrio youth, told me in our interview that MAPA sought to instill pride and a sense of *familia* (family) and *carnalismo* (brotherhood), among its members and especially among youth.[26] Although some of the barrio residents resented the usage of "Chicano" in the chapter's literature and public statements, believing that it was a pejorative term, "Chicano" and "Méxicano" were used interchangeably. There was a categorical rejection of assimilation, and Chicanismo was zealously embraced. Ideologically, while being culturally nationalist, the chapter's stated objectives, mission statement, and more importantly, its actions suggested its commitment to reforming the liberal capitalist system.

Throughout 1968, the chapter's leadership charted a strategic organizing course that included building the chapter's membership, winning support from the barrio residents, developing a high media profile, organizing community projects, and taking on issues via political action. Initially, the interaction between the Mapistas (MAPA members) and the barrio residents was minimal, because of their parochial attitudes. Some residents were suspicious of and cynical about MAPA's political posture, and some especially suspected my intentions, despite the fact that I was raised in the barrio of El Dipo and my parents still lived there. Even though a majority of MAPA's membership lived in the barrio, some of the entrenched business elite adamantly resisted MAPA's entrance into the barrios.[27] Others were still troubled by MAPA's emphasis on politics and its use of movimiento rhetoric that was construed by some as being too militant if not radical. Those averse to MAPA accused it of being comprised of mostly "outsiders" and "troublemakers."[28]

MAPA's meetings were held twice a month in the barrios. Initially, the agenda was fairly innocuous so as not to antagonize those who were distrustful of MAPA's intentions into actively working against it. The leadership felt it needed time to consolidate and build up its base of support among the barrio's residents. Once that occurred, it would be able to fend off the attacks that were sure to come upon taking on "heavy" polarizing issues.

Education became the chapter's immediate focus, not yet as an issue, but rather as a project. In order to foster the people's support, a scholarship drive was organized. In late May, an officers' installation dance was held, and the proceeds were used to set up a scholarship fund. The dance was attended by some 250 people and drew participation from MAPA regional officials, local politicians, and people from throughout the area. It netted a profit, and in June scholarships were given to two Méxicano students from Cucamonga.[29]

During the summer of 1968, Operation Clean-up was initiated in Cucamonga's largest barrio, El Norte. As a "barrio beautification" project, it sought to clean up the barrio's empty lots and streets that were littered with weeds, trash, cans, and bottles. Tractors and large trucks were borrowed from sympathetic contractors and the school district. Contributions were solicited from the owners of the lots that were cleaned. Monies contributed were donated to the local Boys' Club for the purchase of sports equipment. For the next two months, every Saturday, early in the morning, the Mapistas (Arthur Ayala, Roberto Perez, Leo Juarez, Arnold Urtiaga, and I) drove the tractors and trucks through the streets of the barrio, accompanied by forty to fifty barrio youth.[30] The sounds of trucks and tractors and children cheering created the sense of a parade. People lined the street to find out what was going on. They had no idea that what was on display was MAPA's commitment to improving the physical appearance of their barrios. The project was a great success in building up MAPA's base of support and media visibility. The media depicted the project as being illustrative of MAPA's innovative "self-help" philosophy, which emphasized commitment to change via the people's own energies, determination, and resources and not through government funding.[31]

Complementing Operation Clean-up was MAPA's summer recreation program. MAPA members throughout the summer worked with barrio youth in order to alleviate the community's gang and juvenile delinquency problems. Field trips to the beach, a camping trip to the San Bernardino Mountains, a trip to Universal Studios, and weekly recreational activities were organized—sports activities as well as rap sessions on various aspects of the CM. The young people were given heavy doses of Chicano history and politics. The intent was to instill a sense of *orgullo* (pride), carnalismo, and familia. They were exhorted to stop their involvement in "gang banging" and not get involved in any criminal activity. As was the case with Colorado's Crusade for Justice, the intent was to give the rebels, *vatos locos*, a constructive purpose or cause. The youth became a powerful "organizing hook" in getting their parents to become involved with the chapter. Some youth joined the local Brown Berets chapter.[32]

In order to support its diverse programs, the chapter was involved in constant fund-raising via dances, dinners, contributions, and membership. However, when it came to membership, some people when approached were still apprehensive and reluctant to join. By the fall, with a paid membership of some forty people, the chapter was a mix of poor and middle-class Méxicanos, college and university students, and white- and blue-collar workers.[33]

After weeks of research and meetings with community leaders and chapter supporters, MAPA in October initiated its own "barrio renewal" program. The program sought to build curbs and gutters, pave some streets, and build low-income housing for the barrios El Norte and El Dipo. Meetings were held in the barrios with county and Housing and Urban Development (HUD) officials to ascertain the feasibility of securing federal funds for both projects.[34] The curb, gutter, and street-paving aspect of the program failed to galvanize the people's support for multiple reasons. One reason was that some of the barrio residents simply did not understand the HUD guidelines. They fell victims to the old adage "What people do not understand, they fear." A second and more important reason was that some of the economic elite who owned businesses in the area refused to support the project, since it was going to cost them money. They succeeded in defeating the curb and sidewalk project. MAPA lost its first political battle because it was not able to calm the people's trepidation and fears.[35] However, the housing aspect of MAPA's barrio renewal program was supported and was carried over into 1969.[36]

The chapter in 1968 began to gradually flex some political muscle. In preparation for the November general elections, it organized several political forums and conducted a voter registration, political education, and get-out-the-vote drive. A number of Democratic and Republican politicians running for various offices attended the forums and sought the chapter's endorsement. The candidates made their pitches to audiences of fifty to seventy-five people. The politicians were drilled on issues pertinent to the Méxicano community. The purpose of the forums was to instill confidence among the people and make it clear to the politicians that Méxicanos were a power to be reckoned with. Both groups witnessed Mapistas who were articulate, assertive, and knowledgeable in politics. Candidates were endorsed and a voter registration and political education drive was organized for the barrios of Cucamonga and Upland. On Election Day, Mapistas worked the barrio precincts and got out the Méxicano vote.[37]

As part of MAPA's efforts to preserve the Méxicano culture, for Christmas the chapter organized the first *posadas* (Méxicano pre-Christmas celebrations) in the barrios of Cucamonga. Some 200 people from the area participated, going from house to house in Cucamonga's El Norte barrio. Ontario's *Daily Report* in a full-page article provided a pictorial account of the event and reported that "MAPA sponsored the posada ceremony to teach Anglos as well as Mexican Americans something of the traditions and culture of México."[38]

## The Cucamonga Revolt: Instrument of Community Control

After almost a year of intensive organizing, MAPA's leadership felt the time was auspicious for gaining control of the Cucamonga School District. In January 1969, MAPA planned what became tantamount to an electoral revolt. A cardinal problem the chapter had to overcome was the people's apathy. Decades of discrimination and segregation had engendered attitudes of resignation, fatalism, and indifference among many of the barrio residents. The leadership decided that tactically, confronting the district's educational problems was the best way to organize the people and set in motion the drive for control of the school board.

After months of researching the district's various educational problems, the chapter staged several community meetings with school officials that were designed to stir up the people's discontent. The school officials were presented with the results of MAPA's research: the "push-out rate" for Méxicano students was over 60 percent; functional illiteracy was rampant; most teachers and administrators were White, while most of the students were Méxicano; and due to the conservative philosophy of school officials, the district had only one federal program, Head Start.[39]

MAPA also pointed out that even though adjacent school districts had a lower tax base, they had more educational programs than did the Cucamonga School District, which had a rich tax base due to industry moving into the district.[40] MAPA accused school officials of practicing de facto segregation to the degree that few Méxicano parents participated in the White-controlled Parent Teachers Association.

In February 1969, MAPA presented school officials with a series of proposals oriented toward educational change. They included the implementation of a bilingual/bicultural program, the hiring of Méxicano teachers, revision of the curriculum to include instruction on Chicano history and culture, tutorial and remedial reading programs, and the construction of a baseball diamond for the public's use.[41] Anticipating that the school officials would not be interested in implementing MAPA's proposals, the meetings, with an attendance of some 100 people, were used to prepare the community for the upcoming school board elections. MAPA's leadership maneuvered the school officials into showing their antipathy toward MAPA's proposals. The people, angered at their reaction, were ready for the next strategic phase: the election.[42]

While preparing for the school board election that February, MAPA responded to a flood disaster by providing relief assistance to flood victims in Cucamonga. It succeeded in gathering clothing, furniture, food, and money for its flood relief effort. As a result, according to Turi Ayala, numerous Méxicano and White families as well were given assistance.[43] In addition, that month, a blood bank was established for the barrios of Cucamonga and Upland and a tutorial program was set up that took the form of a Saturday school involving seventy-five students and thirty-five tutors. Emphasis was placed on the three R's, with heavy doses of Chicano history and culture.[44]

In the midst of all this activity, MAPA's leadership set up a search for three Méxicano school board candidates through a political action committee. A meeting was held with the only Méxicano on the school board, Juan Martinez, for the purpose of ascertaining if he was going to run for reelection. Initially, he informed the committee that he was not going to run. Shortly after, he and his son-in-law, Joe Sandoval, announced their candidacy. MAPA learned from reliable internal sources that both Martinez and Sandoval were encouraged to run by Superintendent George Scott, who perceived MAPA as a threat both to him and the White-controlled board.

To divide the White vote, MAPA's leadership responded by persuading two Whites to run on the pretense that MAPA was going to give them financial and manpower support. A MAPA committee member actually submitted the filing papers on behalf of one candidate, ten minutes before the deadline. A check for $25.00 was contributed to the other White candidate.[45] At no time, however, did MAPA make an explicit commitment to endorse or support either of the two White candidates. It was all done by inference.[46] MAPA thus reversed the superintendent's divide-and-conquer tactics.

The recruitment of three Méxicano candidates became problematic. The political committee adopted three evaluation criteria: candidates needed to be intelligent and possess leadership qualities; to be committed to the movimiento; and to be supportive of MAPA's educational change proposals. Some of the prospective candidates were afraid to run; others felt they were not qualified. One person who decided to run dropped out just a few days before the deadline. The next day the committee came up with another candidate.

Without any media fanfare, the committee's search finally produced MAPA's three-candidate slate: Carmen Betancourt, a librarian assistant at Altaloma High School; Arnold Urtiaga, a barber; and Manuel Luna, a mason subcontractor. Betancourt had two years of college, and Luna and Urtiaga both had only eighth-grade educations. None of the three had any history of political involvement.[47] When approached to run, Urtiaga expressed surprise that he was asked to run, due to his eighth-grade education and lack of previous political involvement.[48]

In the time remaining before the April elections, MAPA went into full mobilization mode. The people had been well prepared organizationally and politically. The political awakening in the barrios was evidenced by the large number of people who on a regular basis attended MAPA's meetings and fund-raisers, and who volunteered for its various projects. The chains of apathy and alienation had begun to break. As an intrinsic part of its mobilization strategy, MAPA sponsored several election forums. All the candidates were invited to participate. MAPA's three inexperienced candidates were groomed and given access to the questions that were going to be asked by the political action committee members. The intent of this action was to make them shine before the people and the press.

MAPA's strategy was to focus its efforts solely on the Méxicanos who were registered to vote, because the White vote seemed out of reach anyway. Anticipating a backlash from white voters, MAPA did not reveal either that it was running a slate or that it was going to initiate a full-scale voter mobilization among Méxicanos. For weeks, especially in the White areas, MAPA sought to project an image of political neutrality. In a surreptitious manner, it organized a massive voter registration and education drive in Cucamonga's three barrios. Voter registrars were secured from the area's Democratic Party headquarters and Woman's League. Moreover, some Mapistas received training and became voter registrars. The registrars accompanied numerous volunteers, especially youth, who went from door to door identifying those Méxicanos who needed to be registered. The voter registration drive was used to make contact with the voters and further strengthen MAPA's barrio power base.

In spite of bad weather, more than 100 Méxicanos were registered to vote. By election time, Méxicanos constituted some 48 percent of the district's registered voters.[49] However, the voter registration drive also revealed that many of the barrio residents were not U.S. citizens.

Timing being crucial, a couple of weeks before the election, MAPA publicly endorsed its slate. MAPA's get-out-the-vote campaign was predicated on targeting only the Méxicano precincts. Now, precinct captains and block leaders were selected, campaign literature was developed, house-to-house canvassing was conducted, community meetings were held, radio spots were bought, a telephone canvassing campaign was organized, and a vehicle with a sound system canvassed the targeted precincts.[50] Every targeted precinct was canvassed several times. Sample ballots were prepared and distributed indicating where voters needed to mark MAPA's candidates' names. The Méxicano voters were reminded that if there was to be educational change, all three MAPA candidates needed to be supported as a slate.

MAPA's leaders also met with heads of the largest and most influential families in order to secure their support and that of their extended families. Gradually intensifying its campaign activity, MAPA sought to peak at the right time. Meanwhile, up to two weeks before the election, Whites were still not cognizant of MAPA's ongoing, surreptitious, well-orchestrated mobilization; consequently, they did not react until it was too late. Their stereotype of Méxicanos as politically unsophisticated worked in favor of MAPA's campaign strategy.[25]

MAPA's opposition candidates did little campaigning in the barrios. They lacked the leadership and political machinery to run an effective campaign. They also seemed to be conditioned by a history of Méxicanos not voting and by the beliefs that Whites would vote in greater numbers and that they had the superintendent's support. Conversely, MAPA's candidates took nothing for granted and ran scared. Using the chapter's educational proposals as their platform, they walked the Méxicano precincts and participated in telephone canvassing efforts, making direct contact with the voters to explain the importance of the election.

A few days before the election, a letter was mailed anonymously to all the White voters of the district alleging that three Méxicano candidates were MAPA's puppets. The decision was made not to openly respond to the letter. Instead, MAPA accelerated its get-out-the-vote drive and its appeal to the barrio residents' sense of "Méxicanismo." By their final days, the campaigns had become increasingly polarized along ethnic lines.

On Election Day, MAPA established a command post at the contact station located in the heart of the barrio of El Norte to coordinate the block and precinct get-out-the-vote efforts. Some fifty volunteers canvassed the precincts, manned the telephone bank, provided child care while mothers voted, drove the sound vehicle canvassing the precincts, made food for the volunteers, provided transportation to the polls, and acted as poll watchers. Late that evening, at about 11 P.M, the final results came in. MAPA's three candidates had won by a wide majority. Carmen Betancourt was the high vote getter with 247 votes, followed by Manuel Luna with 212 and Arnold Urtiaga with 181 votes. The two incumbents, Paul Makabe and Juan Martinez, received 134 and 93 votes. The three remaining candidates received 88, 70, and 68 votes.[52] Clearly, MAPA's get-out-the-vote effort and divide-and-conquer strategy had made the difference.

Chicano history was made that evening. Never before had Méxicanos in California taken over a school district. Equally important, it was the Chicano Movement's first electoral takeover. At that time, no other movimiento-oriented Méxicano organization in the nation could claim such a political achievement—securing community control of a school district. Only once before, in 1963, had Méxicanos won control of a local governmental entity. This occurred in Crystal City, Texas, with the election of five Méxicanos to the city council.[53] Cucamonga's political victory was the first electoral response to the CM's call for "Chicano Power."

## The Takeover's Political Aftermath

The three Mapista board members took office in July 1969. Their first policy priority was to move on MAPA's bilingual/bicultural education proposal. Unsure of themselves, inexperienced, and concerned about the growing ethnic divisions, the three Mapista board members initially moved with circumspection. The superintendent continued to resist the Mapista board members' attempts to implement the proposals. MAPA's leaders, although trying to appear not to be "pulling the strings," began to voice concern over their procrastination. Before the three Méxicano board members were elected, the MAPA leaders had made it very clear to them that MAPA would not seek to control or direct them, provided they adhered to their agreement to implement MAPA's proposals. The three Mapista board members were warned that if they broke the accord, MAPA would politically mobilize against them.

While Superintendent Scott was on a world tour, the Mapista board members seized the opportunity to appoint principal Ray Trujillo as acting superintendent. By late summer 1969, federal funding was secured and several Méxicano teachers and teacher aids were hired. In September, the district implemented its bilingual/bicultural pilot program without any Title VII funds. Psychologist Manuel Rameriz of Pitzer College was hired as a consultant for purposes of further developing the program.[54] Under his guidance, the district's bilingual/bicultural program was developed and became one of the finest in the nation.

In November 1969, at a private meeting, an ultimatum was given to the three Méxicano board members that, beyond MAPA's proposals, the board had to fire the superintendent. While Urtiaga and Betancourt concurred, the president of the board, Manuel Luna, reacted with ambivalence and concern that MAPA was dictating to him. As a result, Luna and MAPA's leadership became increasingly divided over the board's failure to implement MAPA's proposals.

By January 1970, MAPA's political muscle had grown. After months of organizing, MAPA members from a defunct MAPA chapter in the neighboring community of Ontario were persuaded to become part of the Cucamonga/Upland chapter. As a result of the merger, the chapter changed its name to the West End MAPA chapter, which included the communities of Cucamonga, Upland, Ontario, Montclair, and Claremont. Its membership increased to some 100, making it one of the largest chapters in the state.

To ensure that all the communities were represented, the structure and leadership of the chapter were changed. Now there would be a chapter chair, two regional vice-chairs, treasurer, recording secretary, corresponding secretary, three city chairs, and standing committees on education, fundraising, political action, labor, media, youth activities, and economic development. Each committee had its own chair.[55]

The reorganized chapter once again directed its attention to the Cucamonga School District. On January 13, 1970, at a district school board meeting attended by some 300 people, the newly restructured West End MAPA chapter confronted the board over its unimplemented education proposals. The reluctance by school board president Luna to support their implementation compelled MAPA's leaders to resort to organized pressure. The proposals introduced before the takeover now became "demands."[56] Other CM organizations from the area, such as the Brown Berets, United Mexican American Students, and Movimiento Estudiantil Chicano de Aztlán (MEChA) were brought in to support the demands. From the floor, I demanded that the superintendent resign: "In the name of the people, in the name of change, we demand your resignation."[57]

The call for resignation produced a counter-MAPA petition drive for the retention of the superintendent. On February 24, at a second board meeting held to address MAPA's demands, on the behalf of the anti-MAPA contingent, Carmen Vasquez presented the board with a petition bearing some 200 signatures supporting Scott. She charged that the board represented MAPA more than the community, which brought a denial from board president Manuel Luna: "Mrs Vasquez, MAPA does not control the board."[58] The petition was discounted since the several hundred people present were mostly MAPA supporters, but Luna's comments produced the first public indicator of schisms that had emerged within the chapter.

On May 12, 1969, the board finally took decisive action and fired Scott as superintendent. In a motion made by Urtiaga, seconded by Betancourt, the board voted unanimously to relieve him of his duties as superintendent, and he was hired as a consultant to the district. Principal Trujillo was appointed acting superintendent for the second time.[59] This action allowed the board to expedite MAPA's educational change reforms. For the West End MAPA chapter, Scott's resignation and the changes that followed were major victories that served to enhance its reputation among Méxicanos and Whites alike as a militant organization that had the muscle to back up its politics of change.

## RUP in San Bernardino and Riverside Counties: The West End MAPA Chapter

In the ensuing two years, few areas outside of Crystal City, Texas, experienced more tangible victories than those produced in the West End of San Bernardino County. While the public's focus was on Los Angeles because of the size of the Chicano population and the media presence, Méxicanos there produced few major victories.

Conversely, forty miles south of Los Angeles, during the West End MAPA Chapter's golden years, 1970–1972, the Cucamonga Experiment reached its apogee and marked the rise of RUP in California.

By 1970, the West End MAPA chapter had become one of the largest in the state and second to none in organizing battles won. In 1970, its Labor Committee, headed by Joe Becomo, took on cases involving employment discrimination. In the course of negotiations with Ontario Motor Speedway, city, and Teamster officials, MAPA's leaders threatened to disrupt the grand opening of the Ontario Motor Speedway. Preparations had been made to bottle up and disrupt the flow of traffic on the San Bernardino Freeway with staged car failures and burning cars blocking entry to the Motor Speedway.

MAPA negotiators scored a victory with the Ontario Motor Speedway and the two other entities that it had been negotiating with. The Ontario Motor Speedway agreed to hire twenty-five Méxicanos; the Ontario Airport agreed to hire more Méxicanos; and the Kaiser Steel plant in Fontana agreed to promote Méxicanos to supervisory positions. The chapter also strongly supported the United Farm Workers by organizing several pickets of Safeway markets. In Cucamonga, the Mapista board voted to support the UFW's lettuce boycott. The Mapista school board expedited the hiring of more Méxicano administrators, teachers, staff, and teacher aids, as well as several staff, maintenance, and janitorial personnel.

MAPA's reputation, high media profile, and power image drew a minimum of fifty people to every meeting. Méxicanos from throughout the area would come to the meeting requesting assistance on a variety of issues and problems, including job discrimination, police abuse, and emergency financial aid. Although not always able to handle all of the people's concerns because of its all-volunteer efforts, those MAPA did handle were resolved. One such case occurred in 1970 when a local gang member killed an undocumented Méxicano worker in Cucamonga. The victim's impoverished family did not have the money to return both the body and themselves to México. In less than two weeks, the chapter raised nearly $1,000, allowing the family and the victim's body to be returned to Mexico.

MAPA took a strong position against the Vietnam War. In numerous meetings, MAPA's leaders and others, as well, spoke out against what they considered an unjust war. On August 29, the National Chicano Moratorium Committee held the largest antiwar demonstration yet in Los Angeles. MAPA mobilized a contingent of 150 people from throughout the region. As the march turned into a riot, MAPA members played an important role at Laguna Park in assisting people to exit the park while the police were attacking.

In response to the riot, in September MAPA organized a nonviolent candlelight vigil at De Anza Park in Ontario that was attended by nearly 1,000 people from throughout Southern California. An incident occurred at the vigil in which thirty or so *pintos* (former convicts) sought to take over the religious service and create a confrontation with police. The chapter's security, comprised of Mapistas, Brown Berets, MEChA, and other groups, quickly encircled the pintos and told them in plain Spanish to back off or else—they agreed, thus avoiding a physical confrontation.

However, the pintos retaliated against MAPA's leaders. The next Saturday, unknown assailants went to Cucamonga and unsuccessfully sought to accost the priest at Mount Carmel's Catholic Church as he was returning to his home after hearing confessions. The following Saturday the assailants came back, and this time they tied the priest on the floor as if he had been crucified and placed a moneybag over his head; he was left tied all night. The next morning he was found by Mapista David Hernandez's grandmother, who was partially blind and in her eighties. She knelt next to the priest, thinking he was praying. Minutes later another woman came into church and hysterically untied the priest, and police were called.

The incident was set up by the assailants to appear as if MAPA's leadership had orchestrated it. As they departed from the church, they yelled, "Viva La Raza!" and "Chicano Power!" words commonly used by MAPA's leaders. I was notified Sunday morning of the incident by the church elders, who alleged that I was responsible. A few days later, a town hall meeting was held at the church. I was seated in front of the altar, as if I were on trial. With hundreds of people in attendance, the meeting was almost a kangaroo court in which I had to defend myself. I was informed before the meeting that there was a contract out on my life. Paradoxically, MAPA had been told that those involved in the alleged contract were some of the people we had secured jobs for at the Ontario Motor Speedway a few months before. A few Mapistas with guns, led by Arnold Urtiaga, approached the suspects and warned them that if anything happened to me there would be an in-kind retaliation.

MAPA's adversaries at the church meeting took advantage of the opportunity to make vociferous attacks on me and on MAPA. Without any evidence, they alleged that I was responsible for the incident with the priest and that MAPA was not satisfied with controlling the schools, it wanted to control the church as well. In addition, they accused MAPA of being Communist and radical. A release prepared by MAPA's press person, Felix Martel was the end product of the meeting; it suggested there was an ongoing investigation on the matter. The incident served to further polarize the community. A few weeks later, Urtiaga and others received threats, and their homes were at times staked out by unknown persons. My mother's house, which was in the barrio of El Dipo, was shot at. The shooters were never apprehended; consequently, for a time I carried a weapon for my protection.

In spite of the growing polarization, MAPA continued to gain in membership and strength because of its actions and efforts. In Cucamonga, most of the barrio residents were supportive. MAPA continued with many of its proactive activities, such as supporting the Cucamonga Boys' Club by organizing field trips, cultural and music programs, group counseling, and political rap sessions. The blood bank was expanded to serve the West End. Dances, the annual Christmas posada, Cinco de Mayo, and Mexican Independence Day (September 16) celebrations were all used to reinforce MAPA's strong cultural nationalist orientation.

In its struggle to promote economic empowerment, MAPA's leadership in 1970 organized the Barrio Investment Group (BIG). With twenty-six persons investing anywhere from $200 to $1000, BIG served as the catalyst for MAPA's economic empowerment efforts. Supported by the Housing and Urban Development Federal Housing Association's 235 program, a self-help barrio renewal project was initiated that entailed buying empty lots in the barrio and building low-income housing.

## RUP's Beginnings in San Bernardino and Riverside Counties

The West End MAPA chapter toward the end of 1970 moved to organize the Raza Unida Party (RUP) in San Bernardino and Riverside Counties. Inspired by the electoral success of the RUP in Texas, in October 1970, while I was a graduate student in political science at the University of California, Riverside (UCR), I formed a RUP organizing committee. Initially, it was comprised of a few community leaders and MEChA UCR students. Numerous preliminary discussions and planning meetings were held during November and December.

Between January and April 1971, the RUP committee, spearheaded by the West End MAPA chapter, held two regional RUP organizing conferences at Riverside City College and at San Bernardino Community College.[60] At each, the attendance averaged around 200 people. Representatives came from seventeen organizations from throughout the two counties, including various MEChA and Brown Beret chapters, MAPA chapters, La Confederacion, and faculty from the University of California, Riverside. Barrio residents from various communities from throughout the two counties also attended. At each of the conferences and meetings, I, among others, addressed the various aspects of organizing RUP—the rationale, structure, ideology, strategy and tactics, and finances.[61]

On April 17, the West End MAPA chapter in conjunction with MEChA sponsored California's first major statewide RUP conference, at Chaffey College in Cucamonga. With some 500 people in attendance, the conference was held to develop a plan of action for organizing RUP in California. The conference's major speakers were to include José Angel Gutiérrez, Carlos Muñoz, Bert Corona, and myself. While Corona never showed up, Gutiérrez spoke on why RUP emerged and attacked those who categorized it as racist: "I say there is no such thing as a racist in reverse. It's simply a healthy reaction to racism, to their racism and their hatred. When these liberals say that we are a party of hate, we must reply 'we are a party of hate because we teach the truth about our parties, and because America has been bred not only out of hate, but out of violence. They say we are a party of hate, yet we have no George Wallaces, we have no Agnews.'"[62]

After Carlos Muñoz spoke on the need to build the RUP in California, I spoke further about why Méxicanos needed to form the RUP. I mentioned that Méxicanos in the United States were victims of racism, oppression, and exploitation and said that Méxicanos had been victims of a history of betrayal by both major parties. I said that RUP needed to be different from the existing political parties: "Our concept of La Raza Unida Party is one based on the belief that in order to have political power, we must have economic power. Our party is also one of action, of confrontation. . . . But it must be based on community control and not the control of a few people. Our party will grow as long as there are issues to be confronted, and our party will be at the forefront. It's an organization that functions every day . . . we have to build, to work, so that self-determination may become a reality and not just an expression."[63] My presentation culminated with a proposed plan of action that I had developed which addressed various aspects of what needed to be done to organize RUP in California and strengthen the CM..

## Building a Nation within a Nation: The Trinity Concept

The plan I presented at the Chaffey College conference was called the Trinity Concept for Community Development. It was developed as a result of my studies of social and revolutionary movements and empirically tested as part of the Cucamonga Experiment. Predicated on an ideological eclecticism of cultural nationalism, socialism, and capitalism, the plan called for a holistic, concurrent political, economic, and social change approach to building a "nation within a nation" for Chicanos. The Trinity Concept called for the creation of multiple organizations within each of three sectors—political, social, and economic—with interlocking boards.

Politically, RUP was to be at the forefront of the struggle for self-determination and empowerment. Several other political entities, such as pressure groups and coalitions, would be created that would be RUP "front entities." Until RUP became a certified party, RUP's proposed interim structure included a State Congreso, a State Central Committee; County Central Coordinating Committees; and at the local level "units or *focos*" (units of people formed into trained cadres).[64] The economic and social sectors would each have their own sort of profit and nonprofit corporations. While the social sector would provide the communities with a variety of needed services, programs, and assistance, the economic sector would develop the cooperatives, businesses, industries, and economic infrastructure for people's economic empowerment.

The response of activists to the Trinity Concept was mixed. Some of the conference activists from Los Angeles in particular, using a rather sectarian Marxist analysis, attacked it as being reformist and prosystem oriented. They accused me of trying to organize RUP into a mere community service organization that provided services and programs. I stressed to those critics that the Trinity Concept model had been tested for nearly three years and had met with great success. My words, however, did not convince the activists. The Chaffey conference produced no consensus on what RUP's state-level organizational plan of action should be. The conference did set off a conflict-ridden debate over RUP's role, ideology, and structure, and over who was going to lead the party in California. However, RUP in San Bernardino and Riverside Counties adopted a modified structure of the Trinity Concept that included a two-county central committee with representatives from various supporting organizations and from the several local RUP organizing focos.

With MAPA's leaders overextended, the decision was made to convert the West End MAPA chapter into several local focos. As had the leaders of MAYO in Texas and of the Crusade in Colorado, MAPA's leaders became RUP's leaders in the two California counties. The transition from MAPA to RUP created divisions and conflict within MAPA in the region. At a MAPA conference held that summer in Ontario, for example, I reported that the West End chapter was being dismantled and that its membership was being reorganized into RUP organizing "focos." MAPA's Southern California regional director, Raul Loya, spoke out against the action. After the meeting, he confronted me in a rather bellicose manner and asked me why was I doing it. If I would stay, he offered to work toward my election as MAPA's next state president. My response was that because of time constraints and political priorities, I could not serve two political masters.

Throughout 1971, several regional organizing conferences and community meetings were held throughout the two counties, officers were elected, and focos established. I was elected chairperson of the two-county Central Coordinating Committee, RUP's major regional policy-making arm.[65] It was comprised of the regional officers, one representative from the Corporacion para el Desarrallo de Aztlán (CEDA), Proyecto Acción Social (PAS), and from each local foco, and standing committee chairs. The focos at the community or barrio level were comprised of ten to twenty-five members. These were the units of electoral or direct action. RUP's standing committees included voter registration, political action, economic development, finance, community outreach, and media. At both levels, the principles of democratic centralism and collective leadership were practiced.[66] In the months that followed, maintaining this organizational structure became problematic because of the intensity of the work and limited resources. RUP was never able to establish an office with paid staff. It depended solely on volunteers. My home and the homes of others became RUP's administrative centers.[67]

Early on, a two-county RUP voter registration drive was begun as part of the statewide effort to certify RUP as an official party and be on ballot by 1972. In a matter of a few months, more than 600 Méxicanos were registered by RUP. For the first time in the history of the two counties, Méxicanos were organizing politically in a coordinated manner to empower themselves, build an alternative to the two-party system, and confront local issues. The focos were encouraged to engage with issues plaguing their respective communities. Women played a significant role at the foco level, but RUP's Central Coordinating Committee was male dominated. While it never became an issue that women were underrepresented at that level, by 1972, women took on a more prominent leadership role.[68]

RUP's ideological underpinnings were largely predicated on the Trinity Concept of community development I had presented at the March 1971 RUP conference held at Chaffey College.[69] From 1971 to 1973, RUP's ideology was eclectic and dialectic—a mix of nationalism, liberal capitalism, and socialism. It emphasized preserving the Méxicano culture, heritage, and Spanish language, and adhering to a form of cultural pluralism. The notions of the "melting pot" and of "assimilation" were unequivocally rejected. The liberal capitalist posture reflected the political and economic realities Méxicanos found themselves in. Yet because separatism or proletarian revolutionary struggles were not realistic possibilities at that time, the feeling among most RUP activists was that the liberal capitalist system needed to be reformed to become more socialist. RUP therefore needed to create reforms that would foster a more equitable distribution of wealth and political power sharing among all people. This position engendered the formation of various types of cooperatives—markets, credit unions, farms, and nonprofit social service corporations.

Inherent in RUP's pragmatic and eclectic ideology was the idea of self-determination. For RUP, self-determination meant building a nation within a nation for Méxicanos. The underlying rationale was that the Méxicano population was too small to pursue a separatist ultranationalist course toward creating Aztlán. So, until the material and political conditions changed dialectically, Méxicanos needed to strive to control their destiny by building a nation within a nation, similar to the entity the Mormons had established in Utah. Méxicanos needed to promote their own economic empowerment by developing parallel economic structures such as banks, corporations, investment groups, and businesses. RUP's political role was to be the vanguard party that functioned in both the electoral and social justice advocacy arenas.

When writing the Trinity Concept of Community Development, I was influenced greatly by such theorists as Saul Alinsky, Lenin, and Che Guevara. The document reflected my strong belief that essential for any struggle for change to be effective were organization coupled with strong leadership, impelled by the power of an inspiring vision. Tactically, this meant that the situation or the agenda of the time determines what methods are to be used. Given this view, RUP would determine when it should encourage the formation of other advocacy groups, coalitions, and popular fronts that would ultimately all use both conventional and unconventional methods of protest.

## The Chaffey Union High School Walkouts

For months, RUP's leaders spoke on the need to confront the numerous educational inequities suffered by Méxicanos in the area's local high schools—the high push-out rates, the absence of Chicano teachers and administrators, and the need for Chicano studies and curriculum change. In May 1971, an altercation—almost a riot—occurred involving Chicano and White students at Chaffey High School in Ontario. As RUP regional chairperson, in order to mitigate the matter, I met with several youth leaders from the surrounding communities, including members of the Brown Berets and MEChA.[70] It was decided that, with the school year almost over, action on RUP's education reform agenda should be postponed. In the meantime, the high school students were persuaded to end altercations with White students.

In October, the conditions became auspicious for a massive mobilization against the Chaffey Union High School district's five high schools. That month, RUP initiated the second successful school walkout in the history of the CM (the other was the Cristal walkout organized by Gutiérrez in Texas in 1969). The incident that precipitated the massive walkouts was the severe beating of a Chicano student leader, Roman Montoya, by three White football players at Upland High School. When I was approached on the matter by the parents, I said that RUP would intervene, providing they agreed to assist in organizing other parents; they agreed.[71]

An emergency meeting of the area's various RUP focos was held. In attendance were various MEChA and Brown Beret chapters. RUP's leadership called for using a strategy predicated on a tactical "domino mobilization," that is, one high school at a time, and "graduated intensification." The first walkout occurred in mid-October at Upland High School with some 200 students walking out. Isabele Contreras became the walkout's main student leader. Within a few days, some 1,000 students from the other four high schools joined the districtwide school strike.

During the two weeks the students were out, RUP intensified the conflict with numerous meetings, picketing, a march from all the high schools to the district's offices, community town hall meetings, and massive media coverage. Three ad hoc barrio high schools were set up in community centers located in centralized locations— Cucamonga, Upland, and Ontario. Supervised by RUP and the other groups, volunteer teachers and parents taught math, English, and Chicano history and culture. Student consciousness-raising sessions were also part of the curriculum.

The walkouts served to further polarize the White and Méxicano communities of the area. The local newspapers contributed significantly to the division by running multiple front-page articles on various aspects of the walkouts. Extreme right-wing elements calling themselves "Representatives of the Christian Majority" delivered an "open letter" to my residence and released it to the press; it condemned me for what they perceived as radical action and included a warning: "It is a matter of fact that you are unlawfully attempting to alter our Christian form of government by mob rule and violence. It is too bad that you haven't studied sufficiently to understand that the same anti-Christians who financed recent totalitarian movements are prompting your doomed cause. . . . Perhaps you do not realize that you are 'outgunned' 5 to 1. Continuance of your present approach to violence and intimidation will result in swift retribution. This warning is not intended to be, nor is it, a 'threat' in any manner whatsoever. It is merely a 'promise.' "[72]

On the evening of November 1, the Chaffey Union High School district's school board met to vote on the demands. Just before I left for the meeting, I received an anonymous telephone call warning me that if I attended the meeting I would be killed. As if that was not enough, at the meeting a group of twenty-five Mexican Americans led by Connie Vasquez spoke out against me personally and RUP. She alleged that I did not represent the majority of the Mexican people of the area. The more than 500 parents and students who were supportive of the school strike stood up, gave the Chicano handclap, and booed her down. Police were called in and lined up in front of the school board members. After I implored the people to quiet down, RUP's leaders reintroduced its demands. After some deliberation, in spite of major ethnic tensions and some division among Méxicanos, the board voted to approve all of the demands.[73]

After two weeks of intense pressure, the approval of the demands translated into a major victory for RUP and for the students and parents who stood strong in the struggle for educational change. Unlike most other school walkouts of the time, the victory was attributable to solid parental and student support and well-organized, massive, and escalating organizational pressure.[74]

## The Social/Economic Implementation of the Trinity Plan

From 1971 to 1973, while RUP was being organized politically, efforts were initiated to accelerate the implementation of the social and economic components of the Trinity Concept. In the social area, many of the social, cultural, and recreational activities that characterized first the Cucamonga/Upland and later the West End MAPA chapter continued after the transition into RUP, but not at the same level of intensity. With RUP's leaders busy organizing throughout the two counties, there was not enough time, capable and committed personnel, or resources to replicate the social and economic projects that had been developed in the Cucamonga area.

To resolve the financial resource problems, two corporations were formed, one for profit, Corporacion Economica para el Desarrollo de Aztlán (Economic Development Corporation for the Southwest, or CEDA), the other nonprofit, Proyecto Accíon Social (Project Social Action, or PAS). Each entity was to act as a counterpart to RUP, in that within their respective area, each was to lead the implementation of their respective part of the Trinity Concept plan of action. In the social arena, PAS, as a nonprofit corporation, was to be responsible for the development of educational, cultural, recreational, and social service programs, and economic cooperatives, under the leadership of Vicente Rodriguez; CEDA, a for-profit corporation, was to replace BIG and expand its economic empowerment projects. Support would come from both the community and federal funding.[75]

During the next two years, CEDA became more active. After dismantling BIG in 1971, CEDA was incorporated as a result of the leadership of Alfonso Navarro (my brother). The rational for the transition was that CEDA would ultimately be a "people's corporation," with its capital coming from thousands of barrio investors buying shares for a minimal amount. The intent was to begin to develop the economic infrastructure or substructure for building a nation within a nation. The intent was to put in motion the formulation of a master economic empowerment and development plan for Aztlán that would include numerous affiliated economic entities in the areas of housing, small business, banking, real estate, factories, and media.

Over the next two years, CEDA built two more low-income homes in the barrios of Cucamonga. Coordinated by Alfonso Navarro, the low-income housing self-help barrio renewal program was given wide exposure by HUD as one of its most successful. By 1971, five homes had been built in the barrios of Cucamonga using a Méxicano general contractor.[76] Three acres were bought with the intent of building fifty more units. With the transition to RUP and its increasingly radical posture, however, some of the more moderate investors became disgruntled, pulled out their investments, and left CEDA. With its assets committed to the construction of the two homes, CEDA paid them off by giving them three acres that had been purchased to build low-income housing. This schism marked the beginning of CEDA's decline.

By 1973, the Nixon administration had frozen all funding of HUD's 235 low-income housing programs. As a result, CEDA's fifty-unit allocation was canceled, making it difficult to qualify poor people for conventional loans. Desperate for additional capital, CEDA used the profits from the sale of the two homes to finance two unsuccessful concerts. Without capital, CEDA became moribund in 1973.[77]

In the social arena, PAS was not incorporated as a nonprofit corporation until 1973. With its multidimensional programmatic orientation, it sought to provide the barrios of the area with badly needed social, educational, and cultural services, including cooperatives of a sort. Headed by Vicente Rodriguez, in 1974 it was funded for $35,000 for a drug abuse prevention program by the West End Drug Abuse Council. During this time, PAS also was involved in sponsoring numerous cultural events, such as dances, concerts, Cinco de Mayo fiestas and parades, and posadas. Without a political arm, by 1974 PAS began functioning more as a pressure group in dealing with a variety of issues. However, because of its advocacy role, in 1976 its funds were cut off. Without resources, it continued to exist as a volunteer advocacy group operating mainly in the West End part of San Bernardino County until its demise in 1977.[78]

## RUP's Political Victories, 1971–1973

In spite of a lack of resources and trained organizers, and in spite of myself and other leaders being overextended, RUP in San Bernardino and Riverside Counties was able to score the only electoral victories outside Texas and New Mexico. While Los Angeles congratulated itself for Raul Ruiz's garnering 6 percent of the vote for the Fortieth Assembly District, RUP in Cucamonga in April 1971 was successful in electing David Ortega to the Cucamonga School Board, giving RUP a four to one majority.[79]

With the victory, however, came more division among the four RUP board members. Problems had been brewing since MAPA presented its demands to the Méxicano majority board in 1970. School board president Luna, from then until 1971, continued to try to establish himself as his own man, dictated to by neither MAPA nor, later, RUP. Numerous private house meetings were held to iron out personality as well as other differences between the majority who supported RUP and the minority aligned with Luna. A gap that became unbridgeable came with the board's appointment of Ray Trujillo as permanent school superintendent in 1971.

The working relationship between Luna and me became contentious. That year at a private meeting between us at Luna's home, he presented me with a list of eight complaints or allegations. He basically accused me of using the Méxicano community of Cucamonga and specifically the schools for my own political aggrandizement.[80] I denied the allegations and informed both Luna and the board that MAPA was moving forward with its education reform agenda.

With a growing presence in Ontario, RUP scored its second electoral victory in April 1972. Ontario's population was then 50,000. Méxicanos comprised no more than 17 percent of the population. Initially, RUP had planned to run Rogelio Granados, a Presbyterian minister who had moved from Altaloma to Ontario, but he did not meet the residency requirement. Without a candidate, RUP's political action committee did a search and interviewed several prospective Méxicano candidates. As a precondition for being considered, those interviewed agreed that if they were not chosen, they would not run and would support whomever RUP selected. The committee was able to get away with such a precondition because of its high profile, militant reputation, and the respect and fear some people had for it.

Finally, the committee opted for Gustavo Ramos, a Housing Authority administrator and former high school friend of mine, who was a political neophyte. As Ramos's campaign manager, I had him undergo several hours of candidate instruction and grooming. The instruction was provided by both Jerry Leggett, a minister who operated the Fish Market (a combination church and service center in the barrio of Ontario), and me. Ramos was instructed on the issues, various aspects of local government, and public speaking.[81] Within a few weeks, he had become a viable candidate with cross-over appeal.

The campaign's strategy was twofold: one tactic for Whites and others, and the second for Méxicanos. The intent was not to polarize voters, but to win them over. For Whites, the campaign issues were citizen involvement in the city's various commissions, a change in the city's charter to a charter city, improved transportation, and so on.[82] In the barrios, however, the issues shifted to improving police-community relations, city services, and recreational programs; placement of Méxicanos on the various city commissions; and of replacing the city's at-large system of representation with single-member districts.

Moreover, without a significant number of Méxicanos to elect Ramos, RUP's campaign strategy was also predicated on coalition building. RUP intentionally toned down its nationalist posture and sought support from numerous other ethnic/racial groups. Support was garnered from the city's Blacks, unions, and liberals. One of the community's most influential white leaders, attorney Sam Crowe, who had been a city councilman himself, not only endorsed Ramos but contributed to the campaign by sending out a mailer.[83] RUP maintained a low profile in the White areas, and a high profile in the city's numerous barrios. A massive grass-roots campaign was organized, with precinct captains, block leaders, and an army of some 150 volunteers from throughout the region.

The targeted precincts were repeatedly canvassed on foot, literature was distributed, mailers sent, telephone canvassing done, and vehicles with sound systems driven through the barrios. Even the local barrio Catholic priest, Patricio Guillen, galvanized his parishioners to support Ramos. Numerous town hall meetings were held in the barrios. In a very coordinated manner, the weekend before the election, a massive canvassing blitz was undertaken. With three seats open, Méxicano voters were instructed to vote only for Ramos and no one else.

On April 11, a massive get-out-the-vote drive by RUP's machinery scored an unprecedented political victory. RUP was successful in electing the first Méxicano ever to the Ontario City Council. Its coalition approach coupled with its massive grass-roots effort and "single-shot voting" in the Méxicano precincts was able to deliver 3,383 votes. Out of the thirteen candidates, Ramos came in second. For RUP, it was yet another tangible sign of its organizational power and political prowess.[84]

In November of that same year, Roger Granados ran unsuccessfully for Congress on a RUP write-in campaign against liberal Democrat George Brown. The genesis of the campaign was an unsuccessful attempt by several RUP leaders and supporters to have me run for the Thirty-eighth Congressional District against Democrat George Brown. On February 26, more than 300 people had gathered at the Ontario Motor Speedway Victory Circle Restaurant for a testimonial dinner to honor me as the "Chicano of the Year." The main speakers included José Angel Gutiérrez and Carlos Muñoz. Gutiérrez exhorted Chicanos not to be overwhelmed by the two-party system, while Muñoz warned them about a possible revolution.[85]

At the time, I did not know that in part the event had been staged to get me to run for Congress under RUP. After the dinner that same evening, a private meeting of some of the RUP leaders from throughout Southern California was held at the Holiday Inn in Ontario. For two hours, Gutiérrez and others sought unsuccessfully to convince me to run. They argued that because of my high profile and name recognition, my candidacy would do much to catalyze RUP's formation in California.

A few weeks later, Rogelio Granados, after taking a trip to Texas and consulting with RUP leaders there, decided that he would run himself via a write-in cam-paign. At a meeting of RUP's Central Coordinating Committee, I argued against the proposed write-in campaign for five reasons: (1) Write-in campaigns, especially for Congress, were extremely difficult to organize; (2) Méxicanos were no more than 17 percent of the district population; (3) RUP's various organizing focos were still small, lacking a barrio power base; (4) financial resources for such a campaign were nonexistent; and (5) why run against one of the Democratic Party's most progres-sive, liberal, antiwar congressmen, George Brown, who had been left without a constituency due to redistricting? In addition, I warned them that the campaign could be the deathblow to RUP in the area if not enough votes were garnered; instead, it should continue to build its local power base and work to strengthen the Trinity Concept's economic and social components. My arguments fell on deaf ears. Their emotion and romanticism was stronger than my pragmatism. They voted to support Granados's write-in bid, thinking erroneously that I was going to be his campaign manager.

In June 1972, after much deliberation, I gathered several of RUP's cadre leaders from the various focos at my home in Upland to inform them of my decision to resign as RUP's two-county chairperson. Although the futility of the campaign was a factor, the major reason was that I had decided to take the Ph.D. exams in October. I had completed my coursework in two years, but in spending some twenty to thirty hours per week organizing and professionally playing trumpet in an orchestra, I had neglected my family and graduate studies. I explained to them that if I expected to pass, I needed to cram and isolate myself for the next three months.

Most of those present respected my decision. However, even though I indicated I would support the campaign, some felt betrayed that I was not willing to organize it. Once it became known that I had resigned, some RUP supporters throughout the two counties and beyond felt that I had let them down. Israel Arraiga, a community college professor, replaced me as chair. I had planned after successfully passing both the written and oral Ph.D. exams to assist the Granados campaign. However, I was unable to do so due to a back injury that incapacitated me for weeks.

Granados' campaign was run on a shoestring budget. An office was established in a garage of a residence in Rialto. The campaign strategy relied on Granados speaking at the area's colleges and universities, community meetings in the district's numerous barrios, some telephoning, rallies, some precinct canvassing, and fundraisers. A lot of organizing time was spent on instructing potential voters on the procedures of filling out a write-in ballot.

In September, a small delegation of RUP activists from the area, including me, attended the national RUP convention in El Paso, Texas. Granados played a pivotal role in that he was in charge of the Credentials Committee. In late October, José Angel Gutiérrez came to a RUP rally for Granados in San Bernardino. Gutiérrez stressed the importance of building RUP as an ongoing social movement. Granados vehemently attacked both parties. He said, "We can no longer depend upon the Republican and Democratic Parties to speak and determine our destiny. Both parties are controlled by the rich corporations no matter how often denied."[86]

The election held on November 11 produced no surprises. In spite of being very articulate and knowledgeable on the issues, Granados was not successful in mounting a serious challenge against Brown. Beyond a scarcity of resources—both money and people—the campaign lacked the requisite organization that would give it a "spoiler" capability. Brown won the election decisively. Granados garnered approximately 3,000 votes. Politically, the defeat engendered such disillusionment that several RUP focos became inactive. Meanwhile, RUP's foco in Cucamonga geared up for the April 1973 school board elections.

By April, RUP's Cucamonga foco, plagued by internal divisions, had three candidates running for two seats: incumbent Arnold Urtiaga and challengers Luis Gonzales and David Hernandez. On the eve of the election, Congressman George Brown sent a letter to the district's voters supporting Urtiaga, Gonzales, and Harlan Lee. An anonymous counterletter was distributed bitterly criticizing Brown for being an "outsider." Moreover, the letter said, "We are tired of outsiders coming into our district to run our school board elections." The letter concluded that both Urtiaga and Gonzales were "puppets" of Navarro, even though at the time I was in Texas with my family conducting my dissertation research. While Urtiaga lost, Gonzales and Hernandez won.[87] As a result of the election, the most dynamic RUP foco in the region became inactive, a casualty of infighting.[88]

By the spring of 1973, RUP in San Bernardino and Riverside Counties became moribund. Its demise was a result of too many of its leaders dropping out. Neither Arriaga nor Granados were any longer involved in a leadership capacity, and I was in Texas.[89] Some of the other leaders shifted to developing PAS and CEDA. Without stable leadership, RUP's many focos began to fall apart. As a result, the RUP Central Coordinating Committee could no longer function. In addition, power struggles and the disorganization of RUP statewide fostered frustration among some RUP activists. All these factors contributed to the demoralization of the few remaining RUP activists, which caused them to drop out.

Thus, with the collapse of RUP in 1973 came the end of the Cucamonga Experiment.

*Chapter Six*

---

# A Partido of Clashing Caciques and Ideologies: The Rise of RUP in California, 1971–1972

At about the same time that the Raza Unida Party (RUP) was being formed in San Bernardino and Riverside Counties, Chicano activists from Northern California were likewise exploring the possibly of setting up an alternative to the Democratic and Republican Parties. The unprecedented developments in Texas and Colorado were fostering a contagious excitement, interest, and hope among some Chicano Movement (CM) activists. From 1970 to 1972, numerous RUP organizing efforts sprang up throughout the state—what I describe here as RUP's two golden years of organizing, 1971 and 1972.

## RUP's Emergence: A Product of Discontent

By late 1970, the political conditions in California were auspicious for RUP's emergence. Méxicano activists, after battling a number of social issues such as education, police brutality, and the Vietnam War, and inspired by RUP's success in Texas and its rise in Colorado, began to shift their attention and priorities to the electoral arena. This shift was, in great part, motivated by the alienation and discontent of many of the activists with the two major parties, particularly the Democrats. There had been a long history of political repression and exploitation . . . by the Democratic Party in California.[1] RUP leader Bert Corona testified before the California State Advisory Committee to the U.S. Commission on Civil Rights in Sacramento in 1971; his words illustratrate why countless CM activists joined to form RUP: "Both parties have been guilty of using Spanish speaking and the Chicano vote for their imperative of control of the legislature . . . they are cynical in their dealings with our needs and aspirations . . . Both parties ultimately have shown that they represent the big money interests."[2]

With the rise of RUP, some Méxicano activists saw an opportunity to make the political shift and also to redefine the "Chicano struggle." Here was an opportunity, they felt, to extricate the Méxicano masses from the clutches of internal colonialism. Explaining internal colonialism, political scientists Mario Barrera, Carlos Muñoz, and Carlos Ornelas wrote that "to be colonized means to be affected in every aspect of one's life: political, economic, social, cultural, and psychological."[3]

In 1969, a conference attended by some five hundred activists, at California State University, Hayward, dealt with issues impacting the Méxicano. At the conference, discontent among some Méxicano activists toward both the Democratic and Republican Parties became evident. The idea of forming a political party was examined; some agreed with the idea, but the majority did not. Instead, it was proposed that Cesar Chavez run for governor either as a Democrat or under the aegis of the Peace and Freedom Party. The majority, however, said that they would not support him if he ran as a Democrat. (Although no campaign ever materialized for Chavez, hundreds of bumper stickers reading "Chavez for Governor" were printed and distributed.) One of the main symposium speakers, Rodolfo "Corky" Gonzales from Denver's Crusade for Justice, advocated basing the new party on Chicano nationalism.[4]

The conference was significant in that, even though nothing was decided, the idea of forming a Méxicano political party was discussed in California before RUP's emergence in Texas and Colorado. Nevertheless, after the conference, some activists supported the gubernatorial candidacy of Ricardo Rome, who ran under the aegis of the Peace and Freedom Party.

Concrete efforts to establish a Méxicano political party did not surface in California, outside of San Bernardino and Riverside Counties, until late 1970. Inspired by the partido concept, some sixty activists met in Oakland in October 1970 and agreed to initiate organizing efforts by forming RUP chapters (RUP organizing committees) in Northern California. They, like their counterparts in Texas and Colorado, perceived the two-party system, and especially the Democrats, as being the cardinal obstacles to the struggle for Chicano liberation and self-determination.[5]

That December a second conference was held in Union City. With 450 persons in attendance, the agenda focused on securing reports from the emerging RUP chapters and on developing RUP's platform. Victor Acosta, a longtime activist and one of the founders of the Latin and Mexican American Studies Department at Merriott College, read the preamble and platform for the Oakland-Berkeley chapter. The document criticized the nation's so-called "dark chapters" of history, blatant imperialism, exploitation, and oppression toward the Méxicano. It accused the two major parties, particularly the Democratic Party, of being the primary tools used to oppress the Chicano: "Because we see through the trickery of the Democratic and Republican politicians, and see that these two political parties have completely failed us in their promises, and understand that in reality they have been working for the benefit of the wealthy Anglos by furthering and perpetuating the oppression of the people. . . . Given that these factors of oppression form the common denominator that unites us, therefore, we the people of La Raza have decided to form

La Raza Unida Party, which will serve as a unifying force in our struggle for self-determination."[6]

In the discussion that followed, Ricardo Paniagua Lopez from Stockton commented that trying to distinguish between Democrats and Republicans was like "choosing between Hitler and Mussolini." Numerous activists from a variety of groups and parties supported the proposed preamble. Former Peace and Freedom Party gubernatorial candidate Ricardo Romo was one such ardent supporter.

An important aspect of the conference was that the activists defined "La Raza" to mean those who came from México and Central and South America and their descendants. This description was needed because the Oakland/San Francisco areas had substantial numbers of Latinos from various parts of Latin America who did not identify as Chicano or Méxicano. The definition distinguished California's from the RUP organizing efforts in Texas and Colorado, which were oriented almost exclusively toward Méxicanos. As a result of the conference, a RUP steering committee or chapter was formed for each area to help organize the next meeting, scheduled for January in San José. In addition, support was given to the Oakland RUP chapter's efforts to run candidates for the upcoming municipal elections in Berkeley and Oakland, and to commence a voter registration drive in Stockton.[7]

On February 21, 1971, two RUP conferences were held, one in Stockton and the other in Los Angeles. Some 1,200 activists from throughout Northern California attended the Stockton conference. The agenda focused on fine-tuning the strategy to organize RUP. By then some fourteen RUP chapters had been formed in Northern California. José Angel Gutiérrez, who delivered the keynote address, spoke on the virtues of using "nationalism" as a way to organize RUP.[8]

Later that month, in Los Angeles, some 250 persons, mostly young activists from throughout the Los Angeles area, also came together to discuss the need for an alternative political party. The event came about as the result of a student class project assigned by Bert Corona at California State College, Los Angeles. Corona got the idea after he attended a redistricting hearing in Sacramento, where assemblyperson Alex Garcia had been shunned by his fellow Democrats as he addressed the body. Corona, who also spoke, was furious at the disrespect shown Garcia. After the hearing, he stated that the time had come for Chicanos to support the movement to organize RUP. According to Richard Santillan, Corona said, "We need to consider a new political party."[9]

Concurrently, a RUP regional planning conference was held for San Bernardino and Riverside Counties. The agenda dealt with various aspects of building a political party. Nine workshops were conducted: labor, education, welfare, immigration, penal reform, administration of justice, public health and drug abuse, political representation, and control of the land. The conference's keynote speaker was Bert Corona, who attacked the Democratic Party: "Our job is to unmask the Democratic Party. We must clear this [Democratic Party] out of our mind. Democrats have always put nails on our coffin."[10]

During the next three months, numerous RUP meetings and organizing conferences were held throughout the state. RUP's foco (focus group) in Cucamonga succeeded in electing a Chicano to the school board. On April 17, a RUP state conference was held at Chaffey Community College in Cucamonga (see Chapter Five). The Oakland/Berkeley area held its regional conference on April 20 and also ran several candidates for the city council and school board, though unsuccessfully: Tito Lucero ran in Oakland for councilman at large and received 1,087 votes; Florencia Medina ran for the Oakland school board and garnered about 27,000 votes, or 33 percent, and Trinidad Lopez got some 25,000 votes, or 25 percent. RUP also ran two candidates in Berkeley, Victor Acosta for the city council and Carmen Alegria for the school board, but both lost.[11]

By May, several RUP chapters had been formed in the Los Angeles area. Gilbert Blanco, a community organizer and student at California State College, Los Angeles, formally announced on May 22 the formation of the East Los Angeles RUP chapter. RUP was described as serving two functions: In areas where Méxicanos were a minority, the party would act as a swing vote; and in areas where Méxicanos were a majority, RUP would run candidates and seek community control. That same month, another organizing conference was held at the Euclid Community Center in Boyle Heights. Soon after, several more chapters were formed in Los Angeles County—Labor Committee, City Terrace, La Puente, San Fernando, and others. In June, a conference was held in Los Angeles for the purpose of bringing together all the chapters from throughout Southern California for a major strategy-planning session.[12]

Early in 1971, Chicano activists in San Diego, under the leadership of Herman Baca, also moved to organize RUP. Baca at the time was chair of the National City Mexican American Political Association (MAPA) chapter and in 1970 had founded the Committee on Chicano Rights. As a leader, he was very much a protégé of Bert Corona and of MAPA state chair Abe Tapia. Baca had tried to work within the Democratic Party but to no avail—the party had failed Méxicanos. Baca told me in our 1997 interview: "We thought we could go in and make the party meet the needs of our people, but the attitude, money, power, and co-optation were just too engrained. Pete Chacon won the primary election [1969] soon after he was co-opted."[13]

A countywide RUP organizing committee was formed in San Diego. There was a division of labor among the various groups; for instance, coordinated out of Baca's printing shop were activities for RUP, MAPA, the Committee on Chicano Rights, and CASA (Centro de Acción Social Autonomo) Justicia, an immigrant rights group affiliated with Corona. Throughout 1971, San Diego's RUP activities focused almost totally on registering 10,000 Méxicanos and on educating them politically on the need to build a Chicano party committed to "self-determination."

## MAPA's Dilemma: To Support or Not To Support?

Increasingly, MAPA faced the question of whether it should support RUP's' formation. To support RUP meant to sever its alignment with the Democrats. Bert Corona, longtime activist and former MAPA state chair, by early 1971 made the decision to support the formation of RUP as well as MAPA's efforts to do so.[14] From 1971 and well into 1972, Corona promoted the organizing of RUP. He attended as well as spoke at numerous meetings and conferences statewide. Because he was articulate in both Spanish and English, many of the young activists perceived him to be the leader who could best direct and lead RUP. Texas had Gutiérrez and Colorado, Gonzales; these activists felt that Corona was their counterpart in California. As Chicano historian Ignacio Garcia has pointed out: "Corona turned out to be the a strong catalyst for the party in California in its first year and a half. . . . Corona represented a valuable link to the state's Mexican American middle class."[15]

While Corona's leadership contributed substantially to the formation of RUP, it was not at the same level or scope as that of Gutiérrez or Gonzales. In fact, at no time, especially during 1971 and 1972, did RUP have a single leader in California who commanded the respect, legitimacy, and power to unify the various regional leaders who had emerged. While Texas and Colorado each had a strong, charismatic, and respected caudillo, or political leader, California had none. What it did have was a plethora of regional *caciques* (local chiefs) who each aspired to be California's political caudillo. Corona was more than capable of being that leader, as Garcia points out: "Corona was a formidable spokesman for the partido; his enthusiasm for this brand of third-party politics did not hide any ambitions for leadership."[16]

With Corona and other Mapistas taking on prominent roles in organizing RUP, MAPA's association with RUP became problematic for MAPA's traditional Democratic Party supporters. Early in 1971, Herman Baca, in an attempt to resolve the dilemma, printed and distributed what some called a political manifesto, "MAPA and La Raza Unida Party: A Program for Chicano Political Action for the 1970s," written by Bert Corona. In it Corona posited that MAPA could be a valuable asset in organizing RUP and that the groups needed to coexist and collaborate, since each had a different political role to play. He defined RUP's role as that of a political party designed to realize political control of local governmental bodies and to run candidates at all levels. MAPA's role would be one of "a civic club–membership organization that would help deliver the Méxicano vote."[17]

From July 30 to August 3, MAPA held its state convention in Fresno. Attended by 200 delegates and guests, the convention proved a major setback for RUP. Supported by Corona, Herman Baca ran unsuccessfully for MAPA state president against Democrat Armando Rodriguez. He lost the election to Rodriguez by a mere 20 votes. Some of the more moderate Mapistas accused Baca of engaging in "reverse discrimination" by advocating the formation of a RUP that excluded non-Chicanos.[18] Corona also failed to get the resolution passed that called for MAPA's support in the organizing of RUP. As a result, schisms developed between RUP's leadership and that of MAPA, which was solidly aligned with the Democrats. With Baca's loss and the resolution defeated, some RUP Mapistas left the organization. Corona, however, continued to assist in the organizing of RUP in 1971.

## RUP's Organizing Accelerates in Los Angeles

By the second half of 1971, the struggle to organize RUP had picked up momentum throughout California. In Los Angeles County alone, several additional chapters were formed. Gilberto Blanco and Richard Santillan, among others, continued to organize the East Los Angeles RUP chapter.[19] However, some efforts took a different approach in organizing RUP. For instance, the Labor Committee, which itself was a RUP chapter, and the Lincoln-Boyle Heights chapter were more interested in organizing workers based on labor issues than in moving on an electoral or educational agenda. According Garcia, they "purposely dragged [their] feet on the registration drive and kept arguing at the state conferences that elections were reformist."[20]

The City Terrace RUP chapter, led by Raul Ruiz, editor of *La Raza Magazine*, that summer published and distributed in the community several thousand tabloids that explained RUP's philosophy and platform.[21] Xenaro Ayala, who was a senior at California State College, Northridge, along with Marshall Diaz, Richard Roa, and Eugene Hernandez, were the key leaders who organized the San Fernando RUP chapter.[22]

RUP chapters sprang up in many other areas of the state. In Orange County, Carlos Muñoz, an assistant professor at the University of California, Irvine, and several student leaders formed a RUP chapter. In Northern and Central California, RUP chapters sprang up from Ventura to Fresno to Sacramento to San Francisco. In Santa Barbara, Cireño Rodrigues and others aggressively built the infrastructure to support the formation of RUP in their area.[23] A total of fourteen chapters were formed in Northern California by 1971. Some were cultural nationalist and Chicano based, while others, especially around the Berkeley/San Francisco area, were more Marxist and Latino based. Regardless of their ideologies, all agreed on the need to form RUP.

From the outset, a major concern of RUP organizers was getting RUP on the ballot—qualifying it as an official party. This was and continues to be the most difficult obstacle third parties must overcome. The two major parties, controlling the executive, legislative, and judicial branches of state government, passed legislation specifically designed to thwart the emergence of third parties. In 1971, California had some of the most stringent electoral laws in the nation. RUP had two options for getting RUP on the ballot. The first option was to register in the name of the new party 1 percent of the total number of persons who voted in the last governor's election. The second was to conduct a petition drive and gather the signatures of at least 10 percent of those who were registered in the last statewide gubernatorial election.[24] According to the California Election Code, Section 6430c, if RUP used the first method, it needed to register 1 percent of 6,633,400, the total number of registrants in 1970, or 66,334 voters. With the second method, according to Section 6430d, RUP needed to obtain the signatures of 663,340 registered voters and file them with the secretary of state at least four months before the primary election.[25]

Lacking experience, organization, volunteers, and finances, RUP's chapters in 1971 found the first option easier to achieve, since it required only 66,344 voters to be registered with RUP. However, these same deficiencies became RUP's most serious obstacles in securing the needed new registrations. For the next few months, this drive would become the priority for most RUP chapters. Yet, some RUP organizing efforts, such as the one in San Bernardino and Riverside Counties, sought a balance between securing the new registrations and building up their local organization, advocacy capability, programs, and resources (both people and money). The Labor Committee in Los Angeles shied away from the electoral aspects of RUP altogether and focused instead on organizing workers and initiating strikes; from 1971 to 1973, with its Marxist-Maoist slant, it played a significant leadership role in organizing RUP in Los Angeles County.[26]

## The Forty-eighth Assembly Race: RUP Flexes Its Muscle

In Los Angeles, RUP's City Terrace chapter in 1971 decided to run a candidate in the special election for the Forty-eighth Assembly District. The vacancy was the result of David Roberti's moving on to the state senate. In a district that was heavily Democratic in registration, RUP initiated its first major electoral challenge against the entrenched Democrats. Registered Méxicano voters in the gerrymandered Democratic "safe district" comprised only 18 percent of the electorate.[27] In the district, there were 80,435 registered voters, of whom nearly 50,000 were Democrats. For three decades, the district had been under the Democrats' control.[28] In spite of the numbers and history, the local RUP chapter decided to enter the political arena by running Raul Ruiz in the October 19 primary as an Independent, since RUP was not yet an official party. RUP's leaders felt they could win, but implicit in their strategy was developing RUP's capacity to swing an election.

Ruiz was well-known in activist circles. He was twenty-nine, a professor of Chicano Studies at San Fernando Valley State College, and the editor of the Chicano Movement–oriented magazine, *La Raza*. His testimony had been crucial in the Ruben Salazar inquest—he had introduced graphic pictures that captured what was alleged to have been a deliberate effort by the Los Angeles Police Department to murder Ruben Salazar. To RUP in Los Angeles, Ruiz seemed an excellent choice, since he had good name recognition among Méxicanos in the district, as well as a master's degree, and he was articulate in both English and Spanish. Most of the RUP chapters in the Los Angeles area agreed to support him, especially with volunteers. When I asked Ruiz in our 1997 interview why he had decided to run, he responded: "We thought we could actually beat them . . . and could win. We thought we had the public recognition. We thought that by virtue of our work in the community we could win. It meant getting out there and getting the people to vote for us. We didn't feel that Brophy [Bill Brophy, the Republican candidate] was going to get the Chicano vote."[29] Some Méxicano Democrats, however, perceived Ruiz as a "spoiler" whose candidacy served the political interests and agenda of the Republican minority party.

In the primary, nine other candidates ran against Ruiz: seven Democrats, one Republican, and one Peace and Freedom candidate. The Democrats were Richard Alatorre, Ralph Ochoa, Bruce C. Bolinger, Charles Bono, Paul B.Carpenter, Joe Kailin, and Ysidro Molina. Richard Alatorre was considered the front runner, since he had the support of the senate majority leader, Walter Karabian. Alatorre's most serious threat from within the party was Ralph Ochoa, who was being supported by the speaker of the assembly, Bob Morretti.[30] Ruiz and other RUP leaders perceived the power struggle between the two Democrats as positive. They felt that the divisions within the Democratic Party made it vulnerable to an electoral challenge. Moreover, the election was crucial to the Democrats' reapportionment plans, since there could be a veto by then by Governor Ronald Reagan. Historically, the Republican Party had run only token opposition; this time, however, the feeling was that it could win in the primary with Bill Brophy. The Peace and Freedom Party candidate was John C. Blaine.

In order to win the primary, a candidate was required to garner a minimum of 50 percent of the vote. If no candidate secured the required percentage, then a runoff would be held; those candidates who secured the highest number of votes within each party would face each other in the general election. In order for Ruiz to be placed on the ballot, he needed to garner more votes than did the Peace and Freedom candidate.

Ruiz's candidacy served as a catalyst for RUP's formation throughout the Los Angeles area. The chapter effectively used the election to buttress its voter registration drive.[31] By election time in October, the RUP City Terrace chapter had registered some 2,000 Méxicanos.[32] Ruiz ran on the chapter's platform, mildly reformist in orientation, based on nine points: (1) more Chicano political representation; (2) an end to the Chicano abuse against Chicanos by ruling parties; (3) adequate housing and an end to urban renewal; (4) an end to racist police brutality; (5) an end to consumer fraud; (6) an end to drug trafficking in the barrios; (7) community control of schools and implementation of bilingual/bicultural education; (8) an end to racist job practices; and (9) the promise that all people would benefit from RUP's representation.[33]

While strong in criticism, RUP's platform and campaign literature offered few suggestions for how the issues it raised were going to be resolved. Few references to Chicano nationalism were made, unlike most RUP campaigns in Colorado and Texas. The literature was also void of statements that could be construed as socialist or Marxist in nature. However, it did address the monopolistic character of the two-party system, and especially the hegemony of the Democratic Party. Ruiz during the course of the campaign said: "As far as we are concerned, the Democratic Party is totally irrelevant to the Chicano community. They have proven themselves to be un-responsive to the Peoples' needs, especially to Chicano needs. We are presenting to the community a clear alternative to the Democratic Party. Our source of power will be the people. . . . We don't intend to be elected by an ignorant electorate. We want to educate the community about La Raza Unida and about the nature of the Democratic Party."[34]

RUP's campaign literature homed in on Alatorre. One piece warned: "Don't vote for the puppet. Time is running out for those who claim to represent you when in fact they only speak for those who pull the strings. Cut the ties and burn the myths that hold us back—the Democratic Party. Vote La Raza Unida Party."[35]

The RUP City Terrace chapter with its cadre of thirty-one members was the key organizing force behind Ruiz's campaign.[36] By September, several other RUP chapters had joined in support. In addition, several student/youth organizations, such as Movimiento Estudiantil Chicano de Aztlán (MEChA) from East Los Angeles City College and Cal State Los Angeles, the National Chicano Moratorium, a Chicano law student group, and Carnalismo, a community group, along with individual members of MAPA. The Los Angeles Socialist Workers Party endorsed the Ruiz campaign, while the Communist Party remained undecided, vacillating between Ruiz and Alatorre.[37]

There were, however, some the members of the RUP East Los Angeles chapter who did not support Ruiz's assembly bid. One was RUP leader Richard Santillan, who did not support Ruiz because of differences on strategy. When interviewed many years later, he told me: "When Raul ran in the Forty-eighth, there were mixed feelings . . . in regards to what the outcome would be. I remember that my first reaction was total anger at Raul. . . . One of the things that we had been doing when we went out to register people was that we said we were different. We weren't going to be like the Democrats and Republicans who already knew who was going to run nor meet behind closed doors."[38]

For Santillan, the issue was that Ruiz "never consulted" with the rest of the RUP chapters or with RUP's newly formed Los Angeles County Central Committee. He said that a convention should have been held to allow the people's input in RUP's candidate selection process. Santillan and others felt that Ruiz's decision to run was undemocratic.[39]

In spite of some reluctance by a few RUP activists, Ruiz's assembly campaign resembled a political crusade, bringing together various Chicano activist groups and leaders. Rosalio Muñoz, from the National Chicano Moratorium, explained the short-term goal of supporting Ruiz was to elect him, but the main goal was to promote independent political action. Gilbert Cano, of the National Chicano Moratorium Committee, said: "We thought that this was so important that we dropped everything else we were doing to begin to work full-time to build the Raza Unida Party."[40]

In order to coordinate RUP's get-out-the-vote efforts, the campaign opened three small offices in Los Angeles. Scores of people, mostly young activists, conducted a grass-roots campaign, canvassing targeted precincts by going door to door to distribute bilingual literature. Community meetings, rallies, and a telephone bank were also used to reach the Méxicano voters. Even with no paid staff or professional campaign technicians, and with extremely limited financial resources, RUP's volunteers were determined to send both political parties a powerful message that the Méxicano would no longer be taken for granted.

During the primary campaign, the Democrats showed no signs of feeling threatened by Ruiz's candidacy. To their surprise, Ruiz succeeded in securing a spot on the ballot as an Independent for the general runoff election scheduled for November 16. With a high voter turnout, nearly 44 percent, Ruiz garnered 1,378 votes, nearly 4 percent of the total votes cast. He ran fifth, outpolling four of the seven Democrats. About 60 percent of the votes cast were divided between the seven Democratic candidates, with Alatorre being the front runner. He received 7,685 votes, while Bill Brophey, the Republican candidate, received 12,236; the Peace and Freedom Party candidate, Blaine, got a mere 638.[41]

RUP activists throughout Los Angeles County perceived Ruiz's 4 percent as a major victory. He had outpolled Blaine, ensuring himself a place on the general election ballot. What occurred after the primary was intensified organizing in the barrios. A dramatic increase in the number of volunteers occurred, as *The Militant* reported: "Since the October 19 primary, the level of activity has increased in the City Terrace headquarters. On entering the campaign office one is struck by the constant ringing of phones and the rhythm of mimeograph machines cranking out tens of thousands of leaflets and other campaign materials. Supporters, mostly young, are busy making the leaflets, calling people into the office to distribute them, and looking up telephone numbers of possible campaign supporters."[42]

After the primary, Ruiz intensified his attacks on Alatorre and the Democratic Party. He accused the party of being totally unresponsive to the needs of the Chicano community. He said: "We want to bring the concept of La Raza Unida to more people. The campaign will be a vehicle for building the Raza Unida Party in California."[43] In turn, the Democrats depicted RUP's campaign as merely an exercise designed to benefit the Republicans.

The Democrats brought some heavy political guns into the campaign. Edmund Muskie came into the district on November 7 not only to campaign as a presidential hopeful but in support of Alatorre. Muskie and Alatorre were both greeted by some twenty-five RUP protestors at Our Lady of Guadalupe Catholic Church in El Serrano and at the Morris Steak House in Alhambra. The protestors carried signs that read " Muskie is a carpetbagger," "Democrats No, Raza Unida Si," Alatorre is a Vendido" (a sellout), and "Gringo Go Home."[44]

Before both protest events, RUP activists distributed campaign material in the barrios that read, in part, "El Partido de la Raza Unida has frightened the Democratic Party and is posing a threat to Alatorre's campaign in the 48th Assembly District to the point where he is about to receive outside help. This Sunday, Alatorre, a so-called Chicano who claims to be Italian, will be paraded through the barrio by one of his multimillionaire 'patrones,' Senator Muskie."[45]

RUP's protest was effective in that Muskie canceled a third engagement scheduled for that same day in the district. It was clear from their tactics that the RUP activists envisioned their party not only as an electoral entity, but as one oriented toward direct action and advocacy pressure.

On Election Day, November 16, RUP mobilized scores of volunteers from various Chicano Movement organizations and other RUP chapters in the area to help them get out the vote. The campaign's hard work paid off: While Ruiz did not win, he denied victory to Alatorre, who was favored to win. Instead, the victory went to Republican candidate Brophy, who received 16,346 votes, or 46.7 percent of the vote. Alatorre came in second with 14,759 votes, or 42.17 percent. Ruiz came in third with 2,778 votes, or 7.93 percent. Peace and Freedom Party candidate Blaine garnered only 1,108 votes, or 3.16 percent.[46]

Reaction to Alatorre's defeat was mixed. RUP activists and supporters perceived the victory as indicative of RUP's capacity to swing an election. Had Ruiz's votes gone to Alatorre, he would have been the victor. Ruiz's response was that the election was not so much a Republican victory as a defeat for Democrats: "Brophy did not get more votes than expected. His vote was not surprising. The surprise is that Alatorre did not get the votes the Democrats expected him to. We were responsible for that. We pulled traditional Chicano votes away from him. We stopped their Democratic machine."[47] The bottom line was that RUP had succeeded at being a spoiler, taking enough votes away to deny the Democrats a victory. Historian Gomez Quiñonez has claimed that "it was in this election that the limits of the non-south Texas strategy of La Raza Unida became apparent; to abandon, for the time being, efforts to win seats and to concentrate instead on the role of the 'spoiler' was puerile, especially if the goal sought was increased ethnic representation."[48]

Others within RUP, such as Reggie Ruiz, a campaign organizer, saw the election as an invaluable educational tool. Richard Loa, a RUP leader from San Fernando, said, "Hell, they [the Democrats] had a presidential candidate [Senator Muskie] come into the campaign for them, and spend over $100,000 and still lost in a district that was 2 to 1. You can't say that we didn't scare them."[49]

Most Democrats were surprised and angry at the results. They saw RUP as a spoiler rather than as tipping the balance of power. Assemblyman Henry Waxman described RUP as tantamount to a "neo-segregationist in the Chicano community."[50] This was a rather strange statement coming from him, since he was the chair of the Assembly Reapportionment Committee that had failed to produce new assembly districts for Chicanos. The Brophy victory also affected the state's redistricting politics. The Republicans became even more adamant in their demand for additional Republican districts. This angered the Democrats to the point that they rammed the Assembly Reapportionment Committee's plan through.[51] Statewide, that November, a few RUP chapters either ran or supported candidates. In Stockton, the local RUP chapter ran Tom Oliva and José Correa for the city council. Oliva lost by only twenty-one votes and Correa by thirty-one. The RUP in San Diego was concurrently involved in the election of Gilberto Robledo for mayor. Herman Baca explained in our 1997 interview why RUP got involved in the election campaign: "We got involved both as Mapistas and as organizers for the Raza Unida Party. While MAPA endorsed Robledo we also pulled in those that were involved in organizing and supporting the formation of the Raza Unida Party. We got involved because we needed to make our presence felt. Because he was a Chicano, he was a novelty. We also used the campaign and to run candidates so we could address important issues impacting our communities."[52]

Although unsuccessful, Robledo ran fifth and received some 2,000 votes, most coming from the barrios. The closeness of the election in Stockton and the good showing in San Diego gave many RUP chapters statewide a morale boost.

RUP's Expansion, 1971–1972

Illustrative of the proactive posture of some RUP chapters was the RUP foco in the Ontario area. In October, it carried out a successful walkout that involved five high schools. Another example was that of the Labor Committee in Los Angeles, a RUP chapter that dealt with several labor dispute issues, from attempts by Méxicanos to organize a union and strike against Mejian Chevrolet, to support for the Teamsters' effort to organize workers at Ramona's Mexican Food Products.

Ideologically Marxist (Maoist), the Labor Committee shunned the idea that RUP should be an electoral political party. It did not agree with most other RUP chapters that RUP's role was to conduct voter registration drives, run candidates, and become active in trying to control the flow of public policy. It felt RUP should be a vanguard revolutionary party. It was this sectarian posture that served to foster subsequent ideological schisms within RUP.

By the latter part of 1971, RUP organizing efforts had produced various local organizational structures. In San Bernardino/Riverside and Los Angeles, RUP was structured into chapters, focos, and committees. By the end of the year, several chapters were formed in Northern and Central California: Oakland, Berkeley, Stockton, Sacramento, Hayward, Union City, Gilroy, Hollister, Santa Cruz, San José, Milpitas, Watsonville, Livingston Rio Linda, Los Gatos, and Brodvich.[53] Some of the chapters were integrated into a county or regional structure, for example, the County Central Committee (Los Angeles County) and Central Coordinating Council (San Bernardino/Riverside region).

RUP at this time had no statewide structure, unlike RUP in Texas. The Texas RUP structure was influenced, in part, by state law, which dictated the form and type of party structure. In California, this was not the case. Without a structure mandated by the election code, too many of RUP's regional and local structures varied in composition. Efforts to organize the party were not driven by a common plan of action. Not every region in California in 1971 had an integrated, organized hierarchical structure comparable to those of Los Angeles County or San Bernardino and Riverside Counties. Some areas had loosely structured committees with little or no officer hierarchy or committee infrastructure, in part because activist leaders lacked strong organizational skills. This lack meant they were unable to create a large power base in the communities where they were trying to organize. Compounding the situation, some of the student leaders setting up RUP structures were so sectarian and opinionated in their nationalist and Marxist politics that many barrio residents were turned off. The result was that too many of RUP's local entities were cadre oriented, that is, they were comprised of only a few active members and, with few exceptions, did not develop a power base.

Efforts to organize RUP statewide were also hampered by the prevalence of *caciquismo* (a local leader whose authority is based on personality, a common concept in Latin American politics)—in this case, by multiple local personalities. In general, each perceived himself as destined to be RUP's statewide caudillo or, in José Angel

Gutiérrez's words, "el mas chingon" (a barrio term for the most powerful leader). In fact, when I met Gutiérrez at the Chaffey College conference in April 1971, his first words to me were, "Tu eres el chingon?" (Are you the leader?) I told him I was merely the organizer of the event. But the exchange was indicative of the *personalismo* omnipresent in RUP's leadership ranks.

While Texas had Gutiérrez and Colorado had Gonzales, California had no caudillo. This leadership vacuum precipated power struggles and impeded RUP's statewide development. Parochialism also drove the politics of too many of the caciques. Distrust, petty jealousy, and dislike characterized the thinking of some. For example, RUP's caciques in Los Angeles felt that they should be RUP's leaders, since their area had the largest number of Méxicanos in the state. Yet these individuals had yet to produce any tangible victories or successes. Their attitude fostered divisions among RUP's emerging leaders statewide. The clash of egos largely precluded the development of a working relationship based on cooperation and a willingness to compromise on issues of structure, ideology, and strategy.

RUP's organizational weakness and leadership squabbles became evident in its failure to register enough people to get on the ballot for the 1972 elections. Of the approximately 66,000 RUP registrations needed, by January 1972 only 20,543 had been secured. Of the total, 13,430 came from Los Angeles, 3,520 from Santa Clara, 1,196 from San Diego, and the rest from other counties.[54] Thus, the absence of centralized leadership and organization and of a strategic organizing plan of action, coupled with a chronic lack of resources, caused RUP's efforts in 1971 to get on the ballot for the 1972 general elections to fail.

By late 1971, the structural consolidation of the party became a priority for most chapters. Most of RUP's leadership realized that 1972 was a pivotal year. Their cardinal objective had to be the development of a tight-knit statewide structure.[55] Activist Larry Martinez from Richmond in a letter sent to all the Northern California RUP chapters voiced this concern: "We must develop a unified state plan and discuss *all* alternatives and resolve a unified front."[56]

RUP activists throughout the state spent a great deal of time working to structurally consolidate the party and to define its platform. In order to accomplish this, several regional and statewide meetings and conferences were held in Southern, Central, and Northern California. The agendas focused, in great part, on such items as what constituted a chapter or foco, the consolidation of chapters into a regional structure, developing chapter and central committee operating bylaws and procedures, holding political education sessions and recruitment, fund raising, and defining RUP's platform.

A trend developed that became irreversible, however. More time was spent on arguing and philosophizing about what RUP's structure or ideology should be than on actually organizing in the barrios. For many chapters, students were the major organizing force, which eventually became an organizing problem. Too many student activists, once they graduated, did not continue being active. For them, the exercise had been a mere fad. Others found the intellectual sanctuary of the university or college so comforting that they became "arm-chair organizers" or "ideologues." While still expounding the virtues of organizing RUP, some student activists shifted their focus from actually organizing in the barrios to endless debates over RUP's role, mission, or ideology as a partido. This trend spread to the other organizing constituents within RUP, which in the end contributed to RUP's decline in California.


## The San José State RUP Conference

On April 8 and 9, 1972, a statewide RUP conference was held in San José. This was an important conference in that the agenda focused on developing ways of consolidating the fragmented chapters into a statewide party and designing the template for RUP's platform. Several hundred activists from throughout the state worked on developing a uniform structure, the beginning of a statewide platform, and a coordinated strategy for organizing RUP. The following areas were addressed in workshops: politics, finance, communication, organization and unity, and labor and deportation. In the politics workshop, RUP's rebellion against the nation's two-party monopoly led to a resolution that "La Raza Unida will offer an alternative to the two-party system and will not endorse candidates from any other political party." Some twenty-one resolutions were passed—some were philosophical, attacking the evils of the two-party system, while others addressed the need to include women in leadership roles. Still others were more specific in nature. One, for example, denounced the MAPA convention for not representing Chicano communities, while another decided on Los Angeles as the site for the subsequent RUP state convention.[57]

At the finance workshop, discussion focused on ways of developing the finances needed to sustain RUP's organizing efforts. A resolution was passed that assessed each chapter five dollars per month and called for the formation of a statewide finance committee. The organization and unity workshop moved to have each local chapter designate deputy registrars as well as a quota for RUP registrations needed to meet the mandated 66,000 plus. Another resolution passed that directed individual chapters to develop "service projects," such as free breakfast programs and free income tax services.

During the RUP conference held in April 1971 in Cucamonga, many of the RUP activists from Los Angeles had rejected the idea of using social services and economic development as organizing tactics. When the rationale was presented that these services could help win the support of the barrio residents, they categorically rejected it, on the grounds that RUP was a political party and not a social service or economic entity. Yet, a year later, some RUP chapters discovered, through experimentation, the value of providing services, as RUP from San Bernardino and Riverside Counties had proposed a year earlier.

This rivalry between the various RUP counties or regions became apparent at the statewide conference. At the organization and unity workshop, a resolution was passed that called for the establishment of only five recognized county or regional central committees: San Diego, Los Angeles, Santa Barbara, San José, and Sacramento.[58] In Southern California, the efforts of Orange County and of San Bernardino and Riverside Counties were not included. RUP's leadership from these three counties interpreted the action as purely political, since theirs was the only region in the state producing tangible electoral and change victories.

In the labor and deportation workshop, one resolution passed that called for RUP to support or become involved directly in union organizing struggles of Méxicano workers via the use of boycotts, strikes, picketing, and other direct action tactics. Other resolutions that passed included support for equal rights for women, a guaranteed minimum income, benefits, jobs, and a living wage. On the issue of deportation, no resolution was passed.[59]

In the communication workshop, the discussion centered on finding ways of improving communication between the various RUP entities. One resolution called for the development of five communication centers: San José, Los Angeles, San Diego, Sacramento, and San Bernardino. For reasons unknown, in this case, San Bernardino was included, but not Orange County. Another resolution called for each county central committee to establish a communication committee that would share monthly minutes with other central committees and for each chapter to submit monthly reports to its respective central committees. Lastly, a resolution passed that RUP should have at least two state conferences per year in areas that were in need of organizing.[60] A few days later, another conference was held in San José where Chicano RUP activists butted heads with Chicano Democrats.

## The National Chicano Political Caucus in San José

On April 23, 1972, at the Luxury Hyatt House in San José, approximately 1,000 persons from ten states attended the National Chicano Political Caucus. The caucus was hosted by MAPA, G.I. Forum, Association of Mexican American Educators (AMEA), and the League of United Latin American Citizens (LULAC).[61] While the emphasis was on the Méxicano, there was some participation from Puertorriqueños (Puerto Ricans). The primary object of the caucus was to unify Méxicanos and Puertorriqueños into a powerful voting bloc. The event organizers also invited New Mexico lieutenant governor Roberto Mondragon and Reyes López Tijerina to address the caucus.[62]

Two weeks earlier, at the San José RUP conference, RUP activists had voted unanimously to boycott this caucus, arguing that MAPA and the other host organizations were fronts for the Democratic Party. They warned RUP supporters not to attend: "We state that no individual, group, organization, or partido chapter can address themselves to the Caucus, to this body, or any other splinter group thereof as representing or speaking in the name of El Partido, statewide or nationally."[63]

The San José RUP chapter was quoted in the *San José Mercury* as saying that it was going to boycott the caucus. However, apparently not all were in absolute agreement with the decision to boycott. For instance, before the caucus, RUP Orange County leader Carlos Muñoz wrote a letter of inquiry to José Angel Gutiérrez asking him if he planned on participating and what strategy he proposed for dealing with the matter, telling Gutiérrez, "I smell something rotten in San José but cannot put my finger on it." Moreover, the day the caucus began, RUP leaders Bert Corona and Herman Baca along with some 100 RUP activists decided to ignore the boycott and attend the event.

The caucus led to a confrontation between the Democratic traditionalists and RUP zealots, which resulted in the conducting of two caucuses instead of one. The traditionalist main leader was MAPA state chair Armando Rodriguez. Herman Baca, when interviewed many years later, recalled the scene that produced the two caucuses:

> I remember the caucus was going on. Armando Rodriguez was chairing it and he had the mic. I remember Bert [Corona] walked in and he got a standing ovation. Then somebody from the floor said, "I make a motion that we go on record supporting the Raza Unida Party." That's when all hell broke loose. . . . People started arguing. I ran up there and grabbed the mic [from Rodriguez] and said, "There is a motion on the floor, let's vote on it," and that's when everybody was trying to get the mic from me. They passed the motion and then somebody asked, "What are we doing here at this hotel? Let's go to the barrio." So we wound up in the barrio.[64]

The majority of the caucus participants joined the RUP-initiated walkout. The protestors left the Hyatt Hotel and moved their caucus to the Lee Matheson Junior High School, located in San José's east-side Méxicano barrio.[65] What resulted were two simultaneous caucuses, with contradictory political and partisan agendas.

At the close of the barrio RUP caucus, a press conference was held to present the passed resolutions. Foremost was the resolution announcing the "building of an independent political organization that would lead to the establishment of a national political La Raza Unida Party." The caucus also approved six resolutions that were directed at "all Chicano organizations working for the liberation of Chicanos": (1) A drastic overhaul of U.S. immigration policies that affect Mexican and Latin Americans; (2) an immediate withdrawal of U.S. forces from Indo-China; (3) an end to American imperialism in Latin America; (4) no support by Méxicanos of the two major parties; (5) an end to economic and military aid to Latin American dictatorships; and (6) strong support for Chicana Liberation and equal opportunity for women.[66]

When the RUP-controlled caucus adjourned, the members felt victorious. They felt they had waged war against MAPA and the traditionalists and won. Sam Martinez, head of the University of Washington's Chicano Studies Division, said: "I'm glad we had a funeral for MAPA. It turned out to be a fantastic thing."[67]

The traditionalist caucus likewise produced some criticisms. Reies López Tijerina, who was never really supportive of the idea of forming RUP, addressing the caucus said: "In the Chicano Movement there is more pride than the Blacks, there is too much fire and not enough brains and understanding." He went on to say that RUP was "a young idea, born within the ranks of the young, zealous Chicanos, but today they expressed nothing of unity." Tijerina's agenda for agrarian reform was strongly supported by the traditionalists. David Sierra, national editor for the G.I. Forum, said, "The people who talked the loudest weren't willing to listen to others."[68] Before the caucus, a San José chapter organizer, Enrique Ante, defected from RUP. He was publicly critical of RUP and alleged that he had decided to leave it due to its being infiltrated by leftists who preached a radical socialist philosophy.[69]

As the traditionalist caucus was to adjourn, some twenty-five RUP zealots entered, condemning MAPA. In an official statement released to the press, the traditionalists remarked, "We have acceded to demand after demand, threat after threat only to find it is a one-way street." They concluded, "Our efforts to prevent disunity have brought us to where we must say Basta!" (Enough is enough!).[70]

Thus, the results of the caucuses revealed that RUP zealots and most Mapistas had come to a parting of the ways. Their political agendas were antithetical. MAPA was definitely aligned with the Democratic Party, and the RUP zealots were determined to have Méxicanos extricate themselves from the clutches of the Democratic Party.

## RUP's Contentious State and National Conventions

During the summer months of 1972, RUP held several meetings and a convention. A preconvention meeting was held on June 3 in Los Angeles to plan for the upcoming RUP state convention. Attended by delegates from eleven chapters, the meeting focused on troubleshooting the convention's workshops, general assembly rules, and an assessment of the San José convention and caucus. At the urging of the Los Angeles Labor Committee, the RUP representatives agreed that the same workshops conducted at the San José conference would be held at the convention and that each workshop would be cochaired.[71]

The RUP state convention was held on July 1 and 2 at East Los Angeles City College. Organized chiefly by the Los Angeles Labor Committee, the convention focused on building RUP into a statewide party. Unlike the San José Convention that drew RUP activists mostly from the northern part of the state, some 450 RUP activists from throughout California attended this one.

On the first day of the convention, differences between the regions surfaced. In the politics and strategy workshop, activists differed over the role of the partido. Two schools of thought emerged: Those of Marxist persuasion believed RUP should be a revolutionary party inclusive of all oppressed peoples; and those who were more cultural nationalists wanted RUP to be an electoral party exclusively for Chicanos and reformist in its politics. The debate became acrimonious.

A second major point of contention was whether RUP should support either of the two major parties' presidential candidates. After rancorous debate that included the idea of having a Chicano run for the presidency, the delegates finally adopted the following resolution: "We, LRUP of California, despite relentless pressure from the Democratic and Republican parties, the two party monopoly system of the United States, reaffirm our position that we will not support any candidate for any office from any party other than our own in the 1972 elections."[72]

The convention delegates rejected the idea of running a Chicano as an Independent for president. José Gonzales, a RUP district coordinator from Colorado, was a strong proponent of the idea. Debate made it obvious that Gonzales was at the convention for the purpose of planting the idea that Colorado's Corky Gonzales would run for president. His motion was ruled out of order. As chair of the San Bernardino and Riverside Counties Central Coordinating Committee, I spoke out against the motion on the grounds that we should be organizing and building up the party's infrastructure instead of wasting time and limited resources on symbolic and unrealistic campaigns.

As if these issues were not enough to engender division, heated sectarian clashes occurred between the Maoist-oriented Labor Committee and activists from the Socialist Workers Party (SWP). At the San José conference, the Labor Committee was successful in its red-baiting tactics, which resulted in the exclusion of the SWP and Young Socialist Alliance from participating in the conference. While the groups were not prohibited from participating at the East Los Angeles convention, members of the Labor Committee closed down the SWP and Young Socialist Alliance literature display tables.[73]

The political differences between SWP and the Labor Committee became equally evident in the labor and deportation workshop. The debate on the escalating deportation of Méxicano undocumented workers by the Immigration and Naturalization Services also drew in members of Bert Corona's Center for Autonomous Social Action (CASA). The Labor Committee presented its own position paper on the Dixon-Arnett law, whose emphasis was on employer sanctions. SWP and CASA alleged that the Labor Committee's proposal accepted the deportations of undocumented Raza workers. Pedro Arias from the RUP City Terrace chapter and CASA leader Nacho Uribe were not allowed to challenge the proposal, and both were threatened with bodily harm if they continued to try to do so. RUP leader of the City Terrace chapter, Raul Ruiz, intervened and sided with the ruling of the Labor Committee.[74] Years later when interviewed, Ruiz commented that he and the Labor Committee, among others, were concerned about a possible "takeover" by the Socialist Workers Party and Communist Party.[75]

Three contentious sectarian Marxist groups sought control of RUP: the Labor Committee, SWP, and the Communist Party via CASA. The convention revealed that the Marxist entities had infiltrated RUP and sought to advance their so-called revolutionary agenda in the barrios using RUP as a front. At the other end of ideological spectrum, were the cultural nationalists, who represented a slight majority.

Adding to the precarious situation at the convention was a walkout staged by the delegates from the San Bernardino/Riverside, San Diego, and Orange County regions. Before the convention, the three regions met and formed what they called the Southern Region. The Labor Committee, perceiving this body as a threat to their leadership role and their ability to control the development of the party, refused to recognize the delegates from San Bernardino/Riverside and Orange Counties. The Labor Committee's criteria stipulated that each recognized chapter was allocated two delegates, regardless of how many members it had. They used five criteria for determining what constituted a chapter; it must: (1) have at least five deputy registrars actively registering; (2) have at least ten persons; (3) provide political education classes; (4) pass out only bilingual literature to the community; (5) have a minimum of one monthly meeting; and (6) be a part of the central committee.[76]

Throughout the day the issue was debated, with members of the Labor Committee and Raul Ruiz, who started out trying to mediate the dispute, eventually on the same side, leading to angry exchanges between Ruiz and me. That evening, using a divide-and-conquer tactic, the Labor Committee seated only the San Diego County delegation. In protest, Orange County RUP coordinator Carlos Muñoz and I, along with some fifty convention participants from the three counties, walked out of the convention.

In response to the walkout, Herman Baca delivered a statement to the convention encouraging solidarity with the unseated counties: "We cannot in good faith stay, while the other representatives of our region are being denied their voting rights."[77] With San Diego County joining the walkout, the number of those walking out increased to seventy-five. Years later, Ruiz said, "We [the Labor Committee, among others] thought that you were a Mapista disguised as Raza Unida. . . . I think that your allegiance was being questioned. We thought there was some type of conspiracy. This is why we did what we did."[78] The schisms and conflict that pervaded the East Los Angeles convention, however, were merely an omen of worse things to come. The acuteness of the philosophical and ideological differences between the various regions and chapters suggested that they were irreconcilable.

The leadership and ideological divisions became worse after the convention. The SWP and the Labor Committee power struggle continued. The RUP Central Committee of Los Angeles County met in July and made it clear that it did not support SWP and did not want its support. At a RUP meeting in Los Angeles, a SWP position paper critical of the convention was rejected on the grounds that it denigrated RUP and, in particular, the Labor Committee.[79] SWP's role within the Chicano Movement and RUP would be a point of contention for years to come—one that would foster conflict among the other competing Marxist and nationalist groups fighting for control of the CM and RUP agendas. On August 21, the Southern Region released a position paper on the matters of the East Los Angeles convention, RUP's national El Paso convention, and strategy and tactics. In the "Brown paper," they criticized the actions taken by the Labor Committee and voiced concern over the growing schisms and the negative impact they might have on the upcoming RUP national convention in El Paso that September as well as on RUP's future in California. Moreover, the Southern Region felt that it had been betrayed, since at a meeting held by the Southern Region on June 9, representatives of the Labor Committee had promised that the East Los Angeles convention would be open to all regions and that their delegations would be seated. Specifically, the paper stated: "We are not in disagreement on the end objective of establishing the partido as a viable alternative to the two-party system! We found that our differences have to do with questions of method, tactics, and strategy." In reference to the Southern Region's role at the national convention, it underscored that "all areas of the state must be allowed an equal voice at all times." On the issue of the growing power struggle between Gutiérrez and Gonzales, it was observed that RUP in California needed to remain neutral and build a "collective leadership" as opposed to individual leadership. On the question of ideology, it repudiated sectarianism in any form and expounded on the need to have one party that is nationalist, eclectic, pragmatic, and based on the Méxicano's historical and material conditions. On strategy, it emphasized the need to deliver to the people victories and not just rhetorical pronouncements.[80]

By late August, the California RUP chapters had become further divided over the emerging power struggle between Gutiérrez and Gonzales. Hundreds of RUP activists from throughout California attended the El Paso convention September 1–4. Two individuals from Southern California played significant leadership roles at the convention. One was Roger Granados, who was a write-in candidate for Congress in the San Bernardino/Riverside area and who had been appointed to chair the powerful Credentials Committee by Gutiérrez. The second was Raul Ruiz, who was also appointed by Gutiérrez, as the convention's chairperson. Both ultimately played significant roles in the politics that determined who prevailed as RUP's national chairperson.[81]

As a result of the national convention, RUP in California became even more polarized over ideological differences. Increasingly, RUP became engulfed in battles over which was going to prevail—nationalism or a form of Marxism. What surfaced was a "politic of self-destruction."

## RUP's Electioneering Struggle in 1972

RUP's political activity in California reached its apogee in 1972. In San Fernando, where Méxicanos comprised nearly 50 percent of the city's population, the local RUP chapter ran two candidates, Richard Corona and Jess Margarito, for the city council and endorsed incumbent E. C. Orozco for city treasurer. The traditional White political machine, which felt threatened by RUP's entry into the city's politics, resorted to red-baiting and racial attacks on RUP's candidates. The city's mayor publicly denounced RUP's candidates as radicals and subversives and stated that the partido had no place in San Fernando. RUP's candidates responded with charges of racism, red-baiting, voting irregularities, and lack of sensitivity to the needs of the poor in the barrios.

Beyond fending off the attacks, RUP's candidates stressed such issues as ending drug trafficking, establishing drug rehabilitation centers, bringing better transportation systems to the barrio, equal education, health care, bilingual/bicultural education, better housing, and an end to urban renewal. The results of the election were: Quintin D. Johnson, 2,009 votes; J. B. Van Sickle, 1,807 votes; Richard Corona, 1,007 votes; Jess Margarito, 1,000 votes; Alfred Bernal, 279 votes; and W. C. Godchalk, 192 votes. City treasurer candidate Orozco was reelected. The vilification of the RUP candidates resulted in a large White voter turnout, causing RUP's two city council candidates to lose badly.[82]

Other RUP chapters also ran candidates for their respective local, state, and federal offices. In Ontario, the local RUP foco scored an unprecedented victory with the election of Gustavo Ramos to the city council. In San Francisco, Antonio Baca ran unsuccessfully for the Thirteenth State Assembly District in the San Francisco area. Roger Granados ran unsuccessfully in a write-in campaign for the Thirty-eighth Congressional District, which included parts of San Bernardino and Riverside Counties. In the San Fernando area, Guadalupe Rameriz ran unsuccessfully for the Forty-first Assembly District. In the Los Angeles area, some RUP chapters indicated an interest in running a Chicano for Congress and state assembly; however, they withdrew when Raul Ruiz, former Forty-eighth Assembly RUP candidate, announced in April that he was running for the Fortieth Assembly District.[83]

It was the race for the Fortieth Assembly District that engendered the most interest among RUP activists. Méxicanos comprised nearly 30 percent of the district's population and 18 percent of its electorate.[84] But, as was the case in 1971, some RUP activists in Los Angeles alleged that Ruiz had not consulted with them before deciding to run. They complained that he had decided to run even though he would be running against a Méxicano, there was no consensus within RUP, and it was destined to be a "blunder," explained Santillan more than twenty years later.[85] Xenaro Ayala, a leader from the San Fernando RUP chapter, agreed that Ruiz never requested their input on his running against Garcia, attributing it to "impulsiveness" by Ruiz. Ayala said that this type of lack of control permeated much of the RUP organizing effort—"Let's do it. It's got to be done, so let's do it." He commented that, although they participated in the campaign, it was not with the same intensity and participation as in Ruiz's first race.[86]

In spite of some initial apprehension, most of the RUP chapters in Los Angeles County strongly supported Ruiz's challenge of Alex Garcia. According to Fred Aguilar, RUP leader from the LaPuente chapter, "We and many other chapters worked hard every weekend prior to election to ensure RUP sent a powerful message to the Democrats."[87]

Ruiz explained in our 1997 interview why the City Terrace RUP chapter decided to support him over Democrat Alex Garcia: "We didn't feel that Garcia was a good candidate. He had a personal history, which I don't want to get into, but there were a lot of problems in his personal life."[88] Ruiz was alluding to Garcia's having one of the worst attendance records in the history of the assembly, which put his district at a disadvantage. He was absent 40.7 percent of the time in 1970 and 46.7 percent of the time during the 1971 legislative session. Some people attributed his absenteeism to an alleged drinking problem. In addition, Garcia voted against several educational and minimum-wage bills that would have benefited the Méxicanos of the district.[89]

Because RUP was not an official party, Ruiz ran as an Independent. In order to qualify, he had to be registered outside one of the then legal parties (Democrats, Republicans, Peace and Freedom, and American Independent) for no less than one year. Also, according to the California Election Code, Ruiz had to get 5 percent of the district's registered voters to sign a petition. Complicating the situation, the code also stipulated that the 5 percent could not have voted in the preceding primary election in a "legal" party—this made the pool of potential signers extremely limited. In the case of the Fortieth Assembly District, the number of petition signatures required totaled some 2,000. The code also required that the petitions be secured within a three-week time frame and that all those who signed had to pledge that they would vote for Ruiz.[90] Yet, in spite of these difficulties, Ruiz was able to secure the required 2,000 signatures.

Ruiz's campaign from the outset relied on a grass-roots approach. The petition drive was conducted by scores of volunteers from the community and adjacent colleges and universities. The campaign was much better organized than the one for the Forty-eighth. Door-to-door canvassing was carried out in the targeted precincts; campaign literature was developed and distributed; community meetings were held; telephone banks were established, and a well-coordinated get-out-the-vote drive was organized. The campaign stressed five major issues: rights for all workers; rights for the aged; better education; effective political representation; and the idea that problems should be addressed through separate, independent action and struggle by an independent force such as RUP.[91]

Both the Democratic candidate, Garcia, and the Republican, Aguirre, resorted to depicting both Ruiz and RUP as a radical activist group with Communist leanings. One leaflet distributed by a group called "Concerned Community Chicanos" alleged that from 1968 to 1972, Ruiz was involved with "Communist" causes and groups. It charged that he was corrupting the youth by taking them away from God into sexual promiscuity. In another leaflet, Democrats attacked him as being a "spoiler" who was benefiting the Republican candidate.[92]

Ruiz lost the election to Garcia, but he did much better this time than in his previous bid for the Forty-eighth District. While Garcia garnered 21,328 votes (56 percent), Ruiz received 5,130 votes (13 percent). The election returns brought mixed responses from RUP activists. Some were disillusioned because they felt that Ruiz really had a chance to win. Even years later, Ruiz commented: "Our belief was that we had a better program and we had more years of participating in the community. We should have won."[93]

Others felt that, considering the obstacles the campaign had to overcome, Ruiz had done well. He had shown the promise and potential of RUP and proved that it had some political support in the Méxicano community. After the November elections, strategic planning meetings occurred at both the state and local levels. Until October 1972, RUP had registered only 30,563.[94] After RUP failed to get on the 1972 ballot, another effort was initiated to get the party on the ballot for the 1974 elections. Moreover, the San Fernando RUP chapter in December announced it would run Andres Torres for the Twenty-second Assembly District.

As 1972 came to a close, RUP had yet to become an official party; with the exception of Cucamonga and Ontario, no RUP chapter in California had yet produced electoral victories. Even worse, the clashes of the two caudillos, Gutiérrez and Gonzales, at the El Paso convention precipitated a power struggle that irreparably harmed the emerging Chicano third party.

*Chapter Seven*

---

# A Casualty of the Viva Yo Generation: The Decline of RUP in California, 1973–1981

Driven by rising expectations that the Raza Unida Party (RUP) could succeed in becoming a political alternative to the Democrat and Republican Parties, Chicano activists in California by 1973 had created a semblance of organization, established a leadership, begun developing an organizing plan of action, and run a number of candidates. From then on, RUP in California entered a decline that by 1981 would leave it moribund, despite developments in the Los Angeles County area, where RUP took the lead in organizing the Raza Unida Party statewide.

## Clashing Personalities and Beliefs, 1973–1975

In 1973, RUP in California entered a period of conflict that was the product of personality-driven power struggles and clashing ideologies, which eventually would lead to a politics of self-destruction.[1] The Gutiérrez/Gonzales leadership power struggle coupled with several internal power conflicts involving regional caciques became the two major endogenous antagonisms that set in motion the descent. Moreover, the growing battle over which political doctrine RUP should adhere to served to further intensify the already strained relationship between the cultural nationalists and the Marxists.[2]

Ideologically, RUP was evolving from being cultural nationalist to quasi-Marxist in orientation. This process actually started in 1971 when RUP activists from throughout California tried to provide the party with a platform that complemented their area's or region's ideological agenda. Most of the platforms, however, were merely protests against the nation's two-party monopoly.

For the most part, the proposed platforms contained strong doses of cultural nationalism (Chicanismo) and anticapitalism covered with a veneer of Marxist thought.
While the platforms were emphatically against the two-party system, they differed
on their adherence and commitment to cultural nationalism or Marxism. RUP's organizing efforts in Northern California, while containing some reference to cultural
nationalism, were much more sectarian or Marxist, to the degree that some did implic-
itly espouse a proletarian revolutionary struggle. In Southern and Central California,
with few exceptions, the RUP organizers were essentially cultural nationalist and
reformist. They all concurred, however, on one salient point—their antipathy for the
nation's two-party system.[3]

The following excerpts from platforms or position papers illustrate the diversity of
ideas among the RUP regions throughout the state, particularly their views on what
RUP's beliefs and role as a political party should be.

San Bernardino/Riverside Counties: "Our concept of La Raza Unida Party is based
on the belief that in order to have political power, we must have economic power.
Our party is also one of action, confrontation, and not only of political action. . . .
It's an organization that functions every day . . . we have to build, to work, so that
self-determination may become a reality and not just an expression."[4]

San Diego County: "La Raza Unida is a political party, which gives emphasis to
the Chicano. The goals of this party are to bring respect, justice, and dignity to
the Chicano by way of political representation. . . . By uniting our people, we can
be a viable political force in resolving many of the problems that confront our
communities."[5]

City Terrace (Los Angeles County): "La Raza Unida is the only alternative open to
Chicanos at this time in the struggle for adequate representation of all levels of government. . . . Even if there are no victories initially, Chicanos will demonstrate their
unity and political strength. By pulling away votes from the Democratic Party and
causing them to lose, Chicanos can force the Democrats to become responsive to the
needs of the Chicano community. Chicanos can be the balance of power . . . under
a cohesive and democratically run organization, namely La Raza Unida Party."[6]

Labor Committee (Los Angeles County): "The LRUP is a party that will be responsive
to the needs of the Chicano and all Latin Americans. It is a party in which the
workers, both men and women, will have a direct part in building and directing. It
is a party that will be directly responsive to our community and therefore the most
dramatic of all."[7]

Northern California: "Any person of La Raza registered in La Raza and/or who works
actively to support the program and activities of the party will be considered a
member with the rights to participate in all decision-making processes of the party
on the basis of one person and one vote. By 'La Raza' we mean those people who
are descendents of or come from México, Central America, South America and the
Antilles."[8]

Sacramento: "The party is being formed as an alternative to the traditional stronghold the Democratic and Republican parties have on the United States political system. The Raza people recognize that these two parties have ignored the existing problems of the brown minority. . . . Unifying the brown minorities will be the key factor for organizing 'La Raza Unida.' "[9]

These excerpts buttress the argument that RUP in California during its formative years (1970–1972) was essentially a cultural nationalist and reform-oriented third-party movement. Yet RUP activists with Marxist beliefs increasingly challenged cultural nationalists for the ideological control of the Chicano Movement in general and RUP in particular. RUP's platform in California by the late 1970s would be a hybrid of nationalism and socialism.

## RUP Statewide Participation Decreases

Until early 1973, RUP statewide was essentially a loosely structured state caucus without a permanent chairperson to direct its statewide development. At each state caucus, those present would elect a chair to preside, but only for that particular meeting. This arrangement was designed to mitigate the personality-based leadership that typified both Texas and Colorado. This changed however, during the summer of 1973, when the caucus was renamed the State Central Committee. By 1974, a semblance of statewide leadership had surfaced, with the State Central Committee electing "temporary" state cochairpersons Catarino Hurtado from Fresno and Cecilia Quijano from City Terrace (Los Angeles).

Each chapter was limited to two representatives. The average number of chapters in attendance at the State Central Committee meetings was eight—meaning that only sixteen individuals were actually involved in formulating policy toward the development of RUP statewide.[10] During much of 1973, no common or uniform statewide RUP structure existed. San Diego, for example, called its countywide organizing entity a "committee"; San Bernardino/Riverside Counties used "foco," while the rest used the term "chapter."

By the end of 1975, there were only eight active RUP chapters participating in statewide activities: City Terrace, La Puente, Norwalk, San Fernando, Lamont, Arvin, Shafter, and Fresno.[11] In San Bernardino and Riverside Counties, RUP organizing activity ended in 1973. Such efforts likewise subsided by 1975 in Orange County. In San Diego County, the only RUP countywide organizing committee became defunct in 1975. There, the organizing emphasis shifted to the Ad Hoc Committee on Chicano Rights, which continued to focus on civil rights and immigration-related issues. It subsequently became immersed in the issue of the Rodino bill. Proposed by Democratic congressman Peter Rodino, the legislation called for employer sanctions.[12]

Of those RUP chapters that remained, few were mass based. Instead, they tended to be cadre oriented, made up of a small nucleus of hardcore young activists buttressed by a small number of supporters who participated off and on. Those chapters that did manage to continue organizing began functioning more like pressure groups, addressing local issues or providing social services or both. Some of these RUP chapters were involved in education, police brutality, labor organizing, and support for the United Farm Workers. Some of them provided immigration counseling, job development, free income tax filing, free lunch programs for children, translation of documents, and various cultural activities.[13] The only chapter that combined social services with an emphasis on local issues was the one from San Fernando.[14] During the summer of 1973, for example, it supported the United Rubber Workers Local 621 in its strike for better wages and working conditions.[15]

Between 1973 and 1975, a number of RUP conventions and state meetings were held throughout California. What prevailed at most of them was rhetorical fisticuffs. The debates focused on issues that kept most RUP activists preoccupied, such as the Gutiérrez/Gonzales power struggle, cultural nationalism versus Marxism, reform versus revolutionary party, cadre versus mass-base structure, finances, communication, and a myriad of social issues. More time was spent on intellectualizing about these issues than on organizing RUP's power base—*el pueblo* (the community).

The downward spiral of the party was particularly evident at a RUP statewide convention held in Fresno on August 10, 1973. Only some 150 people were in attendance, most from chapters belonging to the Los Angeles County Central Committee. It was a far cry from the 500 RUP zealots who had attended the statewide convention of July 1972 held at East Los Angeles College. Due to the schism that occurred between the leadership of the Los Angeles County Central Committee and that of the rest of Southern California, there was no representation from the Southern Region at the Fresno convention. Increasingly, the Los Angeles region kept the statewide RUP organizing effort alive.

A paramount concern at the Fresno convention.was the coordination of efforts to register enough people to make RUP a legal political party statewide. The delegates set a statewide goal to register 10,000 by September.[16] There were those who expressed concern over the weak status of the partido and the declining number of those registered in it. They alluded to the lack of a barrio community presence and the need for RUP to change its philosophy and tactics.[17] There was a growing sense of disillusionment within the cadre ranks of the fledgling partido. A content analysis of the state minutes for the period 1973–1975 revealed that state meetings or conventions never attracted more than 200 people, many fewer than at those held during the first two years of organizing RUP. Yet in spite of declining numbers, some diehards continued their efforts to get RUP on the ballot.

The RUP delegates to the State Central Committee took a strong position in support of all political prisoners, specifically Ricardo Chavez Ortiz, Los Tres, and the San Quentin Six. A call was made for their release as well as that of Juan Corona. Furthermore, strong stands were taken against drug trafficking in the barrios and against the liberal capitalist system: "[RUP] understands monopoly capitalism use of repressive drugs such as heroine, barbiturates, and amphetamines as a subtle insidious form of repression of our poor people. We therefore denounce the government of the USA for its involvement in the production, transportation, and distribution of repressive drugs and the profit oriented economic system that produces many of the repressive drugs for the Black market to sell in poor communities."[18]

The delegates also took a very strong stand against the U. S. position on Latin America. Indicative of the increasingly Marxist stance of some RUP activists, the delegates voted to support all nationalist movements against alleged U.S. imperialism in Asia, Africa, and Latin America. Although the convention continued to reveal the differences over ideology and strategic orientation, the Gutiérrez/Gonzales power struggle dominated the debate.

## The Struggle To Become an Official Party Continues

From RUP's inception, many activists propounded the need to get it on the ballot as an official political party. Although the first effort, in 1971 and 1972, failed because RUP was only able to get 35,000 registrants, it did not deter RUP activists from working again for the 1974 gubernatorial elections. Yet a decreasing support base, little or no finances, and weak organization made securing the required 66,000 new registrations impossible. Since 1971 in San Diego County, RUP's county committee had publicly stated that it would not run candidates or assume a very public role until the mandated 10,000 registered RUP voters had been secured.[19] Enthusiasm for organizing, however, was rare among chapters statewide, with the exception of Los Angeles County.

A content analysis of the minutes for both the State Central Committee and Los Angeles Central Committee shows repeated references to strategic discussions on how the local chapters were committed to conducting RUP voter registration drives. However, what becomes apparent is that the organization, finances, volunteers, and in some cases the commitment were just not there. By January 1974, only 20,674 voters had been registered into the RUP. Statewide, the counties that led in the number of RUP registrations were: Los Angeles, 11,951; San Diego, 2,191; Santa Clara, 2,003; Ventura, 926; Fresno, 644; Orange, 481; San Bernardino, 436; and Riverside, 372. These figures were a major disappointment to RUP activists, who thought that the number was much higher than reported.[20] Thus, 1974 was the last year in which a major effort was initiated to get RUP on the ballot via RUP voter registration.

By this time, RUP had resorted to other means to try to get on the ballot. In July 1973, RUP, the Socialist Workers Party, and other third parties became coplaintiffs in a federal suit filed by the Committee for Democratic Election Laws (CODEL) that challenged the constitutionality of California election laws as they related to third parties.[21] In 1971, RUP had been approached by CODEL to join a similar suit but had refused to participate. The state supreme court refused the petition. The election laws were so restrictive that in 1972 California was the only state in which no previously unqualified party could gain official ballot status. The suit alleged that the election codes violated the First, Fourteenth, and Fifteenth Amendments of the nation's Constitution.[22]

Specifically, the suit sought to overturn the law that required the registration of 66,000 people or the signatures of 663,000 voters in order to obtain ballot status.[23] A press release issued by RUP pointed out:

> There are tremendous obstacles in registering people in an unqualified party. These figures show the potential for [RUP] in California and underscore the undemocratic nature of the law, which required a registration of over 66,000 to place the party on the ballot. The unfair election laws have forced us into the courts. The CODEL suit represents our hope of winning a right to be on the ballot. It's a shame that in a state that is supposed to be democratic, parties are forced to go to court for the right to run in elections. If our suit wins, it will give us the opportunity to represent thousands of [RUP] supporters.[24]

The suit sought to democratize California's election laws. The federal court moved rather slowly on the matter. The suit remained in limbo until February 1976, at which time the three federal court judges ruled that any changes in California's election laws were to be made by the legislature and not by the courts, which were comprised of only Democrats and Republicans.

RUP and other third parties pressured the state legislature to look into the matter of reforming the election code. In 1973, a subcommittee on election reform controlled by Democrats voted nine to seven to ease official party requirements for third parties. This somewhat generous act by Democrats was an obvious attempt to curb any serious challenge to their power monopoly. Taking RUP's challenge seriously, using the redistricting process, Democrats in 1973 succeeded in carving out several new state senate and assembly districts for Chicanos. In 1965 there were no Méxicanos serving in the legislature. However, as a result of RUP's threat, by 1974 there were eight serving as legislators, all Democrats.[25]

The action by Democrats took some of the wind out of RUP's organizing sails, and RUP activists were disillusioned. By 1975, after struggling for four years unsuccessfully to get RUP on the ballot, it had become evident to many of the activists that their allegation that the two parties had a monopoly of control was a fact.

## RUP's Symbolic Election Campaigns

In spite of difficulties, from 1973 to 1975, some RUP chapters remained active in the electoral arena. Statewide, as the number of chapters declined, RUP electoral activities mostly emanated from Los Angeles County. Although none of the campaigns were successful, they demonstrated the commitment of Chicano activists to promoting the community's empowerment. As a result of a special election due to the death of State Senator Tom Carrell, in December 1972, the San Fernando chapter formally announced the candidacy of Andres Torres for the Twenty-second State Senate District as an Independent. In order for Torres to get on the ballot, he was required to circulate a petition and secure 500 signatures, as opposed to the Democrat and Republican candidates' 40 to 65 signatures. Torres said that "in two short drives we got nine hundred signatures."[26] Without adequate funding or workers, Torres joined thirteen other Democrat, Republican, and Peace and Freedom candidates in vying for the heavily contested seat. The district was crucial to both the major parties, since each had nineteen seats in the state senate.

What ensued was controversy over charges by Torres that the Los Angeles Police Department was waging an intimidation and harassment campaign against him and RUP. Moreover, while Torres sought to address issues affecting the District's Méxicanos and poor people in general, he found himself under constant attack by Democrats. He was depicted as a radical and a spoiler who had no chance of winning.[27] The outcome of the election proved his running to be symbolic only; Torres was able to garner 2,636 votes, or 3.2 percent of the total. The victor was Democrat Alan Robbins, who received 41,395 votes to Republican Phillip Johnson's 37,348 votes and Peace and Freedom candidate Paula Marsh's 836 votes.[28] While Torres spent a mere $500, Robbins spent $385,041 and Johnson spent $256,904.[29]

Considering the amount of money spent by the two major party candidates and the sophisticated, well-organized campaigns they mounted, Torres and other RUP activists were not completely disillusioned by the election results. They noted that the campaign had been used to organize the disenfranchised Chicano community. In addition, it had served to educate the people as to how both major parties were controlled by powerful economic interests and were insensitive to the needs of the Chicano community.[30]

While RUP in San Fernando was embroiled in the election, the La Puente chapter was engaged in the local race for the city council. The chapter, organized in December 1971, decided to run candidates in 1973.[31] An office was opened to facilitate the organizing of the campaign. The candidate was Ernie Porras, a program coordinator for the Bienvenidos Community Center in San Gabriel. Even though Porras stressed very conventional issues, such as parity in city employment, greater coordination to enhance services to senior citizens, better youth recreational programs, and the need for each councilman to have two assistant volunteer deputy councilpersons,[32] he was labeled a radical and Communist by his opposition.[33] The election results again were essentially symbolic. Porras managed to come in fourth out of a field of five candidates. Out of a total of 2,014 votes cast, Porras garnered only 223 votes, or 11 percent. The winner, Charles Storing, was able to capture 48 percent, or 983 votes. RUP spent only $400 in organizing the campaign.

As the city council campaign ended, the local school board campaign began. Nellie Bustillos was selected as RUP's candidate for the school board. However, out of the city's 9,000 registered voters, only 29.5 percent were Méxicano. The lack of a majority Méxicano voting base coupled with her emphasis on educational issues impacting Méxicanos nevertheless resulted in Bustillos receiving an impressive 650 votes. This campaign like the previous one was used by the chapter to politicize and build its power base among the city's growing Méxicano community, approximately 48 percent of the city's population.[34]

In neighboring San Bernardino County, in Cucamonga the local RUP foco in 1973 scored its last electoral victory by electing two more Méxicanos to the Cucamonga School Board. A few months later, the foco became defunct. Yet for several years thereafter, Méxicanos continued to exercise majority control. In 1974, RUP chapters in Los Angeles took on their greatest electoral challenge.

## Incorporation of East Los Angeles

RUP's electoral apogee in California came in 1974 with the Los Angeles County Central Committee's involvement—and particularly the City Terrace chapter—in the effort to incorporate East Los Angeles into a city with its own elected officials, budget, and administrative infrastructure. The idea of incorporating East Los Angeles into a city had been unsuccessfully tried twice before, in 1961 and again in 1963.[35] In 1971, the staff of the county administrative officer prepared a report on the aspects of incorporation. The report concluded that the proposed city would encompass 6.14 square miles and would have a population of some 86,490 people. Furthermore, that it would include all the unincorporated county territory bounded by the cities of Los Angeles, Commerce, Monterrey Park, and Montebello.[36] Méxicanos would constitute 83 percent of the new city's population, a percentage greater than that of any other city outside of México City, México.[37] Historian Rodolfo Acuña claims that by 1974, Méxicanos constituted 90 percent of the proposed city's 105,033 residents.[38]

For RUP's Méxicano political empowerment agenda, the idea of controlling an urban city in California where Méxicanos were clearly in the majority would be a dream come true. This was to be California's counterpart to RUP community control of Crystal City, Texas. The City Terrace chapter took the lead in preparing for the biggest electoral challenge and the most lucrative politically that RUP would ever undertake in Los Angeles County. RUP, however, was not the only one who had this idea. Some of the more traditional and institutional Méxicano leaders of the area also saw the need for incorporation. In fact, it was not RUP that initially began the movement for incorporation. In 1972, the Ad-Hoc Committee to Incorporate East Los Angeles (ACTIELA) was established. Elected as its chairperson was Esteban Torres, former director of the East Los Angeles Community Union.[39]

In the ensuing months, ACTIELA contracted with the private consulting firm of James P. Hays and Associates to conduct a study on the feasibility of incorporating East Los Angeles. On February 23, 1973, the feasibility study was submitted to ACTIELA. The study's results were highly positive: It would be beneficial to the residents of East Los Angeles to incorporate. The study's rationale for supporting the incorporation was fivefold. First, it would foster greater citizen participation; second, it would give city residents representation; third, it would improve the city's socioeconomic and physical characteristics; fourth, it would give citizens greater control over the city's purse strings; and fifth, it would maximize the benefits of long-range planning. The study's cardinal finding was that enough revenue would be available without an increase in property taxes.[40]

The results of the study were submitted to the county's Local Agency Formation Committee on April 19, 1973. After a series of adjustments to the study's proposed budget, the committee authorized ACTIELA to circulate petitions for incorporation. After several months of gathering petition signatures from at least 25 percent of the proposed city's voters, in March 1974 ACTIELA submitted 8,000 signatures. The county supervisors voted to place the measure on the ballot to coincide with the November elections. With the incorporation measure on the ballot, the next five months witnessed a major political struggle between the traditionalists and the RUP activist forces, as well as those who opposed the measure.

On the proponent side of the political equation were four major competing forces, two of which were supported by ACTIELA. The first, United Democrats for Incorporation, was comprised of the "who's who" of Democratic politics in Los Angeles. It was supported by several very powerful Democrats, among them U.S. senators Alan Cranston and John Tunney. The second ACTIELA-supported group was the Committee for Responsible Government (CRG), comprised mostly of professionals from the area. The third group was RUP, which was made up of activists from the City Terrace chapter, led by Raul Ruiz, former forty-eighth and fortieth RUP assembly candidate. A fourth, minor group came from the Socialist Workers Party, which endorsed two of its own candidates and also supported three of RUP's candidates. Each one of these four competing forces ran its own slate of proincorporation candidates. Further complicating the field were numerous other candidates for a total of thirty-nine, of which thirty-six were Méxicanos.[41]

While the issues and rationales used by the various proincorporation groups may have differed, the groups all agreed on one point—the importance of community control. To them, control translated to local control over the area; the ability to effectively deal with the problems within the proposed community; control of the tax money (only one-third of the taxes generated by East Los Angeles returned to the area); and a quelling of the fear of annexation by the surrounding areas.[42]

RUP's slate included Raul Ruiz, Jorge Garcia, Daniel Zapata, Celia Rodriguez, and Arturo Sanchez. The slate's goals were to: (1) combat unemployment; (2) improve the living conditions of senior citizens; (3) upgrade housing conditions; (4) upgrade and expand recreational facilities; (5) open all phases of government operations to the people; and (6) create alternate structures for providing basic necessities.[43] Even though the election was nonpartisan, RUP's slate of candidates strategically sought to make it a partisan one. They attacked the ACTIELA and CRG for being Democrats. Moreover, they blamed the manifold problems plaguing the proposed city on neglect by Democratic Party officials. They stressed that as Crystal City, Texas, was going through some progressive changes, so would the new city under their leadership.

The anti-incorporation forces were well-organized and formidable opponents. There were three groups that constituted the opposition: the Maravilla–Belvedere Park Property Association, the Montebello Park Taxpayers Association, and the Committee Opposing Incorporation Now. The three groups were comprised of conservative Méxicanos, Whites, businesspeople, and elderly retired homeowners.[44] Although there were several opposition leaders, Arthur Montoya was the most vocal and visible. He and others claimed that East Los Angeles could not sustain itself without raising property taxes and rents. They offered five other reasons why they were so unequivocally against incorporation:

1. Outsiders and militant were attempting to control the area (RUP and the Socialist Workers Party).
2. East Los Angeles did not have a tax base to generate adequate funds for the proposed city.
3. Urban renewal would take place in order to sustain the city.
4. Cityhood would result in inferior services, including law enforcement, which would result in more crime.
5. If the city were incorporated, racism would afflict the non-Chicano population of the area.[45]

They relied on distorting the facts, fear tactics, and red-baiting to win the voters over. The RUP slate refuted, in particular, the issue of increasing property taxes. RUP pledged that it would not raise taxes and would instead rely on other revenue sources, such as revenue sharing.[46]

On November 5, voters defeated the measure. They voted on two items—the incorporation measure and the mayor and councilman who would represent them should the measure pass. Against incorporation, there were 7,197 votes or 58 percent. The "yes" vote was 5,256 votes, or 42 percent of the total vote.[47] On mayor and councilman, no slate as a whole prevailed. Raul Ruiz from the RUP slate was the top vote getter with 2,240 votes.[48] He became known as the mayor without a city to govern.[49] The other four RUP candidates placed seventh through fourteenth, with vote totals ranging from 1,557 to 1,239.

At the crux of the measure's failure were three issues: racism, the specter of higher taxes, and, in the case of RUP, red-baiting. The opponents openly declared, "We don't want to be a part of a Chicano city, a city of welfare recipients and 'illegals'—a city where crime runs rampant." They argued that because the new city would be comprised mostly of poor people, the city administration would have no choice but to increase taxes on homeowners to pay for running the city.[50]

RUP fell victim to the well-orchestrated effort that depicted it as a fringe, radical group that did not have the best interests of homeowners in mind. There were numerous other factors that negatively impacted the election result, such as RUP's lack of adequate resources, the heavy anti-incorporation media coverage, and the lack of a well-organized effort by the proincorporation forces.[51] On the last point,

Gomez Quiñonez was critical of RUP's electoral performance: "Though it was only one of several participants, La Raza Unida of California's influence as a vehicle in local government was tested, and it failed. In the process, LRUP demonstrated some of the most incompetent electoral efforts ever witnessed in Los Angeles."[52]

Thus, neither the RUP nor ACTIETA was able to overcome the fear engendered by the powerful and well-organized opposition. Ruiz commented on RUP's defeat: "We were a player in that particular race. Unfortunately, we were not able to crest the mountain and get the community to totally understand."[53]

As 1975 came to a close, RUP's struggle to pass the incorporation measure and elect its candidates had failed. With the exception of the victories in Cucamonga in 1971 and 1973 and Ontario in 1972, all of the campaigns ended in defeat. The 1974 East Los Angeles incorporation election raised RUP activists' expectations, but in the end the defeat served to accelerate RUP's decline.

## RUP's Sectarian Politics, 1976–1981

As we have seen, the "Viva Yo generation" by 1975 had begun to emerge and replace the Chicano Movement generation.[54] In the face of this new Hispanic ethos, activists in California found it difficult to sell their social justice, change, and empowerment agendas to each other, and more importantly, to the masses of people in the nation's growing barrios.

From 1976 to 1981, the few remaining RUP chapters went through an ideological metamorphosis. After 1975, the City Terrace chapter began to disengage from a lot of the RUP organizing activities due to increasing conflicts over a variety of issues within the Los Angeles County Central Committee.[55] By late 1976, most of the rigid Marxist ideologues had defected to other groups. For example, the Maoist-oriented Los Angeles Labor Committee had left RUP to form the August 29 Movement. RUP had only seven chapters statewide: La Puente, San Fernando, Lamont, Norwalk, Arvin, Fresno, and City Terrace.[56] SWP activists had left the party by 1977. According to the minutes of both the state and Los Angeles central committees, in spite of these departures, the remaining RUP chapters became increasingly anticapitalist. (This pattern also surfaced in New Mexico.) RUP activists adopted a more socialist and Third World perspective, combined with extreme nationalism predicated on nation building. They had embraced Corky Gonzales's call for the formation of a Chicano nation rather than Gutiérrez's nationalist reformist pragmatism. They did not call themselves either Marxists or socialists, however. They felt they needed to create an original ideology. Fred Aguilar, RUP state chair from 1978 to 1980, said when interviewed years later: "The Right was quick to brand us Communist or Marxist. Yet we didn't want to adopt any of those ideologies, because we were just learning."[57]

Scarred by years of electoral failure, the remaining chapters held numerous state and regional conferences and meetings at which they spent countless hours debating and refining RUP's hybrid ideology and strategizing ways to build RUP into an organizational weapon that would lead the struggle for a Chicano nation. Nationalists who were ostensibly reform oriented in their politics left RUP and rejoined the Democratic party. RUP's last few years saw it transformed into a vanguard party of true believers who in most cases eschewed electoral politics in favor of confronting issues. This meant that RUP in California, while described by its zealots as a political party, in practice was nothing more than an interest group. RUP leader Xenaro Ayala said that "the lack of clarity in ideology contributed to the decline of both the partido and the rest of the Chicano Movement."[58]

In 1978, only four chapters participated in the state meeting: La Puente, San Fernando, San José, and Norwalk.[59] The two most active chapters at the time were the La Puente and San Fernando chapters. According to RUP state central committee and Los Angeles County Central Committee minutes, RUP chapters by 1981 had all but disappeared, although that year six paid either in full or in part their chapter dues of five dollars a month.[60] The only chapter that remained active, however, was the San Fernando chapter led by Xenaro Ayala, who became RUP's last national chairperson.[61]

This generally downward spiral of RUP activism and chapter formation showed up in the absence of any major electoral activity during the five-year period. While some discussion occurred, no real effort was ever again initiated to get RUP on the ballot. California's restrictive election laws were too much for the RUP zealots to surmount. This in part was a contributing factor to the decision to opt for a more cadre-oriented partido. RUP, in essence, during these final years took on more the role of a pressure group seeking to address issues and to influence public policy rather than to control it. A content analysis of the minutes further suggests that RUP chapters addressed a variety of domestic issues, including the Bakke decision (affirmative action), immigration, police brutality, and education. Yet no longer did those chapters receive the extensive media coverage of earlier years. Allegedly, they were no longer newsworthy. Without demonstrating a viable power capability and with little or no organizing being done in the barrios, RUP intimidated neither the media nor those in power with its verbal and press release attacks.

## Chicanas' Role in RUP

RUP's Chicana activists also became more pressure-group oriented. RUP's organizing experience in California since late 1970 had been dominated by males. Few women held major leadership positions in RUP. Sexism was thus a problem that pervaded most RUP chapters. While women played important secondary leadership and supportive roles, it was the Méxicano male who tended to usurp the partido's main leadership positions. Most of RUP's candidates and state chairpersons were males, with one exception in 1972, when Cecilia Quijano was elected state cochair. Apart from Texas, this was typical of RUP's organizing paradigm throughout most of the Southwest and Midwest.

In an effort to have a stronger voice within RUP, in 1975 the women from the Los Angeles chapter started La Federacicon de Mujeres Unidas (Federation of United Women).[62] Its key architects were Gloria Santillan, Betty Cuevas, Kathy Borunda, and Maria Sanchez. Richard Santillan, former husband of Gloria Santillan, explained that they organized the federation "because they felt they weren't getting their due within the party. They felt they needed an organization of their own to kind of pressure, push, whatever."[63] The federation was transitory. While there were numerous statements condemning the sexism within RUP, the partido continued to be led by men until 1981 when Irene Rodarte was elected state chair; however, by then there was little of the partido left.

## RUP's Last Electoral Hurrah

During the years 1976 through 1978, the San Fernando chapter was politically resilient, active in both the electoral and the advocacy arenas. When interviewed, Andres Torres commented that they were "the only ones that continued trying to organize."[64] In 1976, the chapter ran two candidates, Marshal Diaz and Xenaro Ayala, for the city council. Their campaign emphasized four salient issues: equal representation on the city council, immigration, full employment, and health care. For the chapter, the election was a valuable organizing tool. During the campaign, Ayala said that "the purpose of the Raza Unida is to politicize people. . . . Especially in this city, the working-class people are the Méxicanos and the Chicanos, the people with no support and no type of power."[65]

RUP's opposition described both candidates as radicals, and thus they were not allowed to participate in some of the candidate forums. As was commonplace with RUP campaigns, they lacked the adequate resources—both people and money—to present a viable threat to San Fernando's White establishment, which controlled the city's politics.[66] The election results proved disappointing. The RUP candidates came in fourth and fifth respectively. The two Whites received 1,100 and 1,200 votes. With Méxicanos making up nearly 50 percent of the city's population, Diaz got 424 and Ayala 385 votes. *The Militant* reporter Miguel Pendas commented, "The RUP chapter in San Fernando is composed of a relatively small group of dedicated activists. Had their resources been greater, they would undoubtedly have reaped even greater results from the election."[67]

The election did not dampen the organizing spirit of the activists of the San Fernando chapter. The chapter ran Andres Torres, who in 1976 was RUP's state chairperson, for the Thirty-ninth Assembly District. In another race, José Gonzales ran for the Sixty-third Assembly District. Both were successful in securing the required number of signatures to be placed on the ballot as Independents. Two other RUP candidates tried to run but were not able to secure the required number of signatures. Lacking the necessary resources and organization to mount effective campaigns, both were designed mostly to buttress the ongoing litigation on California's restrictive election laws. They sought to show the legal and financial difficulties Independent and third-party candidates faced in running for a partisan office. Torres managed to garner only 4.5 percent of the vote, or 3,292 votes, while Gonzales was able to secure only 3.9 percent, or 2,968 votes.[68]

In 1978, Andres Torres again ran for the San Fernando City Council. Using a more grass-roots coalition strategy that embraced more groups and did not accentuate RUP, Torres came very close to winning.[69] He lost the election by a mere fifty-five votes. This suggested that the Méxicano voters in San Fernando were much more willing to respond to a nonpartisan approach than a partisan one.

That same year, Torres made an unsuccessful run for governor. As had been the case in previous elections, the campaign was much more an organizing effort than a serious electoral challenge. Torres told the press that he was aware that he could not win, but that his candidacy for governor would foster enough recognition to help RUP become an official political party. With changes that had occurred in the state election laws, Torres needed at least 99,821 valid signatures to put him on the ballot as a third-party candidate. In August, two weeks before the deadline, he had only 20,000 signatures. His goal was to run and pull a minimum of 120,000 votes, or 2 percent of the total votes cast. This would qualify RUP as California's fifth official political party.[70]

Without the resources—specifically, money, staff, and volunteers—Torres's campaign just could not put it together. After Torres's unsuccessful bid, RUP's electoral focus diminished considerably. In the RUP State Central Committee minutes from 1978 to 1981, there are only a few references to political activities such as voter registration efforts and RUP candidates running for office. One such reference was the San Fernando chapter's effort under the leadership of Xenaro Ayala, when in 1981 it was involved in an unsuccessful recall election.

After four years of a semblance of a RUP movement, RUP's decline accelerated during the next three years, 1978–1981. Without an organized power base in the sprawling barrios of California, the few RUP chapters that did exist were essentially cadre oriented and functioned more as pressure groups than a political party. Several of the remaining chapters were very active in the advocacy arena. Their local issues included immigration, police brutality, a Coors boycott, an end to barrio violence, a Nestle's boycott, youth activities, painting murals, and Becas de Aztlán (a scholarship given to Chicanos by Mexico). Meeting minutes suggest, however, that the chapters were more reactive than proactive.[71]

The minutes further reveal that RUP's State Central Committee meetings continued well into 1981. There was still a semblance of a state structure, including state officers and a few chapters. From 1978 to 1980, Fred Aguilar was RUP's state chairperson. Tony Gonzales replaced Aguilar from the San Francisco chapter, who served throughout 1981. In 1982, Irene Rodarte was elected state chairperson. She became the first Chicana to hold such a high position of leadership within RUP in California. But none of RUP's state leaders were successful in building up RUP's image either in the media or community.

Symptomatic of RUP's decline was its inability to demonstrate any power capability. This became a major preoccupation of RUP's leadership: RUP's cadre infrastructure did not have the capacity to respond effectively either in the electoral arena or in the pressure group arena of politics. With few chapters and supporters, RUP's leadership found it difficult to convince the people in the barrios that it had what it took to defend and advance their interests. As Fred Aguilar explained when interviewed, "Too many of us had full-time jobs and families. It was very difficult for us in leadership positions to do what we had to do. There was just not enough time to do what had to be done."[72] Even though a considerable amount of time was spent on study sessions on a variety of topics and in discussion on revitalizing RUP, no plan of action was ever put into effect.

During the years 1978–1981, RUP in California continued to hold conventions and state meetings, which produced a plethora of resolutions and motions on its "internationalist" agenda. RUP leaders, especially in California, from 1975 on traveled to Mexico, Cuba, China, Lebanon, and Nicaragua. The trend had its genesis with José Angel Gutiérrez's efforts to reach out to Mexico in 1972 and in 1975 to Cuba.

This was indicative of an ideological mix of Marxism and cultural nationalism that had evolved since 1976. Increasingly, RUP activists perceived themselves as revolutionaries preparing for the liberation of the Aztlán. While domestic issues were dealt with, RUP activists between 1978 and 1981 seemed to be more interested in identifying and supporting Third World revolutionary struggles, such as that of the Palestine Liberation Organization. After reviewing the minutes, one may fairly deduce that RUP activists were more intrigued with the romanticism of international issues than with the wearisome struggle to organize RUP in the barrios. While there was plenty of revolutionary fervor on behalf of the oppressed Méxicano, there was no revolutionary "praxis."

Although almost defunct by 1981, RUP refused to support the redistricting coalition Californios for Fair Representation (CFR), and the effort to increase the number of Latino single-member legislative districts. RUP's leadership perceived CFR's actions as buttressing the Democratic Party's hold on the growing Méxicano community. A position paper prepared by Eugene Hernandez made it very clear that RUP would not compromise its political integrity in a process that would benefit the Democrats. With an obvious jab at CFR, Hernandez wrote of "another word on the reapportionment drive by Chicano vendido (sell-outs) democrats and company." He alleged that Santillan and others involved with CFR were "fattening their political pockets in hopes of getting a piece of the political pie for themselves."[73] RUP leaders also took issue with Richard Santillan and me for being former RUP activists who took leadership positions with CFR (I was its state director, and Santillan was research coordinator in charge of developing redistricting plans).

By 1981, other organizing efforts, such as those of CFR, the Committee on Chicano Rights (San Diego) and Congreso para Pueblos Unidos (Congress for United Communities, although statewide, was primarily out of San Bernardino and Riverside Counties), were out-organizing RUP in the struggle to empower the barrios and effect social change. Concomitantly, the more moderate traditional organizations such as MAPA, LULAC, and G.I.Forum, and the newer advocacy groups such as the Mexican American Legal Defense and Educational Fund, National Association of Latino Elected Officials, Southwest Voter Registration Education Project, National Council of La Raza, and the Hispanic Chamber of Commerce had started to rival and displace those entities that were products of the Chicano Movement.

## The Decline of RUP in California

As in most other states, by 1981 RUP in California had become the victim of exogenous and endogenous antagonisms. First, California's restrictive election laws were just too difficult for RUP activists to surmount. After numerous unsuccessful attempts to get on the ballot, many activists became disillusioned and quit out of frustration and desperation. Second, the concerted effort by Democrats to win over the Méxicano community succeeded. The Democrats in 1973 and 1974 in particular initiated a new outreach effort, courting the political support of the Méxicano community statewide. Because of redistricting, Chicano political representation in both the assembly and state senate increased, thus making it very difficult for RUP activists to make the argument that Méxicanos needed political representation. Political co-optation of some RUP activists by the Democrats also contributed to RUP's decline.

Several other exogenous antagonisms also contributed, including the end of the epoch of protest; infiltration and harassment by law enforcement agencies; the emergence of the era of the Hispanic and the Viva Yo generation; and the often hostile and red-baiting media. In some respects, in California, the endogenous antagonisms contributed more to RUP's decline than the exogenous antagonisms.

Of the endogenous factors that contributed to RUP's decline, first, between 1973 and 1981, RUP experienced a leadership drain. Numerous leaders and organizers, such as Raul Ruiz, Herman Baca, Fred Aguilar, Andres Torres, and Bert Corona, by 1981 had left RUP with only a handful of true believers. Some leaders suffered financial problems as a result of losing their job or being blackballed. Others wound up divorced or separated. A few of them even became victims of drug and alcohol abuse. After 1981, only one RUP leader was left to carry on the struggle of building RUP into a viable partido—Xenaro Ayala from the San Fernando chapter, who from then until 2000 has kept the political dream of RUP alive.

Second, power struggles (Gutiérrez verses Gonzales), ideological and strategic differences (Marxists versus nationalists), and myopic parochialism and regionalism also contributed to RUP's decline in California. Third, without the requisite financial resources, RUP lacked organizing and administrative staff, infrastructure, and campaign funds, and thus its organizing efforts relied on volunteers. Fourth, the prevalence of sexism within RUP's leadership ranks resulted in many women dropping out of the partido. Fifth, because its cadre leadership structure in some areas was comprised mostly of students, RUP was never able to broaden its base of grassroots support to include the people of the barrios and the divergent working- and middle-class sectors. Sixth, the Méxicano population was still not large enough to sustain RUP as an all-Méxicano political partido. And last, too many people by the late 1970s perceived RUP as out of sync with what the masses of people really wanted—the materialistic "goodies" of liberal capitalism.

RUP founder and leader, José Angel Gutiérrez, addressing boycotting students in front of Crystal City High School, December 1969. The walkout became the catalyst for the founding of RUP in Texas. Photo courtesy of Oscar Castillo.

RUP Zavala County leader, Virginia Musquiz, explains to a Crystal City voter the procedures for RUP's county write-in campaign in 1970. Photo courtesy of José Angel Gutiérrez.

RUP school board meeting in Crystal City, Texas, summer 1974. The meeting's agenda focused on the appointment of Amancio Cantu as district school superintendent. Photo courtesy of José Angel Gutiérrez.

Texas RUP gubernatorial candidate, Ramsey Muñez, delivering a speech during the 1972 campaign. Ramsey ran again unsuccessfully for governor in 1974. Photo courtesy of José Angel Gutiérrez.

Poster of Colorado RUP gubernatorial candidate, Albert Gurrule, produced for the 1970 election campaign. Photo courtesy of Albert Gurrule.

Armando Navarro at the National Chicano Moratorium Anti-Vietnam War March held in Los Angeles on August 29, 1970. He organized a large contingent from San Bernardino and Riverside counties. Two months later, Navarro began organizing the California RUP in those two counties. Photo from the author's collection.

RUP California leader, Herman Baca, from San Diego registering Mr. Mendoza into the party. Photo courtesy of Herman Baca.

José Angel Gutiérrez (left) and California RUP leader, Raul Ruiz, from Los Angeles presiding over RUP's National Convention at El Paso, Texas, in September 1972. Ruiz was the RUP candidate for the 40th and 48th assembly districts and for mayor in the unsuccessful attempt to incorporate East Los Angeles. Photo courtesy of Oscar Castillo.

José Angel Gutiérrez at one of several press conferences he called during the RUP National Convention in El Paso in September 1972. Photo courtesy of Oscar Castillo.

José Angel Gutiérrez, Reies Lopez Tijerina, and Rodolfo "Corky" Gonzalez (left to right) clasping hands in a gesture of RUP unity during the national convention in El Paso. Photo courtesy of Oscar Castillo.

A RUP contingent from Los Angeles marching in the East Los Angeles Mexican Independence Day Parade in 1972. Photo courtesy of Raul Ruiz.

Texas RUP State Chairperson Maria Elena Martinez (front row, right), New Mexico RUP State Chairperson Juan José Peña (back row, right), and RUP National Chairperson José Angel Gutiérrez (back row, left) at the National RUP Consejo meeting held in Albuquerque, New Mexico, in 1978. Photo courtest of Juan José Peña.

Mexico's President Luis Echeverría Alvarez meeting with Texas RUP leaders in San Antonio, Texas, in 1972. From left to right are José Angel Gutiérrez, Jesus Gomez, Amado Peña, President Echeverría, Francisco Benavides, and Ramsey Muñiz. Photo courtesy of José Angel Gutiérrez.

José Angel Gutiérrez, head of a RUP delegation that traveled to Cuba in 1975, shaking hands with a Cuban government of½cial. Photo courtesy of Abel Cavada.

RUP delegation meeting with Palestinian Liberation Organization leader Yasser Arafat in Beirut, Lebanon, in 1980. From left to right are Larry Hill, Ignacio Garcia, Frank Schafer, Juan José Peña, Danny Osuna, Yasser Arafat, Rebecca Hill, Tony Gonzalez, Miguel Perez, Eddie Canales, and Fred Saint John. Photo courtesy of Juan José Peña.

Mexico's Partido Socialista de Trabajadores (PST) General Assembly held in Mexico City, November 1981. Seated fourth from right is California RUP leader Xenaro Ayala from San Fernando, who became the last RUP national chairperson in 1981 and in 1999 was still serving in that capacity. Photo courtesy of Xenaro Ayala.

*Chapter Eight*

---

# A Vehicle for Self-Determination: The Rise and Fall of RUP in New Mexico, 1971–1984

The states of Texas, Colorado, and California were the pace setters in the development of the Raza Unida Party (RUP). However, by 1971 activists in New Mexico joined in the struggle to build a Chicano political party as an alternative to the major parties. The formation of RUP in New Mexico occurred at a time when the Chicano Movement (CM) was at its apogee and increasingly had taken a posture of political empowerment.

## The Historical Setting: A Template for Governance

The experience of Méxicanos in New Mexico was unique. Whereas in Texas, Colorado, and California, Méxicanos suffered from an internal colonial history of political oppression, disenfranchisement, and powerlessness, this was not necessarily the case in New Mexico. The literature on the Chicano experience in New Mexico is rich with references to its unique historical development. It was the first area of what is today the United States to have been settled by Spanish settlers, specifically Juan Oñate and his expedition in 1598. From then until Mexico lost the Southwest to the United States in 1848, New Mexico was the locus of Spanish and Mexican colonization. From the conclusion of the U.S. war on Mexico to 1972, Méxicano or Hispano elites had always been an intrinsic part of New Mexico's political superstructure and leadership.[1] This was true of no other state.

A contributing factor to this unique political experience was the fact that Méxicanos from 1848 to the 1930s comprised the majority of the state's population. At the conclusion of the U.S. war on Mexico in 1848, Méxicanos in the Southwest numbered approximately 75,000. New Mexico had the largest Méxicano population, numbering some 60,000, compared to California's 7,500, Texas's 5,000, and Arizona's 1,000.[2]

Méxicanos continued to constitute a majority until the 1930s. George Sanchez, in his appraisal of the 1930s, from school and census data concluded that Méxicanos comprised 52 percent of the state's population in 1930, 270,475 persons.[3] However, the influx of Whites into New Mexico by 1940 relegated Méxicanos to a new "minority" status; they composed only 49.1 percent of the state's population.[4]

By 1950, the proportion of the state's residents with Hispanic surnames had dropped to 37 percent. In only ten of the thirty-two counties did Méxicanos make up 50 percent or more of the population.[5] By the early 1970s, when RUP was being formed, the Méxicano population had increased slightly to approximately 40 percent. Thus, Méxicanos in New Mexico always had the numbers to wield political power.

A cursory examination of New Mexico's politics clearly indicates the Méxicanos' political involvement and enfranchisement. Méxicano elites in New Mexico had considerable power from 1848 to the 1970s. Prior to statehood in 1912, Méxicanos were territorial governors and congressmen who controlled the territorial legislature for years; they were the judges, administrators, and county and local officials. In other words, they were part of the political system that participated in and at times controlled the government. Historian Juan Gomez Quiñonez comments on this point: "The positive enumeration of the participating elite in New Mexico included nine members who served as territorial delegates to the U.S. Congress; they provided strong representation in both territorial houses, and their strength was also measured by the number of local offices they held and by their significant representation in the eventual statehood constitution."[6]

This is not saying, however, that the masses of poor people were empowered. The territory of New Mexico in essence had a representative democratic form of government that was controlled by elites for elites. It was the *rico* (rich) Méxicano elite, or *patrones,* as they were called, who controlled the governance process. There was a pattern of competition for power among the sometimes contentious Republican and Democrat Méxicano elites. Impoverished Méxicanos were political pawns for the competing Méxicano and White elites.

Throughout the "New Mexican Experience," Méxicano elites collaborated with emerging White elites to control the politics of the territory. One example was the Santa Fe Ring. According to historian Rodolfo Acuña: "In New Mexico, the Santa Fe Ring controlled territorial politics, while a number of smaller, satellite rings operated at the county levels. Land acquisition was their cardinal objective to the degree that ring members 'grabbed' an estimated 80 percent of New Mexico's land grants."[7] Hence, Méxicano surnames such as Chavez, Otero, Montoya, and Luna are commonplace in the history of the state's politics. Méxicano elites protected their interests by joining the leadership ranks of both major parties.

In spite of this commitment to the two major parties, some Méxicanos during the 1890s participated in the formation of a third party—*El Partido Del Pueblo Unido* (the United People's Party, or PPU). This set an important historical precedent in that prior to RUP's emergence, Méxicanos had already participated in third-party movements. The PPU's political roots were deep in the protest activities of Las Gorras Blancas.

By the 1880s, the economic situation for many Nuevo Méxicanos had deteriorated considerably. Through a variety of legal and illegal means, especially chicanery, poor Méxicanos had lost their communal and private lands to White and Méxicano elite business interests, for example, large land companies, cattlemen, and the railroads.[8] In protest, in about 1887, poor Méxicanos led by Juan José Herrera organized a clandestine armed self-defense group, Las Gorras Blancas, the White Caps.

In 1889, Las Gorras Blancas, armed with rifles and pistols, dressed in long coats and slickers, their faces hidden behind white masks, rode into Las Vegas, New Mexico, and confronted various local officials. Their use of nonconventional tactics such as tearing down fences, burning barns, and destroying railroad ties was condemned as anti-American and revolutionary.[9] Some Whites perceived their actions as a prelude to a war of independence.[10] By 1890, their intimidation and use of violence had considerably slowed the grabbing of land from Méxicanos.[11]

The protest activities of Las Gorras Blancas by 1890 had also created internal problems for the PPU. Formed in 1888 in San Miguel County by a number of disaffected Republicans and Democrats, the PPU sought to directly challenge the Republican Party, which controlled the politics of the county. While some Whites participated, the principal organizers and leaders of the PPU were Méxicanos: Felix Martinez, who was an influential and powerful businessman from San Miguel County; Juan José Herrera, who was head of Las Gorras Blancas and the local Knights of Labor; Lorenzo Delgado, a relative of the influential Republican Romero family; and Ezequiel de Vaca, a descendant of the founding families of Las Vegas.[12] It was a coalition of lower- to middle-class Méxicano Democrats, disgruntled middle-class Republicans, Anglo lawyers and laborers, and a larger and more resentful Méxicano labor constituency.

While the argument cannot be made that it was an all-Méxicano political party, it is fair to say that the Méxicanos' interests dominated PPU. Historian Juan Gomez Quiñonez explains the relationship of PPU to Las Gorras Blancas and its platform: "Ostensibly, the partido adopted as its platform the issues raised by Las Gorras Blancas, especially the issues of land and the common people's mistreatment by the dominant political leaders, both Anglo and Mexican." The partido also favored antimonopolistic positions. As a reform effort, the partido advocated anti-Republicanism, because the Republicans were associated with large land and railroad interests.[13]

PPU not only assumed the moral position of Las Gorras Blancas by embracing the land grant" issue, but took on the problem of local Republican "bossism." Ideologically, with its antimonopoly and anti–big business views, it was a precursor to the Populist Party. At the county level, it presented itself as a reform party committed to the advancement of the common people's welfare.[14]

In 1890, PPU reached its apogee when it won four seats in the assembly in the San Miguel County elections. However, without a majority, implementation of PPU's platform proved to be next to impossible. The influence it had gained was insufficient to overcome the problem of securing the electoral, judicial, and economic rights of the poor when the governmental infrastructure and process favored the rich. Pablo

Herrera, who had been one of the four elected, expressed his disillusionment: "I would prefer another term in prison than another election in to the house."[15]

In 1892, PPU again won control of San Miguel County, but by 1894 it was plagued by internal warfare over the party's platform and by distrust, primarily among its Méxicano leaders. A contributing factor was that it never developed consensus on its platform. Also, its members often did not share the class interests of its constituents; consequently, it began to lose their support.

There were a number of external antagonisms that also contributed to PPU's decline. The Republican Party mounted a fierce attack on it as well as on its support groups, Las Gorras Blancas and the Knights of Labor. These attacks were often supported by organizations such as the Sociedad de Los Caballeros de Ley y Orden y Protección Mutua (Society of Gentleman for Law, Order, and Mutual Protection). The Republicans in 1891 started their own newspaper, *El Sol de Mayo,* to counteract the sometimes supportive newspaper *La Voz del Pueblo.* There were several instances when physical violence and other forms of intimidation and harassment were used against PPU members and those suspected of being supportive of Las Gorras Blancas.[16] The new Populist Party with its stance against monopolies and big business became a competitor.

Thus, by 1896, the PPU had faded into history. The Méxicanos' sense of rebelliousness against their oppression, however, did not stop with the end of PPU, but continued through their involvement with Las Gorras Blancas. In 1903, for example, some 300 men rode for several nights through Anton Chico, destroying fences erected by Whites on what they said was Méxicano land. For years, law enforcement agencies tried to eradicate Las Gorras Blancas, but they did not cease to exist until the mid-1920s or so.

With the decline of PPU, no third party that subsequently emerged stimulated the interest of Méxicanos. For example, the Populist, Progressive, Socialist, and Farm-Labor Parties failed to galvanize strong support. Historian Jack E. Holmes explains why: "Immersed in the highly competitive two party politics of faction and coalition, through which the Republican Party for a time dominated the state, these counties had no ear, for various cultural and economic reasons, for the songs of populism. As a group the Hispanic counties cast about 60 percent of their vote for Republicans and except for a mild flirtation in 1912, refused to trifle with Progressive or other third party candidates."[17]

Méxicanos at the turn of the century became engaged with the issue of statehood. At the state constitutional convention of 1910, 35 of the 100 delegates were Méxicanos. They played an important leadership role in New Mexico's becoming the nation's forty-seventh state. From 1912 to the 1970s, the number of Méxicanos in the state legislature, for example, remained at about 20 percent.[18] While Whites increasingly became politically entrenched, Méxicanos, unlike their counterparts in other states, continued to play a significant political role, and a good percentage remained loyal to the Republican Party. From 1911 to 1928, for example, in the ten counties most heavily populated by Méxicanos, 60 percent cast their vote for Republicans.[19]

Moreover, the political template cast by Méxicanos in 1848 was still in place in the twentieth century. Méxicanos in New Mexico served as lieutenant governors and in the state legislature, courts, and local government as well as in the U.S. House of Representatives and U.S. Senate. One such political leader was Octaviano Ambrosio Larrazola, who as a Republican served from 1918 to 1920 and who in 1928 became the first Méxicano elected to the U.S. Senate. Although born in Sonora, Mexico, Larrazola grew up in Santa Fe, New Mexico. He died in 1929 while serving in the U.S. Senate. Six years later, Dennis Chavez replaced him. Chavez had served from 1930 to 1935 in the U.S. House of Representatives; he went on to serve in the U.S. Senate from 1935 to 1962. As a social commentary on the way the Méxicano was perceived by Whites, Chavez said, "If they go to war they are Americans; if they run for office, they're Spanish-Americans; but if they're looking for a job, they're damned Mexicans."[20] Between 1940 and 1960, Méxicanos ran three times unsuccessfully for governor. However, several were elected as lieutenant governors: Ceferino Quintana (1939–1942); Joséph Montoya (1946–1951 and 1954–1956); and Tibo J. Chavez (1951–1954). In 1964, Congressman Joséph Montoya was elected to the U. S. Senate and served until his defeat in 1976 by astronaut Harrison Schmitt.[21]

Méxicanos served in various other political capacities before the emergence of RUP in New Mexico in 1972. In the state legislature, at times, Méxicanos numbered about a third and on a few occasions served as speakers of the house and as senate leaders.[22] The important point is that in New Mexico, Méxicanos could not make the argument in the early 1970s that they had been excluded from the political process.

Indicative of the Méxicanos' access to the political system was the state's constitution and legislation. The constitution in Section 3, Article VII, protects, among other things, the right of citizens to vote regardless of their "religion, race, language or color," and regardless of their inability to handle effectively either the English or Spanish languages except as may be otherwise provided in the constitution. The fact is, the constitution stressed the virtues of "bilingualism" in education and in the publication of state documents, including voting ballots. This bilingual tradition remained in effect until the early 1970s, when it was made optional. Thus, at the height of the Chicano Movement, New Mexico, relatively speaking, was a pacesetter in the struggle for civil rights and in the quest to preserve the Méxicanos' rich cultural traditions and language. Joaquin Ortega, onetime director of the School of International Affairs at the University of New Mexico, asserted that New Mexico had the most homogenous Spanish-speaking community in the United States.[23] Yet, as George Sanchez wrote, "Almost one-hundred years after becoming American citizens, a broad gap separates them from the culture that surrounds them."[24]

Another third-party revolt that preceded RUP's emergence was the formation of the People's Constitutional Party (PCP) in 1968. The architect of this party was Reies Lopez Tijerina, who was also the founder of the Alianza Federal de Pueblos Libres—the Alianza.[25] Both entities were products of the militancy that pervaded the epoch of protest. They were both impelled by some of the same concerns, such as the issue of land grants, that gave rise to Las Gorras Blancas and PPU. Like Pablo Herrera, Tijerina was a maverick who became a protest leader in defense of the poor who had lost their land to rich land barons or the federal government.

PCP's emergence was due to the Aliancistas' alienation from and discontent with the politics of the state's two major parties. From the time Tijerina founded the Alianza in 1963, to 1969 when he was sent to prison, he was the CM's most notorious and controversial leader. A fiery Pentecostal preacher and a zealous advocate, Tijerina built the Alianza into a formidable organization with a mobilization capability that commanded respect from both friend and foe.

When the Alianza was formed in 1963, it was essentially a moderate pressure group that practiced an accommodationist mode of politics. It was not until 1965 that it began to carry out a militant type of protest that entailed the use of civil disobedience and, eventually, violence. The militant approach became evident when the Alianza organized a massive march to the state capitol in 1965, the occupation of the Echo Amphitheater in 1966, and the Tierra Amarilla Courthouse Raid in 1967.[26] No leader or organization in New Mexico contributed more to the development of the CM in that state than did Tijerina and the Alianza.

The Alianza took its struggle into the electoral arena in 1968. Besides participating in the Poor People's March on Washington, D.C., that same year, Tijerina opted to take the Alianza's land grant struggle into the political arena by forming the PCP. This was the second time that a third party had been formed involving the land grant issue. Although it was oriented toward poor people, meaning that its general appeal was to all the poor, including Whites, its base of support came mostly from Méxicanos who supported the Alianza.

Under the aegis of the Alianza, the PCP that year held several conventions in the northern part of the state. As a result, a rather populist platform was adopted that resembled that of the PPU. It called for bilingual/bicultural education for Méxicano children, civilian police review boards, investigation of land speculators, the end of discrimination in local draft boards, an increase in welfare payments, the pardon of some felons, lowering of the voting age to eighteen, and protecting the rights of those with different life-styles.[27] There was nothing radical or anti–liberal capitalist about PCP's platform.

During the conventions, candidates for both state and county offices were selected. While continuing his activism with the Alianza, Tijerina was nominated to run for governor. From the outset, there were legal problems related to getting PCP on the ballot as an official party. At that time, the state required only that a petition with 100 signatures be submitted to the secretary of state along with the names of the party's officers. In early October, the secretary of state disqualified eight PCP candidates, including Tijerina. His ineligibility was due to a previous felony conviction. Tijerina used the disqualification as an issue through which to vehemently attack the Democrats. After a successful petition filed with the state supreme court by the American Civil Liberties Union on behalf of the PCP and Tijerina in late October, the candidates, with the exception of Tijerina, were put back on the ballot. José Alfredo Maestas replaced Tijerina as the PCP gubernatorial candidate.[28]

Plagued by problems, PCP received only 2 percent of the total vote. According to political scientist Maurillo Vigil, the "PCP challenge was not a serious threat to the major parties . . . as the highest vote a PCP candidate received was 2,884 in the race for State Treasurer." PCP's candidate for governor, Maestas, received only 1,540 votes.[29] PCP failed in its attempt to challenge the entrenched and omnipotent major parties. Part of the problem was that Tijerina had become such a controversial personality, the press and the two major opposition parties depicted him and PCP as fringe and antisystem figures.

While the electoral efforts of PCP were not impressive, the election allowed Tijerina and others to advance their land grant struggle by attacking both political parties. In other words, like other third parties, the PCP sought to educate the electorate as to the virtues of its *causa*. Because of the collective pressure exerted by PCP and the Alianza, Augustus Hawkins, a Black congressman from Los Angeles, introduced a Community Land Grant Bill, and the Presbyterian Church announced plans to restore some of the land that it owned to land grant heirs.[30]

The PCP ran again in 1970, without Tijerina, who was in prison. It ran candidates for both state and county positions unsuccessfully. Although it failed to have any major electoral impact, its candidates did a little better than those in 1968. Its presence was instrumental in helping pressure the state legislature to liberalize the state's campaign laws. But, like so many other third-party attempts, the PCP proved to be transitory. With the release of Tijerina in 1971, PCP was officially disbanded on the grounds that it had served its purpose.[31] Thus, both the Alianza and PCP acted as catalytic agents that helped radicalize New Mexico's political climate, which in turn helped give rise to the CM.[32]

## The Chicano Movement: Precursor to RUP

New Mexico's political climate from 1965 to 1972 was permeated with the protest politics of the CM. Although Tijerina was incarcerated between 1969 and 1971 on charges of destroying federal property, the Alianza continued to function, but weakly. Even after Tijerina's prison release in 1971, the Alianza never regained the momentum necessary to make it a viable advocate for social change. By the conditions of his parole, Tijerina was not allowed to hold any leadership role in the Alianza. By 1972, he had shifted to preaching the cultural gospel of national brotherhood awareness. He underwent a dramatic attitudinal change—he was no longer the firebrand militant on the issue of the land grants.

Impelled by rising expectations and politically alienated, activist youth from the barrios, universities, and colleges in New Mexico from 1967 to 1972 contributed to the climate for change that fostered the emergence of both the CM and RUP. They were influenced not only by the radicalism of Tijerina, but by two other important endogenous antagonisms: Rodolfo "Corky" Gonzales's Crusade for Justice and Cesar Chavez's United Farm Workers (UFW). Gonzales's charisma as a leader and the

Crusade for Justice's cultural nationalist sectarianism, coupled with Colorado's proximity and historical ties to New Mexico, significantly influenced the young activists. While Chavez's UFW organizing efforts were not as strong in New Mexico as they were in other states, the romance of the farm worker movement also contributed to the emergence of the CM in New Mexico.[33]

With the start-up of the Chicano Youth Movement in New Mexico during the late 1960s, a spirit of radicalism began to surface in the barrios in the shape of the Black and Brown Berets. Both were barrio based, and self-defense, paramilitary, and cultural nationalist in orientation. While the Berets organized in the barrios, Chicano students organized in the state's universities and colleges. The Berets, for example, were active in confronting police brutality in Albuquerque. Student organizations, such as the United Mexican American Students (UMAS) at the University of New Mexico, were active on a variety of educational and community issues. Through their activism, Chicano Studies as well as other programs were created, Chicano student enrollment increased, and Chicano faculty, staff, and administrators were hired. This brought some resources for organizing and conducting outreach to the various Méxicano communities and barrios. The Chicano youth activism was complemented by the activist journalism of Elizabeth "Betita" Martinez and Enriqueta Longauez y Vasques through their newspaper, *El Grito del Norte*.[34] Thus, with a climate propitious for change, Chicano activists in New Mexico in 1971 joined the growing RUP rebellion against the nation's two monopolistic political parties.

## The Rise of the Raza Unida Party, 1971–1972

RUP was not embraced in New Mexico until 1971. Why did it take a year for RUP organizing efforts to begin? The answer lies in New Mexico's history of Méxicano political participation. For example, in 1971 Méxicanos comprised approximately 38 percent of New Mexico's population. The state had the highest percentage of Méxicanos and of elected officials in the country. Using 1965 figures, in the state legislature, while New Mexico had twenty-two, Texas had six, California none, and Colorado one. By 1973, the number in New Mexico had increased to thirty-two.[35] In light of such high percentages in population and political representation, one might presume that the idea of Méxicanos having their own political party would be better received there than anywhere else in the country; however, this proved not to be the case, as Acuña explains: "The New Mexico RUP found it impossible to organize because Chicanos often controlled the local Democratic Party machines."[36]

Another important factor against RUP's emergence was that the party was not the product of prominent leaders or organizations. Unlike Texas or Colorado, where RUP was indeed a product of charismatic leaders and strong organizations, efforts to organize RUP in New Mexico resembled the effort in California, with the emergence of multiple leaders and organizations during the organizing process. Chicano activists in New Mexico who were involved in various struggles of the Chicano Movement followed with great interest RUP's development in these three states. In particular, the electoral successes of RUP in Texas coupled with the Crusade for Justice's efforts in Colorado influenced a number of Méxicanos to begin the formation of RUP in New Mexico during the early months of 1971.

RUP in New Mexico sprang from two simultaneous but independent organizing efforts. One was in San Miguel County (Las Vegas), the other in Bernalillo County (Albuquerque). In San Miguel County, RUP's formation started in February 1971, when José Angel Gutiérrez spoke at Highlands University. Pedro Rodriguez, who was the head of Chicano Studies, invited Gutiérrez to speak. Before coming to Highlands University, Rodriguez had been active with the RUP in Texas. During his visit, Gutiérrez met with local Chicano activists, most of whom were students from the Chicano Associated Student Organization (CASO), and convinced some of them to start organizing RUP. Juan José Peña, whose great-grandfather had been a member of the PPU, told me when interviewed that RUP "essentially came to us from the outside."[37]

Political parties are the products of leaders. In the case of RUP in New Mexico, from its rise to its decline several leaders emerged, but initially two stood out: Juan José Peña and Manuel Archuleta. When they started organizing RUP, both were students at Highland University. Peña was a Vietnam veteran and graduate student working on his master's degree. Archuleta was an undergraduate student who was well versed in the writings of the Socialist Labor Party, particularly those of Daniel de Leon, its founder.[38] During the formation of RUP, numerous study sessions were held at which De Leon's writings as well as those of others were examined. According to Peña, "From the very beginning to its decline in 1981, the leadership of the Raza Unida in San Miguel County was ideologically socialist."[39] It was out of San Miguel County that these two student leaders supported by CASO became major leaders in New Mexico in the organizing of RUP. (This was the same county that had given birth to PPU some eighty years earlier.)

Throughout 1971, several house meetings were held, a countywide organizing committee was formed, and research was conducted on the legal requirements to get RUP on the ballot. According to Peña, getting RUP on the ballot at the county level was not that difficult. It merely required that the necessary paperwork be filled out and submitted to the secretary of state, including the names of officers.

By March 1972, a similar RUP organizing effort had begun in Bernalillo County. Efforts to organize RUP there began in late 1971 and were spearheaded by Chris Eichwald Cebada of Cuba, New Mexico, who had been a member of the Brown Berets in Albuquerque and of MEChA at the University of New Mexico.[40] Peña explains that he " was designated to come and visit with the people that were organizing the partido in Bernalillo County. They were ahead of us in that they had registered with the secretary of state and were ready to charter. So I took it back to the San Miguel County organization. They decided to go ahead and let the Bernalillo County charter the [partido] statewide; then San Miguel would come in."[41]

RUP activists from both counties met in July 1972 to formally initiate RUP statewide in New Mexico.[42] Interim state officers to the partido's State Central Committee were elected, including Santiago Maestas, state president; Larry Candelaria, vice president; Dan Armijo, treasurer; and Arlene Candelaria, secretary. A total of twelve persons comprised the first RUP State Central Committee. At a press conference held to formally announce the formation of RUP, Maestas explained why RUP was being organized: "The New Mexico Raza Unida Party recognizes that the two major political parties of the state have failed to protect and defend our people's interest. It has been created out of the need for a truly representative political force to protect and further the human rights, education, and economic interests of our people."[43]

On the issue of land, Maestas said, "The partido's objective is to establish the idea that the natural resources of this state belong to the people of the state." He announced that RUP would begin to circulate petitions in seven counties in order to get on the ballot as an official political party. In 1971, the state legislature had lowered the percentage of petition signatures needed to qualify a third party for official ballot status from the 5 percent to 3 percent of the last votes cast.[44] For RUP activists, this meant acquiring some 10,000 signatures; Maestas reported that they had already secured some 1,000 signatures.[45]

It was in San Miguel County that RUP's political base developed fastest. That summer RUP there elected its countywide officers: Pedro Rodriguez, president; Juan José Peña, vice president; Manuel Archuleta, treasurer; and Federico Trujillo, secretary. Four other persons were also elected to the County Central Committee. Its activist membership consisted of a cadre of university and high school students and community people that included former Alianistas.[46] In the university, CASO students were RUP's organizing catalysts.[47]

From the beginning, no RUP county chapter in the state could match San Miguel's intense organizing for both electoral and social change. A cardinal reason for San Miguel County's success was its adherence to a pragmatic service and advocate approach. Its leadership believed that by meeting the material and everyday needs of the people, it would gain support and gather a mass base for RUP. As a chapter, it provided a variety of volunteer services: distributed clothes to the needy, brought legal aid services to the community, and provided emergency relief. As an advocate, it was always prepared to take on civil rights and social justice issues, such as welfare rights, education, and job discrimination.[48] Peña explained, "Our approach relied on putting a spin on the issues facing the community, not on the use of ideology."[49] Peña and others in San Miguel County followed a rather pragmatic Alinskyst approach, similar in some respects to the Mexican American Youth Organization in Texas.[50]

When addressing the community or the general public via the media, San Miguel's RUP activists refrained from using Marxist terminology or rhetoric. They understood the moderate to conservative political culture and the strong religious inclinations of most Méxicanos in New Mexico. Unlike other Left-oriented RUP activists in California, they were careful not to turn off the people by being labeled a bunch of radicals out to create trouble.[51]

In August 1972, RUP held its first statewide convention, in Albuquerque. Approximately 100 activists from throughout New Mexico representing seven counties attended. San Miguel County brought the largest delegation, forty. Permanent state officers were elected: Juan José Peña, state president; Chris Eichwald Cebada, vice president; Harold Martinez, treasurer; and Nancy Montaño, secretary. A number of resolutions were passed as a prelude to the RUP national convention. They voted that RUP would not support Democrat George McGovern for president of the United States. Furthermore, as a state delegation, they would propose at the RUP national convention at El Paso, Texas, that September that RUP run its own presidential candidate.[52] Peña delineated the underlying rationale for organizing RUP in New Mexico: "Partido de la Raza Unida was founded this summer in New Mexico because the two major political parties were not serving the needs of 'our people. . . . The Chicano, or Indo-Hispano, in the Southwest has been under-represented by both of the major parties. . . . The Partido intends to attempt to fill this vacuum which has existed for a long time and which has been detrimental to our people. . . . The Partido also intends to bring many other issues, grievances, and injustices to light in order that the public may become more aware of them."[53]

Peña acknowledged that in spite of the fact that Méxicanos had a history of political representation in the state, neither major political party had served their interests, especially those of the poor. He described RUP's emerging political role as being multifarious, which is emblematic of most third parties. He emphasized RUP's commitment to the empowerment and franchisement of the Méxicano, and he stressed RUP's educational, pressure, and advocacy roles.[54]

RUP's structure was hierarchical in that it included a county organization or chapter and a state governing body; at the apex was the state convention, which met the last weekend of April of each year. County chapters were given limited autonomy to deal with their particular needs and issues. A minimum of six persons constituted the embryo of RUP's county organization. Once they filed with their respective county clerks, they in essence formed RUP's county central committee and became eligible for chartering by the state central committee. Between conventions, the state central committee of some twelve persons, including one representative from each county chapter, was the main decision-making body. A form of democratic centralism was used in making decisions. In essence, RUP's structural orientation was that of a cadre party of activists.[55]

RUP's platform from the outset was socialist and anti–liberal capitalist. RUP's leaders in both San Miguel and Bernalillo Counties were ideologically socialist in their orientation. In San Miguel, they initially identified more with the Socialist Labor Party line. The leadership of Bernarlillo identified more with the Marxist-Leninist theories of the Communist Party.[56] The reality was, RUP's leaders in both counties were Marxists in theory. They couched their sectarianism in pragmatism. In the beginning, RUP's ideology and practice were reform oriented. While there were some within its ranks who preached the gospel of socialist dialectical materialism, some did propound the virtues of cultural nationalism and of a "separatist" Aztlán. The interest in cultural nationalism was influenced by RUP's leaders out of Texas and Colorado, that is, Gutiérrez and Gonzales.

RUP's evolving platform in New Mexico was much more doctrinaire than that of Texas or other areas. It resembled more the platform developed out of Northern California, especially from the San Francisco area. In the area of labor, it advocated the workers' right to strike, support for the UFW, parity in wages, an end to the exploitation of undocumented workers, a guaranteed annual income, an end to right-to-work laws, and so on. RUP's progressive ideas were manifested in its plank on the economy, which postulated that the capitalist economy could be restructured into becoming more equitable by creating a redistribution of wealth that would break up the nation's monopolies. In education, it proposed that bilingual/bicultural education be extended to all levels and that higher education be made available for Chicanos. It advocated adequate housing, free health care, free legal aid, an end to police brutality, and community control of law enforcement agencies. In foreign policy, it called for the withdrawal of U.S. troops from Indochina. Two other strong planks were a call for equal rights in all spheres of life for all Chicanas, and a call for the honoring of the Treaty of Guadalupe Hidalgo and all land grants.[57]

Politically, the platform called for community control of all institutions; simply put, it called for self-determination, translated to mean "complete political independence."[58] As the years passed, RUP's platform became increasingly anti–liberal capitalist, but still eclectic in its ideological tendencies—a mixture of cultural nationalism, socialism, and separatism.

In September 1972, the New Mexico party sent the third largest delegation to the RUP national convention held in El Paso, Texas. Reies Lopez Tijerina, who had been released from prison in 1971, was invited to attend the convention by both José Angel Gutiérrez and RUP's leadership in New Mexico. Tijerina had come out of prison a different man. At the convention, he sought to be the "unifier" (the convention is thoroughly examined in Chapter Eleven). His leadership role at the convention was problematic to some delegates, since he had never been an advocate of RUP.

The New Mexico RUP delegation's role at the convention, initially, was to act as peacemaker between the contentious leaders Gutiérrez and Gonzales.[59] They were caught in a difficult political situation, since they had respect and admiration for both leaders. Yet as the convention proceeded, the New Mexico delegation sided with Gutiérrez, who was elected RUP's national chairperson. When interviewed, Peña commented that they supported Gutiérrez "because we had been active politically in New Mexico in large numbers for a long time; the vast majority felt that José Angel Gutiérrez's pragmatic approach to the movement was the way to go."[60] The delegation also played an important role in the various resolutions that were passed. One such resolution was that Cesar Chavez should not be invited to participate with the partido, since as a labor leader he had shown loyalty to the Democratic Party.[61]

Right after the convention, RUP in New Mexico continued its dualistic approach of advocacy and electoral action. Even though the RUP national convention produced unbridgeable gaps nationwide within the fledgling Chicano partido, RUP's efforts in New Mexico continued to accelerate, relatively free of internal power struggles. While some two-thirds of RUP adherents supported Gutiérrez and the other one-third Gonzales, at no time did differences foster internal antagonisms that might have threatened to split the partido. This was also true of the ideological differences that existed within RUP's leadership and ranks. There was a sense of respect and tolerance for each other's differences and *politica* (politics).

After the El Paso convention, the partido held several demonstrations in southern New Mexico in response to the killing of Richard Falcon by Perry Brunson in Orogrande, which occurred just before RUP's national convention. These demonstrations were carried out in front of the Otero County Courthouse in Alamogordo where Brunson was being tried. Acting as Brunson's legal counsel was Albert Rivera.[62]

Some RUP activists intensified their efforts to build RUP into a competitive electoral-oriented political party. They worked to expand their organizing efforts into other counties by forming chapters. Concurrently, RUP voter registrations and recruitment drives were initiated to get new members into the already active county chapters. Despite a concerted effort, RUP was unsuccessful in its drive to secure the 10,000 signatures required to get on the 1972 ballot. The required signatures needed to be turned in by September. In spite of the setback, the first RUP electoral challenge occurred that same year, 1972, in San Miguel County.

The San Miguel County RUP chapter for several years had been politically the most active and visible of the county chapters. Its activism was especially apparent in the electoral arena; that summer it decided to run candidates for the county elections. Two of its candidates were for county clerk and probate judge and three for county commissioner. The former two were certified candidates; the latter were write-in candidates. They filed late and were denied ballot access. The chapter litigated the matter, but the court ruling came too late. In the process, however, RUP decided to run the three candidates for county commissioner using a write-in campaign. They were Juan José Peña, Manuel Archuleta, and Pedro Rodriguez.

With hardly any finances and few volunteers, and categorized by the opposition as a radical fringe partido, RUP in its first electoral challenge was a dismal failure. The certified candidates garnered slightly over 200 votes, while the write-in candidates did even worse—they got 60 votes. Political scientist Maurillo Vigil wrote that the results indicated that RUP "had established its small base of loyal supporters, and more importantly that of the 231 [RUP] registered voters in the county virtually all went to the polls."[63] What he did not say, however, was that not all of them voted for RUP's candidates, especially its write-in candidates.

Beyond electoral politics, RUP activists in October 1972 participated in Tijerina's National Congress for Land and Cultural Reform held at the old Albuquerque Convention Center in Albuquerque. Attended by some 1,000 activists, the conference was organized under the rubric of "National Brotherhood Awareness." Peña and other RUP activists from New Mexico at the conference played important leadership roles.

## RUP: An Advocate for Social Change, 1973–1976

Between 1973 and 1976, most RUP chapters functioned as both pressure group and political party, in theory seeking both to control government and to influence public policy. But in practice, most of the RUP chapters' emphasis was on the latter. Statewide, RUP assumed a pressure and advocate role and continued to take on a variety of issues. Out of New Mexico's thirty-two counties, RUP's organizing activity during this time and beyond 1976 was limited to the following seven: San Miguel, Bernalillo, Rio Arriba, Taos, Union, Otero, and Sandoval. While some partido chapters did engage in electoral activity, such as those in Bernalillo, Otero, and Rio Arriba Counties, with the exception of the last, none were successful in electing a Méxicano to any public office. The exception was the election of two RUP school board candidates to the Jemez Mountain Independent School District in 1975.[64] Despite several electoral attempts in these three counties, RUP was never able to realize community control of any local political structure.

While all seven chapters embraced an advocacy posture, the four county chapters (San Miguel, Taos, Union, and Sandoval) were strictly advocacy oriented in their political activities. They did not have an interest in ballot-box politics. Their strategic perspective was that RUP should be a cadre vanguard political party rather than one that was electoral oriented. They thrived by confronting a myriad of issues and community social problems. For example, the Union County RUP chapter was very much involved in fighting discrimination and police brutality; the Taos County chapter fought discrimination. Sandoval was the most passive and least action oriented of the seven chapters.[65]

The two most active RUP chapters to emerge during these three years, both oriented toward social change, were the San Miguel County and Rio Arriba County chapters. Of the two, the San Miguel County chapter was the most tenacious in its struggle to empower and bring about change for the people. While actively involved with providing some services and doing some advocacy, it became engaged in Las Vegas in a school board election in 1973. This nonpartisan election became problematic for RUP. The school board was comprised of liberal Méxicanos who had already instituted various educational reforms. Nevertheless, the chapter made the decision to challenge them and ran two candidates, one of whom was Peña. The two RUP candidates ran on a platform advocating bilingual/bicultural education and recruitment of more Méxicano teachers and administrators into the system. The two opponents who were White were better financed and organized.

As was the case with most RUP organizing efforts, the RUP candidates lacked the money, volunteers, and everything else needed to run a credible and serious campaign. Not surprisingly, with other Méxicano candidates running as well, both White candidates won handily. Yet Peña received 25 percent of the vote, and his running mate got 26 percent—much higher percentages than those of the other Méxicano candidates in the race. According to Vigil, "Had the two [RUP] candidates been running alone against the two Anglos, the race would have undoubtedly been much closer." However, the political reality was that the two RUP candidates had split the Nuevo Méxicano vote, thus allowing the two white candidates to win.[66]

By 1973, RUP's base of support had gradually broadened with the inclusion of more former members and leaders of the Alianza. Tijerina's leadership was in a downward spiral, to some degree induced by the conditions of his parole. This contributed, in part, to the exodus of some Aliancistas into RUP. Another factor was the conflict and schisms within the Alianza itself, which Peña explained in our 1997 interview.

> There was a split over ideology within the Alianza. While Reyes was in prison, the Alianza had passed a resolution . . . in favor of the formation of an independent Chicano nation and of the unification of the Spanish-speaking people of the Americas. When he came out he opposed it. . . . Tijerina had lost control of his organization around this time period, because there were a lot of divisions as to the way the land grant movement should be pursued. In fact, half of the Alianza came into the Partido de la Raza Unida. Santiago Tapia y Anaya, who was one of Tijerina's rivals, brought his half of the Alianza into the partido and so the partido was expanded by [their] presence.[67]

In 1973, the San Miguel County RUP chapter became involved with two major educational issues. The first occurred during the first part of the year with the East Las Vegas public schools. Both RUP and CASO exerted pressure and presented a list of demands to the East Las Vegas School District, one of which included the hiring of more Méxicano teachers. Although there were two Méxicanos on the school board, it was White controlled. With the school superintendent, Fred Pomeroy, and the board not supportive of RUP and CASO's demands, the conflict quickly escalated. The board held community meetings on the matter, especially on the issue of replacing the superintendent. In the process of dealing with the issue, Elizabeth "Betita" Martinez, editor of *El Grito del Norte,* suggested that a "broader based" coalition be formed under a new name that would include others, such as Democrats who were not affiliated with the partido or CASO. The new coalition was named Chicanos Unidos para Justicia (Chicanos United for Justice, or CUJ).

As the issue intensified, a number of incidents occurred that were indicative of the polarization of Whites and Méxicanos. A White sheriff's posse member stabbed Gustavo Cordova, who was from Taos, in the back. In addition, several leaders of the CUJ were shot at, including Peña. The windows of one of his cars were also broken with rocks. He fired at the perpetrators with a rifle as they sped away.[68] The East Las Vegas education issue was diffused with the hiring of José Vasquez as school superintendent. Even though Vasquez was not a supporter of RUP, the issues that had driven the protests were effectively dealt with by his administration. In particular, he was able to increase the number of Méxicano teachers and administrators considerably.

The East Las Vegas issues revealed the tensions between Méxicanos and Whites. They also revealed the willingness of some RUP activists to counteract violence with violence. The fact that Peña had returned fire demonstrated RUP's willingness to use arms in self-defense. Within the San Miguel County chapter, there was a covert Violence Committee chaired by Peña's bodyguard, Patricio Paiz. It was organized to use force only if partido members were attacked with firearms. It was customary for most of RUP's officers and some of its members to carry weapons for protection. In his unpublished manuscript "The Chicano Movement in New Mexico," he writes about an incident related to the East Las Vegas educational issue: "After several threats and shootings, the violence committee determined that one of the Sheriff's Posse members was the ringleader and unleashed a fusillade against his house and forced him to leave town. The violence committee kept observers all around the city of Las Vegas in order to know who came and went in the city and especially to be informed if strangers came into town."

Thus, unlike other RUP entities throughout the Southwest and Midwest, in New Mexico, it was rather commonplace for some RUP chapters to be armed and trained for self-defense purposes. The Otero County RUP chapter, for example, engaged in guerrilla warfare training around Alamogordo. Some of the RUP activists were convinced that ethnic warfare between Whites and Méxicanos was inevitable.

In late September 1973, RUP in San Miguel County again engaged in an educational confrontation. This time it was against Highlands University. In September of 1972, Peña, who was RUP's state chairperson at the time, was hired as a Spanish instructor at the university and became faculty advisor to CASO. In the ensuing months, he had run-ins with the administration because the university was not recruiting Méxicanos into its departments. CASO as well began to pressure university president Frank Angel on the affirmative action issue.

After months of meetings and negotiations, the disagreement only intensified, especially because the administration had failed to renew the contract of Pedro Rodriguez, a RUP leader. CASO and RUP responded by holding demonstrations, and CASO's newspaper El Machete fanned the fires of discontent. This issue opened a Pandora's box of other issues: the hiring of new faculty, the slow implementation of Chicano Studies, and the failure to hire more Chicano professors.

The issue escalated into a confrontation between students and the administration. Students, under the guise of the Chicano Student Justice Committee which included CASO members, held a sit-in demonstration at the administration building after President Angel repeatedly refused to meet with them to discuss their grievances. Its counterpart in the community was CUJ, chaired by Peña, which included both RUP supporters and Democrats. Journalist Richard Everett wrote about the relationship between RUP and CUJ: "Partido de La Raza Unida may not win elections in the near future, but it unquestionably is the most dynamic force in the Las Vegas area today. The leadership and members of La Raza Unida are avowedly and proudly activist. They believe in protesting publicly against whatever upsets them. They frighten a lot of non-activist people . . . La Raza Unida and another organization, known as Chicanos Unidos para Justicia whose leadership is interchangeable and almost identical with the party, have won some victories."[69]

The groups' demands included student control over the hiring of faculty for Chicano Studies, full funding of Chicano Studies, and the hiring of Peña as the director of Chicano Studies. The protests culminated with the arrest of forty-one students. Some $30,000 was raised to free them, class boycotts were initiated, and the student senate passed a resolution that no disciplinary action be taken against those arrested.[70]

After weeks of pressure, the administration acquiesced to several of the demands. According to Peña, they "raised so much hell" that he was given a new contract as a consultant for the 1973–1974 academic year, instructor status in 1974, and the title of Coordinator for Ethnic and Chicano Studies. This was in response to Peña's earlier loss of his National Teaching Fellowship, which had paid his salary as an instructor. Even more significant was the number of Méxicano faculty hired between 1973 and 1975. In 1971 there were only six Méxicano faculty members; by 1975, 68 of 140 faculty members were Méxicano.[71]

In the community the close working relationship between RUP and CUJ proved to be transitory. During the summer of 1973, CUJ separated formally from RUP over differences of direction. David Montoya replaced Peña as CUJ chairperson, and, under the direction of Betita Martinez, CUJ sought to distance itself from RUP. It established a Chicano alternative school and farm cooperative at Montezuma. According to Peña, the split occurred as a result of Martinez's Communist Party agenda, which sought total control of both projects.[72] A former seminary owned by the Archdiocese of Santa Fe was selected as the site for the school. After CUJ organized a march and takeover of the old buildings, the archdiocese acquiesced and allowed CUJ to establish its school and a farm cooperative. By the summer of 1974, unable to secure funding, both projects were abandoned and CUJ soon declined.

The split within CUJ weakened the San Miguel RUP chapter as some of the activists left the group. With its cadre orientation, the loss of any of its activist members greatly affected its advocacy and electoral efforts. While a few activists did return to the RUP chapter, others became victims of burnout. During the next two years, it continued to be active, but at a reduced level. RUP's organizing momentum, however, picked up with the emergence of another dynamic chapter, the Rio Arriba.

Assisted by Manuel Archuleta, Antonio De Vargas, who at the time was a lumberjack, formed the Rio Arriba RUP chapter in 1973. De Vargas was its chairperson from the time of its formation until its demise in 1985. When I interviewed him years later, he explained why he got involved in organizing RUP in New Mexico: "I thought the idea of a Chicano party, independent of the major political parties, was a good one. I thought that it was a good vehicle, if nothing else, if not to win elections at least to apply some pressure at the establishment." To De Vargas, RUP was both a political party and an advocacy pressure group. As was the case with other RUP chapters, it was cadre oriented, with a good portion of the membership being former members of the Alianza.[73]

As a county, Rio Arriba had a rich history that went back to the time of New Mexico's colonization by the Spaniards. Méxicanos continued through the 1970s to comprise the county's largest ethnic population. Of its population of 27,000, about 75 percent was Méxicano, 10 percent indigenous (Jicarilla, Apache, San Juan, and Santa Clara Pueblos), and 15 percent White. Much of the county was land-grant land, given to Méxicanos by the Spanish and Méxicano governments. Yet it was the second poorest county in the state, reflected in an unemployment rate in 1975 of 20.5 percent. The federal government owned 75 percent of all the land, with the rest owned by a few White ranchers.[74]

As in so many other communities in New Mexico, Méxicanos in Rio Arriba County were victims of a modified internal colonial status—modified in the sense that, while some Méxicanos were politically powerless, the powerful were not Whites but other Méxicanos, such as Emilio Naranjo. Barbara Manzanares, RUP chapter vice chair, explained the political paradox in this manner: "In the Rio Arriba County we are not facing Gringo officials. They are Chicanos, of the type who prefer to call themselves Spanish-Americans. . . . We are facing shameless, obvious political corruption. This force is on the brink of completely selling our people and the little land left undeveloped and intact to the big business interests who want to develop the area."[75]

Thus, in a very controlled political climate, the local RUP chapter for the next twelve years was a relentless advocate on a number of local issues, specifically those related to political empowerment, the bicentennial celebration, education, police brutality, and the environment. (As previously discussed, during its formation in 1974, the chapter was successful in electing two of its members to the school board.) In 1976, it threatened to burn the wagons of a cross-country wagon train that was traveling through New Mexico to commemorate the bicentennial; instead, on the grounds that Méxicanos had nothing to celebrate, the chapter opted for a series of protest demonstrations.

From 1975 to 1978 the Rio Arriba RUP chapter was embroiled in a political struggle against the Democratic machinery of Rio Arriba County and Sheriff Emilio Naranjo.[76] He had governed Rio Arriba County for twenty-four years, using material incentives or patronage in the form of jobs. The RUP chapter challenged Naranjo on several issues, engendering a climate of conflict. In 1976, RUP engaged Naranjo by fielding several local candidates, including Moises Morales, for the office of county sheriff, for the November elections; Morales lost. Although never proven, RUP leaders alleged that Naranjo, concerned about the challenge to his power, had Morales's house burned to the ground. Arnold Weissberg of *The Militant* wrote: "A clash with Naranjo is no small political squabble. Naranjo's cops have arrested, beaten, and shot at RUP's activists. . . . Using the bombing of a bar owned by a deputy as a pretext, the sheriffs launched a reign of terror against RUP activists and members of the land grant movement."[77]

For the remaining months of 1976, Naranjo's reign of terror was real and not rhetorical. RUP's leadership and supporters came under deliberate attack. RUP activist Floyd Valdez and two of his brothers, who were arrested by Naranjo's deputies on fabricated drug charges in 1975, were acquitted in 1976. Two weeks after their acquittal, a sheriff's lieutenant and deputy opened fire on Floyd Valdez and two of his companions, wounding one of them. The three were arrested on charges that they had fired at the sheriffs from a moving car. Days later the charges were dropped. RUP responded by holding a march and rally at which Naranjo was hung in effigy.

RUP in Rio Arriba County was persistent in its efforts to destroy the Naranjo political dynasty, particularly what RUP attorney Richard Rosenstock described as

Naranjo's "instrument of terror," the Rio Arriba County Sheriff's Department.[78] In spite of his tyrannical control of the county, RUP consistently confronted him and his machine, particularly on charges of police brutality and general corruption, through direct action and electoral politics.

Naranjo continued to retaliate against RUP's attacks and charges. He went after some of RUP's principal leaders, Antonio De Vargas and Moises Morales, who were jailed on trumped-up drug charges. For example, in late November 1975, Morales was arrested for possession of marijuana. In April 1976, De Vargas was also arrested on drug charges. Both were acquitted, De Vargas in June 1976 and Morales in November 1977, for lack of evidence. In the case of De Vargas, the charges were dropped only after he successfully passed a polygraph test. By the end of 1976, RUP was engaged in an all-out political war against Naranjo's Democratic machine.

Meanwhile, other RUP chapters were involved in either supporting or organizing in the labor arena. RUP chapters in general supported the sanitation workers' strike in Artesia, Albuquerque, and Santa Fe and supported other labor-organizing efforts as well. Even though, as a union, the United Farm Workers because of its Democratic Party affiliation did not support RUP, RUP activists ardently supported it. RUP's Labor Committee, led by Chris Eichwald and Santiago Maestas, sought to organize state workers, especially those involved in social services and corrections. After four years of struggle, Joe Gardinar, also of the partido's Labor Committee, became president of a union at the University of New Mexico.[79]

Yet, by the end of 1976, RUP had failed to significantly expand its overall organizing efforts. Out of thirty-two counties in New Mexico, RUP was active politically in only seven. With the exception of Otero County, all were located in the northern and central part of the state. The reasons were several, but two stand out: (1) A dramatic increase in the number of Méxicano elected officials occurred, which will be subsequently addressed; and (2) with the demise of the epoch of protest in 1974, the level of activism and protest diminished. Both impacted the state's political climate, which was becoming increasingly conservative. What activism continued was largely produced by the few RUP chapters. The remnant CM organizations still functional by 1976 became increasingly Marxist in persuasion.

## RUP's Struggle in the Electoral Arena, 1974–1976

Involved with social justice issues, none of the RUP chapters chose to enter the electoral arena in 1974 except San Miguel County. Encouraged by its showing in the 1973 school board elections, the San Miguel County chapter decided to go after the Las Vegas municipal elections. Strategically, since the elections were nonpartisan, it chose to use subterfuge. It decided to run a full slate—candidates for mayor, four city council seats, and the city police magistrate—under the guise of Pueblo Unido (United Community). But, as political scientist Vigil points out, "The candidates [Pueblo Unido] posed for city offices left little mystery about its true affiliation."[80] Heading the slate was Peña, who ran for mayor. The slate's campaign addressed issues affecting the city's poor, including the passage of city ordinances that would assist the poor, pave streets, and install street lights in the barrio; support would come from redirected revenue-sharing funds. Pueblo Unido's opposition consisted of two slates. One slate, the Greater Las Vegas Ticket, was comprised of Méxicanos who were moderate to liberal in their politics. The second was the United Citizens slate, which consisted of conservative Méxicanos and Whites. According to Peña, both tended to be rather reactive. They waited for the Pueblo Unido candidates to present their positions on the issues; in most cases, they then took the same positions.[81]

In the election, the United Citizens slate was victorious. RUP's Pueblo Unido slate acted again as a spoiler. Because there were several Méxicanos running on all three slates, the White candidates won by 34 and 50 votes over the Méxicanos on the Greater Las Vegas Ticket. The votes won by each RUP candidate were: mayor, Juan José Peña, 362; judge, Arcenio Gardino, 282; city council, Ray Morales, 303, Manuel Archuleta, 371, José C. Duran, 410, and Clemencia M. Jabbs, 215.[82]

Even with RUP's slate receiving no more than 10 percent of the vote, it was obvious that its candidates had spoiled the chances of victory for the Greater Las Vegas Ticket. It drew enough votes from them to give the two White candidates the victory. This election as well as the two previous ones showed the detrimental consequences of Méxicanos "splitting" their so-called ethnic vote.[83] But to RUP, this was not a negative, for it was also part of its strategy to pressure non-RUP Méxicano candidates into becoming more responsive and sensitive to the issues affecting the poor, especially the Méxicano poor. In this respect, like most third parties, RUP sought to bring attention to certain issues and politicize the people. For RUP activists, there was not much difference between a liberal Méxicano politician and a conservative White politician.[84] Ideologically, both adhered to the liberal capitalist system.

Facing a possible challenge by RUP, in 1974 both major political parties had substantially increased the number of Méxicano elected officials. Whereas in 1965 there were twenty-two in the state legislature, nine years later there were thirty-three.[85] Joséph Montoya was elected to the U.S. Senate in 1964 and in 1974 was still in office. That same year, Democrat Jerry Apodaca was elected governor. The increase in the number of Méxicano elected officials continued to obviate RUP's organizing efforts in New Mexico. Its empowerment sell was increasingly difficult in a political setting where Méxicano political representation was proliferating.

RUP's involvement in the electoral arena culminated in 1976 with its running of several candidates for statewide office. By 1975, only 4,800 voters had registered RUP statewide. During that year, the state legislature lowered the number of signatures required for a party to get on the ballot from 3 percent to 1 percent of the last vote cast for governor, but the deadline was advanced to sixty-three days before the general election.[86] In 1976, however, a U.S. District Court ruled that the lack of procedures for independent candidates was unconstitutional. The impact of the decision was favorable to RUP in that it reduced the number of petition signatures required from 30, 000 to 3,000. As a result of the suit, in April, a RUP statewide convention was held in Alamogordo. With some fifty delegates attending, the decision was made to run candidates for state and federal offices.[87]

Instead of RUP running a candidate for governor, it chose to endorse the Socialist Workers' Party (SWP) candidate for president, Peter Camejo. The endorsement resolution read that Camejo was the first Latino to run for president of the United States and that "his ideology is similar to that of the Raza Unida de Nuevo Mexico." Camejo won RUP's endorsement based on his platform—the "Bill of Rights for Working People"—which was in harmony with the Declaration of Human Rights adopted by the partido at its 1975 state convention. That declaration included the people's right to a good paying jobs, a free education through college, and free medical and health care; abolition of private ownership of the land, with those who work it given control; and the right of people to live and work whereever they want to, regardless of economic or political boundaries. A strong position was also taken against any policy that caused "cutbacks" in social services.[88] RUP's platform reflected the variegated orientations of its cultural nationalist and Marxist activists and the strong influence of Socialist Workers' Party within RUP.

Limited in human and financial resources, the RUP delegates voted to concentrate their energies on getting their candidates on the ballot.[89] They decided to run no candidates for either the state house or senate. Ernesto Borunda was nominated to challenge incumbent Democrat Joséph Montoya for the U.S. Senate. Jesus Aragon and Ernesto Hill were nominated for the state's two congressional seats, although Hill failed to run.[90]

In its first statewide and federal challenge to the Democrats and Republicans, RUP's candidates failed to make a dent in their political armor. With more than 400,000 votes cast, presidential candidate Camejo received only 2,462 votes. Republican presidential candidate Gerald Ford carried the state with 211,419 votes. In the U.S. Senate race, RUP candidate Borunda received 1,087 votes to Republican Harrison Schmitt's 234,681. Republican incumbent congressman Manuel Lujan won over both his Democratic Party challenger Raymond Garcia and RUP's Jesus Aragon, with 162,587 votes to Garcia's 61,800, and Aragon's 1,159. RUP's candidate for state corporation commissioner, Sam Sanchez, received only 3,132 votes to the Democratic candidate's 192,767.[91] In Rio Arriba County, RUP's county candidates took some 11 percent of the vote.[92]

RUP's first and last involvement in the statewide electoral arena was a political fiasco. However, state leader Juan José Peña and other RUP activists construed it as "damned good," considering the obstacles its candidates had faced, such as no finances, little organization, red-baiting attacks, stringent petition requirements to get on the ballot, and so on. It is important to note that by 1976, the Viva Yo generation had taken root in New Mexico as well. A false sense of complacency and outright apathy had set in among many Méxicanos. With the Chicano Movement moribund by 1975, RUP in New Mexico, with its cultural nationalist/Marxist ideological posture, was out of sync with the state's moderate to conservative political culture.

## RUP's Eclectic Ideology, 1971–1981

In order to understand RUP's decline in New Mexico it is important to understand what I call RUP's eclectic ideology, which was antithetical to the state's dominant liberal capitalist ideology. During its first five years (1971–1976), RUP had been an ideologically eclectic, cadre-oriented party that had aspirations of becoming a mass-based political party of and for Méxicanos. But RUP evolved into an ideological/doctrinaire third party. RUP leaders and activists during these years claimed that it was ideologically cultural nationalist. However, from the start, there were a number of RUP leaders who were Marxists of a sort in their politics. Peña, Archuleta, and Leocaido Cervantez, among others, during 1972 and 1973, met on a regular basis with Vito Vigil, who had been a member of the Socialist Labor Party (SLP); all were influenced by the writings of SLP leader Daniel de Leon.[93]

The affinity to socialism was evident in the number of activists who were members or supporters of other leftist political parties between 1971 and 1976—namely the Communist Party of the United States of America (CPUSA) and the Socialist Workers Party. Both of these parties as well as others jumped on the RUP organizing bandwagon and infiltrated it in hopes of advancing their own causes and interests. What ensued was a struggle among those holding Marxist, humanist, and nationalist ideas who sought to dominate RUP's vision and agenda for change.

However, between 1974 and 1976, it was the SWP that was the most successful in establishing a strong foothold within RUP, especially among its leaders. Manuel Archuleta as early as 1974 began to make contact with the Trotskyite SWP leaders, for example, Peter Camejo, Harry Ring, and Donald Barnes, and to bring to RUP meetings copies of its newspaper, *The Militant*. During the next two years, RUP activists attended and spoke at SWP meetings and state and national conferences. By 1976, there had been several meetings held that involved both RUP and SWP leaders, including Peña. An amicable and collaborative relationship developed between the two parties that lasted into 1977.[94]

Illustrative of this cordial working relationship was the extensive national coverage given to New Mexico's RUP in *The Militant*. Several feature stories were published in 1976 on RUP leaders Archuleta and Peña.[95] This relationship ultimately engendered both internal and external problems for RUP's leadership. The rather close working relationship allowed SWP to successfully siphon off a small number of RUP's leaders, such as Archuleta, and members. This created problems for RUP in New Mexico when conflicts broke out between RUP in Colorado and the SWP in 1976.

By the end of 1976, some RUP activists who worked concomitantly with what Peña described as the "alphabet soup of leftist" organizations became disenchanted with RUP and left it for more sectarian groups. Other RUP activists who were cultural nationalists and not Marxists burned out on the ideological differences and the lack of successes by 1976 and dropped out altogether. Some, especially students, rejected their activism and embraced the materialism, individualism, and mainstream politics of the Viva Yo generation.

RUP's decline became increasingly evident by 1977. The 1976 elections had failed to build organizing momentum for RUP. Its ideological cleavages continued well into 1977, reaching a breaking point at the National Immigration Conference held in San Antonio. The SWP wound up a casualty of ideological conflicts with other Marxist groups; it was ousted from the conference as a result of sectarian squabbles, especially with CASA, which was supported by CPUSA

After the conference, New Mexico RUP voted to sever its contact with the SWP. It forbade its leadership and members from attending SWP functions and vice versa. This decision caused RUP leader Archuleta and others to leave RUP for the SWP.[96] Peña explained in a bulletin why he was severing his relationship with the SWP: "Because of what I perceive as SWP Anglo chauvinism of its top leadership and much of its young membership, I can no longer work with the organization, and because our political disagreements that the Chicano Movement and in particular the partido de la Raza Unida should organize the Chicano community, and that the SWP should keep to organizing the Anglo community; it is no longer possible to work together on a political plane for political reasons."[97]

Peña's major criticism of SWP was that it wooed away RUP's supporters. He described the taking of RUP's "best fighters" as a "chauvinistic intrusion" on the Chicano's right to organize themselves, based on their own agenda and not someone else's.[98] Although RUP severed its linkages with the SWP, in 1976 it established a cordial relationship with Mexico's Partido Socialista de los Trabajadores (Socialist Workers Party). The two entities exchanged information and worked on transborder projects, such as immigration and transnational corporations.[99]

RUP encountered similar problems with other Marxist activists. From 1976 and well into 1977, RUP lost some of its Bernalillo County cadre to the August 29th Movement. Essentially Maoist in ideology, it sought to make inroads using the Chilili Land Grant issue as a basis. Movement activists believed that the Chicano revolution to form a separatist nation was going to start at Chilili, New Mexico. The August 29th Movement openly advocated the idea of a separatist Aztlán in its monograph *Fan the Flames*.[100] Aztlán would be realized either through armed struggle or by plebiscite. Unable to make any inroads, the movement did not last.

What then was RUP's ideology from 1976 to 1981? It continued to be ideologically rather eclectic, incorporating ultranationalism and Marxism. According to Peña, there was a leaning toward the idea of developing a Chicano nation, combined with Marxist economic analysis. According to political scientist Richard Santillan in 1978: "Within the past two years, the partido has taken a Marxist perspective regarding social change. Partido members in New Mexico felt that the partido in Colorado had influenced the party regarding nationalism as a key for liberation, however, most members believed it must extend beyond merely appealing to ethnicity. Members in New Mexico believed that the partido needed to incorporate all poor people and not simply Chicanos."[101]

Peña, in one of his bulletins on the theology of liberation, writes that he was "strongly opposed to having the Partido de la Raza Unida become a Marxist-Leninist political party." His recommendation was that RUP develop its own ideology, which would allow theists like himself, who leaned toward the theology of liberation, to use Pablo Friere's "conscientization" pedagogy[102] but would still incorporate some aspects of Marxism.[103] However, in another of his bulletins, "The Socialist Worker's Question," Peña openly admitted RUP's adherence to socialism: "Despite the criticism of Partido's "collaboration" with the SWP, the Partido de la Raza Unida will continue to organize and present . . . its socialist position and Latin Americanist and Internationalist positions as an alternative to the straight Marxist-Leninist lines, including those of the Socialist Workers Party."[104]

Integral to RUP's eclectic ideology was its devotion to Chicano separatism. When interviewed, Peña described RUP's ideology as not just socialist, but "independentist": "We wanted to work towards a Chicano nation. Electorally, socially, and politically in the same manner that the [Bloc Quebecois] was working in Quebec."[105] This position continued to be taken by most within RUP's diminishing ranks up to 1981.

In Rio Arriba County, RUP's ideological posture was not as defined as that Peña described. According to Richard Rosenstock, who was RUP's attorney, "it was a mixed bag that included radical, conservative, populist [thinkers], but most importantly, we were flexible in our politics."[106] Antonio De Vargas, who was RUP's driving force in the county, acknowledged the presence of socialist ideas within RUP in Rio Arriba County: "It was more socialist, but not socialist in the sense of the Socialist Workers Party. . . . The socialism that we practiced here was a socialism that came from the villages over the centuries. It was a communal/social type of ideology. It wasn't nationalistic at all . . . as it was else where."[107]

Some within RUP thought that RUP's ideology was neither socialist nor cultural nationalist but "humanist." Rebecca Hill from Alamagorro described it as being "humanist" first, because the partido cared about uplifting the overall human condition of Méxicanos and promoting their welfare.[108]

RUP in New Mexico was never completely clear on its ideological vision. There were differences among the few RUP county central committees. While it was anticapitalist and ostensibly socialist, its ideology was not that lucid regarding strategy. For example, little was detailed as to how RUP was to embark on its nation-building objective. Yet upon the return of the RUP delegation to Lebanon in 1980, some within RUP felt the need for it to become more revolutionary in its actions.

By 1981, RUP's politics reflected a much more internationalist ideological perspective that openly embraced Third World struggles of liberation, such as that of the Palestine Liberation Organization (PLO).[109] To the public and media, RUP in New Mexico was a radical fringe group. This was noted by Acuña: "State officials branded RUP members un-American, radicals, and outsiders."[110]

## The End of RUP's Advocacy Agenda, 1977–1981

RUP's advocacy activity all but disappeared from the political landscape between 1977 and 1981. Whereas in 1975 RUP had seven chapters, by 1981 only two were functional: Rio Arriba and San Miguel. One reason for the decline was that some of the social and legal service programs and agencies that its activists had infiltrated had dried up. RUP's infiltration was part of an effort to surreptitiously direct the resources of these entities toward supporting RUP's organizing activities.

Some leaders relied extensively on these agencies' resources (phones, paper, duplicating machine, pencils, etc.) for assistance in their RUP organizing efforts, and for their paychecks. A few of the principal entities used by RUP were the Chicano Studies Program at Highlands University, chaired by RUP New Mexico state chairperson Peña; Northern New Mexico Legal Services, chaired by Peña; Southern New Mexico Legal Services, chaired by RUP leader Larry Hill; Community Service Center, directed by RUP leader Frank Schafer; and Clinica de la Gente (Clinic of the People).[111]

A case that reflected the financial precariousness of some of RUP's leaders was that of Juan Jose Peña and RUP's San Miguel chapter. With both RUP and CASO in a state of decline, Highlands University president Jesus Aragon decided to deny Peña tenure and cut off the Title VII funding for Chicano Studies. The Méxicano university President did away with most of the changes that both RUP and CASO had earlier brought about. Peña moved to Albuquerque, where he enrolled in a doctoral program at the University of New Mexico. Without Peña and others who acted as the main cadre, there was little to anchor the San Miguel County RUP Central Committee. For a brief period, it became defunct; however, in 1980, the Flores brothers, Lorenzo and Steve, temporarily revived it.

Although the San Miguel chapter had historically been the most prominent committee, by the late 1970s the role went to RUP in Rio Arriba County.[112] The reputation it earned was based on activism and consistency of action. With its proactive advocacy and electoral posture, from 1977 to 1985, it was the last remnant of RUP's original movement in New Mexico to develop an alternative political party for Méxicanos.

Unlike that of some other RUP chapters, the Rio Arriba County membership was a mix of Méxicanos and Whites. While the committee was change oriented, it was less ideology based and more issue directed. From 1977 to 1981, when not battling the Naranjo machine by running candidates, it was busy dealing with a variety of issues— police brutality, the disruptive aspects of tourism, the environment, and others— related to the general development of the county.[113]

In 1977, both De Vargas and Morales filed civil suits against Naranjo and the Sheriff's Department. De Vargas's civil suit was for $54,500 and Morales's for $1 million. De Vargas won his suit in 1978 for the full amount; Morales won for an undisclosed amount.[114] As a result of the Morales suit, State Attorney General Tony Anaya, in 1979, indicted Naranjo on charges related to Morales being set up. He was removed from the state senate temporarily and was replaced by his son. A few months later, according to De Vargas, "the supreme court overturned his conviction and [he subsequently] took his job back as senator."[115] Thus, the political confrontations between Naranjo and RUP continued well into the 1980s.

From 1977 to 1981, everal of RUP's New Mexico leaders participated in delegations that met with Mexico's governmental and political party leaders. In particular, RUP developed a strong collaborative relationship with Mexico's Partido Socialista de los Trabajadores. Some RUP activists went to Nicaragua, where they supported and even fought on the side of the Sandinistas. In 1980, RUP's leadership in New Mexico led a RUP delegation to Lebanon to meet with the PLO.

## RUP's Diminishing Electoral Agenda (1977–1981)

RUP's political coup de grace as a statewide party came in 1977 with the passage of even more restrictive ballot access legislation by the state legislature. As a result of RUP's electoral statewide challenge, the two major parties voted to increase the percentage of petition signatures needed from 2 to 3 percent and to advance the petition deadline to thirty-three days prior to the June primary. Furthermore, procedures for independent candidates required a petition signed by 5 percent of the last vote cast, due in March. To add insult to injury, the legislation provided that third parties were disqualified if they ceased to run candidates for a period of four years. This change in the election laws made some among RUP's leadership and supporters despair of it's ever becoming an official party on the ballot.

This dire political situation further induced RUP's leadership to opt for a cadre party comprised of a few zealots from Rio Arriba, San Miguel, and Bernalillo Counties.[116] In Rio Arriba County, for example, the size of RUP's cadre numbered no more than twenty.[117] The same situation applied to the two other counties. In spite of no longer being on the ballot statewide after 1976, RUP continued to run some candidates and to act as an advocate on a variety of issues.[118] In 1977 at a RUP state convention, a slate of candidates for the 1978 elections was announced: Peña was nominated for the U.S. Senate against Democratic governor Jerry Apodaca, Larry Hill for attorney general, Isabel Blea for governor, Manuel Archuleta for lieutenant governor, and Ernesto Borunda for Congress.[119] Blea was also elected as RUP state chair, replacing Peña, who declined to run again.

Blea's candidacy for governor and her leadership role as RUP state chairperson were major victories for Mexicanas. Since RUP's inception, Blea had played a crucial role in RUP's development. RUP had no written antisexism policy until 1976; that year the State Central Committee took a very strong position against male chauvinism. Part of the resolution passed read: "The Partido de la Raza Unida de Nuevo Mexico recognizes the special oppression and exploitation of women and will struggle for the emancipation of women as part our struggle of liberation. We see the source of the oppression of women as the system and not the men (male supremacy), but within the movement, male supremacy is recognized as a danger within the organization."[120] The resolution stressed the need for males and females to work together for the abolition of male supremacy and the liberation of women and put in place a new leadership training and development program for women designed to promote their leadership skills.

Before 1977, the overwhelming majority of RUP's state leaders as well as its state and federal candidates were male. When interviewed on the matter, Peña commented,

"We had some counties that were male dominated, but we had women active in the majority of the counties that the partido was active in and we had women active in the State Central Committee." Blea took a slightly different view: "Women would do most of the work and the men would take all the credit. That's the way it was then, and that's the way it is now." Rebecca Hill, who became one of the most visible RUP women leaders, agreed with Blea's assessment. She said women had to deal with some of the male chauvinism by seeking to educate the men within the party. "We did most of the work. Women were mostly in the background. There wasn't much leadership as far as women go."[121] Blea acknowledged, however, that some women within the partido did excel as leaders. She mentioned her sister, Josie Blea, who was the main RUP leader in Clayton. But it was Isabel Blea who became the most visible woman RUP leader in the state.[122] Other women, such as Rebecca Hill and Linda Pedro, also contributed to RUP's development.

Before becoming state RUP chairperson, Blea served as RUP chair for Bernalillo County and on the partido's state central committee. To Peña, the leadership role of women within RUP was never an issue. He did, however, concede that there was a time when Linda Macias attempted, as Peña put it, to inject feminism into one RUP agenda; he recalled that some of her suggestions were incorporated, while others were not. He stressed that the genders were equal.[123] When asked in 1977 why she joined RUP, Isabel Blea responded: "I knew something about the evils of capitalism. But since then I've learned a lot more, and I've seen that the only way we'll get [gender] equality is through socialism."[124]

There is no public record either in newspaper accounts or with New Mexico's secretary of state to verify that RUP's 1977 statewide nominees ran in 1978. State officials maintained that election returns sent to me were complete and that even if a candidate ran on a write-in campaign, the results would have been recorded.[125] The responses of former RUP leaders to the lack of corroboration were mixed. Some, like Blea, said that they had run, but on a write-in campaign since RUP was not on the ballot. She claimed that she was the highest RUP vote getter, receiving some 200 votes statewide, adding, "It was just too difficult to try get votes."[126] Juan José Peña was adamant that he along with some others were on the ballot, but he could not remember the number or percentage of votes he and the others received.[127] Several others could not remember which of these two scenarios was the case. The fact was that by 1978, RUP was inconsequential in terms of statewide elections and posed no threat to either of the two major governing parties.

At the state senate level, RUP's sole candidate for District Five was Antonio De Vargas. Since 1974, RUP had been a thorn in the side of the Naranjo Democratic machine in the Rio Arriba County area. Without much money, and with limited organization, a hostile red-baiting campaign, and a conservative political climate, De Vargas was the David battling the omnipotent one-party Goliath, as the election returns confirmed. After a hard-run campaign, Naranjo was the victor, with 5,022 votes to De Vargas's 808. The Republican candidate came in second with 3,882.[128]

By 1980, only the Rio Arriba and San Miguel County chapters were still functional, and the Rio Arriba County chapter was the only one to run candidates. It ran a total of four: Linda Pedro for state senator against RUP's archenemy, the Democrat Naranjo; Moises Morales and Patricio Valdez for the county commission; and Susana Valdez for county clerk. Out of 16,365 eligible voters, Democrats numbered 12,542, Republicans 2,642, RUP 887, and Independents 794.[129]

Even though RUP organized a vigorous campaign, it lost to Naranjo's machine, which garnered him 5,985 votes; Republican Samuel R. Ziegler received 2,651 votes; and RUP's Linda Pedro got 990 votes. RUP's other three county candidates were soundly defeated by the Democrats. Moises Morales secured 1, 447, Patricio Valdez 750, and Susana Valdez 1,230 votes.[130] Regardless of the fact that Rio Arriba County had a high percentage of Méxicanos, RUP's electoral showing for the state senate and county offices reflected the omnipotence of the Democratic Party and Naranjo's machine.

## RUP's Demise

As 1981 came to a close, so did the struggle to build an alternative Méxicano political party in New Mexico. The last gasp came with the resignation of Peña as RUP's national chairperson. Like so many other RUP activists, he became a victim of burnout. In his case it was severe. When asked why he resigned, he responded: "I had no job, no money, no place to live, no resources, and I was going through a divorce. In other words, I was in dire straits."[131] By the time he resigned, there was little left of RUP in New Mexico. After nearly ten years of struggling to organize RUP as a viable alternative to the state's two-party system, only the Rio Arriba County chapter continued, running candidates unsuccessfully until 1982.[132] However, in 1984, it was dismantled as an RUP chapter, and its members supported Rev. Jesse Jackson's bid for the Democratic presidential nomination.

What kind of legacy did RUP in New Mexico leave? To Peña, RUP meant that Méxicanos had created the largest political organization via a political party in New Mexico's history.[133] RUP in New Mexico was an expression of the discontent, frustration, and anger that existed against a two-party monopoly. Its greatest legacy was that it continued the Méxicano's long and rich historical tradition of resistance and struggle.

As with RUP organizing efforts in other states, the reasons for RUP's decline and ultimate demise in New Mexico are both endogenous and exogenous. In that state, the foremost endogenous factor was the Méxicano's rich history of political participation and representation. Politically, internal colonialism was not a factor. From 1848 until RUP emerged in 1972, Méxicanos had been part of the elite—active and viable participants at all levels in the governance of the state. It was not the discontent of the many that launched RUP's development, but that of a few disenchanted young CM activists.

The endogenous factors that contributed to RUP's demise included: (1) failure to develop a sufficiently strong mass power base; (2) lack of support from the various segments of the Méxicano community; (3) conflicting ideologies and schisms; (4) Méxicanos who were part of a rather moderate to conservative political culture; (5) the decline of the Chicano Movement; and (6) RUP's inability to amass the requisite resources—in both money and people—to get on the ballot and run viable campaigns.

RUP's demise, however, was also a result of several exogenous factors, the most salient of which was New Mexico's election laws. Lacking resources, RUP was never able to secure the appropriate number of petition signatures needed to get on the ballot as an official party. The single-member district system and the state's rather prosystem political culture precluded a serious challenge to the party monopoly. The reluctance of mass media to cover RUP events made it difficult for partido activists to disseminate their message. When RUP did receive coverage, it was sometimes depicted as radical. Yet, in spite of all these obstacles, a few RUP zealots since the partido's demise in 1984 have continued to struggle for its revival.

*Chapter Nine*

---

# Instrument of Change and Service: The Rise and Fall of RUP in Arizona, 1971–1974

Arizona was not immune from the Chicano Movement's contagion. The state's Chicano activists became involved in the struggle to form the Raza Unida Party (RUP), even though Arizona did not have the large Méxicano population concentrations of Texas, California, and New Mexico. The Chicano Movement (CM) turned many of Arizona's activists off to the nation's two major parties and turned them on to the idea of forming a Chicano political party. Arizona has a rich tradition of labor and *mutualista* activism (*mutualista* refers to a brand of self-help, fraternal organizations). The news of the Cristal, Texas, takeover and of RUP's emergence in Texas, Colorado, and California, led Méxicanos in the state, especially around the Tucson area, to organize RUP beginning in 1971.

### The Historical Setting in Tucson:
### Before the Chicano Movement

The rise of RUP in Arizona, specifically in Tucson, as elsewhere, was a result of discontent with the two-party system. The discontent of Tucson's activists, however, had its roots in the state's history of relegating Méxicanos to an internal colonial status. As was the case with Méxicanos in Texas, California, and Colorado, Méxicanos in Arizona were never viable participants in the process of statewide governance, from 1848, when Arizona together with New Mexico became a territory of the United States, to statehood in 1911, to the early 1970s.[1]

The Méxicano population of Arizona in 1848 was only about 1,000 and was concentrated around the Tucson area. A flood of Whites, primarily Southerners, into the new territory was impelled by their pursuit of mineral wealth, railroad expansion, and agricultural development that in turn fostered a need for cheap labor.[2] By 1870, Méxicanos constituted some 30 percent of Tucson's population and a majority of Arizona's population. It was during the 1880s that a few Méxicanos, chiefly from Tucson, were elected to the legislative assembly.[3] Méxicanos during these years were the ones who gave political life to Tucson by developing the city and school infrastructure. At this time, they had access to the process of governance.

By the 1890s, with the influx of Whites from the East and Midwest, Méxicanos in Tucson began their journey into demographic minority status. White settlers soon became the majority, and it was they who were in total control of the city and school politics.[4] As David Weber writes: "Anglos held firm control of Arizona throughout the territorial period. From 1863 to 1912, no one of Spanish surname served in an important territorial office, either elective or appointive."[5] Carey McWilliams suggests that, as a consequence of the 1848 war, Whites felt "a measureless contempt for all things Mexican."[6] Hence a paradox developed: While Whites hated Méxicanos, they needed them as a source of cheap labor. And, according to David E. Camacho: "One may infer that La Raza were unable to control their destiny because of their inability to break from their traditional role of servant to master."[7]

The first major Méxicano resistance in Arizona came in 1894 when in the Tucson area some Méxicanos organized La Alianza Hispana Americana (the Alliance of Hispanic Americans). Formed initially as a *mutualista* organization, it sought to relieve the Méxicano's repression by providing its members with death insurance and other forms of aid.[8] However, until its demise in the 1960s, it also developed a quasi-political and advocacy function, seeking to protect and advance the interests of the declining Méxicano population of Arizona, especially in Tucson.

The Méxicano's resistance from the early 1900s to the early 1970s occurred in both the labor and political organizing arenas. During these years, Méxicanos were victimized as an "inferior race" and despised, ostracized, and exploited, working hard for starvation wages.[9] Méxicanos responded by becoming involved in numerous strikes—for example, Clifton-Morenci (1903 and 1915)—in the labor movement of Arizona's mine workers. In some cases, the workers and leaders were Méxicanos, many of them from the ranks of mutualista organizations. Méxicano workers resisted their exploitation by joining a number of unions, including the Industrial Workers of the World in the 1930s and others in the years that followed.

Politically, Méxicanos in Arizona were relegated to a powerless internal colonial status. Even though La Alianza had linkages to both major parties, neither sought to mobilize Méxicanos politically. From the 1890s to the 1930s, while some Méxicano elites engaged in politics, the majority of Méxicanos were disenfranchised and alienated from the political process. Their powerlessness was evident at the statehood constitutional convention held in 1910 in Tucson. Of the fifty-two delegates who participated, only one was a Méxicano; the rest were White. For years, Whites had opposed statehood for fear that Méxicanos would dominate the new state.[10] This fear was based on the gradual Méxicano population increases that occurred due to the exodus produced by the Mexican Revolution—from 14,171 in 1900 to 114,173 in 1930.[11]

This fear became even more apparent with the forced repatriation of Méxicanos in the 1930s; this nation's own form of ethnic cleansing had cut the Méxicano population by some 14,000 by 1940.[12] In spite of the reverse exodus (repatriation) to Mexico, Méxicanos regarded Franklin Roosevelt and the Democratic Party as saviors.[13] Numerous changes in the areas of education, jobs, and housing during the post–World War II years (1945 to the 1960s) improved the socioeconomic status of Méxicanos in Arizona. In addition, during these years the Méxicano population had rebounded— from 128,318 in 1950 to 194,356 in 1960.[14] While poverty was still pervasive, a small middle class had emerged and Méxicanos gradually became politically more active.

In the 1960 presidential election, some Méxicanos showed their support for Democratic presidential candidate John Fitzgerald Kennedy by becoming involved with the Viva Kennedy clubs that emanated from Texas. Moreover, in 1961, while Méxicanos in California had formed the Mexican American Political Association and, in Texas, the Political Association of Spanish-speaking Organizations, Arizona Méxicanos established their own political organization, the American Coordinating Council on Political Education.[15] By 1962, it had grown to ten chapters with a total membership of 2,500. That year, it made political history by orchestrating the first political takeover of a local government by electing five Méxicanos to a seven-member city council in the city of Miami. The Council was nonpartisan, but most of its membership was solidly committed to the Democratic Party.[16] Its life, however, proved short; it declined by the end of the decade.[17]

By the late 1960s, in spite of Arizona's rather conservative and often racist political climate, Méxicano political participation resulted in a few Méxicanos being elected to the state legislature. In 1950, there were no Méxicanos in the state legislature, but by 1960 there were four and by 1965 six.[18] All those elected were Democrats, suggesting the powerful hold the Democratic Party had over the Méxicano. At the local level of politics, Méxicanos by this time had generally become more participatory and active. But in Tucson, their political situation was poor. Raul Grijalva, who became one of RUP's major leaders in Arizona and now serves as a Pima County supervisor, explained that immigration from the East and Midwest had considerably changed the demographic face of Tucson, relegating Méxicanos to a minority: "By the sixties there had been a whole different political shift. We had few if any [Méxicanos] in elected positions. All the issues relative to the school system had begun to become important issues. . . . It was generally a negative thing going on in the community."[19]

The increasing realization of their powerlessness by some Méxicanos fostered frustration and discontent and by the midsixties had served to heighten expectations.

## The Chicano Movement in Arizona: Struggle for a Cause

By 1967, the political unrest and discontent to which Grijalva alluded became the basis for the emergence of the CM in Arizona. As was the case in other states, exogenous and endogenous antagonisms that fostered the epoch of protest also created a climate of change in Arizona. Particularly, the activism of Tijerina and the Alianza in New Mexico, Ceasar Chavez's United Farm Workers (UFW) in California, and Rodolfo "Corky" Gonzales's Crusade for Justice in Colorado acted as endogenous catalytic agents that triggered the rise of the CM.[20]

As in Texas, Chicano youth became the avant garde of the emerging CM. From the barrios to the universities and colleges, the youth became infused with the spirit of the Movimiento. In the words of Raul Grijalva, who at the time was a student leader of the Mexican American Student Association (MASA): "We were the point of the Movimiento."[21] Chicano students at the University of Arizona at Tucson, in 1967, under the leadership of Sal Baldenegro, formed MASA, the result of Baldenegro's exposure earlier that year to the emerging Chicano student movement in the Los Angeles area, where he lived with his mother while attending El Camino College.[22] He had returned to Arizona inspired and committed to organizing a student organization in Tucson.[23]

In 1968, MASA's leaders sought to start a chapter at Arizona State University in Phoenix. They made contact with a number of students, who were led by Alfredo Gutiérrez to form their own student organization. According to Baldenegro, "Because of the rivalry between the two universities, they chose to name their organization the Mexican American Student Organization (MASO)."[24] By 1970, MASO had become Movimiento Estudiantil Chicano de Aztlán and for the next three years was active in a number of issues and actions, among the occupation of the president's office at Arizona State University, the struggle to establish Chicano Studies, the provision of assistance to Chicanos por La Causa in organizing walkouts, the participation in organizing a school board election, and the support of UFW labor organizing activities.[25]

In 1968, MASA began to involve itself in community issues. One such issue was assisting the UFW on a consistent basis in its organizing activities around the Tucson area. It also participated in and organized pickets and marches and distributed literature, among other activities. By late that year, MASA's growing militant posture had created some internal divisions. Some of the students wanted MASA to be more educational and less advocacy oriented. Essentially middle class and moderate in their politics, they argued that MASA's focus should be developing tutorial programs and scholarships. The conflict escalated to the point that Baldenegro came under serious attack. He was threatened with impeachment by his fellow members for making radical speeches at the university that allegedly did not reflect the views of MASA's membership.[26] Grijalva explains the crux of the issue: "The traditional argument during those times was for working through the system as opposed to taking the system head on."[27] Before MASA's membership could take any action on the matter, Baldenegro resigned as its president.

With his resignation, ten other members left MASA and formed the barrio/university-based Chicano Liberation Committee (CLC).[28] In 1969, it confronted university officials on a variety of issues. After resorting to pressure via protests, it was successful in realizing a number of campus reforms, which included development of Mexican American Studies; programs for the enrollment, retention, and recruitment of Chicano students; recruitment of Chicano faculty and administrators, and diversity in staffing.[29] Realizing the importance of being connected to the community, the CLC by 1969 had established a major presence in the barrios of Tucson.[30] When interviewed in 1998, Frank de la Cruz, who was a member of both groups, said that compared to MASO, CLC "was much more barrio oriented. It had a stronger commitment to dealing with many of the problems of barrios."[31]

Increasingly, in 1969, CLC took activism into the barrios of Tucson.[32] A small neighborhood office called the Chicano House was established for purposes of organizing and developing community programs.[33] According to Lupe Castillo, "The house was owned by Salomon [Baldenegro's] mother. She loaned it to us and we developed various kinds of community projects and did our organizing from there."[34]

The office was shared with another barrio activist group called the Young Mexican American Association, which two years later became the Brown Berets led by Jorge Villarreal, a former Vietnam veteran and a pinto (former convict). A collaborative and coalitional relationship developed between the various participating groups.[35] The Chicano House also sponsored a number of self-supported community programs: childcare, recreation, cultural and educational conscious-raising instruction for young people, and so on. The programs were funded through tithes and fund raising.[36] For the next year and a half or so, in most cases, the two entities were indistinguishable.

When the CLC became engaged in an issue, the other entities housed at the Chicano House would support it. The relationship between the CLC at the university and the Chicano House in the barrio gave the leadership of both entities resources to draw on from each other. When CLC brought in a speaker at the university; the speaker was expected to contribute a percentage of the honorarium to the Chicano House; it was used to support community activities.[37]

In 1969, CLC became engaged in the Tucson and Pueblo high school walkouts. The elementary and high schools were full of educational problems. The high schools were plagued by high drop-out rates, an irrelevant curriculum, and relatively few Chicano teachers or administrators, among other problems. The elementary schools shared many of the same problems as well as being housed in badly deteriorating facilities. Influenced by the walkouts of East Los Angeles, the high school students decided to stage their own.

They contacted CLC leadership and requested its organizing assistance. The result was a massive walkout by hundreds of students. The students presented a number of demands that included bilingual/bicultural education; establishment of Chicano Studies; hiring of Chicano teachers, administrators, and staff; and physical improvements in some of the schools in the barrios.[38] The walkout lasted several days and had a polarizing impact. Some of the more conservative Méxicanos became upset with the students and at CLC. The school administration effectively used some of these individuals to create divisions within the Méxicano community, with the intent of diluting support for the students.

While the walkouts failed in their demands, they succeeded in building CLC's activist stature and reputation. In addition, they fostered an awareness of the Méxicano's educational needs.[39] In explaining the failure of the Tucson walkout, Grijalva pointed out that an "intense debate" had ensued in the Méxicano community. There were persons who attacked CLC for using the students and accused the group of being Communists and of having no regard for the students' welfare. "At the time, we felt we lost. Numerically, in terms of the turnout and the kids that responded, it was a tremendous success. From an organizing perspective, it was good. The fallout from it was that we had to spend about six months being defensive because they were trying to kick students out of school. We got caught up in their process. We couldn't break away from it because we had a responsibility to defend these kids that we had asked to go on the line."[40]

The debate on the walkouts lasted for about a year. However, some of those who had been critical of CLC's alleged radical action changed their minds when the administration began to implement bilingual/bicultural education and hired Méxicano teachers and staff.[41]

By 1969, the CM in Arizona emanated primarily from Tucson and Phoenix. In great part this was ascribable to the activism of both CLC and MASO. However, with the emergence of the Movimiento Estudiantil Chicano de Aztlán (MEChA) in California in 1969, both MASO at Arizona State University and CLC at the University of Arizona in Tucson in 1970 converted to MEChA. At the University of Arizona, MASA continued in a low-key fashion until its demise in 1971, while MEChA continued to intensify its struggle for change.[42]

While Arizona's Chicano youth movement gained momentum, another byproduct of the CM in Arizona was the formation of the Southwest Council of La Raza in 1968. Funded by the Ford Foundation for some one million dollars, it was based in Phoenix until 1972 when it underwent a name change and became the National Council of La Raza. With its general purpose being to promote community and economic development, its primary function was to provide assistance to community service organizations in proposal writing, leadership training, funding allocation.

The Southwest Council of La Raza and its leadership were helpful in strengthening the CM's various struggles for change in Arizona. Its founder and leader, Maclovio Barraza, who was known for his progressive politics, contributed greatly to the growing activism among Méxicanos there. In addition, he was an inspiration and mentor to Salomon Baldenegro, who became Arizona's main CM leader and the founder of RUP in Arizona. For several years, Baldenegro accompanied Barraza to speeches he gave at demonstrations and to other forms of political activity. Baldenegro's disdain for the Democrats in part began with a speech given by Barraza in 1967 in which he berated "the Democrats for taking for granted the Méxicanos in Arizona."[43]

## El Rio Coalition: RUP's Precursor

RUP's birth in Tucson was a result of many years of frustration over the Méxicano's sense of political powerlessness. However, the precipitant that gave rise to RUP was a community issue that fostered a long, drawn-out political struggle in which the CLC became engaged. The issue was a proposal by CLC and community people of the west-side barrio called El Hollywood to convert the city-run El Rio Golf Course into a people's park. From the spring of 1970 to the early part of 1971, CLC was immersed in a struggle against city officials who opposed the conversion.

The struggle began with the request from barrio residents to the Chicano House for assistance on the matter of building a community park. With CLC agreeing to take on the issue, the El Rio Coalition (ERC) was formed representing some 10,000 mostly barrio residents.[44] Within weeks, a petition drive was organized that was successful in securing 1,500 signatures requesting that a park be built from land taken from the El Rio golf course.

That June the ERC presented the petitions to the city council. With only one Méxicano, Ray Castillo, on the Democrat-controlled council, the coalition's request failed.[45] Throughout, even though he was Méxicano, Castillo was the biggest and most vociferous opponent of ERC's proposal. The city council's inaction escalated the issue, and, for the next six months, the ERC attacked the recalcitrant city council. The pressure came in various forms of protests, marches, sit-ins, vigils, and press conferences that kept the issue alive for months. In our 1998 interview, de la Cruz described some of the ERC's direct actions: "The city council kept putting us off. We started having some of these marches. Some of them had up to two thousand people. We started going to the golf course and picketing, blocking the driveway, trying to talk the golfers into not going there. We would go on the golf course and interrupt their golf game. We would sit in at the coffee shop so the golfers couldn't use it. We had around five arrests for trespassing. A few weeks after that we had a few scuffles with the police and a few more people were arrested. Every weekend until January of the following year we would picket or do something."[46]

Throughout the course of the struggle, the city officials' lack of respect for the barrio residents' concerns and interests became apparent, as well as the barrios' lack of power. The demonstrations had been successful in mustering large numbers of people—anywhere from 200 to 2,000. However, by January 1971, the ERC's ranks had dwindled to some fifty picketers. In spite of the decrease in direct action activities, ERC leaders continued to meet and pressure the city council.[47] Yet the city's public officials were determined not to give in to what they perceived as an unreasonable proposal.

In January 1971, ERC's pressure and resolve finally broke the intransigent city officials. They capitulated to ERC's demand to build a people's park on a thirty-eight-acre parcel, including the building of a community center.[48] The people responded with jubilation, feeling that an unprecedented victory had been won.[49] Years later, Baldenegro remembered, "We won the issue and were successful in getting a community center that was named El Rio Community Center and a *parque* [park], the Joaquin Murrieta Park."[50] During the groundbreaking ceremonies, the ERC protested to city officials for not being formally invited to attend.[51] This issue became the springboard Baldenegro used in early 1971 to launch RUP in Tucson.[52]

## The Emergence of RUP: A Profile of a Partido

The El Rio Golf Course issue raised the level of expectations of both activists and people in the barrios of Tucson. In what can be described as a state of euphoria, some people became so excited with their victory that they asked, "What do we do now?" The Chicano House's leadership answered the question with a proposal to form a Chicano political party. After four years of student and community organizing, much of the cadre that had made up the core of MASA, CLC, and Chicano House's leadership by early 1971 began the move to organize RUP in Arizona.

Working still under the aegis of Chicano House, Salomon Baldenegro, Raul Grijalva, Lupe Castillo, Frank de la Cruz, and a few others had totally despaired at the insensitivity of the two party-system, particularly the Democrats, towards the Méxicano.[53] De la Cruz explained that with the political happenings in Texas with RUP, coupled with increasing resistance from local city officials to some community issues, they had numerous discussions on the prospects of forming RUP in Arizona. They were turned off by the Democratic Party's lip service and the Republican Party's opposition to anything Chicanos proposed.[54]

However, in developing RUP's organizing strategy for Arizona, they were cognizant of the demographic differences between South Texas and Arizona. Outside Tucson, there were very few Méxicano population concentrations in Arizona. Moreover, their perception of RUP's role in Arizona differed from that in Texas. Grijalva explained, "We decided to go into elective politics more in the sense of an educational tool rather than an opportunity for winning."[55]

Motivated by RUP's successes in Cristal, Texas, Baldenegro found RUP simply "an idea whose time had come."[56] He officially promulgated the formation of RUP on February 22, 1971, at a meeting of the Pima County Young Democrats held at the Tucson Press Club.[57] At no time during its three years of life would RUP ever go beyond Tucson. The decision to keep the organizing focused on the Tucson area was made by the CLC organizers, who felt they did not have the manpower, resources, and networks to coordinate a statewide effort.[58] Strategically, they felt that if RUP could be made to work in Tucson, others around the state would then join the struggle to build it into a statewide party.

At that meeting of Young Democrats, Baldenegro explained the rationale behind RUP's formation. He said that activists of the CM in Tucson had written off both the Democrats and Republicans and had opted to form their own party. Their reasoning was that neither of the two major parties were "interested in working toward achieving social justice for the millions of Chicanos in the United States."[59]

> The two major parties are active and conscious collaborators in the racist society, which keeps the Chicano in a position of colonialism. . . . There is no qualitative difference in the racism perpetrated by the Democratic Party and that perpetrated by the Republican Party, although the Democrats would have us believe that their racism is more benevolent than the Republicans are. The Democratic and Republican parties are the same animal with two heads controlled by the same moneyed interests, who, because they are rich

exploiters, have no interests or desire to see the Chicano achieve the slightest degree of self-determination.[60]

In addition, Baldenegro pledged that RUP would not be elitist, that it would be involved in the Chicano struggle for justice and equality, and that it was going to be engaged in the upcoming local city council elections.[61]

The reaction to Baldenegro's announcement was mixed. The White-controlled media was critical of the RUP idea. An editorial in the *Arizona Daily Star* concluded: "What they [Méxicanos] need is justice. La Raza Unida is not likely to achieve much of it for them. . . . For Mexican Americans it is a case of cutting off one's political nose to spite one's political face."[62] The media were not the only ones to receive the news of RUP's emergence in a negative manner. When Grijalva was asked about the reaction of the average Méxicano in the street, he said: "At first they didn't understand what Salomon and us were trying to push. They felt that we were going up against the established political order, the parties, and that was something perhaps bigger than what we could handle. There was confusion among some people as to what we were trying to do."[40]

Operating out of the Chicano House, CLC became the sparkplug for organizing RUP. On February 27, a closed conference involving 125 persons was held in Tucson in the schoolyard of Manzo Elementary School. The conference agenda focused on pulling RUP together organizationally in Arizona.[41] Those in attendance included young people from the barrios, MEChA students from Tucson's local university and community college, and some middle-aged community residents. During the discussion on strategy, some of the participants expressed concerns about the way RUP was being organized. Hector Morales, director of the Tucson Committee for Economic Opportunity, admonished the new party supporters for stressing dogma, for the unquestioning acceptance of partido leaders, and for not involving more people from the barrios in the development of RUP's platform.[42]

Yet the overwhelming majority of the conference participants did not share Morales's skepticism. They drafted and adopted a platform, which in part read: "We have decided to form our own political party to work toward our liberation, our goal of complete self-determination, complete freedom and justice. . . . La Raza Unida Party will not support any candidate of the Democratic and Republican Party nor any individual who supports these parties."[43]

Baldenegro, Grijalva, and de la Cruz, who drafted a good part of the platform, described it as ideologically rather eclectic and reformist. It was a hybrid of liberal capitalist, socialist, and nationalist ideas and beliefs. The platform reflected RUP's commitment to work and to using the existing governmental superstructure to bring about change. More specifically, its planks on social service and job training programs reflected its reformist posture. But its socialist and progressive ideas became evident in planks on national health care (establishment of free health clinics); a guaranteed national income; community control of all local institutions; free prekindergarten schools; access to a free higher education, and support for the UFW and *pinto* (released convict) programs. The platform's cultural nationalism was reflected in its strong plank on bilingual/bicultural education and support for Chicano Studies programs. The CM's cultural renaissance, "El Plan Espiritual de Aztlán," developments in Texas, and even the Cuban revolution drove their nationalism.[67]

While Tuscon's RUP activists had some sympathy toward Third World struggles, their priority was the domestic struggle in the United States. Lupe Castillo described RUP's ideology as a combination of socialism and nationalism. "Activists that were Marxist and nationalists worked closely together and shared ideas. They interacted with other Black and White radicals, especially on the issue of the Vietnam War."[68] For very practical reasons, Baldenegro and other RUP activist leaders believed that the priorities were with the people in the barrios. They believed that the barrios were this nation's Third World and needed to be addressed first. What was important was the nature, obstacles to, and complexity of the struggle that needed to be waged domestically if social change and empowerment for Méxicanos was to be realized.[69]

But nationalism was the most prominent ideology, as Grijalva explained in our 1998 interview: "We were very much nationalist. That was one of the criticisms we were receiving from some of the other activist groups that said we were nationalist and isolationists, i.e., it is hard to build coalitions with the party people because they wanted to be on their own."[70]

RUP's nationalism reflected the historical experience of the area. Tucson's proximity to the United States–Mexican border coupled with its rich Méxicano heritage, traditions, and culture rekindled *orgullo* (pride) in being Méxicano and further supported RUP's nationalism. Unlike California and Colorado, where many activists were not fluent in Spanish, most RUP activists in Arizona as in Texas were both bilingual and bicultural. Their nationalism was predicated on the principle of self-determination— the idea that Chicanos needed to control their destiny, particularly at the community level.

Like its ideology, RUP's strategy and tactics were hybrids. It relied on running and endorsing candidates and concomitantly on the use of pressure tactics when dealing with a number of issues. RUP organizer Frank Wood told the press, "We're going to step on a lot of toes as we wage our campaigns, but we're willing to sacrifice elections in order to bring out the true and important issues." Baldenegro added that the partido "will be prepared to deal with everyday social problems of our community 24 hours a day, every day of the year, not just during election time."[71]

Because RUP was established only in Tucson, its structure was very localized. An exception was the small city of Douglas, where for a brief time a local RUP organizing committee was formed by Frank Barraza, who was on the city council.[72] Unlike RUP structures in other states that were more centralized, in Tucson RUP was rather loosely organized, lacking a formally defined structure, and without bylaws. Without an elected president or chairperson, it operated as a county committee, and the decision-making process was essentially democratic centralist. However, there was an implicit understanding that Baldenegro was, according to Grijalva, "our public persona." His power to lead was predicated not on any constitution, bylaws, or organizational hierarchy, but rather on his "persuasion powers." Grijalva further explained that Baldenegro was in a position to dictate because of the quality and independent nature of RUP's other cadre leaders and members. Ultimately, Baldenegro's power was "based on his ability to keep everybody together."[73] According to Cecilia Baldenegro, "Everyone knew Salomon was the main leader."[74] Thus, unlike Texas and Colorado, Arizona did not develop a strong caudillo type of leader.

Yet RUP's leadership can also be described as elitist in that it was led by a cadre of no more than five individuals who were all leaders. De la Cruz said that "RUP's leadership nucleus were the same people involved with the other groups. It was the same people who just wore different hats."[75] RUP's cadre leadership reaffirms my dictum that in the history of social movements, change is always made by the few in the name of the many.

Women were very much involved in the development of RUP in Arizona. Initially, when MASA was formed, women played a secondary leadership role. However, with the formation of CLC and the Chicano House, according to Lupe Castillo, "Women played a very strong leadership role. In many instances, they were the sharpest organizers, not interested in being in the limelight, but ensuring the organizing got done."[76]

By the early 1970s, women like Lupe Castillo and Raquel Rubio Goldsmith, among others, began to hold leadership roles equal to the men's. To a major degree because of their progressive beliefs, they had equal input in the making of decisions and formulation and implementation of ideas. They were capable and assertive, successful in "sensitizing" the men to the importance of being more inclusionary of women in leadership roles.[77]

## RUP's Political Struggles

No concerted effort was made to expand RUP beyond Tucson to other parts of the state or to get it officially on the ballot as a legitimate political party. Activists in most other areas, Phoenix, for example, never got into the RUP-organizing contagion. Their activism was much more oriented toward promoting educational change, supporting the UFW (which supported the Democrats), and other social justice issues. Some activists within MASO, for example, were well connected in the Democratic Party. Since the Southwest Council of La Raza, which had offices in Phoenix at that time, was a strong supporter of the Democrats, according to Castillo, "They exerted a lot influence in terms of determining the Chicano agenda, especially around the Phoenix area."[78]

Another reason that RUP did not pick up any organizing steam outside of Tucson was that, in the words of Grijalva, "it was ideological as well," that is, some of the other organizations throughout the state thought that RUP had gone too far and created problems by "taking on the two-party system." Outside Tucson, many of the CM activist leaders, such as Alfredo Gutiérrez in Phoenix, directed their activism toward educational and social justice issues. They were not willing to buck the

Democrats. Other CM activists across the state did not support RUP for fear of alienating the Democrats and losing funding support for their projects and programs.[79] Understanding the conservative political culture of the state and the iron control of the Democratic Party over many local Méxicano elites, as well as RUP's image as a radical party, it is not difficult to see why RUP never extended itself beyond Tucson.

## Baldenegro's City Council Race

On March 25, 1971, a few days prior to Baldenegro's council candidacy announcement, RUP organized a Vietnam Moratorium demonstration in Tucson involving some 200 protestors, a protest consistent with Baldenegro's long history of antiwar activism. There was a noon rally at Santa Rosa Park and a march and protest at the Selective Service Board and Marine Corps Recruitment offices.[80] The war protestors, mostly Méxicanos, demonstrated their antipathy for the war with placards, shouts, and slogans. One speaker declared, "The Selective Service has a contract with school boards. The contract says that you will not be educated, that you will not get to college; it guarantees that your blood will flow—to make some gringos richer."[81] This action was indicative of RUP's adherence to a strategy predicated on the concurrent use of pressure/advocacy and electioneering.[82]

Late in March 1971, Baldenegro, at the age of twenty-six, formally announced his RUP candidacy for city council for Tucson's Ward One. He called his candidacy on the RUP ticket "inevitable in the face of the inaction of the present City Council with regard to the problems of the poor." In explaining his decision to run, he stated: "I have lived here for more than 20 years. I am Chicano. I am poor. I not only speak the language of the people, I understand the daily problems they face because I face them, too."[83]

From the outset, the election was a political long shot because (1) Tucson had a complex single-member district (ward) system of local government in which candidates running for a particular ward had to run at large, citywide; (2) the election was partisan, meaning that Baldenegro was challenging the candidates of both the Republican and Democratic Parties; (3) RUP lacked resources and citywide organization, and Baldenegro's radical image made him vulnerable to red-baiting attacks from the opposition; (4) even though Méxicanos and other minorities constituted an overwhelming majority of the First Ward's population, it had been represented by a Republican; (5) Baldenegro faced the difficult task of running against a liberal Democrat, Ruben Romero, who was well financed. Republican opponent incumbent William Ruck had been appointed to the seat.[84]

In spite of these formidable obstacles, Baldenegro used the election to build RUP in Arizona. To him, the election was a tool designed to organize and politicize the people on the issues impacting their lives and, if he was elected, to begin instituting community control and bringing about major changes. He strongly felt that Méxicanos, Native Americans, and Blacks were not being adequately represented in the council. In reference to his platform, he said that the people from the barrio would decide what the issues would be.[85] With a campaign theme of social justice, he reminded the voters and media that "the poor in Tucson [needed] moral leadership, not political pimps."[86]

The fledgling RUP mounted a grassroots political campaign that relied on door-to-door canvassing of the ward's barrios and poor areas. Baldenegro focused on the issues he felt were important to the Méxicanos and other poor people of the Ward and did not skirt or minimize RUP's role in the campaign. In fact, he made it clear that he was running under the RUP label.[87] Several Méxicano organizations supported his campaign: El Rio Coalition, Chicano House, Centro Chicano, Centro Ruben Salazar, New Party, MEChA at the University of Arizona, MEChA at Pima College, Young Mexican American Association, Pima County Welfare Rights Organization, and University Educators for Baldenegro. Some of the literature put out by the campaign suggested his support was broad based and multiethnic and multiracial as well.[88]

Yet the labor unions, such as the AFL/CIO, endorsed the Democrat, Romero, and mounted an effort to mobilize their Méxicano members in the barrios. Grijalva explained years later that going against labor was "tough." Even though for years Baldenegro and others working the campaign had been strong supporters of the UFW, the unions "chose to be neutral. They sat it out."[89]

Thus, while his campaign message focused on the Méxicano, Baldenegro still sought the votes of Blacks, poor Whites, and sympathetic liberals. Johnny Heard, head of the Black Student Union, was one of his main campaign managers. He was also successful in securing contributions from some sympathetic liberal Jews, and he received input on campaign issues from some of the White professors at the University of Arizona.[90] Having been influenced by Saul Alinksy's *Reveille for Radicals* and *Rules for Radicals*, Baldenegro was a pragmatic organizer who did not allow his nationalism to become an obstacle to securing support from divergent sectors and groups.

His broad-based appeal became evident in the debates and community forums in which he participated. In one candidates' debate, Baldenegro said he felt that there were two Tucsons—"the one the tourists see, the downtown area and the university, and the neglected Tucson." The solution, he argued, was to establish "some sort of equilibrium between the two."[91] He further claimed that he more than the other two candidates personified and internalized the true "life-style" of the people in the First Ward. He also pledged that neither Democrats nor Republicans would control him.[92] Indicative of this was his refusal to be bought off by influential Democrats who offered him $15,000 in program money for one of the groups with which he was associated, provided he would pull out of the campaign.[93]

In spite of an aggressive get-out-the-vote drive by RUP that included radio spots in Spanish and scores of volunteers canvassing the barrios and other targeted areas of Tucson, Baldenegro lost the election to another Méxicano, Democrat Ruben Romero. With a voter turnout of 68 percent, some 68,405 voters, Baldenegro received 5,862 votes from the four east-side and north-side wards. According to Rosales, he lost Ward One, which was approximately 90 percent Méxicano.[94] Democrat Romero, who ousted the Republican incumbent, Vice Mayor William Ruck, received 27,801 to Ruck's 26,214 votes.[95]

At the core of Baldenegro's loss was the power of the major political parties. De la Cruz explained one of the lessons learned—"finding out how huge and powerful the Democratic and Republican Parties are and how difficult it is to challenge them."[96] However, there were several other major factors that contributed to Baldenegro's loss. First, his opponents perceived him as an unorthodox, radical, rabble-rouser activist who was antiestablishment and never wore a suit. Second, his campaign message and his focus on the issues were primarily directed at the Méxicano and poor. Third, the liberal Democrat Romero successfully used character assassination against Baldenegro, accusing him of being a "draft dodger." The issue played well in Tucson's conservative political culture. Fourth, the campaign had insufficient resources. The Democrats in particular were well entrenched and had access to money, while Baldenegro was extremely limited in finances.

The media as well homed in on Baldenegro's alleged negatives. The *Arizona Daily Star*, in an article a few days before the election, wrote: "Baldenegro is appealing for votes on the strength of his Mexican heritage and his contention that the city government has been unfair to his fellow West Side residents. His chances of winning in a citywide vote are remote."[97] To Baldenegro the organizer, his defeat was nothing more than another stage in the continuing struggle to promote social justice and to politicize and organize the people under RUP.[98] Grijalva's opinion of RUP's election performance was positive. He explained that overall, considering that Baldenegro had never before worked a campaign, he had done well. He further explained that "in terms of percentages we did really good, we had a good message, it scared the heck out of the Democratic Party. We had very limited resources, the difference was that we put in a lot of sweat equity."[99]

The next RUP electoral battle occurred in 1972 in a race for the school board in Tucson. The sole RUP candidate was Grijalva. The election, which was citywide, did not engender the publicity or excitement that Baldenegro's had the previous year. Since the election was nonpartisan, Grijalva for strategic reasons chose not to run under the aegis of RUP. He had learned from Baldenegro's election that RUP was perceived by too many people, including Méxicanos, as too radical. Furthermore, if they wanted to win or do well, they had to deemphasize their involvement with RUP and not make the election a partisan one.

Grijalva explained that, "consciously, we decided to not press the usage of Raza Unida—that we were not going let it become a pressing issue." The campaign issues were bilingual/bicultural education, Chicano Studies, more Chicano and minority teachers and administrators, and the district's use of funds.[100] Grijalva's radical image and inadequate resources coupled with the fact that he had to run citywide contributed to his defeat. Nevertheless, he felt that RUP had done well by addressing the various educational issues.[101]

RUP used the loss to convince the Mexican American Legal Defense and Education Fund (MALDEF) to file a suit against the school district on grounds that the at-large election discriminated against Méxicanos, who were a minority. RUP's intent was to push for the establishment of single-member districts. By dividing the school district into districts, or wards, partido activists felt they could elect Méxicanos to the school board. RUP was informed by MALDEF, however, that more research needed to be done on the issue in order to file a suit and that a candidate would have to run again in 1974 in order to show there was a clear pattern of discrimination.

## RUP's Declining Years

For the next two years (1972–1974), RUP went into a decline. After Grijalva's school board election, RUP's leaders began to abandon the partido. In a major story in the *Arizona Daily Star*, Baldenegro was described as an activist who had "mellowed," but he was quoted as saying that he felt politicians were *"muy perros"* (extremely mean). When asked if he would run for public office again, he replied that if he did he would run as a RUP candidate.[102] A content analysis of local newspapers revealed that during RUP's last two years, while some electioneering occurred, RUP's leadership shifted to a service and advocacy approach.[103]

RUP in 1973 challenged the Democrat-controlled South Tucson City Council. This was one instance in which RUP became politically active outside Tucson; South Tucson is a very small, incorporated community no larger than one square mile with a population that was at that time 90 percent Méxicano. The idea to expand RUP's organizing efforts to the southern part of Tucson was proposed by Grijalva in 1971 and subsequently supported. Grijalva and de la Cruz began preparing for the challenge in 1971 under the auspices of CLC by opening an office right in the heart of the barrio next to an infamous bar.

RUP's organizing strategy was to gain a political foothold in the community by establishing El Centro (The Center).[104] In order to win the people's confidence and support, El Centro provided a variety of social programs and addressed numerous social issues impacting Méxicanos.[105] The programs were designed to offer the people badly needed services: A bilingual preschool was established, and legal and social services were also provided.[106] On the issue side, Castillo explained, the town's police and city officials had a reputation for corruption. She said later, "It was a real challenge for us to try to politicize and organize a community that few had an interest in creating change."[107]

With El Centro providing services, CLC was able to develop a base of support and access to resources badly needed for organizing purposes. The Southwest Council of La Raza provided some funding for El Centro's programs. Much of the cadre was comprised of students, and the programs gave them parttime jobs that enabled them to continue their education and activism.[108] The Centro was also involved in providing continuing support for the UFW, demonstrating against the Vietnam War, and acting as a pressure group on issues when deemed necessary.

By 1973, with CLC replaced by RUP, it was decided that the timing was propitious for RUP to mount a political challenge to the Democratic Party–controlled council. RUP would field two candidates, Raquel Livas and Francisco Moreno. The corruption among city police officials became one of the main issues on which RUP's candidates focused. RUP's grassroots campaign received considerable media play, and RUP's two candidates were endorsed by the local White-owned newspaper.

Even though the race was nonpartisan, it turned into an unofficial partisan political battle between Democrats and RUP activists. With three seats up for grabs, the Democratic candidates won in a clean sweep: Reynoldo Santa Cruz was the top vote getter with 570 votes, followed by Daniel Eckstrom, who polled 547 votes. Julia Velez finished third with 506 votes. Of RUP's two candidates, Livas got 131 and Moreno 120 votes, not even close enough to boast that RUP presented a serious challenge to the Democrats.[109] RUP lost because the Democrats were well entrenched and had in place "a good old boys' network" that proved to be impregnable. This was to be the last political campaign in which RUP would run candidates in Arizona. As de la Cruz explained many years later: "We thought we had a chance to win. We were very disappointed at the results."[110]

In 1974, RUP leader Grijalva ran for a second time for the Tucson school board and won. Again, since the election was nonpartisan, RUP was totally deemphasized.[111] He ran as an individual on a platform of coalition building, of building bridges on issues with other ethnic and racial communities, a much more middle-of-the-road image and approach. In explaining why Grijalva decided to dissociate himself from RUP, Castillo said: "Raul simply wanted to win. So he ran a populist campaign. He forged a powerful, well organized, grassroots multi-ethnic coalition."[112]

Grijalva explains that a major difference between the 1972 and the 1974 elections was the sophisticated use of the "science of electioneering." The campaign strategy involved grassroots, door-to-door canvassing, targeting of precincts, use of mailers, extensive use of media, coalition building, and a focus on issues of popular concern. Grijalva's victory helped put to rest the RUP in Arizona. RUP activists had tasted victory not under the banner of RUP, but rather through the pragmatic tactic of using issues of popular concern. Because of Grijalva's victory, RUP was informed by MALDEF that the basis for the suit proposed in 1972 against the school district was moot.[113]

RUP continued functioning as a committee until 1974. By then, RUP's leaders had moved on to various other community-based organizations and programs or simply just dropped out and quit. For example, in 1973, RUP's leadership had established an alternative bilingual/bicultural preschool, Escuela Analco, which meant "barrio school." Coordinated by RUP leader Raul Grijalva and Tony Bracamonte, a service worker at the Centro Aztlán, a fund drive for $10,000 was initiated.[114] According to Cecelia Baldenegro, a leader in RUP and other groups: "The Raza Unida Party here in Tucson was only one project of many we were organizing, all at the same time. It was a question of not having enough time and resources to do everything we had to do."[115]

Although RUP was moribund by 1974, Baldenegro and a few others continued to identify themselves as RUP supporters for a few more years. Baldenegro, for example, during 1973 and 1974 served as Arizona's representative in RUP's National Congreso de Aztlán. He continued to be consulted by the first RUP national chairman, José Angel Gutiérrez, then by his replacement, Juan José Peña from New Mexico, as if he were still actively organizing RUP in Arizona. He was consulted on a variety of domestic and foreign policy matters involving RUP until he broke away in 1979 due to differences with RUP's growing "internationalist" politics, namely the 1980 meeting of a RUP delegation with Yasir Arafat in Lebanon (see Chapter Eleven).[116] Baldenegro said in our interview: "I have always believed that Chicanos first have to fight the struggle here in the United States, not abroad."[117] Yet both he and his wife, Cecelia Baldenegro, remained registered as RUP until the mid-1980s.

Even though RUP's existence in Tucson proved transitory, the fact that it presented even a potential political threat to the Democrats is part of its success story. As a result of its work, changes occurred that enhanced the Méxicano's struggle for political empowerment.[118] By 1973, the number of Méxicanos elected to the state legislature had increased to eleven, whereas in 1965 the figure had been six, all Democrats. In addition, Democrat Raul Castro was elected governor in 1974. Cecilia Baldenegro commented that "too many Chicano Democrats, who were friends and who identified with the philosophy [cultural nationalism] of the partido were being elected."[119]

With its demise by 1974, RUP in Arizona left a legacy of struggle for the empowerment of the Méxicano. The question is why it ended. The reasons can be traced primarily to endogenous factors, along with a few exogenous factors. Foremost was the exodus of RUP's true-believer activists, which began in 1972 right after Grivalja's unsuccessful school board bid. They left to work other agendas or with other groups. RUP's unsuccessful bid to replace the Democrat-controlled city council in South Tucson in 1973, however, proved to be the killing blow. RUP's small cadre had fallen victim to burnout, frustration, and disillusionment. Their abandonment of RUP left a leadership void that was not filled. Concurrent endogenous antagonisms included the Gutierrez/Gonzales power struggle; the decline of the Chicano Movement; the lack of finances; RUP's inability to expand its base beyond Tucson; RUP's leaders overextending themselves to work on concurrent agendas; the small statewide Méxicano population; the loyalty of Méxicano activists, organizations, and unions throughout the state to the Democratic Party; and RUP's failure to produce tangible electoral victories.

RUP's dissolution was also significantly impacted by exogenous factors, as was the case in Texas, Colorado, California, and Mew Mexico. These included Arizona's omnipotent two-party system; Arizona's conservative political culture; Tucson's cumbersome city council ward/at-large system; the at-large election system used by Tucson's school board and South Tucson's city council; and the media coverage that often depicted RUP as a radical political force.

RUP's ultimate legacy in Arizona, in the words of Lupe Castillo, was that "it was successful in breaking down many of the obstacles that Méxicanos faced politically, and in the end it was instrumental in unleashing an empowerment movement that continues today."[120]

## Chapter Ten

# Pressure Group, Service Provider, or Partido? The Rise and Fall of RUP in the Midwest and Utah, 1972–1976

The Midwest and Utah never became a fertile political region for organizing the RUP.[1] Historically, the Midwest had not been part of Mexico's lost territories. It was never colonized by the Spaniards or occupied by Mexico. The colonizers had been the French, and most of the Midwest had been part of the Louisiana Purchase of 1803. Displacing the indigenous peoples, White settlers by the latter part of the nineteenth century had consolidated their power. It was not until the early 1900s that Méxicanos in search of work began to settle in the Midwest and Utah.

### The Historical Setting

With the emergence of the Chicano Movement (CM), some Méxicano activists in the Midwest became infused with a new sense of purpose, a revitalized pride in being Chicano, and a willingness to confront the superstructure that had kept them subordinated. A major catalyst in the propagation of the CM in the Midwest was the La Raza Unida Conference held in 1967 in El Paso, Texas. With Méxicanos from the Midwest participating, the defiance and the call for change spread quickly to their home states.

Concurrently, the student activism emanating from California and Texas by 1968 triggered student activism among the few Méxicano students attending universities and colleges in the Midwest. Inspired by a sense of cultural renaissance, students pushed for cultural and Chicano Studies programs; student, faculty, and staff recruitment among Méxicanos; and a collaborative relationship with the community. The Chicano Youth Liberation conferences of 1969 and 1970, held in Denver, Colorado, by the Crusade for Justice, further inspired the Chicano cultural renaissance and raised the level of activism among the youth in the Midwest.[2] However, their activism was constrained by their small numbers within the universities and the region as a whole.

Méxicanos in the Midwest did not have the population numbers or density of some of the states in the Southwest. Not until the early part of the twentieth century had they arrived in any numbers, fleeing the violence of the Mexican revolution and Mexico's wretched poverty. They had settled particularly in Illinois, Michigan, Kansas, Ohio, and Indiana. Initially, agricultural and railroad work drew them to the Midwest. Beginning around the 1920s, barrios began forming around the migrant workplaces—factories, meat-packing houses, agricultural centers, railroads, and so on—in such cities as Chicago, Kansas City, Detroit, and St. Louis; there, Méxicanos became victims of exploitation and powerlessness.[3]

As the demand for cheap labor increased in the region, so did the Méxicano population. Table 2 provides a 1960 population and percentage breakdown of each state.[4]

In the 1960s, for example, the Méxicano population in the nine Midwestern states totaled some 145,000.[5] By the early 1970s, only 10 percent of the total Méxicano population lived outside the Southwest.[6]

## The Rise of RUP

Between the years 1968 and 1972, the CM in the Midwest experienced considerable growth. With the emergence of RUP in 1970, the organizing contagion that had begun to permeate the Southwest spread as well to various states of the Midwest. However, it was not until 1972 that some young Chicano activists in the universities and colleges and community activists in the barrios became politically excited enough to jump on the RUP-organizing bandwagon. From 1972 to about 1979, RUP organizing efforts occurred in Illinois, Wisconsin, Michigan, Ohio, Indiana, Kansas, Nebraska, and Iowa. In the West and Northwest, some RUP organizing activity occurred in Utah and Washington. In all these states, RUP activists were determined to connect with RUP's struggle in the Southwest.

Initially, in some of the Midwest states, it was the student sector that was the avant garde for organizing RUP. In those states, many of the RUP leaders and organizers came from the leadership ranks of various student organizations, such as Movimiento Estudiantil Chicano de Aztlán (MEChA), United Mexican American Students (UMAS), and La CAUSA (Chicano Association of United Students for Action). According to Pat Velasquez, a student leader with La CAUSA at the University of Nebraska: "As student activists, we were very much influenced by the Raza Unida Party events occurring throughout the Southwest. We wanted to be a part of the struggle. So we started to organize the partido in 1972."[7]

In some other states, however, RUP leaders and supporters came from the communities and barrios. Some were farm workers; others were blue-collar workers who also became protagonists for organizing RUP.[8] According to Ernesto Chacon, who became

TABLE 2.   1960 Méxicano Population of Midwest States

| State | Number | Percent of U.S. Total |
|-------|--------|----------------------|
| Illinois | 63,063 | 3.6 |
| Michigan | 24,298 | 1.4 |
| Kansas | 12,972 | 0.7 |
| Ohio | 9,960 | 0.6 |
| Missouri | 8,159 | 0.5 |
| Wisconsin | 6,705 | 0.4 |
| Nebraska | 5,858 | 0.3 |

one of the most prominent RUP organizer-leaders in the Midwest, "In Wisconsin and some other states it was the farm worker that was at the forefront of the organizing for the Raza Unida."[9] Their involvement was a result of the fact that many of them had roots in Texas, being products of the migrant stream of farm workers. As farm workers from Crystal City and other parts of South Texas traveled to their seasonal work in the Midwest, they were instrumental in propagating the good news of RUP's electoral successes in South Texas.

Still others, especially those in Nebraska, had a close relationship with Méxicano activists from Colorado's Crusade for Justice. As a result, RUP organizing committees were formed in some states by 1972. A major stimulating force was RUP's national convention, held in El Paso, Texas, that September. Several Midwest delegations participated: Illinois, Indiana, Kansas, Michigan, Nebraska, Wisconsin, and Missouri.[10] Most of the delegates from the Midwest were students and community people. At the convention, a RUP leader from Illinois, Arturo Vasquez, explained that Méxicanos from the Midwest were involved with the partido because "one can voice the wants and needs of Midwest Chicanos for independent political action for the kind of change and benefits we desire."[11] Even after the national convention, the Midwest was not exempt from the ongoing power struggle between Gonzales and Gutiérrez. At a Congreso de Aztlán meeting held in Chicago in 1973 that was attended by supporters of both leaders, the meeting was adjourned after a pro-Gonzales proposal was introduced by the Illinois delegation; it called for the elimination of the position of national RUP Congreso chairperson, a post held by Gutiérriez.[12]

## La Raza Unida: Party or Organization?

In spite of the power struggle, for the next three years efforts to organize RUP continued. From the outset, most community and student activists realized that the idea of organizing a "partido" in the Midwest was not realistic or practical. Without the requisite population base, they could not challenge the hegemony of the two major parties. Consequently, what RUP had done in Texas was not politically replicable in the Midwest. Initially, with the exception of a few states like Illinois and Michigan, where activists pushed RUP's electoral agenda, most of RUP's activists pragmatically opted to form not a political party, but rather an organization. Others—for instance, Ohio, which by 1972 had adopted the name La Raza Unida de Ohio—were social service and program driven.[13]

Hence, activists with divergent interests adopted the concept of La Raza Unida and put their energies into building two types of organizations: one was a pressure group oriented toward social change; the other was a social service and program development agency. The latter model was buttressed by the formation of the Midwest Council of La Raza, which had been formed as a result of a conference held at the University of Notre Dame. Its orientation was similar to that of the Southwest Council of La Raza, with its focus on development of programs and funding. Thus, under the rubric of La Raza Unida (LRU), activists in the Midwest connected with RUP's struggle in the Southwest.

## Five LRU Case Studies: Diversity of Focus

Four Midwest states and one in the West offer similar but still distinctive examples of both the LRU and RUP.

### Michigan

In the state of Michigan, Ruben Alfaro, inspired by the concept of La Raza Unida, organized LRU. The concept behind the LRU in Michigan was not that of a political partido, but that of an "organization of organizations."[14] Juarez described it as "an umbrella organization that brought different groups together periodically to battle some common interest issue."[15] A paper by RUP organizer Ricardo Parra suggests that developing an "organization rather than a party might have been due to the thinking of the leadership, who felt that more reform and benefits might come about through a nonpartisan pressure organization than by finding out how weak their constituents' voting power was.[16]

Alfaro started organizing LRU in Michigan using issues related to the farm workers, many of whom were migrants or ex-migrants from South Texas. LRU's purpose was to improve the conditions of farm workers, particularly in the employment arena. Initially, committees were set up in different communities. In a very short period of time, the committees turned into chapters, and LRU was transformed into a statewide nonprofit organization. Olga Villa Parra, who was a student organizer for LRU at the time, explained that as a new organization, "its focus was on dealing with the social, employment, and educational needs of the people, especially those who were migrants. That kept us preoccupied."[17]

As the organization grew, it became more assertive in its demands. At this time, a few committees sought unsuccessfully to run candidates for local office. Most of the committees functioned as pressure groups rather than as social service agencies. Marches and protests at the state capital were organized. They protested the deplorable living conditions of farm workers. They lobbied and made demands for the state to produce more jobs and better services for Méxicano workers.

By 1973, the idea of building LRU into an umbrella organization had gained momentum in other Midwest states, such as Ohio, Iowa, Wisconsin, and Nebraska.[18] Networking, the sharing of information and advocacy support, became important inducements for Méxicanos in other states to build LRU in their respective states and communities. In most of these states as well, LRU was formed as a nonprofit organization. While in some states it did function at times as a pressure group seeking to effect social change, its primary orientation in most states was that of a social service program provider.

RUP's growth and development in Michigan was very much influenced by RUP's activities and politics in Texas. Through a combination of migrant farm workers propagating news of RUP's activities and José Angel Gutiérrez's several visits to the state, efforts to organize RUP commenced around 1972.[19] In Michigan, students and community people were at the forefront of organizing RUP. Especially in Lansing, Michigan, community people sought unsuccessfully to give RUP an electoral emphasis by running some candidates for local office.[20] Because of the small size of the Méxicano population, RUP there never took on the semblance of a political party.

Ideologically, RUP in Michigan was cultural nationalist. Again, it was influenced by Texas RUP and Gutiérrez. Few of the leaders were cognizant of Rodolfo "Corky" Gonzales or of his separatist politics. They were practical and reform oriented. Their main concern was ensuring that they addressed the educational, job, health, cultural, and other social issue concerns that affected Méxicanos.[21] While RUP in Michigan never developed Marxist tendencies, some of its organizers were critical of liberal capitalism and saw that the struggle was one "between the haves and have-nots."[22]

*Illinois*

In Illinois, Chicano activists in 1972 sought to form RUP as a political party. In great part, this was because Illinois, especially in the city of Chicago, had the largest concentration of Méxicanos and Latinos of any state in the region. In 1960, Illinois had more Méxicanos of foreign stock than Colorado and New Mexico combined.[23] As Richard Parra explained, "Unlike other states in the Midwest, because of Méxicano density in Chicago, RUP there developed an electoral approach to its development."[24] An organizing problem for RUP activists there was that too many of the Méxicanos were not U.S. citizens, making them ineligible to vote. Although it never became a certified political party, RUP in Illinois did become involved in running candidates for public office—unsuccessfully. In addition, Méxicanos there had much more political experience than those of other Midwest states; they experienced, participated, and were a part of Chicago mayor Richard Daley's Democratic machine.[25]

In 1973, for example, Angel Moreno ran unsuccessfully as an independent under the guise of RUP for the Seventh Congressional District. The fact that he got on the ballot was a success, considering the internal and external difficulties he had to overcome. He was required to submit nominating petitions bearing signatures of at least 5 percent of the district's registered voters, which amounted to 6,700 names. Although he lost, his campaign was used to organize and politicize the 200,000 or so Méxicanos that resided in the district.[26] Concomitantly, beyond its electoral function, RUP was involved in a number of social justice issues.

In Illinois, RUP activists actually called themselves El Partido de La Raza Unida. Politically, as a developing partido, the RUP nationalists developed their own platform, which included such planks as: community control of schools, programs for migrant workers, an end to discrimination in employment, greater Chicano control of television and other media, better health and housing programs, and support for bilingual/bicultural education. The Marxist chapter's program of action repudiated most of these goals as too reformist; it set forth the virtues of a proletarian class struggle.

*Nebraska*

Student activists from the University of Nebraska in Omaha organized RUP in 1972. The students were members of La CAUSA. In 1972 and 1973, RUP coexisted with a number of other activist-oriented groups. Excited by RUP's political developments in Texas and Colorado, a core group of students who were working at the Chicano Awareness Center, a multiservice center that housed several other groups, opted to form a RUP organizing committee. RUP in Omaha never developed an electoral agenda. Pat Velazquez, who was one of the leaders, explained that it took on a much more social justice and cultural thrust because of its strong nationalist posture. Issues of education and culture became the focus of its activity, because "the Chicano community in Omaha comprised only 3 percent of the city's population. This translated to only 10,000 Chicanos. From the onset we recognized that we just did not have the population base, especially when all of the local elections were at-large."[27] By late 1973, after being involved in a variety of local issues, RUP declined—a victim of a scenario similar to that in Arizona. The leaders simply moved on and continued to deal with social justice issues and social service/program development elsewhere; consequently, the partido experiment in Nebraska was short-lived.

*Wisconsin*

Throughout much of the Midwest by 1975, RUP was in a state of decline. Once the funding sources started to dry up, LRU organizations began to decline as well although many of its leaders and supporters continued to be supportive of RUP. This became evident in the various newsletters that were published during the time that LRU was functional.

Wisconsin's LRU in the long run was perhaps the most dynamic and successful. As both a pressure advocacy organization and social service provider, it had the most successes and lasted the longest. Formed around 1972,[28] Wisconsin's LRU continued to function until 1979.[29] All this time, while there were several leaders, the primary organizer and leader was Ernesto Chacon, a veteran activist with years of community-organizing experience. Recognizing that Méxicanos did not have suffi-cient numbers in Wisconsin to politically challenge the Democrats and Republicans, Chacon and others working with him decided against building La Raza Unida into a political party. Instead, as in other states, they decided to form a multifunctional advocacy and service organization that would at times endorse local candidates.

As an advocacy pressure group, LRU took on a myriad of issues and causes, from education, police harassment, immigration, discrimination, and jobs, to bettering the services and working conditions of farm workers. It also addressed issues that were national or international in scope. With fourteen county chapters that were grass-roots oriented, LRU relied on direct action protest and traditional lobbying methods to advance its interest as an action-oriented pressure group. Indicative of its mass base, the Jefferson County LRU had some 300 members.[30] As Chacon explained in our interview, "The use of direct action tactics quickly got the attention of the politicos. When we had to we used picket lines, marches, demonstrations, to get their attention to our concerns."[31]

A few of Wisconsin's LRU committees by 1975 had become incorporated as non-profit service and program organizations. In Jefferson County, LRU in 1975 opened an office, and that year it received a small government grant of $10,000 to assess the Méxicano population's problems in the county. Its programmatic priorities were to provide services, particularly in the fields of education, manpower, and health. Yet its main leader, Alcario Samudio, publicly acknowledged its pressure role and his intent to transform it into a political force in the county: "We're not gonna go and bow our heads."[32]

Ideologically, LRU in Wisconsin was cultural nationalist and reformist. Because many of the migrant farm workers came from South Texas, for example, from Crystal City, Cotulla, and Carrizo Springs, the LRU was very much influenced by RUP's development in Texas, by Gutiérrez the leader, and by the Tejano (Texas) Méxicano culture. According to Chacon, "We followed a strong nationalist line. We felt too many of our young people were losing their Méxicano identity so we sought to stop the as-similation of our people."[33] Consequently, LRU sought to reinforce what was Méxicano by holding numerous cultural events, which encouraged a cultural renaissance.

By 1979, however, LRU in Wisconsin had become a casualty of the changing conservative times. Funding had practically dried up, and some of both the service and advocacy committees had become defunct.

## Utah

As was the case in the Midwest, RUP in Utah became a pressure group rather than a political party. Influenced by RUP developments in Texas, Hector Rodriguez of Provo led the effort to establish RUP statewide in 1975. The impetus to organize, however, was driven by an issue that evolved from an unfriendly encounter between Rodriguez and officials from the governor's office. At its crux was Rodriguez's charge that state officials were spending monies elsewhere that had been earmarked for

Chicano areas. He aslo charged that some Méxicanos were "on the take." When he brought these allegations to state officials in August 1975—and also identified himself as representing RUP—he was asked to leave the office and drop the issue. As a consequence of the verbal altercation, Rodriguez lost his job as executive director of La Raza Organization, a social service agency.[34]

In 1975, Rodriguez convened a statewide meeting in Midvale and with some fifty persons from eight counties took the steps necessary to form RUP in Utah. Jesse Hernandez from Layton was elected state chair and Gloria Rodriguez, a doctoral candidate at Brigham Young University, was elected secretary. RUP was loosely structured, with organizing committees at the county level. From the outset, the intent for RUP was that it be strong enough to affect the political balance of power statewide. Both Rodriguez and Hernandez believed that the Méxicano base of 10,000 to 18,000 was large enough to accomplish this goal. RUP's ideology was ostensibly cultural nationalist and reformist, strongly influenced by Gutiérrez and RUP in Texas. While its cardinal goal was to become a political party, RUP's advocacy activities and priorities lay in education, housing, and employment.[35]

For about two years, RUP in Utah functioned as a pressure group, taking on a variety of issues.[36] Without a large enough population base, it declined by 1978, partly because other advocacy and social service organizations had more clout and support in Utah's Méxicano community. RUP took a rather adversarial stance in its dealings with other organizations, such as La Raza Oganization and particularly SOCIO (Spanish-speaking Organizaiton for Community Integrity and Opportunity). In a letter Hector Rodriguez sent José Angel Gutiérrez dated May 7, 1976, he attacked Abelardo Delgado and me, co-chairs of the National Chicano Forum:

> As you remember some time last year I called you and mentioned to you that Armando Navarro was in this organization of SOCIO, and that people here in Utah were not too happy with this group. . . . We failed to get on the ballot because Abelardo as State Chairman of SOCIO refused to sign our petition and passed the word to several county chapters to stay away from the Raza Unida petition. . . . We (Raza Unida Party) have a good chance of getting support. . . . I will meet with the Republican Gubernatorial Candidate Vernon Romney (he is Attorney general) who gave me big support.

Without a population and concentration base, and with an organizing straegy that divided rather than unified, RUP in Utah was a transient political effort propelled by the personal agenda of its leader.

In the end, although RUP never scored any major political victories in the state or became a leading organizational force, it served as confrontive force for social justice issues.

## Profile of a Partido Movement that Became an Organization

It is informative to compare the Midwest's La Raza Unida (LRU) and RUP in terms of leadership, ideology, organization, and strategy and tactics.

In the Southwest, RUP had many leaders and organizers, some of whom became prominent in the CM. In the Midwest, the leaders and organizers never achieved great notoriety. No strong regional leader ever emerged. Yet, as Chacon observed, "We had many competent and very skilled local organizers that were able to organize our people under very difficult situations."[37] Of those leaders that did emerge in different states, none were able to overcome the problems of distance, insufficient resources, ideological and strategic differences, and parochialism. (Of all these leaders, Chacon was the most prominent and visible, the moving force behind regional meetings and the RUP organizing effort in the Midwest.)

These problems impeded efforts to unify and consolidate either RUP or LRU on a regional scale. Consequently, no local or state leader ever reached the stature of a Gutiérrez or Gonzales at a regional level. Chacon from Wisconsin, Olga and Ricardo Parra from Indiana, Angel Moreno and Art Vasquez from Illinois, and Gilberto Martinez from Ohio were a few of the major RUP leaders from the Midwest. Ruben Alfaro from Michigan was another major leader who was instrumental in organizing RUP as an organization and not as a political party. Chacon explained that in Wisconsin they were blessed with more organizers than leaders.[38] Trained as a professional organizer, Chacon more than anyone had the leadership and organizing skills to unify LRU at a Midwest regional level but was unable to do so because he was too preoccupied with various ongoing organizing projects.[39]

Moreover, on the issue of the leadership role of women, both RUP and LRU leadership in the Midwest were male dominated. The men had the most visible or "out-front" leadership role. The women generally took on a more secondary leadership role. Velasquez explained that in Nebraska many of RUP leaders came from the student ranks, and at that time there were very few Chicanas enrolled in the universities.[40] Yet in Wisconsin, according to Chacon, "Women like Irma Guerra played a key and crucial leadership role. They brought new ideas and energy to the organization."[41] From the perspective of Olga Villa Parra, who herself became one of the most prominent LRU leaders, "Feminism for Chicanas that were involved with the Raza Unida was not a priority. The reason was that there was so much need that the struggle for justice was a much more important priority."[42]

In spite of divided leadership loyalties, most RUP and LRU organizing efforts in the Midwest were inclined to be strongly cultural nationalist in their ideological posture. Their adherence to Chicanismo was very much a product of the influences of both nationalist leaders.[43] Velasquez explained that RUP in Nebraska adhered to and supported Gonzales's ultra nationalism: "We had him come every chance we had to make a speech. He was inspiring."[44] RUP in Illinois had a strong current of progressivism in its politics. Ricardo Parra in a paper on Midwest organizations wrote that "Illinois is a progressive oriented partido that is interested in promoting political education and awareness of La Raza as to the social, economic, and political contradictions that must be challenged and is thereby taking actions to combat the oppressive forces that enslave la Raza."[45]

This progressivism, however, became so doctrinaire that the original RUP organizing committee split into two chapters, one cultural nationalist, the other Marxist in orientation. The nationalists wanted to develop RUP into a partido that was active in elections, while the Marxists wanted to develop RUP along the lines of the Communist Party. In a letter written by Angel Moreno to José Angel Gutiérrez in November 1973, this split was discussed. Moreno attacked Art Vasquez, Magda Rameriz, Felipe Aguirre, and Ramiro Borja as the leaders of the Marxist RUP chapter. Because of the ideological divisions, Moreno wrote, "After a little over one year we as El Partido de La Raza Unida de Chicago have not done a goddamn thing as far as organizing a working Partido."[46]

The states of Michigan, Wisconsin, Ohio, Indiana, and Minnesota were all ideologically influenced by the cultural nationalism emanating from Texas.[47] They took on a very reformist work-within-the-system approach. They were more preoccupied in trying to meet the needs of the people rather than in devising radical ideas of social change.[48]

Generally speaking, most of the activist groups in the other states were adherents of cultural nationalism. Many Méxicanos through the CM had rediscovered their cultural roots in Mexico and identified as Chicanos."[49] In Nebraska, however, RUP activists were more ultranationalist. They were very much influenced by the separatist nation-building nationalism of Corky Gonzales.[50]

RUP never became an official statewide political party in any of the Midwest states. While groups in some states sought to project the image of a statewide operation, in most cases, they were not. Such was the case in Illinois and in Nebraska, where RUP was limited to Omaha. RUP was loosely organized, followed a cadre approach, and never developed a mass following.

However, in Wisconsin, RUP developed as a movement organization comprised of thirteen chapters, all with a membership base that drew from the communities. RUP in Michigan likewise envisioned itself as an organization of organizations, which did have a statewide structure comprised of several local coalition committees. With RUP's expansion to other Midwest states, similar structures developed. Thus, on a regional basis, RUP never reached the level of organization where all the states were well integrated and had a regional strategy.

RUP in the Midwest never took on the semblance of a regular political party. For all intents and purposes, strategically and tactically, RUP functioned as a pressure group or a social service provider.[51] As the former, it employed direct action methods oriented toward changing public policy in the areas of farm workers' working conditions and programs, police abuse, discrimination, education, housing, and so on. As the latter, it was more concerned about developing and implementing social, educational, and cultural programs. Of the two models, the pressure group orientation was more evident in Wisconsin than anywhere else in the Midwest.

Thus, strategically, RUP activists in the Midwest never moved to put RUP on the ballot as an official party. Yet RUP in some states maintained an intentional strategic political façade. RUP activists in various states periodically invited Gutiérrez, Gonzales, Tijerina, or Muñiz from Texas to give political talks to seminars, meetings, and conferences. In most cases, they were used for consciousness-raising purposes and to remind the Democrat and Republican Party officials that neither party was meeting the manifold needs of the growing Méxicano community. However, RUP electoral activity in the Midwest proved almost nonexistent, with some few exceptions.

## RUP's Decline in the Midwest

With the CM moribund by 1974 and RUP in a state of rapid national decline everywhere, by 1976 RUP declined as well in the Midwest. According to Juan José Peña, who later became RUP's national chairperson, efforts to organize RUP that began in late 1971 declined in 1973; by 1976, RUP was no longer operating in most Midwest states.[52] Both in Nebraska and Michigan, for example, RUP lasted no more than two years; yet in Wisconsin it managed to survive for some six years.

In the Midwest, although RUP was a transitory political phenomenon, its imprint remained in the Méxicano's quest for political power and change. So powerful was its impact that scores of communities from Wisconsin to Michigan got organized and became effective agents of social change. RUP's legacy to the region was that it politicized Méxicanos, helped foster a cultural renaissance that rekindled their pride in being Méxicano, and was beneficial in helping them get better organized and more involved.

RUP's rise and decline in the Midwest was linked to that of RUP both in Texas and Colorado. When RUP in these two states seemed vibrant and dynamic in the early years of the 1970s, some Méxicano activists were swept into the RUP euphoria. But as RUP began to decline by the mid-1970s in these two states, so did RUP in the Midwest. What remained of RUP between 1976 and 1981 was not enough to sustain or impel development. Without the charismatic leadership of Gutiérrez and Gonzales, RUP's few remaining activists shifted their focus away from the partido.

RUP's decline in the Midwest was precipitated almost entirely by exogenous antagonisms, the foremost being (with the exception of Illinois) the lack of both a substantial Méxicano population and a concentrated one. These two factors made it impossible for RUP to take on a formal partido role. Elections are won by a plurality of votes. Lacking the population and density to have a strong political power base, RUP had no realistic chance of becoming an official political party.

RUP's decline was also a product of other endogenous factors: (1) No leader of the stature of Gutierrez or Gonzales emerged to consolidate the region; (2) few if any funds for coordinating RUP across the required distances at either the regional or, in most cases, the state level; (3) at no time was a formal RUP organizing plan of action ever devised; (4) financial and manpower resources were lacking; (5) in some states, RUP depended on students for both leadership and support; and (6) RUP lacked support from existing traditional Méxicano organizations. In light of these challenges, RUP activists opted to create social service and development entities that were supposedly RUP oriented and supportive.

RUP's decline in the Midwest was not influenced by the myriad of constraints that confront third-party movements. One can argue, however, that the presence of rigid election laws and single-member congressional districts in Illinois did impact RUP's development; the Midwest's White-dominated moderate to conservative political culture also contributed to RUP's ultimate demise.

As a third-party movement, RUP in the Midwest never came close to developing into a serious electoral challenge or threat to the region's two-party hegemony—the Democrats and Republicans.

*Chapter Eleven*

---

# Rationale for Expansion: RUP's National and International Politics

After two years of struggling to build the Raza Unida Party (RUP) into a viable political party, in 1972 its national leadership also began to expand its presence in both the national and international arenas. Driven by the organizing dynamism of the Chicano Movement (CM) as well as its own successes, RUP held, in El Paso, Texas, a national convention. Activists from eighteen states gathered for the purpose of transforming and expanding RUP into a national partido. They were not satisfied with merely building a county or state party, they sought to challenge the hegemony of the Democratic and Republican Parties at the regional and national level. Concurrently, in Texas, RUP planted the seed for its entry into the international arena.

## RUP's National Politics: The Leadership Power Struggle Begins

RUP had been in existence only a little more than two years when in 1972 it decided to hold its first and what would be its last national convention. Two questions arise in weighing the practicality of holding such a convention. First, Why would a third party that was only on the ballot in the state of Texas in 1972 move to organize itself into a national party? And second, Why hold a national convention when the party is, at best, regional?

The decision to have RUP go national and the decision to hold a national convention were intertwined. Both ideas were, essentially, the result of a power struggle between José Angel Gutiérrez, founder of RUP in Texas, and Rodolfo "Corky" Gonzales, founder of RUP in Colorado. The two had been battling over who would be RUP's undisputed leader since the party's early development in 1970.[1]

The power struggle between the two began almost immediately after Gutiérrez in January 1970 led the emergence of RUP in Texas and Gonzales in late March followed suit in Colorado. When RUP surfaced in South Texas that January with strong electoral victories, Gonzales, driven by the belief that he was the CM's most prominent leader, moved expeditiously to thwart Gutiérrez's leadership challenge by also forming RUP in Colorado. Historian Ignacio Garcia explains that Gonzales's motivation to form RUP in Colorado "was undoubtedly influenced by the presence of Texas RUP."[2]

During much of 1971, both caudillos sought to consolidate and concomitantly expand their power bases. Gutiérrez had argued that RUP's development in Texas should be on a gradual and systematic county-by-county basis—in particular in those counties that were predominantly Méxicano. At a RUP state convention held in October 1971, however, Mario Compean's strategy to have RUP go statewide prevailed over Gutiérrez's county-by-county approach.[3] Gonzales, on the other hand, that same month at a RUP conference held at Pueblo, Colorado, told the conference participants that RUP should run a slate in the presidential elections of 1972. He felt that the election could be useful in educating Méxicanos across the country about RUP's nationalist separatist agenda. There were, however, those who felt that Gonzales had another motive for pushing the national agenda. Garcia writes, "Though he did not suggest it outright, Gonzales wanted to be the candidate." Backed by a small delegation from Texas, Compean, who attended in place of Gutiérrez, expressed his reservations about Gonzales's idea, stressing that RUP did not have the resources or the capacity to challenge the two major parties nationally.[4]

It was in 1972 that the power struggle between the two charismatic leaders became overt. With Tijerina no longer a leadership factor within the CM and Chavez preoccupied with the United Farm Workers' struggle, the political leadership of the CM was up for grabs. Understanding the importance of timing, Gonzales called for a RUP national convention. Gutiérrez did not receive the idea well. To him, it was premature, since the only victories RUP could claim were those in Crystal City[5] and Cotulla.[6] Even as late as June 1972, at a meeting held by the Crusade for Justice in El Paso, Texas, Mario Compean, who represented the Texas RUP, again warned that RUP was not ready to go national. The delegates nevertheless overwhelmingly approved the Gonzales proposal. Not willing to be left out of RUP's leadership, Gutiérrez reluctantly agreed to support Gonzales's call for the convention. According to historian F. Arturo Rosales: "If Gutiérrez questioned the viability of a statewide party, he definitely was at odds with a national-level organization. But he had traveled throughout the country, mainly to college campuses, encouraging students to form local chapters of the LRUP; he was therefore partially responsible for these aspirations. Besides, since he had wanted a leading role for himself in the Chicano Movement, he could only ignore the Colorado LRUP initiative at his own peril."[7]

At a subsequent meeting involving Gonzales, Gutiérrez, and Tijerina, the agenda focused on RUP strategic matters, including the idea of holding a national RUP convention. All three leaders agreed that 1972 would be a pivotal political year due to the November presidential elections and that a convention should be held in El Paso sometime in September. Gutiérrez explained in our 1997 interview: "When we decided to do it, I remember he [Gonzales] said, 'Why don't you take care of the mechanics? You just put it all together and we will make sure that we get the word out and get the people there.' So I said fine, ok. So the next thing I did was to start working with other groups in El Paso to make sure that we had a binational thing. We wanted to have a convention both in Juarez and in El Paso."[8]

Questions pertinent to RUP's national leadership and structure surfaced shortly after the initial meeting. It was agreed that RUP's leadership would be shared among the three men. According to Gutiérrez, "There would be the party chair and then there would be the head of the Congreso [the proposed national steering committee of RUP], two different positions. . . . Two people, but pretty much equal in what they had to do."[9] Garcia has another version of what was discussed: "Gonzales quickly laid down the hierarchy: he would be the national chairman, Gutiérrez the vice-chairman, and Tijerina the elder statesman of the party."[10] Initially, Gonzales's division of roles was not an issue. This was evident from Gutiérrez's willingness to be the convention's organizer.[11] Gutiérrez explained the circumstances behind his decision: "I kind of always assumed that would be the case. Since I was always taking orders from them and I was always playing the supportive role and I was a very young man. . . . I admit I was inexperienced, I wasn't polished as they were. It provided me with a break to be a player in the action."[12]

Gutiérrez became the engineer and mechanic of the most powerful Méxicano political gathering in the history of the United States. He was responsible for raising the money to pay for the convention, which in the end totaled some $35,000. In addition, he was responsible for logistics, sending out invitations, securing the facilities, setting up the various planning and on-site convention committees (credentials, media, etc.), and putting together the convention program. Regardless of the fact that he was working without paid staff and was overextended due to other organizing responsibilities, using his RUP network of volunteers from Texas, he pulled it all together, but not without conflict.

In late June, RUP of Colorado held a conference in Denver. The conference became an organizing tool for Gonzales's quest to become RUP's national chair. Four planks that he considered to be integral to RUP's national agenda were adopted: (1) RUP's platform would be inspired and based on the tenets of "El Plan Espiritual de Aztlán"; (2) RUP would continue its opposition to U.S. involvement in the Vietnam War; (3) RUP would struggle for the nationalization of the schools; and (4) RUP would be the political voice and representative of Chicano people. Gonzales also reiterated his stance that RUP would never negotiate with either the Democratic or Republican Parties, since it had been implied that a Chicano presidential candidate might be selected at the RUP national convention.[13]

Being an admirer of Saul Alinsky, Gutiérrez was cognizant of the organizing principle "He who organizes controls." And that is precisely what he did, especially when it came to formulating the convention's program and schedule. Gutiérrez recalls, however, exactly when his clashes with Gonzales surfaced: "There was no objection to me paying the bills. There was no objection to me booking places . . . [or] printing agendas and things. It's when I started doing these invitations that it caused a problem, and I remember I was very embarrassed because . . . I had invited Cesar, Bishop Flores. I had mailed a letter inviting Nixon and McGovern to come to the convention. I felt I would be maximizing opportunity."[14] Gutiérrez also sought to invite prominent leaders from other ethnic and racial communities, such as the Southern Christian Leadership Conference's leader Joséph Lowery as well as Native American leaders.

The issue of who would be invited exposed the differences between the two leaders. Gutiérrez's invitation to Nixon and McGovern became a major point of contention. In letters sent in early July inviting them to address the convention, Gutiérrez stressed RUP's important political role in determining the outcome of the presidential election. Both letters reflected Gutiérrez's "balance-of-power strategy," which was predicated on the premise that RUP votes would be a factor in determining the outcome of the election.

Gutiérrez proposed this strategy in an open letter to the San José National Chicano Political Caucus, which was held in San José on April 21 and 22, 1972: "We need to keep White America divided evenly between Democrats and Republicans. And we need to shift our bloc of votes from election to election." In addition, he explained that a mere "shift of 5 percent" in the Chicano vote in the states of California, Texas, Illinois, and New Mexico could determine the outcome of the 1972 presidential elections. This shift in turn would impact the electoral college. At the Texas state RUP convention held in June, Gutiérrez again emphasized his balance-of-power strategy by mentioning the possibility of RUP's supporting either Nixon or McGovern.[15]

Gutiérrez's strategy was not at all radical. It was based on conventional, accommodationist politics buttressed by pragmatism. The letters Gutiérrez sent to Nixon and McGovern clearly reflected this; for example, in the letter to Nixon, he wrote: "Our party organization is such that, rooted deeply in Texas and California Chicano barrios, the Chicano votes our Party represents nationwide will play a significant role in the outcome of the November National Presidential election."[16] Furthermore, he alluded to RUP's being "established and registered in five states," when, in fact, it was recognized as an official third party only in Texas.[17] Gutiérrez's pragmatism comes through loud and clear. He wanted to bring RUP into the mainstream of the nation's politics, where it could bargain for concessions from either of the two major parties.

Gonzales's vision for RUP was categorically opposite to that of Gutiérrez. Since RUP's emergence in Colorado, he had held steadfast on his position of "no compromise" and "no negotiation" with either political party.[18] In speech after speech, he propounded his doctrinaire position that RUP must become an "independent" political party with no loyalty to any other party. He was adamant that any collaboration with either party was tantamount to an act of "political prostitution." His acrimony toward both major parties was based on his notion that the two were the same animal.[19] For him, Aztlán would never become a political reality if RUP became contaminated by the oppressive virus of liberal capitalism.

The conflict between the two leaders was further exacerbated by the issue of Cesar Chavez addressing the convention. Gonzales responded with an emphatic no to Chavez speaking there because of his affiliation with the Democrats as well as his unwillingness to support RUP openly. According to Rosales: "Those ties to the mainstream party were anathema to Gonzales and the Colorado LRUP."[20] When Chavez's people learned that he was going to be denied the right to speak, the invitation was not accepted. Gutiérrez reported that he "felt very embarrassed" about the whole thing.[21]

By August, the war of words between the two leaders had escalated. That month, Gutiérrez continued to move forward with his balance-of-power strategy. In a letter to McGovern in August, Gutiérrez, disappointed with McGovern's lack of response to a previous letter inviting him to address the convention, reaffirmed the important political role that RUP was going to play in deciding the results of the November elections: "It is with deep regrets and diminished hopes that we send this letter to you. Our organization, Cuidadanos Unidos, earlier in the primary campaign, supported your bid for the nomination and made a healthy contribution toward that end. After the nomination we were prepared to send additional money and letters of support. Today we are sending neither money nor expressing support. . . . We, however, still have an open mind. The burden of convincing us to make the extra effort to vote for you is all yours."[22] Gutiérrez closed by reminding McGovern that up to that point, Republicans had been more interested in hearing from RUP than had Democrats and that he could lose several key states by his failure to meet with RUP.[23]

A meeting attended by Gutiérrez, Gonzales, and Tijerina almost turned violent over the issue of RUP's leadership, according to Garcia: "The breaking point came shortly before the national convention convened, when Gonzales and Tijerina engaged in a virulent confrontation that almost turned into a fistfight."[24] Gutiérrez told me: "When we were in the room, they got into a shouting match and basically Reies walked out saying things to Corky and Corky was saying things to him and then he turns to me and tells me that he is the one that is going to get elected and that he could handle it by himself"[25] Gutiérrez responded by saying that he too would place his name in nomination and added, "I'll win."[26] Gutiérrez recalls that when Gonzales told him there was only going to be one leadership position and that he wanted his support, he responded, "I'll let you know." After contacting several of his confidants, such as Mario Compean, Angel Gonzales, Lupe Youngblood, and Jesse Gamez, however, he was convinced he could win himself, so he "decided to go for it."[27]

Nita Gonzales, daughter of Corky Gonzales, as well as other Crusade leaders when interviewed unequivocally repudiated Gutiérrez's account. Nita Gonzales's response was: "That's absolutely bullshit. Anybody that knows Gutiérrez knows that he is not that way. He absolutely plans and is very practical and he was planning long before then to be chairman of this party [RUP]."[28] Sal Carpio, who was a RUP congressional candidate in 1970 from Denver, buttressed Nita Gonzales's assessment of Gutiérrez: "José would be the kind who'd make a move after he counted how many votes he had. Corky wouldn't give a damn about the votes."[29]

By late August, various states, such as Texas, Colorado, California, New México, and Illinois, had held state conventions in preparation for the national convention. There was a feeling of anticipation among the hundreds of RUP activists across the country that history was in the making. That month, Tijernia wrote to Gutiérrez reaffirming his participation and his commitment to get people to attend the convention.[30] Gutiérrez in late August put out several press releases announcing the particulars of the convention. In them, he emphasized the invitations to Nixon and McGovern.

## RUP's 1972 National Convention: One of a Kind.

September 1–5, Labor Day weekend, some 3,000 Méxicanos from eighteen states gathered in El Paso to formulate national directives and strategies for RUP. Never before had so many Méxicanos gathered with such a political agenda.[31] There was a feeling of purpose among the delegates, who had traveled from as far as Washington, D.C., Maryland, and Rhode Island, and from Minnesota, Illinois, Wisconsin, and Nebraska.

Gutiérrez in a press release circulated just a few days before the convention alluded to the far-flung communities of the delegates: "This fact has led many to believe that La Raza Unida will have great influence in deciding the outcome of traditional two-party elections, even in communities where Spanish-speaking people are not in the majority."[32] RUP activists traveled to El Paso as if on a national Chicano political pilgrimage. Those who were involved in the CM perceived the convention as the most important political gathering ever to have been orchestrated by Méxicanos.

Yet even before the convention started, it was rocked by controversy. On August 30, RUP leader Ricardo Falcon, while traveling to the convention in a two-car advance party, was shot and killed in New Mexico, the victim of a racist incident.[33]

For Colorado's RUP delegation, the loss of Falcon was devastating, since he was one of the partido's main leaders. Upon learning of Falcon's death, Gutiérrez on behalf of convention delegates called a press conference, at which he issued a press release demanding a federal investigation into what was described as "this wanton racist murder."[34] Gutiérrez sent telegrams to President Nixon, Attorney General Richard Kleindienst, Democratic presidential candidate McGovern, New Mexico lieutenant governor Roberto Mondragon, and Mario Obledo, general counsel for the Mexican American Legal Defense and Educational Fund, asking for a federal investigation.[35]

The death of Falcon impacted Gonzales's game plan as well. Going into the convention, Gonzales was at a disadvantage. His network of Crusade for Justice supporters was not enough. Vigil's job in El Paso was to do the advance intelligence and put in motion Gonzales's campaign, but Falcon, who was to play a significant role, had now been killed. Vigil and other Crusade leaders found themselves responding to the murder—contacting Falcon's family, investigating what happened, and putting out news releases.[36] In a press release issued by the Colorado delegation, it was alleged that "after having been shot, no medical attention of any kind was given to Falcon and no ambulance or doctors were sent to the scene." Furthermore, "residents of Orogrande [the site of the shooting] refused to let members of Falcon's group use telephones, including pay phones."[37]

Vigil and others adjusted and did what they had to do to push Gonzales's candidacy for chair. Gonzales arrived that evening and called for a meeting of the Colorado delegation for Saturday to deal with Falcon's death as well as the convention. Falcon's close friend José Calderon, from Greeley, Colorado, gave an emotional memorial address at the convention: "When we die, let us die as Ricardo did. Let us die fighting in the barrios, in the jails, in the college campuses, in the fields, in the streets for our Raza. . . . And if we should die, let us die as Ricardo did and not like the many of us who die in Vietnam fighting for hate and Imperialism."[38]

In response to Falcon's death, the Colorado delegation put out a press release describing the shooting as "a racist act of cold blooded murder [that] should be known as such."[39] McGovern set a telegram that read: "I am shocked at the killing of young Richard Falcon. I assure you of my efforts to see that justice is done in this act of insanity. I am contacting the U.S. Attorney General to see that immediate action be taken to initiate investigative proceedings."[40] Lieutenant Governor Roberto Mondragon likewise sent a telegram, calling for an investigation by New Mexico's attorney general and stating that he was in support of a federal inquiry into the matter.[41]

Anger and frustration accompanied the opening of the convention on Friday, September 1; Gutiérrez was elected unanimously as convention chairperson.[42] In describing the reaction of some of the delegates, Rosales writes: "As LRUP members arrived in El Paso's Liberty Hall Coliseum where the meeting was held, excitement and anticipation tinged the air as delegates milled around discussing the debate between the two competing philosophies represented by Gonzales and Gutiérrez."[43] According to Garcia, Arizona RUP leader Salomon Baldenegro "was surprised on his arrival to find that the discussions, conversations, and gossip revolved around who would emerge as the leader of the conference and whose philosophy would prevail."[44]

Being the organizer of the convention and the convention chairperson gave Gutiérrez a tremendous advantage over Gonzales. For weeks he had gone in and out of El Paso putting the convention together. Moreover, he traveled extensively to states in the Southwest and Midwest to solicit the support of RUP's leadership for the convention. This gave him the opportunity to also solicit support for his bid to become national chair. He arrived at El Paso a few days before the start of the convention and set up his command post at the historic El Paso Del Norte Hotel.

As the convention delegates arrived, especially key RUP regional or state leaders, Gutiérrez greeted them at his hospitality room at the hotel, where he personally solicited their support. Gutiérrez's election strategy was taken right from the pages of traditional politicking—collect political IOUs, offer free drinks, have designated operatives lobbying, and so on. His sales pitch was that RUP was at the threshold of its development, that his strategy had produced tangible political victories, and that he was the best and most competent person to lead RUP in the struggle for the Méxicano's empowerment.[45]

Gutiérrez was also in charge of security for the convention. After receiving several death threats, he brought in the Barrio Club from his hometown, Cristal, as part of the convention's security. Carlos Guerra recalls: "I feared for his life . . . because there had been some death threats and we knew that Corky had some goons that tended to harass people. . . . The rumors were that there was going to be some problems at the convention. . . . So more than anything, it was a lot of precaution and concern that they were going to disrupt the convention, because we knew we had the votes."[46]

Gutiérrez was in complete control of the convention's agenda, credentials, administration, logistics, et cetera. As part of establishing their credentials, delegates were required to sign a two-part loyalty oath. Gutiérrez wanted to ensure that registered "Democrats, Republicans, socialists, and communists" were excluded from the convention. The Socialist Workers Party (SWP) protested and challenged Gutiérrez's oath requirement, unsuccessfully. They were also excluded from the Texas RUP delegation and were not permitted to sell their materials at the convention unless they were willing to turn over the proceeds to convention organizers.[47] Gutiérrez also selected people who were loyal to him to head all the important convention committees. For example, Rogelio Granados from the RUP San Bernardino/Riverside Counties region of California was appointed as chairperson of the Credentials Committee.[48]

Saturday September 2, the convention opened at the Sacred Heart Auditorium, where a number of roll calls involving state chairpersons and voting delegates were taken; Table 3 provides a breakdown of the delegates.

The politicking between the competing forces was intense. Of the two, Gutiérrez appeared to be the better organized on the convention floor. Gonzales, on the other hand, always accompanied by an entourage of security guards, relied on the use of group persuasion, which to Gutiérrez supporters was nothing more than group intimidation. The Gonzales contingent cornered delegates wherever they could—in the hallways, lobby, outside—in order to convince them to vote for Gonzales.

Regardless of the strong-arm tactics by Gonzales, Gutiérrez managed to score another major victory. Believing that, as conference chairperson, he would be constrained in his ability to politic for the national chairmanship, in a somewhat Machiavellian manner he maneuvered to get California RUP leader Raul Ruiz nominated as temporary convention chairperson or vice chairperson. Gutiérrez, who knew that Ruiz leaned toward Gonzales, when interviewed years later said: "I knew he [Ruiz] was skilled and I knew he had these feelings [supportive of Gonzales]. I figured, hell, neutralize him. . . . If I neutralize him by giving him this position and he is attacked, he'll come over to my side because he'll have no other side to go to."[49]

Ruiz recalls his reaction to the nomination: "It passed through Corky's group and was accepted almost immediately—yes, its okay, Raul will be acceptable." There was no objection to Ruiz because he was not perceived as being in the Gutiérrez camp, since he had had much more contact with Gonzales than with Gutiérrez prior to the convention. "I was, like, the guy that people felt would be fair," said Ruiz.[50]

That Saturday, each of the leaders addressed the convention for some forty-five minutes.[51] Dressed in his traditional black pants and black shirt, with a black armband,

TABLE 3   State Delegations at RUP's National Convention, 1972

| State | State Chair | Delegate Votes |
|-------|-------------|----------------|
| Arizona | Salamon Baldenegro | 34 |
| California | Rudolfo Quiñonez | 66 |
| Colorado | Salvador Carpio | 39 |
| Indiana | Ricardo Parra | 13 |
| Kansas | Magdalena Vargas | 23 |
| Maryland | Lupe Adelano | 13 |
| Michigan | Desiderio Ortiz | 23 |
| Nebraska | Vino Guevarra | 13 |
| New México | Juan José Peña | 40 |
| New York | None | — |
| Rhode Island | None | — |
| Texas | Mario Compean | 65 |
| Washington | Baco Salazar | 13 |
| Wisconsin | Ernest Chacon | 13 |
| Wyoming | Dolores Arenas | 13 |
| Washington, D.C. | Thema (no last name) | 13 |

Source: MEChA, "La Raza Unida Convention, El Paso, Texas, September 1, 2, 3, & 4," report, University of Colorado at Boulder.

Gonzales spoke first. He delivered a "no compromise" speech against Gutiérrez's balance-of-power strategy. He congratulated Gutiérrez and Ruiz for being elected chairman and vice chairman of the convention, briefly eulogized Ricardo Falcon, and then proceeded to hammer away at Gutiérrez's strategy: "A very important part of the Chicano Movement is La Raza Unida. A few years ago, La Raza Unida was just a dream. No one thought that we could have the courage to come forth. This is a historic day, we have all taken part in creating history. It is a concept of self-determination that brings us together and we must take La Raza Unida in the direction of honesty and not prostitution. When we leave here, we will leave as a united independent party; we do not want to compromise or negotiate with any other political party."[52]

He vehemently attacked both McGovern and Nixon as being stew from the same pot. He used his famous image of the major parties being a two-headed monster eating from the same trough and alluded to the Méxicano *vendidos* (sell-outs) who were being used by the two parties. After addressing some of the salient issues plaguing the community, he concluded with an exhortation for unity. The delegates responded with a standing ovation and chanted, "Viva la Raza y Que Viva Corky" (Long live our people and long live Corky).

As Gutiérrez, who was equally passionate and articulate, addressed the delegates, various accounts suggest that delegates were anticipating a regurgitation of his balance-of-power strategy, but in a calculated manner he avoided any mention of it, knowing full well the divisions it had already created. Instead, in a carefully crafted presentation, using an admixture of Spanish and English as a way of demonstrating his fluency in both languages, he emphasized the importance of unity within the partido:[53]

> We must resolve our own problems within this political party. Que va ser nuestro y de nadie mas no de (That's going to be ours and no one else's). Some say it is impossible y que nos vamos hacer garras (and we'll tear each other up). Ask these same people if they saw fighting at the gringo conventions and they'll say, "Oh, that was discussion, argument." In that case he doesn't know Mexicans. We're not fighting, nos estamos poniendo de acuerdo (We are reaching a consensus). We will leave here a united party. We should have one priority, to learn about each other—in public and in private—love, learn, respect, and I hope, to fight for one another. . . . We should stop concerning ourselves with Chicano power . . . and build power for Chicanos here today.[54]

When Gutiérrez finished his address, the delegates gave him a standing ovation also, with chants of "Viva la Raza Unida." However, an interesting situation developed: Some of the Texas delegates began to chant, "We want Ramsey [Muñiz], We want Ramsey." That evening at a dance, RUP gubernatorial candidate Muñiz addressed about 1,000 Méxicano workers who were engaged in a strike against the Farah Manufacturing Company. The night before, he had spoken at a rally at a park. On the third day of the convention, he traveled to Lubbock, where he addressed a Texas state conference of the Cursillos de Cristianidad, a Roman Catholic evangelical group.

Muñiz had sought desperately to attract some media coverage for his gubernatorial campaign, but he was unable to do so because he spoke late at night when few media representatives were present; besides, the media was focused on the outcome of the convention. Journalist Tony Castro reported that "in the end, Muñiz never addressed the convention. He was the victim of political jealousies within the party—he was in competition with other Texas Chicano leaders, many of whom had already spent years trying to establish themselves—and of a struggle among the delegations for control of the party."[55]

After both Gonzales and Gutiérrez had spoken, Tijerina spoke. Tijerina's role at the convention was rather a symbolic one, since, while never opposing the RUP, he never embraced the idea or actively supported it. Moreover, he never endorsed the notion of Aztlán or the use of the term "Chicano." Since his release from prison in 1971, he did not seem to be the same leader. While he still preached on the issue of land grants, gone were the fiery militant speeches or threats of violence. His new image was that of a mellower reformer with a message of "brotherhood awareness." Tijerina had participated in the preconvention meetings with Gutiérrez and Gonzales. At the convention, his role was that of "special guest." His presentation focused on his new theme, and he called for a national conference on unity in November 1972.[56]

Tijerina underscored the importance of unity before that of organizations or leaders and warned the delegates about getting into a fight over doctrinaire ideas of purity. He sought to project the image of the unifier. Upon completing his "unity" speech, he was joined at the podium by Gonzales and Gutiérrez, and all three in an act of solidarity raised their linked hands. The delegates responded with cheers and a standing ovation, as if beseeching them to accept the unity they were symbolically projecting.

Cesar Chavez was scheduled to speak but never showed up. *Washington Post* reporter Tony Castro noted that "there are indications that la Raza Unida rank-and-file members are discontented with what they view as Chavez's failure to assist La Raza efforts in California." Muñiz reflected the anger of some delegates toward Chavez and his endorsement of McGovern when he was quoted as saying, "If Chavez shows up to rap for McGovern, he'll be booed."[57]

Ruiz did an excellent job of chairing the volatile and often quarrelsome convention. Points of order, calls for information, and out of order claims abounded during the debates on some 500 resolutions that were up for consideration; the results would form the basis for RUP's national platform. California RUP leader Fred Aguilar told me later that "Raul Ruiz did a tremendous job simply because he was as neutral in that chair as neutral could be. I know there were occasions where we got on him and he said to us, 'Look, we're here as La Raza Unida and that's who I have to do it for and I have to be blind when I am up there, as blind as the lady of justice can be, that's what I have to do.' "[58]

In another strategic maneuver, Gutiérrez outflanked Gonzales by pushing through the use of the "unit rule." According to Garcia, "The voting on most of the resolutions was lopsided because the convention had decided to call for a unit vote, which meant that each delegation would cast all its votes for the resolution that the majority of its members favored."[59] Even with strong resistance by the Gonzales forces, Ruiz was able to steer the convention into passing the rule. It was a major victory for Gutiérrez, for it gave the states with the largest delegations—California, Texas, and New Mexico— much more power and leverage with their votes. On some of the resolutions passed, there was bitter maneuvering. The Illinois delegation, for instance, at one point accused Ruiz of trying to influence the vote. They resolved that RUP's Congreso de Aztlán should have the opportunity to amend at a later date all resolutions passed at the convention. This was important, since the Gutiérrez forces were outvoting those of Gonzales. Passing this resolution would mean that Gonzales could have all unfavorable decisions overturned later, since he felt confident he could control the Congreso. The state RUP chairperson from New Mexico, Juan José Peña, introduced an amended motion that allowed each state delegation the opportunity to clarify the accepted resolutions before they were presented to the Congreso.[60]

After exhaustive debate dealing with scores of proposed resolutions, the delegates passed a number of resolutions that became the basis for RUP's platform. The platform included planks on distribution of wealth, bilingual/bicultural education, independence for Puerto Rico, immediate withdrawal of U.S. forces from Vietnam, free health care, and a guaranteed annual income.[61]

The convention delegates also discussed endorsing one of the major party presidential candidates as well as RUP running its own presidential candidate. Gutiérrez backed away from both options and focused instead on winning the office of chair. He modified his strategy because he was well aware of the resistance to his balance-of-power strategy, even by the Texas delegation. However, some of the Muñiz for Governor delegates supported the idea of negotiating with the Democrats. They felt they could negotiate a quid pro quo: McGovern supports Muñiz, and in turn Muñiz supports McGovern. A day before the start of the convention, Muñiz publicly threatened to withhold support for McGovern unless McGovern endorsed him.[62] Even Chicanos in the Communist Party who were in attendance pushed the idea in their newspaper, the *People's World*, that in order to stop the reelection of Nixon, RUP needed to endorse McGovern.[63]

Like Gutiérrez with his balance-of-power strategy, Gonzales never brought up his idea of running a Chicano for president, since he felt this could distract from solidifying the partido and electing him national leader. At a late Sunday session that dragged on until 4:30 A.M., the partido delegates refused to endorse either McGovern or Nixon for president. They decided that RUP would sit out the 1972 presidential election and instead focus on state and local elections.[64]

On that Monday, after weeks of preparation and campaigning, Gutiérrez the adroit organizer prevailed over Gonzales the ideological idealist. During the previous two days, Gonzales supporters had pushed for a bifurcated leadership structure—a national RUP chairperson and a national Congreso chairperson. On the stage, behind the podium, a large banner read, "Unidos Ganeremos" (United we will win). With Ruiz presiding over the election, each of the two contenders gave a five-minute nomination speech. The results of a roll call vote were not close at all. Gutiérrez received 256-1/6 votes to Gonzales's 170-5/6 votes, with one abstention and fourteen No votes, from delegates representing sixteen states and the District of Colombia.[65]

The *Denver Post* reported that "it was believed that a coalition of delegates from Oregon, Wyoming, Nebraska, Kansas, Missouri, and Maryland gave Gutiérrez the necessary margin of votes to win the chairmanship."[66] Gutiérrez won these states solidly. As to the other states: Texas's 64 votes went to Gutiérrez; California's delegation voted 48-1/2 for Gonzales and 17-1/2 for Gutiérrez; New Mexico, 26-2/3 for Gutiérrez and 13-1/3 for Gonzales; Arizona, 21 for Gutiérrez and 13 for Gonzales; Utah, 7 for Gutiérrez and 6 for Gonzales; and Washington, D.C., 9 for Gutiérrez and 4 for Gonzales. Gonzales took Colorado's 39 votes, Illinois's 21, Nebraska's 13, and Mississippi's 13.[67]

With Gutiérrez clearly taking the majority of the votes, the Colorado delegation made a motion to have the vote made unanimous as a gesture of unity. Some members of the California delegation, upset with the results, spoke out against the motion and then walked out.[68] Gonzales quickly joined Gutiérrez at the podium, gave him an embrace, called them back, and made a call for party solidarity and unity.[69] Gonzales in a moving message accentuated the importance of adhering to democratic principles. He thanked all his supporters and reminded the delegates of the unprecedented historical event they had all participated in. He concluded his address by exhorting delegates to hold fast to their principles and not allow the CM and RUP to be "prostituted" by politics.[70] Again, the delegates responded to Gonzales's symbolic gesture of unity with jubilation; however, the commitment to unity would not carry over to the rest of the convention. The Monday session was plagued by conflict. In an obvious affront to the Texas delegation and Gutiérrez, who had invited him, the convention's delegates voted not to allow Auxiliary Bishop Patricio Flores from San Antonio an opportunity to speak. Disregarding his reputation as a progressive bishop, some RUP delegates led by the Colorado delegation felt that he to was too friendly with the Democrats.[71] Furthermore, other non-Méxicano speakers who had been invited to speak by Gutiérrez, such as Joséph Lowery from the Southern Christian Leadership Conference, were also not allowed to speak.[72]

The last major item on the agenda was the Congreso de Aztlán. Gutiérrez's idea of having the Congreso function as a national steering committee rather than a fullfledged congress comprised of numerous entities prevailed. The Congreso was to be the equivalent of the major parties' national executive committees, with each state having three representatives to it. Each state delegation caucused and elected their representatives. In a move to strip away Gutiérrez's power, the convention delegates voted to elect a Congreso chairperson at the first Congreso meeting.

The Illinois delegation successfully persuaded the delegates to require that the national chairperson and the Congreso conduct all party business through individual state chairpersons.[73] It was agreed that the Congreso would have its first meeting on November 24 in Albuquerque, New Mexico. Gutiérrez's final words were conciliatory in nature. He sought to downplay the conflict between the two leaders, applauded the skill and leadership of his opposition, emphasized the importance of putting aside differences, and called for unity in the building of the partido.[74]

The convention proved to be the apogee of RUP's struggle to become an alternative political party for Méxicanos in the United States. While Gutiérrez triumphed over Gonzales, what followed with the effort to establish the Congreso was the politics of self-destruction.

## Tijerina's Conference on Tierra y Cultura

The splits produced at RUP's national convention spilled over into Tijerina's National Congress for Land and Cultural Reform held in Albuquerque, October 21–22. With some 2,000 activists from throughout the nation representing various political persuasions, the conference's theme was "Unity, before Ideas, Leaders, or Organizations." The agenda, however, was really designed to restore Tijerina to a major leadership role within the CM as well as to promote his new mainstream and ostensibly prosystem image. Even though Tijerina continued to preach on the land grant issue, the claws and fangs of El Tigre (the tiger) were gone.

Besides activists, Tijerina invited and showcased several mainstream Democratic business and political figures, which set off a firestorm of protest from many of the pro-RUP activists in attendance. As reported by the newspaper *El Grito Del Norte*, some of the activists openly criticized Tijerina for inviting two individuals who had allegedly been involved with the Central Intelligence Agency. This combination of political activists did not mix well at all. The end result was more conflict and division.

From the first day of the conference, RUP activists pressured Tijerina to entertain a resolution of support for the partido, but he refused to do so. José Angel Gutiérrez came on stage and in effect supported Tijerina's decision on the grounds that Tijerina had the right to set the rules, since it was his conference. Most of the RUP activists who were strong supporters of Gonzales openly disagreed with Gutiérrez's remarks. Tijerina reacted with anger toward the assertive activists: "Estos niños no saben nada" (These children know nothing). He also stated, "The Partido de La Raza Unida wasn't with me in Tierra Amarilla," and "if you want to take over, you can pay the $2,000 for this place."[75] Tijerina walked out of his own meeting, as did others, leaving it in disarray.[76] Angered because he walked out, some activists acknowledged his past contributions but declared that they could not follow him as a leader anymore.[77]

An incident between the Aliancistas and Brown Berets, who had been providing security for the conference, added to the conflict. Fearing the Brown Berets were going to support the resolution the next day, the Aliancistas threw the Brown Berets out of their headquarters. The Berets left and denounced the Alianza and Tijerina. Further exacerbating the growing conflict was that neither Cesar Chavez nor Corky Gonzales, who were scheduled to speak, showed up.[78] Gonzales, angry over Tijerina's having invited Democrats, wrote to him: "In the past years, I have dissociated myself from these people who confuse and mislead the gullible members of our Raza. I can no longer bargain with despotic government representatives. . . . I want no part of alignment with political prostitutes. . . . I have no intention of creating reaction for the profitable benefit of professional program managers."[79]

The conference concluded with RUP activists taking control. After consulting with Tijerina and others on the impasse, New Mexico RUP state chairperson Juan José Peña wound up chairing the rest of the conference. The result was that the participants, many of them from New Mexico, passed a number of resolutions—from unanimously endorsing RUP to showing support for the case against the killer of Ricardo Falcon.[80]

Gonzales's supporters scored a three-fold victory. First, they obviated Tijerina's quest to reassert himself as the CM's *lider maximo* (maximum leader). Second, Gonzales's supporters prevailed in controlling the conference agenda and prevented the formation of a coalition comprised of bureaucrats and mainstream politicians and activists. They were so effective that Tijerina publicly accused RUP activists from Colorado of deliberately stirring up trouble.[81] And third, Gonzales's supporters demonstrated to Gutiérrez and his supporters that the struggle to control RUP was far from over—that in reality it had just begun. This became very evident at the first Congreso meeting, held in New Mexico that November.

## El Congreso: A Victim of the Politics of Self-Destruction

The idea of establishing a Congreso came out of the Second National Youth Liberation Conference, held in March 1970 in Denver. It was to be the people's congress for establishing Aztlán. Gonzales, visualizing the building of a nation, perceived it as a governing body that would be broad based, comprised of representatives from different groups. RUP was supposed to have been merely its political arm. The CJ newspaper, *El Gallo,* throughout RUP's six years of existence, reminded readers of RUP's role: "From its inception, our political movement [RUP], as conceived, was to be the political arm of a total liberation struggle for the Chicano."[82] Ernesto Vigil held the same view: "We had hoped that the Congreso de Aztlán would be something like our government in exile, except that we were not in exile, we were within the geographical boundaries of the country that conquered our territory. It was to be a congress of an occupied nation. I think for us and for Corky, our concern was actually more centered on the Congreso de Aztlán than on the partido."[83]

Gutiérrez, on the other hand, trying to build a political party that emulated the nation's two major parties, perceived the Congreso as part of the party's structure. Perhaps due to his political science background and organizational skill, he saw the Congreso as being essentially the partido's national steering committee, equivalent to the Democratic or Republican national committee.[84] He wanted a smaller body of decision makers that would be responsible for guiding the development of building a national party.[85] Gutiérrez, Garcia told me in our 1998 interview, "wanted RUP to be all encompassing within the Chicano Movement."[86] Guiterrez's view of the Congreso reflected his pragmatic approach to working within the political system and his reform ethos.

Gutiérrez perceived each entity as separate, with its own leadership, and equal in leadership potential. When Gonzales tried to consolidate them into one, Gutiérrez, not agreeing with the Gonzales model, decided to run for RUP national chair and to push his own model; he prevailed in both. The election of Gutiérrez and adoption of his Congreso model raised the question of what kind of political party RUP was to be.

Gutiérrez was a strong believer that RUP should be a party that would challenge whenever possible both major political parties. He envisioned a party that would run its own candidates and employ a balance-of-power strategy whenever needed. At the San José National Chicano Caucus in 1972, he said: "We need to keep White America divided evenly between Democrats and Republicans and we need to shift our block of votes from election to election as needed for maximum feasible benefit."[87]

Gonzales's idea was a partido that educated and politicized the Méxicano masses by engaging in issues, direct action, and, lastly, elections. José Calderon, when interviewed years later, supported Gonzales's perspective: "Corky was emphasizing that Raza Unida should not be a power broker, that it should be used primarily to educate and raise consciousness. And that the way you do that is through organizing. We used elections just as another tactic as part of a larger strategy."[88] Ernesto Vigil felt that for RUP to even try to compete within the two-party system was "an exercise in futility," since "it would not resolve the questions of social inequality."[89] Gutiérrez's victory over Gonzales, which appeared to indicate that he had prevailed, did not.

The first Congreso meeting was held in Albuquerque, New Mexico, November 24–26, 1972. Gutiérrez presided as chair over twenty-six delegates representing ten states.[90] As a result of the splits that had occurred at RUP's national convention and Tijerina's conference, there was a major confrontation between the two power factions, which set in motion the "politics of self-destruction." The split that developed was severe and irreparable.[91]

Hours were spent defining and debating what the function of the Congreso would be. One of the questions that again surfaced was whether the Congreso would be the party's top policy-making executive committee and governing body.[92] Gutiérrez's supporters felt that the Congreso should be solely RUP's executive committee, whereas Gonzales's continued to push for his version of the Congreso as an all-encompassing entity. Ernesto Vigil explains the feelings of the *corkyistas* (supporters of Rodolfo Corky Gonzales): "It concerned us greatly, especially when we felt that the partido would be called into existence and its first gathering would be radically different than what we had foreseen or what we wanted." In other words, the Congreso meeting they were attending went against their perception of what the Congreso should be—an all-inclusive body, not merely a few representatives of one entity.[93]

The political *movidas* (maneuverings) by both power factions culminated in a showdown on the last day of the meeting. Gutiérrez, strongly supported by the Texas delegation, circulated a proposed structure for the Congreso and RUP. The corkyistas took issue with his action and proposed that a new agenda on structure be drafted by all the states present.[94] A frustrated Gutiérrez called for an adjournment of the meeting, since, as he explained, he had a plane to catch before a storm came in.[95] The delegates from Maryland, Wisconsin, Oregon, Michigan, and Texas likewise said they had to be back by Monday, so they also had to leave. The motion to adjourn was defeated by the corkyistas. Gutiérrez left, but the meeting was not adjourned. Since Gonzales's supporters controlled the meeting, it continued until November 28.[96] What transpired after Gutiérrez and the other delegations departed was tantamount to a political coup. A quorum still existed that included the delegations from New Mexico, Colorado, Nebraska, Illinois, and most of California. Angel Moreno from Illinois was elected temporary chairperson, and a California delegate, Cruz Olmeda, replaced Herman Baca, another delegate from California, who had also left. With most of the gutierrista supporters gone, the corkyistas, led by Ernesto Vijil and José Calderon, hammered out a series of decisions that would only create a bigger gap between the two camps.

A Congreso structure was approved that divided the nation into five organizing regions: Pacific Coast, Mountain States, Midwest States, Northeastern States, and Gulf States. Each region in turn was part of a *consejo* (council), with two representatives from that region. The proposed structure sought to neutralize Gutiérrez's power by placing Texas with the Gulf States region. Moreover, officers for the Congreso were elected: Gutiérrez remained as chair; vice chair, Tito Lucero (California); treasurer, Connie Martinez, (Colorado); recording secretary, Nancy Montaño (New Mexico); corresponding secretary, Joe Trujillo (New Mexico); and parliamentarian, Angel Moreno (Illinois). Adding insult to injury, they voted to establish the partido's office in New Mexico and called for the next Congreso meeting to be held there, February 17–19, 1973.[97]

Gutiérrez as well as the *gutierristas* across the country reacted with anger. Gutiérrez categorically rejected the decisions made after his departure as illegitimate and as an orchestrated strategy by Gonzales's supporters to take over the Congreso. Years later, in our interview, he commented on the issue: "I had to deal with people who were there as obstructionists and negativists. They did some crazy things. . . . They wanted to put Cristal and Texas in a region with Atlanta, Alabama, and Mississippi so I couldn't organize in their areas. . . . It was insane. I told them that they didn't want this to work."[98]

As a result of the actions proposed at the Albuquerque meeting, skirmishes took place in letters sent by both sides, accusing each other of numerous improprieties. In an effort to preempt Gutiérrez, Tito Lucero sent out a letter dated December 28, 1972, to all Congreso representatives requesting a comprehensive list of all the active RUP organizing committees or chapters in their particular state.[99] In response, Gutiérrez, the duly elected national chairperson, sent out a scathing letter advising all state RUP officials to disregard any correspondence sent by any of the officers elected at the Congreso meeting in Albuquerque. Lucero responded to Gutiérrez in a public letter dated January 24, 1973, in which he defended what had transpired at the Congreso meeting. Furthermore, he accused Gutiérrez of trying to run the Congreso using a form of "one-man rule" to override the decisions made at the meeting.

Gutiérrez responded to Lucero in a letter written in Spanish that was subsequently published in *El Gallo:* "For example, the five states voted to put the national office in New Mexico. I live and work in Crystal City, Texas. How are we going to operate an organization if the head is in one state and the body is somewhere else?"[100]

The war of words that continued over the next two years was self-destructive. Moreover, the battle between the gutierristas and the corkyistas carried over to other factions within the CM. Movimiento newspapers began taking sides and adding to the sensationalism of the growing rifts within RUP. Each side seemed preoccupied with attacking the other instead of the gringo and the system that continued to oppress and exploit Méxicanos. The polarization became so intense, it was next to impossible for any RUP activist to remain neutral. Each side lined up its supporters to do battle for control of what was left of RUP.

After the Albuquerque meeting of November 1972, only four more Congreso meetings were scheduled: Denver, Colorado, August 1973; East Chicago, Illinois, September 1973; Crystal City, Texas, January 1974; and San Antonio, Texas, July 1975. The Congreso meeting scheduled for February 1973 in Albuquerque never took place, due to the severity of the divisions between the two factions.

The increasing conflict manifested itself at the third Congreso meeting, held in Denver in August in conjunction with a RUP state conference in that city. Since the meeting was called and organized by the existing Congreso board, which happened to be top heavy with corkyistas, most of the gutierristas, including Gutiérrez, did not attend. As a result, Gutiérrez was censured on the grounds that he as the chairperson could no longer legitimately act in the name of the Congreso, since he had ignored the decisions made by the majority of the its delegates.

Two weeks later, in September, Gutiérrez called for a Congreso meeting to be held in East Chicago, Illinois. The meeting became a political showdown and in many ways was a repeat of the first Congreso meeting in Albuquerque. RUP's leadership from Colorado complained that Gutiérrez had not officially invited the delegates from Colorado, Illinois, and New Mexico, among other states. They alleged that they learned of the meeting from the Indiana delegates. Gutiérrez subsequently described the meeting as a "bitter struggle at the national level between opposing delegations."[101]

Gutiérrez proposed a number of structural changes to the Congreso. One was the creation of a *consejo*, or council, which he had introduced earlier. Essentially the Consejo would be comprised of three delegates (later expanded to four) from three states that were arbitrarily picked by him; its function would be to advise him on matters pertinent to the governance of the partido.[102] The delegates from Colorado, Illinois, California, and New Mexico countered by taking the position that a national partido did not exist and that the Congreso's structure should be used merely for communication purposes. The Illinois delegates went on to introduce a proposal that would do away with the position of national chairperson of the Congreso. At this point, impasse was reached. Gutiérrez, furious at the suggestion, adjourned the meeting.[103] According to Peña, "The results of the meeting were devastating. The rupture within the partido became final."[104]

Gonzales's supporters left disgruntled, and in a letter Gonzales informed Gutiérrez that RUP from Colorado would no longer participate in the Congreso. The message was loud and clear—as long as Gutiérrez was heading it, they would not support the Congreso. Some of Gonzales's supporters continued working within RUP, while many others in the Midwest shifted their activism to organizing social service programs and dealing with local issues.[105]

In a desperate attempt to save the Congreso, Gutiérrez called for another meeting. Attending the January 1974 meeting in Crystal City, Texas, were delegates from six states. They discussed and took action on such issues as opening immigration centers for the protection of undocumented workers, promoting unity among the major organizations and leaders, and running voter registration drives.[106] However, the issues that had divided the Congreso, such as structure, officers, and ultimately the direction of RUP, were not discussed. The last Congreso meeting of record was held in July 1975 in San Antonio, Texas. Only the states of Texas, New Mexico, and California sent delegates to the meeting. By 1975 all of the other states that had originally been part of the Congreso had dropped out. Ironically, after some three years of internecine conflict, at no time did the Congreso ever really exist.

By 1973, Gutiérrez began to rely much more on the Consejo, which by 1976 included, besides himself, only four other persons: Juan José Peña (New Mexico), Maria Elena Martinez (Texas), Fred Aguilar (California), and Salamon Baldenegro (Arizona). Having virtually no money for travel, Gutiérrez and later Peña, from 1978 to 1980, relied on conference calls to conduct business for the Consejo, which during these years was renamed the National Executive Committee.

## National Conferences to Revitalize the CM and RUP

A cardinal function of the Congreso was to ensure that RUP held national conventions. Yet, due to the conflict and divisions that existed for some four years, no national conference or convention had been organized since RUP's national convention and Tijerina's Conference on Land and Culture held in 1972. While the CJ and other entities held numerous conferences and RUP had small state conventions, none were designed to revitalize and reunify RUP or the CM. It was not until 1976 with the National Chicano Forum and 1977 with the National Chicano and Latino Immigration Conference that efforts were once again initiated to bring together activists, particularly RUP's leadership, for a major political gathering. At both conferences, RUP leaders and supporters played a pivotal role.

## The National Chicano Forum

By 1976, the situation with RUP and the rest of the CM had reached a state of crisis. With RUP shattered by divisions and the CM moribund, a National Chicano Forum was held May 28–31, 1976, in Salt Lake City, Utah. The research and planning for the forum began as early as 1975 under my direction. At the time, I was an assistant professor of political science and director of the Hinckley Institute of Politics Minority Leadership Training Program at the University of Utah. Being a former organizer and chair of California's San Bernardino and Riverside Counties RUP Central Coordinating Committee, I was deeply concerned about the internecine fighting that had all but destroyed the movement to make RUP a viable political party.

With the input of students, faculty, and community people from Salt Lake City, a plan of action was devised that entailed conducting research and interviewing activist leaders from throughout the Southwest. The objective was to ascertain the status of RUP and the CM. During the summer of 1975, several Chicano interns and I traveled to California, Texas, and Colorado and met with many of the top activist leaders, including Gutiérrez, Gonzales, Corona, Ruiz, and Baca. The research showed that RUP was internally self-destructing and the CM was all but dead. What also became evident was that the battle of conflicting personalities had expanded to a battle of conflicting ideologies.

By late 1975, with the support of student leaders, I organized the National Chicano Forum Steering Committee. The committee included students, faculty, and community people from Salt Lake City. Abelardo Delgado, a poet, and I cochaired the committee. A letter of invitation sent by the committee stated the purpose of the forum: "Our rationale for organizing a national forum is predicated on the premise that the Chicano Movement in 1976 is in desperate need of 'unity' and 'redirection.'" The letter also stressed that the function of the committee was merely to act as a "neutral facilitator" in the pursuit of revitalizing in particular the overall Chicano Movement.[107]

*The Militant* reported that the forum's purpose "was to bring together activists of all political persuasions for a free exchange of views. It sought to promote greater unity within the movement by clarifying goals and methods as well as initiating united action where it can be achieved."[108] Juan José Peña wrote in his unpublished paper "Raza Unida on Youth": " Under the planning of Armando Navarro and Lalo Delgado

[they] wanted to try to heal the wounds of the Chicano Movement and have us forget about ideology." There were some activists, however, who perceived the forum as part of a power play or even part of a CIA effort.

A few days before the start of the forum, a conservative group of Méxicanos calling themselves Concerned Citizens held a press conference in Salt Lake City. They alleged that many of those who would be in attendance and had financed the event were "Communists." The police department had also been informed that various terrorist groups were going to be present. The police were put on a state of high alert, since they had allegedly received information that various institutions were going to be bombed. As the hundreds of Chicano activists arrived, they were greeted by a city that was, in the minds of some, under a state of siege.

The three-day forum drew some 600 activists. The program included workshops on various aspects of organization and ideology, along with speakers, poetry readings, art displays, and musical performances. The keynote speaker was the eminent labor organizer and intellectual Ernesto Galarza. Chavez, Tijerina, José Angel Gutiérrez, and Gonzales, the CM's "four horsemen," were invited to speak; however, none agreed to attend. While Gonzales and Gutiérrez had initially agreed to speak, their ongoing conflict influenced their decision not to participate. Tijerina declined because he was angry over the fact that Gonzales and other CM members did not support him while he was in prison. Those who attended were the primary and secondary leaders of numerous movimiento-oriented groups, especially RUP. The forum also attracted Chicano and Latino activists from the Socialist Workers Party, Communist Party, CASA (Centro de Acción Social Autónoma), and the August 29th Movement.

The forum's two major workshops were "Ideology—What direction will the Chicano Movement take?" and "Organization and Action—How shall we get there?" At the workshop on ideology, heated debate took place between the nationalists and Marxists. As a result of their intransigence, no consensus was reached as to what ideology would guide the CM and RUP. Some RUP leaders sought to bridge or find a friendly compromise between the opposing ideological forces. Texas RUP leader Armando Gutiérrez exhorted the participants to consider the relevance of Marxism to the Chicano struggle and stressed there was no contradiction between Marxism and nationalism. His view was buttressed by New Mexico RUP leader Juan José Peña.

At the workshop on organization and action, RUP activists argued that they needed to support RUP's struggle to become an alternative political party and that it should be made the political arm of the CM. CASA activists disagreed and instead propounded the Communist Party line regarding the need to organize the Méxicano working class in a class struggle movement. The debate became argumentative, and efforts by RUP activists to get a consensus on their agenda of RUP being in the political vanguard of the CM ended in failure.

CASA ultimately fostered so much conflict and polarization that in the end, much like the two previous national meetings, the National Chicano Forum ended in a stalemate. While the forum did not produce a consensus on ideology or organization, *The Militant* praised its "comradely atmosphere," which "was particularly impressive in that the gathering was held under intense pressure." Thus, for RUP activists, another opportunity was lost to rebuild RUP into a viable party. For the sectarian Marxist groups, the meeting merely provided another forum to dialectically advance their proletarian revolutionary agendas.

## The National Chicano and Latino Immigration Conference

The next national meeting of Chicano activists occurred in October 1977 with the National Chicano and Latino Immigration Conference held in San Antonio. The conference was the result of several concurrent factors. With RUP in a state of decline, some activists had shifted their organizing from politics to social justice issues. By 1977, the issue of immigration had become a priority for some RUP activists. In response to increased deportation of Méxicanos and a proposed immigration policy by the Carter administration, Gutiérrez issued a call for action at a Chicano leadership summit meeting that was held on May 5, 1977, in Ontario, California.

That month, forty-five Chicano leaders from throughout the Southwest gathered to discuss what could be done to consolidate what was left of the CM. In some respects, it was a continuation of the National Chicano Forum agenda. The meeting was organized and chaired by me under the aegis of the National Institute for Community Development, which I had established in January of that year. Instead of talking about ideology and organization, the activist leaders addressed the issue of immigration and concurred unanimously that what was needed was a national conference on the emerging immigration crisis. Gutiérrez was commissioned to draft a "Call for Action."[109] Part of the letter sent out by Gutiérrez to numerous activists across the country read: "A crisis for all Spanish surnamed persons within the United States of America is rapidly approaching. The very same man our Raza supported for the Presidency now seeks to deport us. The Carter Administration is designing a new immigration policy. We are the main targets. The phobia mongers insist our people, because of our numbers, birth rate, geographic spread and undocumented status threatens the very underpinnings of this society."[110]

On May 23, RUP's leadership in Texas held a conference in San Antonio at which the call to action was discussed and endorsed. During the weeks that followed, numerous organizations from throughout the Southwest, including RUP, prepared for the conference. By the time the conference was held in October, scores of organizations and leaders endorsed the conference and actively supported it. The broad response suggested that Méxicano activists had shifted the focus of their activism from the electoral arena to the immigration advocacy arena. This also reflected RUP's declining organizational leadership role.

October 28–30 in San Antonio at the El Tropicano Hotel, 1,500 activists from throughout the nation attended the National Chicano and Latino Immigration Conference. Activists from thirty different states representing groups of different ideological persuasions participated in the largest ever Méxicano conference on immigration. They gathered for the purpose of formulating a strategic response to Carter's immigration policies.[111] Prior to the passage of numerous resolutions critical of the policies, the conference was rocked by a destructive internecine conflict. The underlying issue was the apparent omnipresence of the Socialist Workers Party (SWP). Trotskyists, Stalinists, and Maoists grappled for the organizational leadership of the Chicano struggle. RUP from Texas had provided the forum, and the ideological groups used it to advance their own agendas. In explaining the prominence of the SWP, political scientist Mario Barrera wrote: "With La Raza Unida party disorganized and internally divided, José Angel Gutiérrez, who had issued the call for the conference, had come to rely on SWP activists and resources to organize the conference."[112]

After a rambunctious ten hours of debate, conference organizers Compean and Gutiérrez exhorted the conference participants to return to the issue of immigration. Failing to win support for the exclusion of the SWP, the CASA activists walked out of the conference in protest. Antonio Rodriguez, head of CASA, remarked before they left, "We have to tell you, unfortunately, that based on certain principles, it is possible that we may not continue in this process while the Socialist Workers Party is included."[113] Despite all the disruptions, a ten-point plan calling for total amnesty of all undocumented workers was endorsed. Moreover, a call was made for a nationwide protest to be held November 18–20 against the Carter Plan.[114]

The conference revealed several conditions. First, the conference illustrated the extent that Marxist ideas had penetrated the Chicano activist sector. Second, the conference witnessed the prevalence of the "politics of self-destruction," which had become insuperable and irreconcilable. And third, the conference demonstrated the declining leadership strength of both Gutiérrez and Gonzales and of RUP as a national or even a regional third-party movement.

### Gutiérrez's Resignation as RUP National Chairperson

From 1976 to 1981 RUP maintained the masquerade of being a national partido. However, at best, RUP during these years was limited to three states: New Mexico, California, and Texas. RUP had become defunct in Arizona in 1974 and in Colorado in 1976. Most RUP organizing efforts in the Midwest had also disappeared. From 1976 to 1981, only a handful of RUP zealots, led by Juan José Peña, Fred Aguilar, Maria Elena Martinez, Xenaro Ayala, and a few others, kept up the political facade that RUP was national. It was during these years that Gutiérrez's leadership as RUP national chairperson declined, and subsequently he resigned.

According to Peña, Gutiérrez resigned in 1976 during a conference call between him and other RUP leaders. During that same call, the participants held a quick election and Peña was elected national chair; Maria Elena Martinez, vice chairperson; Fred Aguilar, treasurer; and Salomon Baldenegro, secretary.[115] However, when interviewed, Gutiérrez said he did not officially resign until much later, more like 1978 or 1979. Research conducted did in fact reveal that he did not officially resign until January 20, 1979, via a letter sent to then Texas RUP state chair Maria Elena Martinez, which read in part: "I hereby submit my resignation as National Chairperson of the Raza Unida Party to you elected State Chairpersons from your respective states effective January 20, 1979. I feel this action is necessary to effect needed change in our party direction, organization and structure. My service to the Raza Unida Party in the past has been a rewarding and fulfilling experience equal to none other. . . . The future work of the National Party is crucial to its survival."[116]

In our 1998 interview, Gutiérrez recalled informing the RUP National Executive Committee at a meeting that he attended in Albuquerque, New Mexico, in 1976 of his intention to resign as national chairperson:

> They invited me to Albuquerque and I went. I remember we had a very frank discussion and I said I am tired of this bullshit. Nobody seems to want to work with me. They keep making me the object of the problem. So why don't I just resign? Why doesn't somebody else take over or why don't we have another convention? I don't remember what the actual decision was, but I do remember that Juan José took it upon himself to say that he was the national chairman for about a year and I didn't protest. I don't remember ever resigning to anybody.[117]

From 1976 to 1979 when Gutiérrez resigned, it was sometimes difficult to know who was in charge of the partido. Peña during this time took on a high-profile and active role at the regional and national levels.[118] This was understandable, since Gutiérrez from late 1975 to the time he officially left Cristal in early January of 1981 was under constant attack by a number of political forces, including those within RUP in Cristal.[119]

## RUP's Last Convention

In spite of RUP's rapid decline, in 1980 it held a national convention in Albuquerque, New Mexico. Attended by some 100 persons, this convention was a far cry from the 1972 convention that drew some 3,000 people from eighteen different states. Most of those who attended the 1980 gathering came from four states: California, New Mexico, Texas, and Colorado. However, Colorado did not have official delegate status at the convention, since RUP had been defunct there since 1976. Led by Ernesto Vigil, the small delegation was given observer status. Although not interested in participating with RUP, the CJ activists were interested in networking.[120]

Russell Means from the American Indian Movement was present, as well as some representatives of México's Partido Socialista de Trabajadores (Socialist Workers Party, or PST). José Calderon, who had left RUP in Colorado in 1974 and by 1980 had embraced the Maoist-oriented Communist Workers Party, was asked to leave the convention, as was Manuel Archuleta from the PST.[121]

Indicative of RUP's separatist inclinations, the convention delegates deliberated on the "National Question." Four major strategic options were discussed: (1) Should Méxicanos in the United States remain part of the United States? (2) Should Méxicanos

establish a separate state? (3) Should Méxicanos seek a reunification with México?
(4) Should Méxicanos establish a "free state"? A resolution was passed that read: "We
as Chicanos, members of the [RUP], reaffirm our right to establish and/or create the
independent nation of Aztlán." Discussion was also held on establishing a capital for
the nation of Aztlán, but the motion was tabled as "premature." Several other resolutions were passed, including one that called for the reestablishment of the Congreso de
Aztlán. RUP's national officers were elected: Juan José Peña, chair of the RUP Central
Committee; Maria Elena Martinez, vice chair; Isabel Blea, treasurer/secretary; and
Xenaro Ayala, foreign affairs secretary. The convention adjourned with only a handful
of delegates who had stayed to the end[122]

## RUP in Foreign Affairs

No entity in the history of the Chicano experience spent as much time trying to enter
the arena of foreign affairs as did RUP.[123] The architect was José Angel Gutiérrez, who
believed that Méxicanos in the United States had reached a point in their development
when they could play an important role internationally, and that RUP was the vehicle
to use.[124] From 1972 to 1980 and even beyond, RUP activists ventured into foreign
political affairs.[125] They started with México in 1972 and went as far as Lebanon in 1980.
RUP's leadership was determined to catapult the CM into recognition by sympathetic
and supportive governments, such as those of México, Cuba, and others of the Third
World.[126]

### RUP and the México Connection, 1972–1975

Gutiérrez first realized the importance of international connections in 1963, during
the first takeover of the city council in Cristal by Los Cinco.[127] He was in charge of
working the media aspects of the takeover ,and he found that "the Mexican press was
thirsty for information. It was than I realized there was an interest on us."[128] However,
it was not until the second Cristal revolt, in 1970, that the Spanish-speaking media
from México reacted with great interest. By 1970, Gutiérrez had become a seasoned
and accomplished activist leader who knew how to work the media. As he told me
in our 1998 interview, "My job when I became the head of the partido was to use the
media in our public relations."[129]

  With so many inquiries coming from México regarding the Cristal takeover and
the emergence of the first Méxicano political party in the United States, Gutiérrez
by 1972 cleverly initiated what I call the "politics of *acercamiento*" (rapprochement)
with México. For years, assisting Gutiérrez on the Mexican government side was
Jorge Bustamante, a sociologist at the University of Notre Dame. Bustamante acted
as a liason and broker at many of the meetings with México's government officials.[130]
From 1972 to around 1978, Gutiérrez was *the* Chicano connection to México.

Gutiérrez orchestrated the first meeting with México's president Luis Echeverría Alvarez and other government officials during his visit to San Antonio, Texas, in June 1972. The delegation of RUP leaders met with government officials for the purpose of conducting discussions on various issues of common interest. Gutiérrez, in particular, was interested in securing economic as well as technical assistance from the government of México. The RUP delegation presented Echeverría with a painting of Emiliano Zapata that had been painted by an artist from Cristal.

President Echeverría, in a gesture of goodwill, reciprocated by agreeing to donate to Cristal a bust of Benito Juarez, the nineteenth-century statesman and president of México, and some 2,000 books to Cristal's library. He also agreed to send Pedro De Koster, director of industry, to ascertain what kind of technical assistance the government could provide Cristal in the development of new industries. The president exhorted RUP leaders to "keep on winning." Several weeks later, De Koster and other Mexican government officials visited Cristal.[131]

The reaction of some gringos to the Mexican government's overtures was one of concern. A letter to the editor in the San Antonio Express on June 23, 1972, read: "It seems that José Angel Gutiérrez and his gang are planning (and apparently succeeding) to make Crystal City (and all of Texas, with their political aspirations) a suburb of Mexico. All this, while every phase of their lives is U.S. tax-funded."

During the subsequent four years, 1972–1976, Gutiérrez and other RUP leaders attended various meetings with President Echeverría and others from his administration. When interviewed, Gutiérrez alluded to meeting personally at least seven times with Echeverria both in the United States and in Mexico at Los Pinos, the president's official residence, the National Presidential Palace, and the president's private residence. The Echeverría administration, which was nationalist, anti-imperialist, very pro–Third World foreign policy, and to some degree *anti-Yanqui*, took notice of the potential political, economic, and social importance of the Chicano.[132]

Echeverría's administration sponsored numerous educational and cultural exchange programs in Mexico. It was during this period that Gutiérrez secured fifty scholarships for Chicano students under the aegis of the Becas para Aztlán (Scholarships for the Southwest) program. He also got the Mexican government to commit a million dollars toward RUP's economic development projects; however, according to Gutiérrez, "It never materialized because we could never break through the presidential bureaucracy." Echeverría's administration funded a feasibility study for a health clinic that was subsequently built and also helped diplomatically with RUP's trip to Cuba.[133]

RUP's relationship with the Echeverria administration also came under fire from the Marxist elements within the CM, including Juan Gomez Quinonez. Some questioned the value of RUP's relationship with a government they perceived as being a corrupt one-party dictatorship—Partido Revolucioñario Institucional (Revolutionary Institutional Party, or PRI). But to Gutiérrez the pragmatist, the positives far outweighed the negatives: "I knew we had to have a foreign policy. We could not have pretended to be an alternative political party if also we did not have an alternative foreign policy."

He wanted the Mexican government to assume more responsibility for improving the Méxicano's general welfare in the United States.[134] Gutiérrez believed that the government of Mexico had for too many years essentially abandoned its people in the United States.

Gutiérrez was determined to change the negative image Chicanos had of Mexico and vice versa.[135] As a result of RUP's involvement with the so-called Mexican connection, it succeeded in an unprecedented fashion in bringing a new awareness to the Méxicano in Mexico of the political, cultural, and social renaissance engendered in the United States by the CM.

### RUP's Connection to Cuba, China, and the PLO, 1975

While continuing to strengthen RUP's ties with Mexico, Gutiérrez moved to expand the partido's international connection—this time with Cuba. Invited by the government of Cuba, who paid most of the expenses of the Mexico-to-Cuba leg of the trip, a sixteen-member RUP delegation left for Cuba in April via Mexico City. During its ten-day stay, mostly in Havana, the delegation met with high-ranking government officials and was exposed to various aspects of the Cuban revolution. Upon the delegation's return to the United States, Gutiérrez at a press conference made controversial statements praising Cuba's revolution. The most controversial was his claim that he was going to create "many little Cubas in South Texas." Attacks against him and RUP in general were abundant.[136] His remarks were not well received by many Whites in conservative, patriotic Texas, especially among the Democratic Party leadership.

In 1975, RUP's leadership also began to court other countries. Fred Aguilar from California and a few others toured for several weeks the People's Republic of China. The RUP activists went to learn more about Maoism and the Communist Chinese revolution. That same year, Aguilar was part of an eight-person RUP delegation from California that went to Lebanon and met with Yasir Arafat and other leaders of the Palestinian Liberation Organization (PLO). The dialogue with Arafat focused on sharing information about each other's movements. The PLO officials asked specifically about RUP and the CM.[137] Even though the trip was not well publicized and did not produce anything substantial, it illustrated the growing international perspective within RUP.

### RUP's Ties with Mexico's PRI and the PST, 1976–1980

Even after José Lopez Portillo replaced Echeverría as Mexico's president in 1976, Gutiérrez continued to maintain the connection to Mexico. While Portillo was a presidential candidate, Gutiérrez met with him in Juarez, Mexico, in 1976. A few months later, Gutiérrez orchestrated another meeting with Portillo in Hermosillo, Mexico, involving a delegation of RUP leaders and scholars, of whom I was one.

Each of us made a short presentation on the status of the Méxicano in the United States. The meeting was designed to ensure RUP's continued access to Mexico's president. During the next six years, while the relationship between RUP and Portillo continued, the direct access and close working relationship were gone. It became far more bureaucratic, according to Gutiérrez.[138]

Portillo, however, implemented a much expanded policy of reaching out to Chicanos in the areas of education, culture, and immigration matters. For example, he increased the number of Becas para Aztlán from 50 to 250.[139] In the area of immigration, as the attacks on Méxicano immigrants in the United States increased, his administration set up new mechanisms to study the issue.[140] Throughout his six-year administration, Portillo continued to adhere to a form of nationalism that was anti–United States and to maintain a Third World foreign policy posture, which was helpful in keeping the Chicano agenda a priority for Mexico.

During the next three years, RUP leaders met on several occasions with Portillo and government and PRI officials. One such meeting occurred in 1978 in México City at Los Pinos as part of Solidarity Week, organized by the Portillo administration. A California RUP leader recalled: "We had a delegation of some thirty Raza Unida people. We were treated as dignitaries; we were provided with a military escort to Los Pinos, where Portillo was waiting for us."[141]

Gutiérrez also arranged several meetings with Mexico's young Marxist Partido Socialista de los Trabajadores (PST, the Workers Socialist Party). It was a strategic move, since the PST was a left-wing satellite party of the PRI. For RUP it was an important contact; PST had funding and access to the PRI's leadership. Gutiérrez explained: "As a result of electoral laws or *apertura* (opening) as they called it, Echeverría allowed more political parties to compete out in the open. This meant that these new parties had money, subsidy, and now we could be out in the open."[142] Gutiérrez and other RUP leaders in 1976 participated with the PST in a massive demonstration in Mexico City protesting the lack of democracy in Mexico. When interviewed, Gutiérrez, commented on the parallels between the two young parties:

They were young like we were. So in a sense it was kind of, here are the young people of the respective countries trying to change their country. They were trying to change Mexico and we were trying to change the United States. We were both minority parties. They were numerically nobodys in Mexico and we were nobodys in the United States. In some areas they had potential, just like we had potential in certain areas. We just had a lot of things in common.[143]

From 1976 to 1980, Gutiérrez and other RUP leaders enjoyed a rather amicable relationship with the PST while still having meetings with Portillo and other leaders of the PRI. In late 1978, a meeting was held between RUP and PST leaders in San Antonio, Texas. At the meeting a joint statement was signed by PST foreign secretary Carlos Olamendi and RUP's Gutiérrez condemning the Carter administration's immigration policies.[144] As a result of the meeting, RUP agreed to participate in November in a series of activities, sponsored by the Portillo administration, that commemorated Solidarity Week between Méxicanos and Chicanos.

While in Mexico City, the delegation met with President Portillo and leaders from the PST. California RUP leader Andres Torres explains the perception one PST leader had of RUP: "I'll never forget it. Before concluding a long discourse delivered by Rafael Bustamante, chair of the PST, he said to us, "Pero compañeros, debemos de comprender algo, ustedes no tienen un partido politico" (But comrades, we need to face one fact, you do not have a political party).[145]

In early 1980, both parties held another symbolic event commemorating RUP's tenth anniversary, this time in the center of the International Bridge in Laredo, which separates Mexico and the United States. Representatives of both the PST and RUP attacked U.S. imperialism. Preceding the gathering, a meeting was held in Laredo, Mexico, where Gutiérrez underscored the seriousness of the growing immigration crisis when he stated at a press conference that Méxicanos had become undocumented in their own land.

By 1980, only Gutiérrez and a handful of RUP leaders continued to nurture an amicable relationship with both parties. Part of the rationale was that they were in desperate need of financial resources. They figured that either Mexico or a combination of other countries could provide RUP with the badly needed resources or that they could at least set up mutually beneficial collaborative economic ventures.

Unfortunately, in the end, the meetings with PRI and PST officials never produced financial returns for RUP. In fact, the RUP leaders had to cover most of their own expenses when they attended these meetings. Furthermore, Mexico's changing political climate did not help matters. As a result of U.S. pressure, in 1978, the government of Mexico cut off the funding to the PST. This impacted RUP in that its leadership had been working on an economic venture with the PST to sell them video and audio equipment. Without its subsidy, the PST could not afford to buy the equipment from RUP.[146]

*RUP Expands Its Internationalist Role*

In its efforts to make RUP financially stable and viable, the leadership expanded its international agenda to include other governments. Aguilar explains that during the late 1970s, "part of our agenda was always trying to figure out ways of developing cooperative economic ventures."[147] The two RUP leaders who headed much of the economic effort were Larry Hill and Frank Schaffer Corona. They and others were instrumental in forming various RUP-controlled for-profit organizations. One such entity was Vista Multimedia, based in Albuquerque, New Mexico; however, it failed when the PST lost its funding in 1978. Another failed import/export venture was Virgin Industries, which was to have imported Chinese goods into the United States from the People's Republic of China.

Alianza Latina-Americana (Latin American Alliance) was set up by RUP, according to Peña: "It was supposed to have been our umbrella organization for establishing partido businesses." In 1978, the Alianza came close to becoming the broker for the sale of Libyan oil in the United States. After months of meetings between Schaffer and Libyan Embassy officials, RUP succeeded in concluding the oil deal; unfortunately, that year the United States expelled all Libyan diplomats from the country and placed an embargo on Libyan oil. Without the capital from the oil venture, RUP could not follow through with its other business venture with China.[148]

That same year, RUP activists from New Mexico traveled to Nicaragua to join the Sandinista revolution. For the next three to four years, several RUP activists assisted the Sandinistas in fighting their war. According to Peña: "The partido had eighteen people with the Sandinistas in Nicaragua. This is something known by very few. Ernesto Eichwald, Chris Eichwald, and a number of other people here in the partido when the revolution broke out . . . went down to Nicaragua and served with the Sandinistas until the Sandinistas came to power. . . . Later on, many of these people came back to New Mexico."[149]

Concurrently, RUP expanded its contacts to include the PLO and some countries in the Middle East. In 1975, a RUP delegation met with the PLO, but not much was done to foster a working relationship until 1978. RUP's interests were both economic and political. On the economic side, RUP was interested in developing some import/export ventures with the PLO. On the political side, RUP by 1979 had taken a very open pro-Palestinian posture. It was during this time that Fred Aguilar, RUP state chairperson for California, because of his involvement with PLO and Libyan connections was kidnapped for a few days and then released by agents, whose connections were unknown.[150]

In 1980 the PLO invited a RUP delegation of nine persons to meet with Arafat and other PLO officials in Beirut, Lebanon.[151] Although the government of Lebanon paid for the round trip from New York to Lebanon, the actual trip was coordinated under the auspices of the Arab Red Crescent Society, an affiliate of the International Red Cross.[152] RUP leaders, such as Peña, saw parallels between the struggle of the PLO and that of Méxicanos in the United States in that "Palestinians were being denied their civil and human rights." Rebecca Hill, the only Chicana in the delegation, said: "We felt that we both had the same fight. They learned about our struggle that Chicanos were being thrown out of their own homeland. So they invited us on a fact-finding mission so we could come back and tell the world that there are two sides to every story."[153]

During the eight-day stay in war-torn Beirut, the RUP delegation was exposed to various aspects of the Israeli/Palestian conflict. The delegation toured refugee camps, guerrilla camps, and hospitals; witnessed car bombings; and was shot at by Israeli forces. According to Rebecca Hill, the delegation came close to getting killed after a car bomb went off at a military checkpoint just a few minutes after they had passed it. She said that "several people were killed in the explosion."[154] During the time the delegation was in Beirut, Peña and Schafer visited various embassies, including Iran's, with the intent of negotiating the release of two Chicanos and a Native American who were captives as a result of the Iranian hostage crisis. Finally, facilitated by the PLO, a meeting was held with Iranian officials, and they initially agreed to release three hostages, only to renege on the accord, according to Peña, because of pressure exerted from the U.S. State Department.[155]

The delegation was not able to meet with Arafat until the evening before the delegation left Beirut. Due to the threats on his life, security was tight. Before the meeting, the delegation was driven around Beirut for nearly six hours, as various ploys were undertaken to deceive possible followers. The meeting lasted three hours, from four to seven in the morning. According to Ignacio Garcia, a delegate, "Arafat spent a lot of time asking us about the United States."[156] There was some discussion as to what each group could do to help the other. An informal trade accord was concluded by which RUP would be able to sell goods produced by the PLO in the United States.[157]

Upon their return to the United States, according to one delegate, they were asked by the FBI to turn over their film and documents and questioned on the purpose of their trip. The delegation held a press conference in Washington, D.C., but it was not well attended by the press. "It really didn't matter what we said, the press was so pro-Israeli," stated Hill. Garcia, a journalist by trade, wrote a piece, which newspapers refused to carry.[158]

For a few, the return to the United States was a nightmare. Some lost their jobs, while others were harassed by FBI and law enforcement agencies. Banks refused to make loans to a couple of them. The pressure, personal problems, and burnout took its a toll on the few remaining RUP leaders. Unable to find a job, living practically out of his car, and going through a divorce, Peña decided to resign in early 1981 as RUP national chairperson; he chose not to remain active in RUP. For everyone in the delegation, the trip left vivid memories of the tragedies of war.

In the end, the delegation failed to accomplish anything concrete. Garcia explains that (1) we were "out of our league" and did not have "the experienced leadership of a José Angel Gutiérrez"; (2) there was no collective agenda, and some of the delegates "had their own agendas"; (3) they did not know what they were doing; and (4) the delegation was "comprised of remnants of what was left of the partido."[159]

The Lebanon trip expedited the demise of RUP. Xenaro Ayala from San Fernando replaced Peña as RUP national chairperson by way of a simple phone call. Unfortunately, there was little left of RUP at the national level for Ayala to lead.

# Chapter Twelve

## Profile of a Chicano Partido: The Unfinished Partido Experiment

Until 1970, at no time had Méxicanos ever opted to rebuke the nation's two-party dictatorship by forming their own political party. While some electoral flirtations with third parties had occurred—for example, the United People's Party in the 1890s and the People's Constitutional Party in 1968—these experiments were multiethnic, coalitional, and reform oriented. From 1970 until its demise in 1981, the Raza Unida Party (RUP) was indeed an unprecedented third-party movement, in that Méxicanos organized it for Méxicanos. For eleven years, RUP labored to give Méxicanos a political alternative to the Democratic and Republican Parties.

### RUP's Ascent: A Product of Rising Expectations

Like other third-party movements in U.S. politics, RUP's emergence was a product of a climate of change that was permeated with discontent, frustration, and rising expectations. I have argued that, in most cases, third parties in the United States are products of political alienation due to the monopoly of control by the nation's two major political parties. Many of those I interviewed felt that both parties were, using a term of the sixties, "irrelevant," meaning they did not serve the interests of Méxicanos.

Each of my fifty-six interviews of RUP leaders uncovered frustration with the way both political parties had historically treated Méxicanos in the United States. Many leaders used words and phrases like "neglect," "insensitive," "didn't care," "took advantage of us," "were racist," and "represented the ruling class" to describe the reasons why they opted to participate in the organizing of RUP. The words of Cireño Rodriguez, a RUP activist from Santa Barbara, seem to embody the major reason for their involvement: "We believed that neither the Democratic nor the Republican Party was paying much attention to the needs of our community and that we needed to make a statement with a third party. We were students, very idealistic, and we thought of ourselves as progressive. For us, it was important to make a statement, not necessarily to win an election, but we needed to make a statement that they couldn't take our vote for granted anymore. That we were here and we were organized."[1]

Others alluded to how their activism and involvement in the Chicano Movement (CM) had facilitated their crossover to RUP. Many were veterans of activism with movimiento-type organizations. The omnipresence of Chicanismo inspired many activists to join the RUP struggle.[2] The CM by 1970 had radicalized many of the activists. Their political attitudes, beliefs, and values by 1970 had become increasingly critical of the nation's liberal capitalist system; this applied particularly to activists involved with the Mexican American Youth Organization (MAYO) and the Crusade for Justice (CJ). They wanted to extricate Méxicanos from their dependency on the two-party system. In the context of the epoch of protest, 1956–1974, the idea of a Chicano political party was unique, timely, and long overdue.

Due to the CM, by 1970, Chicano activists were caught up in the maelstrom of rising political expectations. Gutiérrez's call for the formation of RUP in January coupled with RUP's electoral successes in South Texas in April heightened expectations. Eddie Montour from Pueblo, Colorado, explained that many activists welcomed the idea of a Chicano political party: "We didn't believe Democrats or Republicans had anything to offer."[3]

Also contributing to the rising expectations of Méxicanos in Colorado was Gonzales's decree to form RUP in March 1970. The concurrent RUP organizing efforts in Texas and Colorado convinced some Chicano activists from other states to join the third-party bandwagon. In describing the organizing contagion that resulted from both states' organizing efforts, Herman Baca, RUP leader from San Diego said: "It was very exciting. Here was self-determination in action and staring us in the face."[4] What enticed Ignacio Garcia to get involved was "the boldness of the idea, the fact that there was an alternative."[5] Thus, RUP's rise was a result of disenchanted Chicano activists whose expectations had risen to a point at which they believed that it was imperative to bolt the two major parties and form an all-Méxicano political party in the United States.

## What Kind of Third Party was RUP?

A summary of some of the points made earlier in this book should help determine what kind of third party RUP was. In the United States, the two major parties have made it almost impossible for a third party to mount an effective challenge against them. There have been, however, a number of third parties that have, if only symbolically, managed to compete in the arena of electoral politics. These exceptions have been useful to both major parties, allowing them to market the notion that the United States is a viable representative democracy. In reality, while the U.S. party system allows third parties to compete, the two major parties through their monopoly of control make sure that such parties do not stand a chance of winning.

In spite of the absolute power both major parties wield, third parties have played significant roles in U.S. politics. Some have actually been instrumental in pushing though political, social, and economic reforms that have made liberal capitalism more tolerable for the nation's poor and working classes.

RUP was unlike other third parties. It was the first political party representing a single ethnic group to emerge in the United States. Some people would dispute this claim, reminding us of the racist, all-White parties, such as the Nazi-oriented National Socialist Party of America. The fact is, however, that White supremacist entities are a hybrid of various White ethnic groups, for instance, German, English, and so on. While some Latinos (non-Méxicanos with roots in Latin America) did participate in RUP, the overwhelming majority of RUP's supporters and leaders were Méxicanos. RUP was essentially a third-party phenomenon that emanated from the Southwest, where Méxicanos comprised some 85 percent of the Latino population. The symbolism used, from its logos to its historical and cultural trappings, was Méxicano.

With reference to the two third-party models I examine in the introduction, Issue Reformist (IR) and Sectarian Doctrinaire (SD), I suggest that RUP was a combination of both. Those who identified with José Angel Gutiérrez and the Texas model of RUP were practitioners of the IR model, while those who identified with Rodolfo "Corky" Gonzales and the Colorado model as well as those who comprised its leadership from 1976 to 1981 were proponents of the SD model. While still very Méxicano oriented, RUP's new leadership during these years became much more doctrinaire in its commitment to forming a Chicano nation that would be ideologically socialist. This dual political personality led to conflicts among activists and contributed to RUP's decline.

## RUP's Eclectic Ideology

Political scientists and sociologists would generally agree that an ideology is a belief system or vision that dictates direction, justification, and even strategy. Ideology is a vital ingredient to the formation of any social movement that seeks to bring about major social change. During RUP's eleven years of existence, there were three major ideological currents that permeated its politics and development: (1) cultural nationalism; (2) Marxism (sectarian ideologues); and (3) ultranationalist socialism. At its inception, ideologically RUP was mainly cultural nationalist in its orientation.

Cultural nationalists identified with Chicanismo. Historian Ignacio Garcia, in explaining RUP's rise, writes: "A political 'consciousness' of being *Méxicano* in the United States gave rise to a militant ethos that became the impetus for this social upheaval [the Chicano Movement]."[6] "El Plan Espiritual de Aztlán," produced by two National Youth Liberation conferences and Corky Gonzales's poem "Yo Soy Joaquin," buttressed this cultural nationalism. To many activists, "Chicano" was the truncated version of "Méxicano." Regardless of its origin, "Chicano" denoted the Méxicano's experience in what some considered, with historian Rodolfo Acuña, "occupied America."

To many activists, Chicano and México were synonymous concepts. Activists rediscovered their cultural roots, heritage, history, and language as a part of the historical experience of the Méxicano, first in the Southwest, then in México, and finally in Latin America. To these activists, Chicanismo was a newfound cultural *orgullo* (pride) predicated on *carnalismo* (brotherhood), *familia* (family), and a reinvigorated sense of positive identity. A "cultural consciousness" of what it was to be a México in the Unites States was what impelled Chicanismo.

Cultural nationalism repudiated the White ethnocentric-imposed stereotypes of Méxicanos as servile, inferior, and fatalist. Chicanos adopted México philosopher José Vasconcelos's call for a "Raza Cosmica," with its emphasis on *meztizaje* (Spanish and indigenous parentage), and its dialectical development of *La Raza de Bronze* infused Chicanismo with a powerful sense of "nationalism." To many Chicano activists, nationalism fostered a geographical loyalty to Aztlán and conjured up a love of being a Chicano, as well as feelings of allegiance and loyalty to a people, public spirit, civic participation, and the rejection of White society. It categorically rejected the liberal agenda that said Méxicanos should culturally and politically integrate, assimilate, and accommodate the political system. They espoused a form of "cultural pluralism" that allowed them to maintain their culture amidst a culturally diverse nation.

Cultural nationalists did not have a well-defined ideology that spelled out a coherent set of beliefs, direction, justification, and strategy. While in many instances they were critical of the liberal capitalist system, most did not have solutions or alternatives to the complex issues confronting Méxicano communities. In most cases, they were militant reformers who merely wanted to create some degree of change and access into the system without appreciably altering it. Because of their adherence to the use of unconventional protest, they were perceived as militants and radicals.

Within RUP's cultural nationalism there were two schools of thought: cultural pluralism and ultranationalism. RUP activists who were cultural pluralists were militant integrationists who were proud of being Chicano, were assertive in their quest to reform the liberal capitalist system, and in the end followed a modified form of liberal capitalism. Conversely, ultranationalists were hypercritical of liberal capitalism and were extreme advocates of Chicano nationalism and practitioners of confrontational protest tactics in their struggle for a separate Chicano nation. They did not provide a well-defined alternative to liberal capitalism.

Marxism was the second ideological current that impacted RUP. There were various schools of Marxist thought that the RUP sectarian doctrinaire activists professed: Trotskyism, Marxism-Leninism, and Maoism. While all were categorically anticapitalist, they differed dramatically as to how and who would lead and precipitate a proletarian revolution. Ultranationalism and reform of the liberal capitalist system were anathema to their struggle. While they all preached that the working class would lead the struggle, they differed on ends and means. Many of the RUP sectarian ideologues were members of other political parties and organizations, such as the Young Socialist Alliance, Socialist Workers Party, Communist Party USA., CASA, October League, and

August 29th Movement. All sought to infiltrate RUP with the intent of advancing their sectarian doctrinaire agenda.

The third ideological current to surface by the mid-1970s within RUP's ranks was socialist ultranationalism. Those who identified ideologically with this politic were culturally and politically ultranationalist and economically socialist. They were ardent nationalists who advocated separatism and the establishment of a Chicano homeland—Aztlán. They went beyond the ultranationalist in that the socialist ultranationalist was more ideological and had a better-defined overall direction. Unequivocally anti–liberal capitalist, they believed that Aztlán would be a working-class democracy buttressed by a socialist economic system not necessarily Marxist in nature. Hence, their ideological inclinations were essentially social democratic. Like ultranationalists, they believed strategically in the use of nationalism to organize the Méxicano. They did not seek to create a partido that was working class, that is, one that would seek to represent the interests of Whites, Blacks, or anyone besides Méxicanos.

So much ideological diversity made it difficult to achieve consensus on anything. RUP began as an Issue Reformist (IR) third party that was cultural nationalist, which sought to work within the confines of the liberal capitalist system; toward its end, it had evolved to a Sectarian Doctrinaire (SD) third party.

## Ideological Profile of RUP's Leaders: Caudillos and Caciques

RUP's early cultural nationalist posture was largely the result of its two chief architects, Gutiérrez and Gonzales. According to Crusade for Justice leader Ernesto Vigil, both leaders were ardent cultural nationalists; where they differed was on strategies and tactics.[7] José Angel Gutiérrez, when questioned on the matter, said: " Well, we were very Méxicano. To us it wasn't an issue of just bilingual education because we spoke Spanish. We acted on it because we just wanted to maintain what we had. . . . Back then, Tejas was more Méxicano than California." While occasionally alluding to Aztlán and at times even being hypercritical of liberal capitalism, he was not a ideologue or separatist but a nationalist, pragmatic reformer, and cultural pluralist who believed in the notion of community control.[8]

Most of those I interviewed concurred with this characterization of Gutiérrez. New Mexico RUP leader Juan José Peña described Gutiérrez as a "radical pragmatist." California RUP leader Fred Aguilar described him as being much more a "capitalist" than anything else.[9] Another California RUP leader, Raul Ruiz, said, "José never had an ideology."[10] Yet Texas RUP leader Mario Compean challenged these characterizations of Gutiérrez and said that "he unquestionably tended towards socialism."[11] Historian Ignacio Garcia offers a nutshell comparison of Gutiérrez and Gonzales: When activists wanted to hear about the spiritual or ideological aspects of Aztlán, they wanted Corky Gonzales, "but when [they wanted] somebody to negotiate for Aztlán, Gutiérrez could deliver."[12]

Cireño Rodriguez, a RUP leader from Santa Barbara, said that Gutiérrez "was an integrationist in that he wanted to organize people to use the system, but I never heard him reject the whole concept of Aztlán."[13]

Others interviewed to some degree agreed with Rodriguez's characterization. They perceived Gutiérrez as a militant integrationist and cultural pluralist who sought to maximize what the system had to offer Méxicanos to better the quality of their lives. While accepting the cultural pluralist notion, RUP leader Marta Cotera from Texas said, "We struggled so that we could successfully integrate ourselves into the system."[14] Former Texas state RUP chairperson Maria Elena Martinez explained that RUP in Texas never advocated overthrowing the existing liberal capitalist system "and supplanting it with another system."[15]

Corky Gonzales was the main RUP leader of those who were ultranationalist. His nationalist zeal was illustrated both directly and indirectly in the documents he produced. They were strongly grounded in Chicanismo, from his epic poem "Yo Soy Joaquin" to "El Plan Espiritual de Aztlán." His writings adulated and propounded the virtues of preserving the Chicano culture and the richness of the Méxicano heritage and Spanish language. To him, cultural nationalism was the "key to unity," the "common denominator" for unifying the people in the struggle to build a homeland for Chicanos. To him, nationalism came first out of *la familia*, "then into tribalism, and then into the alliances that are necessary to lift the burden of all suppressed humanity."[16]

Ideologically, by 1968 Gonzales was a declared separatist who openly and in an intransigent manner preached the virtues of building Aztlán. Unlike Gutiérrez, he was not interested in gaining access to the system and extrapolating whatever reforms he could. Instead, to him, Chicanismo was grounded on self-determination. Lita Gonzales, Corky Gonzales's daughter, explained: "The whole focus and direction of organizing for political power was for nation building. We were very nationalistic and organized towards that end."[17] Several of the RUP leaders I interviewed perceived Corky Gonzales as an "ideologue" who was resolute and not willing to negotiate or compromise his principles. Some said that "compromise" was not a word in his lexicon. In Texas, according to Compean, "One feeling among the rank and file was that Corky was a romantic."[18] Political scientist Richard Santillan described Corky as initially a strong nationalist who with time became increasingly internationalist with his reaching out to other struggles for liberation in the Third World.[19] Peña explained that what "Corky wanted to do was set off a confrontation and conflagration between Chicanos and the mainstream society, whereas Gutiérrez wanted to utilize and absorb or capture the resources of the mainstream society."[20] Baca described Corky as "nationalist in proposing nation building." But he remarked that Gonzales's ideology was completely alien to the majority of the Méxicanos "he was trying to nation build for and with."[21] California RUP leader Xenaro Ayala explained that some activists within RUP saw Corky as "more revolutionary than Gutiérrez."[22] Ruiz's view on Corky's nationalism was that he "brought pride in culture, pride in identity, strength to our presence, more than anybody else."[23]

The majority of those interviewed said that Gonzales differed from Gutiérrez in that Gonzales was much more zealous and clearer about his ideas. Even if building a Chicano nation sounded unrealistic to others, he believed in the dream and he was willing to fight to make the dream a reality. Thus, while Gutiérrez at times sounded like an ultranationalist, Gonzales was adamant and lucid about his ultranationalism.

When I asked those I interviewed to describe their ideology at the time of their involvement with RUP, the overwhelming majority responded "cultural nationalist." Yet most were unclear as to what the term meant. However, based on their understanding of the concept, the great majority were of the "cultural pluralist" type. Only a small minority identified or described themselves as what I have labeled "ultranationalist." Some of the RUP cultural pluralists were José Angel Gutiérrez, Herman Baca, Mario Compean, Ramsey Muñiz, Carlos Guerra, Lupe Youngblood, Raul Ruiz, Ernesto Chacon, and myself. RUP leaders such as Corky Gonzales, Arturo Vasquez, Ernesto Vigil, José Calderon, Eddie Montour, and Albert Gurule were ultranationalists.

With cultural nationalists in the majority at least until 1975, the Marxist RUP leaders were a minority. None of the RUP leaders interviewed, however, identified themselves as Marxists. Yet my investigations revealed that several RUP leaders were Marxists at one point or another in their politics or involvement with leftist-leaning groups or parties, including Bert Corona, Gilbert Blanco, Manuel Archuleta, Chris Eichwald Cebada, José Calderon, and Richard Santillan. Even though they were doctrinaire in their views, they did not supplant or seriously challenge the cultural nationalist sentiment that pervaded RUP until 1976, when they reached the apex of their influence.

By this time, RUP's cultural nationalist posture had become more doctrinaire; a transition was made to a more socialist ultranationalist posture. No longer were the two cultural nationalist titans the idea purveyors. To some degree, this was the result of the devastating impact of their power struggle and the growing influence of Marxists within RUP's leadership ranks. Gradually, RUP's new leadership began to take a more socialist ultranationalist position. The cultural pluralist and ultranationalist perspectives were replaced by a dialectically evolving blend of nationalism and socialism. The socialist aspects were evident in a 1976 New Mexico RUP document: "We feel that the present economic system and the accompanying political system [liberal capitalism] of the western world are the major obstacles to resolving the most basic needs of mankind, as the system not only permits, but rather promotes, hoarding of money and resources which are desperately needed to work on the abolition of human misery in the U.S. and on the earth."[24]

In particular, between 1978 and 1981, RUP's leaders such as Juan José Peña of New México, Fred Aguilar and Andres Torres of California, and Maria Elena Martinez of Texas all propounded a separatist nation-building agenda. Various documents indicate that RUP's so-called internationalist approach was compatible with the nation-building design of the PLO and of the Quebec separatist party, the Bloc Quebecois. The trip to Lebanon by some of RUP's leaders in 1980 reflected their redefined objective of building a Chicano nation, Aztlán.

As ideology is a requisite for any social movement, so is leadership, the ability of a person to lead and give direction and influence and motivate others to follow a prescribed direction, cause, or interest. RUP initially was essentially the creation of two major caudillos and a plethora of regional or local caciques. Gutiérrez's and Gonzales's leadership contributions reinforced the opinion that for a third party to surface, exist, and be viable, it must have a charismatic leader or leaders. No organization in the history of Chicano politics had ever attracted the quality of leadership that RUP had gathered. Leaders emerged from within its ranks as well as from the ranks of other CM organizations.

Much of the leadership during the RUP organizing years tended to be young, well-educated students who before joining RUP were registered Democrats. Table 12.1 provides a profile of the fifty-six RUP leaders I interviewed in depth; their number varied from state to state.

Table 4 reveals that most of the RUP leaders interviewed were in their midtwenties. Their average level of education was fourteen years, and approximately 50 percent were students. It is important to note that those who were not registered Democrat were either registered Independent or not registered at all. The high percentage of student participation reflects their being the avant guard of RUP's third-party movement in many states.

Table 4 does not address the percentage of women leaders. Sexism was very much part of RUP's experience. The patriarchal aspects of Chicanismo contributed to the lack of Méxicana access and mobility within RUP's leadership ranks. With the exception of Texas, in every state males overwhelmingly constituted RUP's top leadership. The women interviewed said that women were generally relegated to either a secondary leadership role or a supportive role. Most of the males, when interviewed, said that women were indispensable and the backbone of the partido.

## RUP's Structure: Mass-Based versus Cadre

The history of revolutionary and reform social movements demonstrates that without solid organization no movement can endure. Organization is power, and power is organization. This principle applies to any third-party movement. RUP never developed a consistent and well-organized structure. Its structure was dictated either by state election laws, as in Texas, or by the whims of its state or local leadership, as was the case with most states. This translated to RUP's developing a structure that was theoretically a mass-based partido in Texas; and everywhere else a cadre-based partido.

In Texas, RUP's mass-based structure allowed for state conventions, a state central committee, and county central committees. A state central committee was led by a hierarchy of officers, including a chairman, and had few members, since only 26 counties of the 254 in the state had central county committees. Only in those counties where there was a fairly large number of Méxicanos were attempts made to structure RUP at the county level. Unique to RUP's structure in Texas was that in some counties or cities local political organizations were formed, such as Cuidadanos Unidos, Barrios Unidos, and Familias Unidas. These grass-roots political organizations were the organizing and issue-oriented arms of RUP at the local community level.

TABLE 4   Profile of Fifty-Six RUP Leaders

| State/Region | Median Age | Years of Education | % Registered Democrats Prior to RUP* | % Students* |
|---|---|---|---|---|
| Arizona | 24 | 15 | 80 | 100 |
| California | 30 | 14 | 86 | 43 |
| Colorado | 23 | 15 | 13 | 25 |
| Midwest | 26 | 13 | 80 | 40 |
| New Mexico | 22 | 13 | 60 | 40 |
| Texas | 25 | 14 | 74 | 53 |
| South/Midwest | 25 | 14 | 66 | 50 |

*Percentages are rounded up.

In no other state did RUP have a formal structure as comprehensive as that in Texas. In most other states, such as California and New Mexico, it was loosely structured, in some cases with a semblance of a state structure—a state central committee and local chapters. Some of the local chapters, for instance, in California, were city based, while in New Mexico they were county based. In most cases, RUP's chapters developed in few cities or counties. In Colorado, Arizona, and the Midwest, RUP never established a formal statewide structure similar to that in Texas. Particularly in Arizona and the midwestern states, RUP's structure was essentially decentralized, local, and loosely organized.

At the national level, RUP's Congreso never became institutionalized. At best, it functioned as a weak regional steering committee. The power struggle obviated any consolidation of RUP as a partido at either the regional or national levels. The so-called eighteen state delegations that participated and voted at the 1972 national convention had all but disappeared by the midseventies. Thus, structurally, RUP never became a consolidated party at any level.

Moreover, RUP's initial intent was to form a mass-based political party. This was very much the case in such states as Texas and some counties of Southern California and Illinois. Meanwhile, in such states as Colorado, New Mexico, and Arizona, and in Northern California, members opted for building a cadre/vanguard-oriented party, comprised of a select group of highly committed and trained activists. Thus, RUP never developed a centralized, mass-based mobilization capability.

## RUP's Strategy and Tactics: Reform or Revolution?

Indispensable to any third-party or social movement is the presence of a well-thought-out strategic and tactical plan of action. In other words, once it defines its vision, a movement must delineate a course of action that will spell out how it intends to attain it. In the case of RUP, none of this was accomplished because of power struggles and ideological cleavages. Consequently, RUP never consolidated and developed a common course of action.

During its first six years (1970–1976), there were several concurrent strategies that conflicted with each other. The Gutiérrez "balance-of-power" strategy was predicated on the notion that RUP would become a reform-oriented third party that would accept and work within the existing liberal capitalist system. Strategically, it would run candidates against both major parties, and whenever politically expedient, it would use its power base to negotiate a deal with either the Democrats or Republicans. Imbued with a powerful spirit of pragmatism, this scenario complemented the cultural pluralist perspective of change. Everyday issues were taken care of by its local political pressure organizations, which at times resorted to the use of direct action tactics, such as marches, picketing, and sit-ins.

Against this plan were those who from the onset proposed that RUP be the revolutionary vanguard for building a Chicano nation, Aztlán. After the 1972 RUP national convention, RUP activists became preoccupied with what role, direction, and type of party RUP should be. The debate picked up momentum as Marxist elements within RUP sought to take on a more proletarian socialist revolutionary posture. Concomitantly, some of the doctrinaire activists who were also cultural nationalists tended to support Gonzales's ultranationalist idea of RUP as a vanguard party for self-determination rather than reform. The various trips by RUP leaders to Mexico, Cuba, the People's Republic of China, Lebanon, Nicaragua, and other countries were illustrative of RUP's "separatist" course of action.

By the time the RUP delegation returned from Lebanon in 1980, some of the RUP activists were preaching the need for RUP to use "revolutionary" tactics in pursuit of an independent Chicano nation. My research on this matter, however, never revealed the type of tactics—for instance, guerrilla warfare, terrorism, sabotage, general strikes, assassination, rural or urban uprisings, or a combination of these—they proposed to use against the giant of liberal capitalism. The very nature of such a proposal served to only divide the few RUP zealots that were left even further. However, never did their revolutionary rhetoric and lexicon translate into action or, as Paulo Friere would say, "praxis." Thus, while they dealt with some issues using protest or direct action methods, they never took on a revolutionary vanguard action mode.

## RUP's Legacy: Views from Its Leaders

RUP's legacy is multidimensional. First, it dared to challenge the awesome power wielded by the nation's two-party dictatorship. However, it eventually realized that such a challenge was doomed to failure. Second, although it failed, it was a party that "resisted" the two-party status quo and sought to give Méxicanos an alternative. Third, the ideas and changes enacted improved, to an extent, the Méxicano's quality of life. Fourth, its political activities and Méxicano political representation, especially at the local level, increased significantly. Fifth, like many other third parties, it provided its own prescriptions for remedying many of the problems facing Méxicanos in the United States. Sixth, it was an effective training ground for leaders. In short, RUP's legacy was one that defied the hegemony of the country's dictatorial political party system.

These points were made by some of the RUP leaders I interviewed on the question of RUP's gains for the Méxicano community. For example, RUP left Ernesto Vigil from Colorado with the hope that, "next time around, if there comes a time when the social conditions are right, . . . we learn from the mistakes of the past."[25] Carlos Guerra from Texas said that RUP created a political revolution led by Méxicanos for increased political representation in Texas: "Because of what was done by the Raza Unida, the number of Méxicanos elected into public office dramatically increased."[26] Herman Baca from California was more pointed on the issue of increased Chicano representation. He said RUP's legacy was both positive and negative. "Positive in that every Hispanic political prostitute you see in office today is a benefactor of the work done by Raza Unida. Raza Unida was like a battering ram that opened the doors to both major parties. . . . The negative is that it failed. It failed because of our immaturity and because maybe it was premature."[27]

## RUP Today: Its Embers Continue to Burn

RUP never completely became defunct, although it had very little structure, leadership, support, or organized activity between 1981 and 2000. It is important, however, to note that a handful of activists, led by Xenaro Ayala from San Fernando, California, and Enrique Cardiel from Albuquerque, New Mexico, in the last few years have been working to revitalize what is called, in the 1990s, El Partido Nacional de la Raza Unida (PNRU). It has been Ayala's tenacity, from the time he took over in 1981 as RUP's national chairperson to the present, that has kept the dream of building a Chicano political party alive. Cardiel joined the PNRU in 1992 and since then has been the New Mexico representative to PNRU.[28]

As of 1998, the partido had no elaborate formal structure. There were no chapters to speak of, except for two small organizing committees—one in San Fernando, California, and the other in Albuquerque, New Mexico.[29] There was a third committee based in Phoenix, Arizona; however, it went out of existence in 1997. Neither of the two existing committees organizes political campaigns or creates massive protest mobilizations. Their purpose has been to act as a "germinating" force in the redevelopment and revitalization of RUP. I was unable to find out how many members each committee has. While they periodically meet and have an occasional conference, their focus in the last few years has been on developing a blueprint, of sorts, that addresses questions of ideology, party structure, and strategy.

Both Ayala and Cardiel point out that many years have been spent on delineating PNRU's ideology. Yet it is apparent that its nation-building or separatist agenda of the late 1970s continues to be the focus of the few activists. It is also clear that these activists still adhere, but much more emphatically, to RUP's old "socialist ultranationalism." According to Ayala: "There has been a process that we've undertaken as an organization very consciously to develop a Chicano/Méxicano ideological position of what it is that we want. . . . We are moving towards becoming what we consider to be revolutionary nationalists who also accept the principles of socialism. . . . We understand that we have to create change and that the change is not going to come out of the capitalist system. We are committed to the dream of Aztlán. That's our conviction and goal."[30]

Cardiel added that he joined RUP because of its ideology. He commented, "Those of us who are involved in the partido have a passion to make real change and not just to react to every piece of oppression that is thrown at us." He described himself as an advocate for "national liberation."[31] Ayala further explained that ideologically there were two schools of thought on the concept of national liberation: creation of an independent Aztlán or at the appropriate time a reunification with Mexico.[32]

A number of documents buttress both Ayala's and Cardiel's ideological positions. In a document entitled "Re-Emergence of El Partido Nacional de La Raza Unida," article three of the introduction reads: "Who we are and what we want. The question is no longer whether we want Liberation and Self-Determination, but how and when. It also has to be clear that there is no longer the question of whether this is our land or not. . . . There is no longer the question as to what Chicanos Méxicanos want, we want Liberation, self-determination and a country free of exploitation, free of inequalities, and free of privileged classes."[33]

When asked just how they intended to create Aztlán, they had no definitive answers. The literature, as well, does not define the methods or tactics to be used. The two PNRU committees, however, have developed a working relationship with other nationalist organizations such as the Union del Barrio, Brown Berets, National Chicano Moratorium, and some MEChA chapters.

Thus, while the RUP of the seventies has been defunct since 1981, according to its true-believer proponents, out of its ashes, is rising a new PNRU—ready to take form when, in the words of its leaders, "the conditions are suitable."

## Why Did RUP Decline? Views of RUP's Leaders

Why did RUP fail as a third party?[34] Clearly, some of the most salient factors that contributed to its decline were the limited Méxicano population (in 1973, no more than seven million) coupled with scarce resources, lack of organization and leadership in some areas, conflicting "isms" and agendas, and prevalent power struggles. When I posed the question to the fifty-six RUP leaders I interviewed, their answers were as diverse as they were numerous. Some focused on the internal factors, others on the external, as the root cause for RUP failing. In the context of RUP's decline in Texas, Mario Compean alluded to the "state apparatus" and all its "forms" and the Democratic Party's ability to co-opt RUP's leadership and supporters: "What they did was very effective. One was co-opt, and two, who they couldn't co-opt they cut off from getting any resources."[35] Eddie Montour from Colorado said that he thought that the major problem was the lack of an independent financial base—this ultimately led to the leadership suffering from burnout. "We needed an economic base and we didn't have it. We were always having to do fund-raising," he explained.[36] Andres Torres from California emphasized the power struggle between Gutiérrez and Gonzales as well as the Democratic Party's ability to co-opt RUP's leadership. On the latter, he said, "From the political electoral standpoint, it was probably the one thing that contributed most to the decline of the Raza Unida Party."[37] Others mentioned the changing political climate, burnout of activists, ideological cleavages, and power struggles.

RUP's decline was a product of many exogenous and endogenous antagonisms, examined state by state in the chapters here. Combined, they created obstacles that became virtually insuperable. However, at the crux of why RUP declined was its inability, like all previous third-party movements that failed, to break the monopoly of power and control wielded by the governing Democrat and Republican Parties. In no state did RUP develop the capability to seriously threaten and challenge the two-party hegemony. The nation's two-party dictatorship was evident in the number of institutional obstacles third parties had to face when challenging the two major parties. These exogenous obstacles were deliberately created by the two major parties so as to perpetuate their control over the nation's local, state, and national institutions. Third parties, as explained in the introduction, have historically been victimized by a multiplicity of external factors and obstacles that serve to perpetuate the longevity of the two-party system. RUP was no exception.

*Restrictive Election Laws*

It was in the area of ballot-access laws that the two-party dictatorship became clearly evident. Like all third parties, RUP had a very difficult time trying to get on the ballot. It did manage to get on the ballot in a few states: Texas in 1972, 1974, and 1978; and once in New México in 1976. In Texas, RUP in 1972 faced the difficult challenge of having to come up with some 23,000 petition signatures. RUP in Colorado in 1970 traveled the easiest electoral path to official party status—its candidates, who ran as Independents, had to secure only 500 petition signatures. In California, several attempts were made to certify RUP as an official party. The activists, however, never came close to bringing the required 66,000 registered voters into RUP; the alternative was to secure 660,000 petition signatures. The highest number of registered voters RUP garnered was in 1972, when it was able to register some 35,000 into RUP. The few candidates who ran for partisan offices did so as Independents. In New Mexico, RUP failed to get the required 10,000 petition signatures to get on the ballot; in 1976, it managed to get its candidates on the ballot, but only after a joint suit was won. Activists in Arizona never even tried to get RUP on the ballot. They feared that they did not have the resources or manpower to carry out the effort. In the Midwest, no major effort was initiated to put RUP on the ballot. Even RUP's candidate who ran in Illinois ran as an Independent.

Once RUP was on the ballot, the difficulties did not end. Staying on the ballot became a major problem. In Texas, RUP was decertified in 1978 because its gubernatorial candidate, Mario Compean, was not successful in securing the required 2 percent of the total popular vote. In Colorado, RUP failed to secure the minimum of 10 percent of the 1970 popular vote, so consequently it never became an official party; RUP candidates, however, continued to run as Independents until 1976. In 1976, RUP in New Mexico, via litigation, *McCarthy v. Evans*, succeeded in getting its candidates on the ballot as Independents only once. Thus, the use of restrictionist election laws was a major obstacle that RUP was never able to circumvent.

### The Two-Party Political Culture

This nation's political culture is antithetical to the formation of third parties. RUP was not able to overcome the inherent political biases integral to the nation's political culture. This view of party politics has been deeply ingrained in the minds of most people in the United States by way of an extensive political socialization process. People have been conditioned to accept the ingrained myths that third parties are not viable alternatives; that if they vote for a third party, their vote will have been wasted; and that third parties have no chance of winning against either one of the two major parties. This socialization process is such that the nation's educational system and media act as agents in conditioning people to accept the legitimacy of the two major parties. Most people die thinking that the nation's only two legitimate political parties are the Democrats and Republicans and that third parties are essentially nothing more than political gadflies.

If the idea of supporting a third party is difficult for most people to entertain, for Méxicanos it is even more so. For Méxicanos, since the Great Depression, the idea that the Democrat Party is the party of the poor and the Republican Party is that of rich has been inculcated. The Méxicano has been courted by the Democrats since the days of Franklin D. Roosevelt and his New Deal and the courtship continued well into Lyndon Johnson's administration with his War on Poverty. Although the political socioeconomic conditions for Méxicanos in the United States were deplorable, the various liberal reforms enacted by, for example, the administrations of presidents Roosevelt, Truman, Carter, Kennedy, and Johnson were sufficient in the 1970s to keep the majority extremely loyal to the Democratic Party. During the time that RUP was being organized, about 85 percent of Méxicanos were registered Democrats. Indicative of this deep loyalty to the Democratic Party during 1960 was the emergence of the Viva Kennedy Clubs, which were organized by supportive Méxicanos.

RUP was never really able to undo this political acculturation. During its eleven years of existence, few Méxicanos were supportive of the idea of an alternative party. This was particularly true among the middle- and upper-class Méxicanos. Few were willing to cross over into the uncharted waters of building an alternative Chicano political party that was depicted by its adversaries as radical and militant.

The RUP advocates also faced the political reality that too many Méxicanos were not registered to vote and were simply too alienated politically to believe that a third party like RUP could do anything to ameliorate their impoverished condition. RUP had the overwhelming challenge of trying to change attitudes such as suspicion, distrust, and a detachment from politics. These feelings that were so commonplace among many of the poor Méxicanos had to be replaced with new ones that led them to support and participate in RUP. Thus, in great part, RUP failed because it did not have access to the media, educational institutions, churches, and other agents of socialization that form and maintain the nation's political culture

### Lack of Access to the Media

In this nation's politics, the media has become the fourth branch of government. It has the power to create or destroy leaders and movements and has become one of the most important socialization agents of political control. In particular, when Karl Marx said that religion was the opium of the masses, he was wrong. In the 1970s, the electronic media, especially television, became the new opium of the people, duped into buying their slanted liberal capitalist and system status quo reporting. This applied equally to the print media. Without having complete access to public exposure via the electronic and print media, RUP was unable to educate the great majority of Méxicanos about its ideas, program of action, and leadership.

In the 1970s, most of the print and electronic media were owned by non-Méxicanos, which factored into why RUP was not able to secure positive media coverage. Even the emerging Spanish-language television networks were cautious. They did not want to project the image that they were supportive of RUP in any way. They did not want to take on the Federal Communications Commissions that regulates television and radio. The reality was that Whites owned and operated most stations, and they were biased in favor of the two major parties.

The media did provide some coverage when RUP was involved in an issue that was controversial and, according to their criteria, "newsworthy." In Colorado and Texas, major newspapers like the *Denver Post, San Antonio Express,* and *Corpus Christi Caller-Times* did cover some of the campaigns and issues RUP was engaged in, but their coverage of the two major parties was far more extensive. In Texas in particular, the print media coverage of RUP at times was inflammatory and detrimental. In cities such as Los Angeles, Albuquerque, and San Diego, the major newspapers would occasionally do a story on RUP.

Some media portrayed RUP as a radical party that was Communist and antisystem. This did not sit well with Méxicanos who shared a moderate to conservative political culture. The electronic media was far less generous with its coverage of RUP than was the printed media. RUP was plagued by the anti-third-party bias that perceived any third party as not worthy of coverage, especially one that was Méxicano. Prejudice also played into the equation of RUP's inaccessibility to the media and the predominance of negative coverage. As an alternative, RUP relied on publishing its own partido newspapers, such as *La Verdad* in Cristal and *El Gallo* in Denver, to counter the negative publicity of the White-controlled media. Thus, without equal access to the media, RUP could not get its political message out to Méxicanos. Ultimately, the slanted, biased, and often red-baiting coverage contributed to RUP's demise.

## The Tyranny of Single-Member Districts

The "winner takes all" single-member district system of elections is another obstacle that helps perpetuate the two-party system. In a single-member district system, the candidate with the most votes, or a plurality, wins the election.

RUP's candidates were victimized by the omnipresence of the single-member system. RUP was not successful in electing anyone to a position higher than county judge; that judge was José Angel Gutiérrez. This situation applied to both partisan and nonpartisan elections. Regardless of the percentage RUP candidates received, it did not have an impact on the results of the election. (The only exception was in California with the Ruiz campaign for assembly who as a spoiler contributed to the defeat of the Democrat.) RUP candidates found the path to political victory difficult if not impossible to travel. Even in heavily populated Méxicano areas, RUP candidates were not able to compete with the two-party candidates and the plurality system of "winner takes all." Thus, the presence of single-member districts contributed significantly to RUP's failure to score a sufficient number of electoral victories.

## The Supremacy of Two-Party Financing

The monopoly of the two-party system over finance campaign laws greatly affects the capacity of third parties to raise monies for their candidates. In 1974, the Federal Election Campaign Act (FECA), passed by both major parties, was designed to limit the influence of wealth or "fat cats" in the electoral process. Without getting into the complexity of its provisions, the act provided public funding to both major and eligible third parties. The reality is, however, that very few third parties qualify. The fund-raising capability of the two major parties is so phenomenal that it is tantamount to a monopoly.

Although for RUP candidates fund-raising became an insurmountable obstacle, public funding from FECA never really was a hurdle, since RUP never developed to the point that it challenged the two major parties in presidential elections. Simply stated, RUP never reached a level of growth and development that qualified it for federal public funding. There was an exception, however, when RUP in Texas in 1972 and again in 1974 garnered some 6 percent of the popular vote, thus qualifying it to receive some money.

RUP's partisan and nonpartisan campaigns were difficult to run due to the scarcity of campaign funds. All RUP campaigns and activities were financed through small individual contributions. It never had powerful special interests or fat cats pumping in money, the lubricant, into its small political machinery. RUP depended on dances, dinners, raffles, and so on, as other means by which to raise the needed resources. Many times individuals covered the RUP costs out of their own pocket. RUP's opponents did not have this kind of financial problems. Whereas local Democrats and Republicans spent several thousand dollars running their high-powered, high-profile campaigns, RUP candidates in most cases spent only hundreds in relative obscurity. Thus, RUP was the victim of a two-party system that has a monopoly over fund-raising and public funding.

### A Victim of Law Enforcement Infiltration

RUP, like other third parties, became the target of the FBI's Counter-Intelligence Program (COINTELPRO), formed in the sixties. Rationalized as being needed to protect the nation's national security, COINTELPRO directed its surveillance efforts at both Left and Right radical groups. However, it particularly, targeted those groups of the Left, such as the Black Panther Party and Communist and Socialist Workers Parties. FBI agents and paid informers infiltrated those groups with the intent of seeking intelligence as well as of destabilizing them via the use of trickery and the sowing of intergroup hatred and violence.[38] The paramount objective of COINTELPRO was to neutralize the targeted group as well as its leadership.

The CM and RUP were not exempt from the scrutiny and infiltration of COINTEL-PRO. For several years, the FBI, along with other law enforcement agencies, targeted persons and groups that they suspected of being a threat to national security and public safety. From its inception in 1970 until its demise in 1981, RUP and its leaders, Corky Gonzales, José Angel Gutiérrez, Juan José Peña, Raul Ruiz, Herman Baca, Ernesto Vigil, Fred Aguilar, Andres Torres, and many others, were closely monitored. Most of those interviewed alluded to this fact.

This was confirmed in 1977 when the Chicano Legal Defense Fund, a nonprofit organization committed to halting government surveillance, filed a lawsuit against the federal government. That year in July as a result of the suit, it received some 800 FBI documents that revealed numerous incidents in which RUP in Texas was a target of FBI and law enforcement surveillance, infiltration, and harassment.

Between 1972 and 1974, burglaries of RUP offices occurred in San Antonio, Kingsville, Crystal City, and Corpus Christi, Texas, all of which resulted in a loss of partido files. The IRS audited all RUP officeholders in Zavala County between 1972 and 1976. In 1974, in Starr County on the day prior to the local elections, two RUP candidates were arrested on trumped-up drug charges. On several occasions over a period of four years, José Angel Gutiérrez's residence and vehicle were broken into, with important records and documents taken each time. In one case, Gutiérrez's vehicle was stolen on election eve. In 1974, in the middle of the night, agents of the Texas Department of Public Safety were caught secretly photographing the inside of classrooms in the junior high school in Crystal City.[39]

By 1977, RUP in Texas was under a state of siege. The following incidents illustrate this charge: A former RUP candidate for lieutenant governor was indicted on drug charges; several RUP local officials from Crystal City were indicted on charges of misuse of funds; RUP was publicly lambasted by Democratic officials as being communistic; and the attorney general and IRS agents were virtually employed full-time in the procurement of information to indict José Angel Gutiérrez.[40] In addition, by 1977, Ramsey Muñiz was also charged and convicted on drug-related charges. Several RUP activists initially said that he was framed and a victim of entrapment. It was quite clear that RUP's politics made it a target for destabilization by law enforcement entities.

In Colorado, New Mexico, and California, RUP leaders were subjected to similar types of harassment and investigation. In Colorado, by 1972, the Crusade for Justice and RUP were under siege by law enforcement agencies. By 1973, some sixty-one mostly RUP leaders had been arrested on a variety of charges. In 1974, six RUP activists were killed in Colorado as a result of a bomb blast. RUP leaders at a press conference alleged that the police along with right-wing extremists were responsible for the bombing of the two cars. Police officers alleged that all six were killed when the bombs went off accidentally. The killing of Ruben Martinez by police in 1973 and the bombing of the Crusade's headquarters were indicative of the state of siege.[41]

When investigating several of the crimes, the main witnesses were police officers who had infiltrated the Crusade and RUP. RUP leaders alleged that Denver police had infiltrated both groups with undercover agents. The agents posed as members of the Crusade and RUP for the purpose of propagating false information with the objective of creating confusion, distrust, and division within their organizational ranks. With every incident and arrest, the media took the opportunity to depict both entities in a negative and radical light.

RUP in New Mexico and California had problems with law enforcement agencies as well. In New Mexico, between 1975 and 1977, some forty activists, many of them RUP organizers, were arrested. RUP experienced similar situations in California, but they were not as severe as those of Texas and Colorado. Several RUP leaders when interviewed told of how they and the RUP chapters became victims of police harassment, intimidation, and infiltration. They gave example after example of how their political campaigns and fund-raisers were monitored by the police. They recalled how some RUP leaders were kept under surveillance and specifically referred to a Los Angeles Police Department undercover officer who had infiltrated their chapter. The infiltration and harassment of RUP by law enforcement agencies further hastened RUP's decline.

*Democrat Party Co-optation*

RUP became the victim of co-optation by the Democrats. Due to the threat that RUP posed, Democrats by 1973—in most states where RUP was active and had a substantial Méxicano population—moved aggressively to neutralize RUP's potential threat. Legislative districts were redrawn so that a few Méxicano Democrats were able to win, former RUP leaders and supporters were co-opted, and the Democratic Party revitalized its political marketing efforts to project itself as the partido that cared about the welfare and needs of the Méxicano.

In Texas, in late 1976, the Democratic Party encouraged the formation of Mexican American Democrats as a countervailing political mechanism to RUP. RUP quickly found itself unable to compete with the Democratic Party's ability to offer incentives and inducements to Méxicanos, such as jobs, support for running campaigns, appointments, and support for proposals. Thus, the awesome power wielded by the Democratic Party and its ability to co-opt issues and leadership contributed to RUP's decline as well.

## The End of the Epoch of Protest

RUP was a product of the epoch of protest (1955–1974). It was also during this era that the Civil Rights, New Left, Vietnam Antiwar, Black Power, and Chicano Movements emerged and declined.[42] For Méxicanos, a dialectical change occurred by 1975 that ushered in a new epoch—the Viva Yo generation.[43] The militancy, radicalism, and Chicanismo that characterized the CM gave way to an accommodationist, reform, and more conservative Hispanic[44] mode of politics. The ethic of the CM was quickly replaced with that of the eighties, known as the "decade of the Hispanic." Thus, without the spirit of radicalism of the epoch of protest and the energizing force of the CM, by 1975 the RUP became a historical anachronism unable to overcome the Viva Yo generation's moderate to conservative politics.

## Prevalence of Internal Strife

Among the endogenous antagonisms that contributed as much as the exogenous problems to RUP's decline and demise was the pervasiveness of strife within its leadership ranks. Any social movement, political party, or any other change-oriented entity that is consumed by an internal war will self-destruct. The power struggle between Gutiérrez and Gonzales contributed significantly to RUP's decline. Likewise, the strife produced as a result of petty jealousies among regional and local caciques, conflicting ideologies and strategies, parochialism, differences in political culture, and feelings of distrust all contributed to RUP's internal strife. For all the repudiating by some RUP activists of the Mexican crab syndrome (the gringo perception that Méxicanos cannot work together but instead pull each other down), some lived up to it. Thus, the debilitating and devastating effects of the "politics of self-destruction" contributed to RUP's fall.

## Insufficient Financial Resources

A lack of resources was a major factor in RUP's decline. In a capitalist society where money is the medium or lubricant that greases both the political and economic machinery, no third party can expect to be competitive without having some capital at its disposal. Without the requisite finances, no party can sustain its organizing, office, and staff, and provide financial support for its candidates and issue campaigns. This was very much the case with RUP: It never had the requisite financial resources or access to a financial base. What motivated RUP was a fervent idealism predicated on pure commitment, passion, and determination. While in the short term, RUP was able to sustain some of its organizing, in the long term, it was fated to fizzle out.

Throughout RUP's organizing history, it never had the full-time organizers, an organizing budget, or the offices and administrative staff that are required to sustain and expand organizing, and it never had access to big PAC monies. It was totally dependent on volunteers, who in most cases paid for their own gas, meals, hotels, and other costs associated with attending and organizing meetings and conferences. Thus, without the financial lubricant, RUP was trying to fight the two-party giant with commitment and hope.

## RUP's Radical Eclectic Ideology

It is important to emphasize that RUP's lack of a well-defined ideology grounded on the people's support also contributed to its decline. RUP's eclectic ideology never became the common denominator needed to unite the various RUP organizing efforts. Contributing to RUP's internal strife were the ideological differences that permeated much of RUP's history. The existence of two subtypes of cultural nationalist and the presence of conflicting schools of Marxist thought contributed to power struggles, divisions, and conflicts that debilitated RUP's capacity to organize.

Few RUP leaders and organizers realized that two—ultranationalism and Marxism —of the three ideological currents that permeated RUP were antithetical to the Méxicano's political culture. After decades of socialization, from the poor to the middle class, Méxicanos overwhelmingly supported liberal capitalism and adhered to it ideologically. Thus, the lack of consensus on an ideology that was not antithetical to the people's experience and culture also contributed to RUP's decline.

## Lack of a Viable Organizing Strategy

The leadership and the ideological conflicts that permeated RUP obviated the formu- lation of a viable organizing plan of action. Its strategies were as diverse as its leaders and their ideological inclinations. There was no common plan of action as to how RUP should be organized and developed. The leadership struggles and ideological cleavages precluded a consensus. Some wanted to run candidates, others wanted to take on issues, and still others could not decide what RUP's role was to be. The absence of a consensus on the type of partido–mass-based reformist versus cadre/vanguard revolutionary—precluded a unified organizing approach.

Even in elections, with some exceptions, RUP ran candidates without understand- ing what it took to win. Too many of the electoral campaigns were symbolic. With the appeal exclusively to Méxicanos, little was done to promote coalition building with other ethnic or racial groups. Running candidates where Méxicanos were a small minority was suicidal without support from others and without organization and finances.

A related problem was that in those few cases where RUP candidates won, once in power, in most cases, they did not have a proposed agenda or plan of action for what needed to be done and how to do it. They had few ideas or the administrative and political skills and experience to put into effect major policy changes. This applied as well as to those who were ideological zealots who preached Aztlán or proletarian revolution. Thus, RUP had the rhetoric but lacked the blueprint, knowledge, and leadership to actualize it.

### Need for More Trained Organizers, Leaders, and Administrators

A fine line separates the organizer from the leader; RUP had too many leaders and not enough organizers. While all organizers are leaders, not all leaders are organizers. The role of the leader is to be the up-front or visible person who articulates and appears to lead the charge. The role of the organizer is that of the mechanic or technician. The absence of competent, disciplined, and committed organizers who could train others debilitated and impeded RUP's organizing efforts. As to the administrators, in those communities where RUP won control, there was always a critical shortage of competent trained administrators and technicians. A related problem was that many who were recruited were not RUP zealots, and some were lacking in technical and administrative know-how.

Both Gutiérrez and Gonzales could be described as capable of being leaders and organizers. However, few others were as able to do both. At best, some were semi-competent organizers who sought to be leaders. And too many that were the leader type failed dismally at being organizers. With some exceptions, too many of RUP's leaders and organizers sought to convert the masses of Méxicanos with the rhetoric of self-determination and pie-in-the-sky solutions. Too many times they tried to declare victories what were in fact defeats. It is difficult to convince the oppressed that they were victorious in an election when RUP's candidate garnered only 6 percent of the vote.

The problem was that too many of the RUP leaders were political neophytes. Some would make intimidating pronouncements to the press, as if they had the masses behind them to carry out their threats, when in fact they did not. Some of RUP's leaders tried to lead without having the skills, expertise, and experience to do so. Not enough leaders or organizers possessed the organizing experience or technical knowledge needed to motivate the people, organize them, run campaigns, take on issues, raise money, and develop literature. Moreover, too many RUP leaders and organizers suffered from what Lenin described as the "infantile disorder of the Left." That is, some RUP leaders were politically immature and unsophisticated in the practice of their sectarian politics. Armed with their rhetoric about the oppression of the ruling class, the proletariat, and Aztlán, instead of converting the Méxicano in the barrio, too often they alienated them. As a result, RUP activists would go into the barrios ill-prepared to market one of the most difficult products to sell—the development of a new political party.

In the end, RUP's decline was attributable to a multiplicity of factors. Its failure was not surprising, in light of the external omnipotent power wielded by the two major parties and the internal political liabilities Méxicanos faced during those years. Despite its failure, RUP left a mark on Chicano political history that cannot be erased. It left Méxicanos an ember of hope that has continued to burn—that someday soon, RUP or a facsimile of it will rise again to challenge the hegemony of this nation's two-party dictatorship.

*Epilogue*

---

# Prospectus for a New Partido and Movement

In spite of the powerful legacy left by the Raza Unida Party and the Chicano Movement, upon entering the new millennium, Méxicanos and other Latinos find themselves in the midst of an unprecedented crisis that is a result of the liberal capitalist system and its two-party dictatorship. This political reality raises two interrelated questions: (1) How is it possible to effect change within the confines of the liberal capitalist system? And (2) how is it possible to effectively challenge the omnipotent power and control of the nation's two-party dictatorship? For Latinos, in particular, it is critical that during the next few years intellectual dialogue, debate, and research be directed toward answering these two questions. I write to foster this change.

## Arguments Supporting the Need for Major Change

In this epilogue, I posit the idea that while it may seem Latinos in the United States have made great strides as a people, the reality is that the change is more illusory than substantive. The following arguments buttress my assertion that unless the liberal capitalist system and its two-party dictatorship undergo major change, the overwhelming majority of Latinos in the twenty-first century will be relegated to an increasingly apartheid and South African–syndrome existence. Moreover, without major changes occurring within the liberal capitalist system, the United States will decline as a superpower.[1]

Argument 1: *The dramatic growth of the Latino population will increase its prospects for political change.*

Both the browning of the United States and the re-Méxicanoization of the Southwest are contributing to the demographic changes occurring in the country today. The former denotes that people of color are fast becoming the nation's majority population. Some one hundred years ago, Latinos in the United States, who at that time were mostly Méxicanos, numbered only 100,000; at the close of 1999, the number had increased to some 31 million. This means that the United States is the fifth largest Spanish-speaking country in the world. Demographers predict that by no later than 2004, Latinos will replace Blacks as the nation's largest minority. One publication went so far as to predict that by 2005, the Latino population would reach 50 million.[2] Other demographers predict that by the year 2050, Latinos will comprise some 25 percent of the national population, nearly 100 million,[3] with most concentrated in the Southwest. (Mexico's current population is 95 million.)

In California alone, in 1999, Latinos numbered nearly 11 million, constituting a third of the state's population.[4] Whites in California that same year became a minority; making people of color the new majority.[5] Latinos are projected to reach majority population status in California by 2020; by the year 2030, Latinos will make up some 60 percent of the state's population. In New Mexico, in 1999, Méxicanos were approaching 50 percent of the state's population. Consequently, in the very near future, Latinos will compose clear-cut majorities in California, Texas, New Mexico, and quite possibly even Arizona. One must also consider the rapid growth of the Latino population in the states of Colorado, Florida, Illinois, Michigan, New Jersey, Washington, and Nevada.[6] Even in the state of New York, Méxicanos in 1998 numbered 306,000.[7]

By 1999, in numerous counties and local communities throughout the Southwest, Méxicanos constituted new majorities. In California's Imperial County, the number of Méxicanos reached 58 percent, while in Los Angeles County, Latinos made up some 45 percent of the 7 million population. In Texas, Méxicanos were the majority population in San Antonio, El Paso, and Laredo, as well as in scores of counties and local communities in South Texas; cities such as Dallas and Houston had substantial Méxicano populations. New York, Miami, and Chicago also had large Latino population centers.

There are three major variables driving this demographic transformation: (1) the immigration from Mexico and Central America, (2) the high birthrate among Latinos, and (3) White flight in key states.[8]

Efforts by both federal and state administrations to curb immigration from Mexico and Central America have failed and will continue to do so. This became evident in 1999, when U.S. efforts such as militarizing the U.S./Mexico border under Operation Gatekeeper, passing increasingly restrictive immigration laws and propositions (e.g., employer sanctions and Proposition 187 in California), and conducting aggressive border patrol enforcement efforts (e.g., raids on businesses and homes) all failed. The inflow of human capital is guaranteeing the demographic transformation of this nation. Annually, conservatively speaking, some 600,000 mainly Méxicano immigrants, about half of them undocumented, leave their homeland, fleeing economic and political repression, drawn to the United States in pursuit of a better life. It is estimated that the total number of undocumented immigrants in the country is about 6 million.[9] Regardless of restrictive immigration laws passed, number of border patrol officers hired, military personnel assigned, iron fences erected, and sophisticated infrared electronic equipment used, the exodus from Mexico and other parts of Latin America will continue to intensify in the years to come.

Even if the federal government completely sealed the U.S./Mexico border, the Latino population increase would continue, due to the high birthrate in the U.S. Latino community. According to the U.S. Bureau of the Census, Latinas have more children than do women of any other racial or ethnic group in the nation. In 1990, the median birthrate for U.S. women between the ages of fifteen and forty-four was 67.0 per 1,000. The rate for White women was 65.2; African American, 78.4; Asian American, 58.1; and Latina, 93.2.[10]

In reaction to the Latino presence in the United States, some states, such as California in the mid-1990s, experienced White flight and some Black flight, due in California's case to economic recession and changing demographics; thousands of Whites left the state and moved to the Northwest or Midwest.[11] In some counties, cities, and neighborhoods, such as the Compton and Watts areas of Los Angeles, where Blacks once constituted the largest minority group, Latinos have become the new majority. Moreover, some Blacks were part of a "reverse migration," meaning that some left California and resettled in the South. By the late 1990s, however, with an improved economy, the out-state migration slowed to a trickle.

Thus, as long as the immigration exodus and high Latino birthrates continue, both the browning of the nation and re-Méxicanoization of the Southwest will intensify and, unfortunately, so will the exploitation of Latinos.

Argument 2: *Latinos, more specifically Méxicanos, continue to be an exploitable commodity in the U.S. labor force.*

Ironically, while racist and anti-Méxicano nativists were extending their tentacles of prejudice throughout the nation, in 1999 several state governors and farmers—responding to an acute farm labor shortage—proposed a new Bracero Program (guest-worker program). Despite double-digit unemployment in most agricultural communities, they claimed there was a shortage of agricultural workers, which could be mitigated by the reestablishment of this program. The program would allow hundreds of thousands of Méxicano farm workers into the country to work on a temporary contractual basis.[12] If the proposal is implemented, the influx of Méxicanos and others will not lessen as long as their respective countries adhere to a market economy, which fosters greater poverty, inequality, and class conflict.

Virtually no one from the nation's two major parties has spoken out against the capitalist system's need to exploit workers. While some may espouse the need to prevent the violation of human rights, they never attack the liberal capitalist system for being the greatest violator of all. The "new world order," the "new market economy," and trade agreements such as the North American Free Trade Agreement are products of the two major party hegemony. Moved by the nation's powerful corporate forces, neither Republican nor Democratic politicians are willing to admit that, as long as this nation remains capitalist, it will need access to cheap, exploitable workers and new markets, all at the expense of U. S. workers.[13] For Latinos both in the United States and Latin America, especially in Mexico's *maquiladoras* (factories in Mexico located close to the U.S. border), this has translated to continued exploitation. The minimum wage in Mexico in 2000 was a little less than four dollars per day.[14]

In the United States, one has merely to look at the various sectors—agriculture, service industries, construction, and light manufacturing—to conclude that this country's economic growth will continue to be increasingly dependent on Latinos, especially Méxicanos, as a source of exploitable cheap labor. Few other ethnic or racial groups in the country are willing to take on the burdensome, backbreaking work Latinos perform. Just look at who picks the grapes, lettuce, and vegetables, or who does the arduous jobs in construction. Méxicano farm workers are still caught up in the powerful currents of the "migrant stream." Despite tenacious efforts by the United Farm Workers Union, *compesinos* (farm workers) continue to work for substandard wages under unsafe and inhumane working conditions.

While Latino service, garment, and construction workers increasingly are becoming unionized, with few exceptions they still work for subsistence wages and few benefits. Still others are victimized by inhumane (e.g., below minimum wage) and dangerous working conditions. Like many non-Latino workers in this country, Latinos live precariously from paycheck to paycheck, always wondering if they are going to have a job the next week. From the sweat and hard labor of Latinos and other exploited workers, the liberal capitalist system has grown and prospered, yet the two major parties have done little or nothing to better the fate of these workers.

The liberal capitalist system and its two governing parties have fostered gross class inequalities and a plethora of social problems at both the domestic and international levels. Both major parties have embraced the creation of a new world order that is predicated on "Pax Americana" control.[15] The world's future under a new world order of capital globalization looks bleak.[16] By the close of 1999, the globalization of capitalism had created chaos worldwide and greater world poverty. The outcomes were a wider rich-poor class gap, hunger, economic instability, global warming, and the shrinking of natural resources (such as is caused by deforestation) induced by multinational corporate greed, insufficient food production, overpopulation, unemployment, AIDS epidemics, and global ethnic/racial conflicts (e.g., "ethnic cleansing"). This worldwide spread of capitalism has produced a few nations that are the haves versus many nations that are the have-nots. This growing doom becomes more evident when one considers that the world's population is expected to reach 10 billion by 2050.[17]

Thus, the entire world in the twenty-first century will be in desperate need of an economic alternative to liberal capitalism, one that is more egalitarian and committed to saving humanity and the planet itself.

Argument 3: *Méxicanos are under a state of siege by nativist forces.*

In the year 2000, Latinos, especially Méxicanos, found themselves under a state of siege.[18] The 1990s activated powerful nativist political forces that sought to contain what they perceived as the growing threat of a *reconquista* (reconquest) of the Southwest by Méxicanos. What these nativists feared was the emergence of a Bloc Méxicano separatist movement similar to the Bloc Quebecois (Free Quebec) movement in Canada. This was the cardinal message of one such group in California, especially evident in its draconian racist propositions. Moreover, numerous White right-wing militias emerged that were preparing for what they consider to be an inevitable race war.

In the 1990s, Latinos were besieged by political attacks from nativists. Particularly in California, both political parties, but especially the Republicans, helped create or induce a climate of fear, hatred, and racism toward Latinos. Politicians from both parties used the Méxicano immigrant as a scapegoat for explaining the state's socioeconomic ills. Using nativist rhetoric and justifications, politicians pandered to the fears of an electorate that was becoming increasingly anti-immigrant and politically alienated. The most blatant perpetrator was the Republican Party, led by then governor Pete Wilson, whose rhetoric was ethnocentric and nativist to the core.

Between 1994 and 1998, a nativist crusade emerged and unleashed a firestorm of racism and xenophobia in California via the passage of three propositions. Proposition 187, passed in 1994 with 59 percent of the voters supporting it, sought to deny children born to undocumented parents the right to an education and social services. For some five years, Proposition 187 was caught up in litigation battles. In 1999, newly elected Democratic governor Gray Davis decided to resolve the legal impasse by submitting the controversial measure to a federal court for mediation.[19] After weeks of negotiations, the state agreed to drop its legal fight for Proposition 187.[20] Soon thereafter, however, Proposition 187 supporters vowed to fight on. In January 2000, they announced the launching of a new campaign, this time calling for a state constitutional amendment.[21]

The proponents of Proposition 187 followed up with Proposition 209, an anti–affirmative action initiative, which sought to put an end to the consideration of race and gender in hiring and admissions. Again strongly supported by Governor Wilson and the Republican Party, the initiative passed, receiving nearly 55 percent of the vote.[22] Its passage has since fostered an epidemic of proposed state and federal legislation calling for the dismantling of all affirmative action programs in such states as Washington, Texas, and Florida. The nativists rejected the principle of equal opportunity and sought instead a return to the good old days of White male control. While appeals were made in the federal courts, the Supreme Court ruled that Proposition 209 was constitutional. Without affirmative action, the employment prospects for Latinos and Blacks for better-paying jobs were in danger of becoming fewer. Energized by the victory in the courts, Proposition 209 architect Ward Connerly in 1998 made it known publicly that he intended to lead a crusade against ethnic studies programs.

The nativist crusade next targeted bilingual/bicultural education. Impelled by the "English Only" proposition that was approved by California voters in 1986, in 1998, nativists succeeded in getting Proposition 227 on the ballot. For the third time, Republicans were in the forefront of a nativist movement, this time calling for the elimination of bilingual/bicultural education. Their attack was obviously directed at the Méxicano. These xenophobic and racist forces pandered to the fears of the White and even the Asian electorate. The proposition passed, with some 61 percent of the electorate voting for it; as was the case with the other two propositions, it is being contested in the courts.

In California, while Republicans were in the lead on all three propositions, Democrats strategically kept a low profile. They did not want to offend their White, Méxicano, or Latino constituents. The Democrats, allegedly the party of the poor and working class, did not stand up and take a leadership role in defeating the three propositions, all either unconstitutional or totally racist in their underpinning. At the federal level, the contagion reached the Democratic White House and the Republican-controlled Congress. During the 1990s, the Clinton administration proposed and passed legislation that was nativist inspired—including welfare reform and restrictionist immigration laws that produced the militarization of the U.S./Mexico border, Operation Gate Keeper, doubling the size of the border patrol, and so on. Concomitantly, by the late 1990s, several states as well as Republicans in Congress put forth legislation similar to Proposition 209. To date, neither party has really represented the interests of poor people, Latino or otherwise.

Thus, in the 1990s, the two major parties, especially the Republicans, chipped away at the few gains made by Latinos and other minorities and gave rise to a destructive nativist politic of "immigrant bashing" that will continue to intensify as the Latino population increases.

*Argument 4: Latino elected officials have yet to provide the leadership needed to effectively deal with the crises afflicting the Méxicano/Latino community.*

With few exceptions, Latino politicians have become the buffers or the political-conflict managers in a neocolonialist situation. Most of them dance to the financial tune of powerful special interests. They espouse the same tired capitalist policies that have yet to work and have no answers for the complex issues plaguing U.S. society today. Most are ideological clones of their White counterparts.[23] Despite the fact that Latinos hold office at most levels of government, replacing non-Latinos, they have yet to make a major policy difference that would improve the people's overall quality of life. As Los Angeles County supervisor Gloria Molina explains, "You're not going to see them pontificating from the podium at a Chamber of Commerce luncheon for [an immigration bill]."[24] But even when Latino politicians are in ethnically safe districts, few choose to be advocates for the Latino community. They tend to be pragmatic politicians who are political climbers guided by personal ambition—higher office or appointment. Their paramount concern is to not alienate those constituencies and special interest contributors whom they feel they need. There are also Latino politicians who have succumbed to the temptations and vices of power, such as drugs, alcoholism, and corruption. Adding to the list of why most Latino politicians are ineffective advocates for the Latino community is the fact that many of them, like their White counterparts, are mediocre politicians at best. They have little or no training in how to govern, and many are therefore not prepared to provide the leadership needed desperately by the Latino community. Without a change-oriented agenda, they have become practitioners of the politics of the status quo.

Given the Latino population explosion, the increase in Latino political representation in the 1990s was inevitable. Nationally, the number of Latino elected officials increased from 4,625 in 1994 to 5,400 in 1997.[25] By the year 2000, there were twenty-one Latino congressmen, and former congressman Bill Richardson was secretary of energy. From California to Florida, political representation increased at the state level. In California, Cruz Bustamante was in 1998 elected lieutenant governor. That same year, Antonio Villaraigosa was elected speaker of the assembly by the Democratic-controlled legislature. On the Republican side, Rod Pacheco served for several months as Republican minority leader, until he was replaced in 1999 by a more conservative White politician. By the close of 1999, California had six Latinos in the state senate alone and a total of twenty-three in the legislature.[26] The state Democratic Party chairperson was Art Torres, a Méxicano. In the mid-1990s, Cuban Tirso del Junco was the state Republican chair. Concomitantly, Latinos from Texas to California made their political presence felt by taking control of city councils, school boards, and in some instances, county governments.

As the overall number of Latinos in the United States dramatically increases, the number of Latino politicians will also surely increase in the twenty-first century; however, if the present trend continues, their policy impact will be negligible. With some exceptions, until now, Latino politicians have not offered the leadership, ideas, or vision needed to fend off nativist attacks, to effectively address the myriad of social problems plaguing the nation's barrios, and to engender the changes needed. A case in point is Texas attorney general Dan Morales, a Democrat and the state's highest ranking Méxicano elected official, who spoke out against affirmative action programs. He was quoted as saying that young Texans did not need quotas but "hard work, sacrifice, commitment, and perseverance." In that spirit, his office went on record that it would no longer defend college racial preference programs in court.[27]

Moreover, in 1997, an article in *U.S. News and World Report* noted that Cruz Bustamante, who at the time was Speaker of the Assembly, "is a mainstream Democrat, not a militant Latino."[28] The point of this article was that "California's new generation of Latino leaders . . . steers clear of incendiary politics. The key reason . . . [is that] most Latino lawmakers in California owe their victories to the votes and donations of non-Latinos." The perception among many, including scholars and journalists, is that Latinos have made great political strides, and they are on the verge of achieving great power. One has only to walk the streets of our barrios to see that their notion does not take into consideration the overwhelming number of Latinos who have yet to taste the sweet fruits of community and political empowerment.

As the crisis confronting Latinos worsens in the twenty-first century, Latino politicians will ultimately have to decide whom they will serve: Latinos and other poor communities or the big-money interests that run the White-controlled Democratic and Republican Parties. In 1999, some Latino politicians began to assume major leadership roles as advocates. Democratic congressman Luis Gutierrez from Illinois, for instance, is one politico who has taken on an advocacy and leadership role in confronting several issues impacting Latinos, particularly immigration. Two other Democratic congressmen who on occasion spoke out strongly on Latino-related issues were California's Xavier Becerra and New York's José Serrano. In California, Los Angeles County supervisor Gloria Molina in 1999 took a bold stand when she accused her fellow supervisors of being "racists" regarding a hospital issue. Senator Richard Polanco, that same year, mobilized support for troubled Los Angeles Unified School District superintendent Reuben Zacharias, who ultimately was forced to resign.[29] Two California Democrats, Lieutenant Governor Cruz Bustamante and assembly speaker Antonio Villaraigosa, openly took on Democratic governor Gray Davis over his decision to submit Proposition 187 to a federal court for mediation.[30]

Thus, it is apparent that by 1999 the seriousness of the issues compelled some Latino politicians to speak out more aggressively in support of the Latino community. Overall, however, there was an absence of consistent advocacy and action among politicos on issues impacting the Latino community.

Argument 5: *The re-Mexicanization of the Southwest will continue to exacerbate ethnic/racial conflicts.*

The re-Méxicanization of the Southwest will continue to heighten conflicts between Méxicanos and other ethnic and racial groups. Conflict between Latinos and Blacks increased during the nineties as the economic, social, and political pies shrank. This was evident in the high number of physical conflicts, fights, and riots that occurred in prisons and schools. The conflict between these groups spilled over into organizations, as Latinos and Blacks found themselves competing for the same old crumbs, with fewer and fewer crumbs available. In California, some Latinos openly exhibited their resentment of the Asian business presence in the barrios in the form of grocery and liquor stores, among others.

In the year 2000, Latinos and Blacks found themselves engaged in conflict over an agreement consummated by the National Association for the Advancement of Colored People (NAACP) with NBC: The television power agreed to give Blacks more access to both the "creative and business ranks of the network." Latinos, Asians, and Native Americans were openly angry about the final agreement. They felt that the NAACP had used them as part of the coalition negotiating with NBC and left them out of the final negotiations, with the result that they gained nothing for their respective communities.[31] Although the issue was supposedly resolved a week later when an accord was signed by all parties, as resources become scarce and other ethnic and racial communities perceive that Latinos are getting a better deal, tensions will undoubtedly heighten.

In all probability, the results of the 2000 census will contribute to the tensions between the various communities, for it will determine not only the allocation of resources but the scope of ethnic and racial political representation. Due to their growing population, Latinos stand to gain additional seats at both the federal and state levels, while Blacks stand to lose seats. The bottom line is that the ethnic and racial relations of this country, especially if the economy goes into a tailspin, have the potential to become confrontive and bellicose . Neither of the two major parties has done much or offered solutions to improve the nation's deteriorating race and ethnic relations. This is becoming more evident with the increase in the number of hate crimes, particularly against Méxicanos.[32]

Thus, if ethnic and race relations do not improve in the coming years, it is quite possible that in the twenty-first century, this nation will not be exempt from the "Kosovo syndrome" that in the 1990s plagued several countries and regions of the world. This argument is not so far-fetched, considering the number of White militias in the United States that are preparing for what they see as an inevitable racial war.

Argument 6: *The number of Latinos living below the poverty level in the United States continues to increase.*

In 1998, Latinos had the second highest poverty rate among ethnic or racial groups, 25.6 percent; the White poverty rate was 8.2 percent. That same year, it was reported that some 31 percent of Latino children lived in poverty.[33] While the national average household income was $38,900, it was only $28,330 for Latinos.[34] In California, in 1998, the White median income was $27, 000; for Asians, $24,000, for Blacks, $23,000; and for Latinos, $14,500.[35] While it was reported that the U.S. economy was on an upswing, Latinos' lives were still dramatically poorer than those of other minorities or of Whites. The income gap continued to widen between the rich and poor, especially in California.[36]

For those Latinos living in the barrios, the poverty syndrome was becoming un-bearable. Increasingly, survival was difficult due to increasing crime and gangs; an epidemic growth of drugs and alcohol abuse; a lack of affordable housing, health care, and child care; high unemployment and underemployment; and growing police and border patrol abuse. In California, for example, some 50 percent of the inmates in the Youth Authority were Latino.

Thus, the barrios in the 1990s, despite a semblance of prosperity and better times elsewhere, were still plagued by economic and social internal colonialism. Increasingly, they were becoming powder kegs of discontent, alienation, and frustration ready to explode.

Argument 7: *Latinos in the United States continue to be denied a quality education at all levels.*

As 1999 ended, Latinos faced a devastating crisis in education. During the nineties, many enclaves of Latinos became war zones rather than places of well-being, especially the schools. In the barrio schools, instead of Latino children having computers, they had weapons detectors; instead of lesson plans, they were Mirandized; and instead of teachers, they had armed police officers. These realities speak to the racist manner in which this country allocates educational opportunities. This is not to say, however, that only Latinos suffer educational inequities. But study after study illustrates that Latinos have been systematically relegated to a marginalized, segregated, inferior education. Schools in the barrios are inferior due to numerous factors: inadequate budgets, substandard and run-down facilities, inadequate material and equipment, overcrowded classes, outdated curricula, elimination of bilingual and bicultural programs (in California, as a result of Proposition 227), and insufficient qualified teachers, administrators, staff, and aids.

These factors have contributed to functional illiteracy, push-out and dropout rates of 40 percent and higher, and a student population unprepared for the rigors of higher education. One study in 1999 concluded that two-thirds of Latino students are not prepared to go to a college or university.[37] For example, on the Scholastic Assessment Test, Latinos scored in the twenty-fifth percentile, that is, well below the median, on both verbal and math measurements.[38] This outcome is due in great part to the schools Latino students attend not offering test preparation courses and to Latinos many times not having the financial means to pay for the courses out of their own pockets.[39]

In 1999, the doors to higher education were closing to many Latinos. While the institutions of higher learning during the sixties, seventies, and eighties exhibited a semblance of an open-door policy, that all ended in the nineties as a result of Proposition 209 in California in 1996, which phased out the use of race- and gender-based admissions and hiring. With affirmative action policies diluted if not eliminated altogether, the enrollment of Latinos fell dramatically in universities such as the University of California, Los Angeles, and the University of California, Berkeley, dropping 50 to 60 percent in 1998.

The passage of Proposition 209 created a wave of similar legislation throughout the nation. In an effort to ensure diversity, Méxicanos and Blacks successfully pressured Texas governor George Bush to accept their admissions proposal, which would guarantee spots in the University of Texas system to the top 10 percent of graduates from every public high school in the state.[40] In California, Governor Gray Davis in 1999 successfully pushed a similar admissions proposal, although it called for only the top 4 percent of students graduating from each public high school in the state. Both the Texas and California admissions plans are highly discriminatory and elitist in that they will prevent scores of minorities, in particular Latinos, from attending state universities.[41] Moreover, many universities put in place discriminatory admission requirements designed to exclude minorities, such as increasing tuition fees; they threatened to dismantle Chicano/Latino studies programs and failed to expand or create recruitment and retention programs for Latinos and other minorities.

The number of Latinos admitted to graduate schools also declined after Proposition 209 passed. For example, on the national level, between 1996 and 1998, the number of minority applicants to medical school fell 13 percent. In California, the decline was 25 percent.[42] Adding to the crisis in higher education was the low number of Latino faculty and administrators employed and promoted in most of the nation's universities and colleges. In California, at the close of 1999, the number of Latino faculty employed by the University of California was only 4.5 percent,[43] not commensurate with the state's population, which was nearly 33 percent.

The response by both the Democratic and Republican Parties to this educational crisis has not been to build more community colleges and state universities, but to build more jails and prisons. Neither party has developed a scheme by which to ensure equal educational access to people of color. Instead, they have jumped on the bandwagon, calling for more police in the streets, more stringent prison penalties, and better protection of the U.S. borders from "those people," meaning those immigrating to the United States from other countries who are non-White, especially Latinos. Their failure to encourage true education reform speaks to their adherence to the philosophy that if you keep people uneducated, you can keep them under control and powerless.

Thus, as Latinos entered the new millennium, their educational status was problematic, to say the least. Increasingly, they were being relegated to an apartheid status. Latinos were not only becoming more segregated but also were falling victims to a seemingly orchestrated effort to deny them access to a higher education.

*Argument 8: Latinos are becoming increasingly dissatisfied with the two major political parties.*

Both major parties suffer from a chronic lack of leadership. Increasingly, scores of voters are registering as Independents and with third parties. A poll taken by the Times Mirror Center in 1995 concluded that voters wanted more choices when it came to political parties. Nearly six out of ten voting-age people favored the creation of a third party.[44] During the last three decades, an increasing percentage of voters in California left the Democratic and Republican Parties and either registered as members of minor parties or declined to state a party affiliation. The *California Journal* reports that "at the beginning of the 1990s, more than 89 percent of the registered voters listed themselves as either Democrats or Republicans. In 1967, 97 percent of California voters were registered with one of the two major parties. By 1999, that figure had dropped to 82 percent." Voters declining to state any party preference were 13 percent.[45] This all translated to an increase in the number of voters registered in third parties. Some 5 percent were registered as Libertarians or Greens.[46] The country's growing voter alienation was further evident with the election of the Reform Party's Jesse Ventura as governor of Minnesota in 1998[47] and of Audie Bock to the California assembly in 1999, making her the first Green Party candidate in the country elected to a state legislature.[48] The alienation also is reflected by the choice of most people to vote less often. The voter turnout for the 1998 national and state elections was the lowest since 1942, with only 36 percent of those eligible voting.[49]

Latinos are not exempt from the growing political alienation from the two major parties. In 1994, a survey conducted by the Times Mirror Center for People and the Press found that 54 percent of Latinos want a third political party and 19 percent had cast their ballots for Ross Perot in 1992. Of those surveyed, 66 percent identified themselves[50] as Democrats, 28 percent Republicans, and 6 percent undecided.[51] Indicative of the growing number of Latino Independents, a survey taken in January of 2000 found that only 45 per cent of Latinos were committed Democrats, 30 percent were hard-core Republicans, and 25 percent were "up for grabs." On the positive side of the political equation, by 1999 the electorate included some 6 million Latinos registered to vote, a figure expected to increase to some 7 million by November 2000. California governor Pete Wilson's nativist politics have engendered so much fear that nationwide, some 3 million immigrants became U.S. citizens, and many of them registered to vote. It is fair to say that the Latino electorate will continue to grow dramatically. The crucial question is, Will it continue to support the two major parties or will it embrace a new partido?

## What Needs to Be Done: Partido Options

The eight preceding arguments are only a few illustrations of why Latinos in the twenty-first century must struggle to formulate and implement alternatives to the present liberal capitalist system and the two-party dictatorship that maintains it. Answering the question of what needs to be done is crucial to the well-being of the Latino community in the United States. The crisis Latinos faced in the nineties is sure to worsen in the twenty-first century. I would argue that as the Latino population increases, the plethora of social problems facing the nation are sure to become more acute. I would also argue that these same social problems could well produce the conditions or climate of change, namely, the chronic discontent, that will motivate Latinos to exit from both major parties and either join an existing third party or create a new one of their own. As long as the present two-party dictatorship refuses to create a perestroika (a restructuring of the political system) and glasnost (an opening up of the political system), the people, especially Latinos, will have little or no chance to reform the nation's political party system. Latinos live and work in the most powerful liberal capitalist country in the world. Notwithstanding, it is also important to understand that the United States is on the verge of entering a state of decline. Consequently, strategically, Latinos must begin to examine the implications of such a decline and to politically plan for change.

From my perspective, Méxicanos and other Latinos, who will increasingly comprise the overwhelming majority of the population in several states, will have four major strategic political party options in the twenty-first century.

Option 1: *Do nothing and perpetuate the two-party dictatorship.*

Under this option, Latinos would continue to work within the confines of the current two-party system. In other words, they would continue to support the maintenance of the status quo. Ideologically, Latinos would continue to adhere to the liberal capitalist system, which as I have argued has so far not worked for the majority of Latinos. They would accelerate their efforts to become viable constituencies within the Democratic and Republican Parties, hoping to exercise enough power to push through their own policy agenda. Latinos would work within the two major parties' ideologically moderate to conservative platforms that in the 1990s became more and more anti-Méxicano, antipoor, and anti–social justice in their politics. Latinos would operate within a two-party system that is White, male dominated, and controlled by powerful plutocratic and special interests. And lastly, Latinos would be willing to share power and work within the structural and leadership confines of the major parties. Simply put, Latinos would perpetrate the two-party dictatorship that has failed to ameliorate the lot of minorities, the poor, and even the middle class.

Option 2: *Seek Latino control of the Democratic Party wherever possible.*

Instead of opting to work with both major parties, this scenario's strategy would be for Latinos to affiliate only with the Democratic Party. The cardinal objective here would be to seek its control in those states and areas where Latinos constitute a majority. The Republican Party has been purposely excluded as an option because of its conservative to reactionary racist and antipoor politics. The Democratic Party, while liberal capitalist in its ideology, has on a few historical occasions (e.g., Roosevelt's New Deal, Johnson's Great Society) displayed a willingness to humanize and reform itself. With Latinos in the ensuing years becoming the majority population in several states, they could very well take control of the Democratic Party's local, county, and state apparatuses. In other words, they would bore from within. Latinos would seek to control the Democratic Party clubs and the county and state central committees. This strategy could also facilitate Latinos taking control of the party's leadership positions, platform, and finances, enabling them to, in conjunction with other supportive constituencies, make major policy changes that could ideologically transform the party into a more progressive social democratic or labor party. While a difficult strategy to implement, given present political realities, this is nevertheless an option worth consideration.

Option 3: *Reject the two major parties and support one of the existing third parties.*

In this scenario, Latinos would reject both the Democrats and Republicans and instead support one of the existing Sectarian Doctrinaire (SD) third parties. Latinos would become a viable constituency in a third party whose platform is committed to a progressive reformation of the liberal capitalist system, meaning one committed ideologically to social democracy or its more doctrinaire relatives, socialism or Marxism. The benefits of supporting an already existing third party are several: (1) It is already officially on the ballot; (2) it has a standing structure; (3) it has an established leadership; (4) it has a platform that addresses the manifold needs and interests of Latinos; and (5) it has access to some operating resources.

Third-party options exist, from the environmentalist Green Party, to the social democratic New Party and Peace and Freedom Party, to the Marxist Socialist Workers' Party. The Libertarian and Reform Parties should not be considered viable options for Latinos and poor people, because they are nothing more than ideological deviants from the present two major parties. They are both liberal capitalist in their platforms, and neither offers a viable alternative to the Democrats and Republicans. If none of the existing SD third parties appeal to Latinos and others as well, then the alternative is to form a new SD partido. A multiethnic-based partido would be impelled by a social democratic or socialist mission to create a society that is just and equitable in the distribution of the nation's wealth; it would be democratically pluralistic.

Option 4: *Form a Latino or Méxicano partido.*

The option to form a new partido has two suboptions. The first would be the formation of an all-Latino partido. The second would be the formation of an all-Méxicano partido. Forming a Latino partido would entail the coalescing of Méxicanos, Puertoriqueños, Cubanos, Centro (central) and Sur (south) Americanos, and other Latinos into a unified political power bloc. It would thus be third party established along ethnic lines. This all-Latino partido could be either SD or Issue Reformist (IR) oriented. Political, economic, and social conditions would ultimately determine the type of partido that should be formed and its ideological underpinnings.

A form of Latin America nationalism, *"somos un pueblo de la Raza Cosmica"* (we are one community of the cosmic race), could well permeate such a partido's change platform. Strategically, in addition to seeking political control of local and state governments, it could also opt to affect the balance of power of the nation's overall politics. The partido would need visionary leaders willing to supplant their own particular ethnic interests with those of a unified Latino community. The coalescing of the Latino community's diverse political agendas, particularly between the conservative Republican Cubans and the more moderate to liberal Méxicanos, Puerto Ricans, and Central Americans, may be easier said than done.

The second suboption would require Méxicanos to again move to form a new SD or SI political party or to seek a revival of the Raza Unida Party (RUP). Given, however, the heterogeneity of Latinos and the inherent tensions and divisions that exist within the group,[52] Méxicanos might opt for their own partido, as they did in 1970 with RUP. The difference this time would be that Méxicanos would have the requisite numbers and concentration, especially in the Southwest, to sustain a viable political party of their own. I would argue that, based on current and projected demographics, RUP as a partido was at least thirty years too early in its emergence. With Méxicanos comprising a minimum of 85 percent of the Latino populations in California, Texas, New Mexico, Arizona, and Colorado, the political timing for such a partido endeavor is auspicious. Strategically, with Mexico's political parties making inroads to organize Méxicanos in the United States, depending upon the ideological agenda and objectives of the new partido, a collaborative alliance with one of Mexico's parties could be politically a beneficial move.

The question is, Would the partido be IR or SD? The former would mean that the change agenda would try either to reform the liberal capitalist system by seeking merely to engender microchange or to become more social democratic and seek macrochange. It would seek to play the political game of affecting the balance of power, a political force for advancing either agenda. In essence, it would follow the RUP model developed by José Angel Gutiérrez.

Conversely, the latter would follow a separatist agenda predicated on the politics of nation building. It would be at the vanguard of the struggle to create a separate and sovereign Méxicano/Latino nation, Aztlán. Ideologically, it would blend ultranationalism with either a social democratic or Marxist framework. Strategically, although conditions would determine its modus operandi, it would function similarly to Canada's Parti Québécois. This partido dichotomy in essence would pick up where RUP left off in 1981.

As a scholar and former community organizer, I do not endorse the first option. My preference lies with the remaining three options. The first option should not be considered, given the various arguments that have been made in this epilogue. The issues confronting Latinos in the twenty-first century will be numerous, complex, and severe; yet neither the liberal capitalist system nor its two-party dictatorship has the will, commitment, or interest to resolve them. I believe that the remaining three options should be considered, intellectually and politically debated, and further developed before deciding on a strategic course of action.

With the innumerable obstacles each partido option would confront, would any of the three options have a chance of succeeding? I would argue that, unlike the situation Méxicanos faced in organizing RUP in the 1970s, the conditions in the twenty-first century are much more auspicious for success. Today, there is a larger Latino population base that is more concentrated, especially in the Southwest, to draw from. In addition, the class and race situation is deteriorating to the point that the nation is becoming increasingly beset with acute social, economic, racial, and ethnic conflicts. Moreover, Latinos possess a financial base that in 1999 was characterized by a purchasing power of $375 billion; this will increase by 2010 to more than $1 trillion. Another positive factor is the powerful Latino mass media that reaches millions of people daily. The changing circumstances also point to the increasing number of Latino intelligentsia who could provide the leadership and technical know-how needed to create a powerful third-party movement. Enhancing the Latinos capability in the United States is it kinship to Latin America. It could very well develop political collaborative relations, *acercamientos*, with Latin America and other third-world countries that would render various forms of support. Lastly, there is the likelihood of a political climate that will require Latinos to take bold political steps. All of these factors could help challenge the third-party constraints outlined here.

Rest assured, however, that Democrats and Republicans will resist with all their power the implementation of all three strategic options, particularly Option 4, which calls for the formation of an SD separatist partido. Regardless of which partido model Latinos go for, it is important to note that the plutocratic powers that govern this nation will most assuredly react, given the current and especially future Méxicano demographic realities. One must remember the dictum, "Power is never given, it is taken." This nation experienced a civil war because of the politics of secession. Both governing parties will use all their legal, political, and extralegal means to stifle the emergence of either type of Méxicano partido. They are cognizant that throughout the world, numerous ethnic communities, impelled by nationalism or Moslem fundamentalism, are struggling for self-determination.

It is imperative to remember that because of the dialectical dynamism of politics and history, what today might seem next to impossible can tomorrow become a reality. After all, no one, including the Central Intelligence Agency in 1991, was able to predict the downfall of the Soviet Union. Political conditions and material goods are always changing, which means that nothing in political life is permanent. I maintain that politics by its very nature is dynamic and always in a state of flux. Nevertheless, cognizant of all the obstacles and constraints impeding third parties in the United States, I am convinced that Latinos need to rebuke the present do-nothing politics of both major parties and consider adopting one of the last three strategic options.

## Building a New Movement in the Twenty-first Century

At the close of 1999, exacerbating the crisis of the Latino community was the absence of a Méxicano or Latino mass movement comparable to that of the Chicano Movement of the late 1960s and early 1970s. This was manifested by the absence of Latino national, state, and, in some cases, local advocacy leadership. Those who projected themselves as such leaders were exponents of liberal capitalism and did not have the power base, following, and skills to alter the crisis. At best, they were reformers who were not apt in the politics of change. While Latinos had numerous organizations, none had the mass base, the resources, or the political and ideological inclination to efficaciously challenge the myriad of issues facing Latinos at all levels. Many of them could not because they were dependent on funding provided by corporations, foundations, and federal and state agencies. Moreover, a few, political in their orientation, were recipients of funds from the Democratic Party. Strategically, Latinos had no agenda and lacked the mobilization capability to demonstrate organized power. Few Latino politicians, scholars, and activists had the solution to the complex issues facing Latinos and even fewer sought an alternative to liberal capitalism or the two-party hegemony. Although in the mid-1990s there was a wave of activism due to the nativist attacks (e.g., Proposition 187), by the late 1990s there was a growing apathy and complacency in most of the Latino communities of the nation. Latinos suffered from what I call the "Rodney Dangerfield syndrome," which denotes that Latinos do not get respect because we do not have what I call a "fear factor" of power.

All three partido options require that they be an integral part of a new movement. Neither option by itself has a possibility of achieving fruition. Whichever option is entertained, it must be understood in the context of a larger social movement that also seeks to change the liberal capitalist system. Movements are products of many different disenchanted groups that complement each other in the pursuit of major change by sharing a similar vision. More specifically, according to scholars James Wood and Maurice Jackson, "social movements can be defined as unconventional groups that have varying degrees of formal organization and that attempt to produce or prevent radical or reformist type change."[53] Norman I. Feinstein and Susan S. Feinstein further write, "The essence of a movement's activities is to convert an unorganized collectivity into an organized one."[54] Therefore, regardless of the option pursued, without the presence of a social movement, no third-party movement launched by Latinos will have much of a chance of prevailing or even of surviving. RUP as a third party emerged as a result of the Chicano Movement, whose decline contributed significantly to RUP's end.

One asks, then, How does a community go about creating a new movement? (This complex question will be the focus of my fourth book, tentatively titled *What Needs to Be Done: The Building of a New Movement*.)[55] My formula for building a viable and powerful new mass movement begins with taking some very basic steps. Latinos must adhere to what I call the three Rs of change. First, Latinos must recommit to creating *una nueva causa* (a new cause or struggle). Second, Latinos must reorganize, because *organización es poder* (organization is power). And, last, Latinos must remobilize, for through *un renaciminto de activismo* (a rebirth of activism), change will be possible. For Latinos to extricate themselves from the clutches of a two-party tyranny, they must transform the liberal capitalist system. However, this will not be possible if the apathy and complacency that permeates much of the Latino communities today is not replaced with the invigorated activism of a new movement.

My paradigm for creating a new movement requires six independent variables. First, a climate of change must exist that is permeated by discontent and frustration among the people, especially the intelligentsia. Second, a cadre of competent and committed leaders and organizers must be formed. Third, these leaders and organizers must be ideologically impelled by the power of a new vision that provides an alternative to the present liberal capitalist system. Fourth, the formation of an infrastructure of new and revitalized organizations and coalitions, including a new partido, must be the new movement's foundation. Fifth, the new movement's strategic and tactical aspects will be both conventional (ballot box) and unconventional (direct action), but ultimately will be determined by the nation's political climate and conditions at the time. Sixth, if it is to have a chance for success, the new movement must develop a power capability that brings together all of the first five ingredients coupled with the requisite independent financial resources to sustain it.[56]

In the twenty-first century, Latinos will have within their grasp the opportunity to transform themselves from an oppressed, powerless community into one of great power and change. The Chicano Movement and the Raza Unida Party left us a historical template by which to better prepare for the many challenges that lie ahead. Latinos are at a historical juncture that requires us as a people to evaluate our past and present, and to define for ourselves our future.

# Notes

## Introduction

1. Here, I am able to provide only an abbreviated examination of the divergent aspects and difficulties of third parties, to provide a context for the difficulties faced by the Raza Unida Party.

2. Quoted in Everett Carll Ladd, *The American Polity: The People and Their Government*, (New York: W.W. Norton, 1989), 487.

3. Ibid., 488.

4. Edmund Burke, *Thoughts on the Cause of the Present Discontents*, vol. 2 of *The Works of Edmund Burke* (London: Rivington, 1815), 335.

5. Ibid.

6. Alexander Hamilton, James Madison, and John Jay, *The Federalist Papers*, ed. Clinton Rossiter (New York: New American Library, 1961), 79.

7. James MacGregor Burns, *The Deadlock of Democracy: Four Party Politics in America* (Englewood Cliffs, N.J.: Prentice-Hall, 1963), 27.

8. Frank J. Sorauf and Paul Allen Beck, *Party Politics in America*, 6th ed. (Glenview, Ill.: Foresman, 1988), 23–24.

9. E. E. Schattschneider, *Party Government* (New York: Farrar and Rinehart, 1942), 1.

10. Frank J. Sorauf, *Political Parties in the American System* (Boston: Little, Brown, 1964), 1.

11. William Chambers, "Party Development and the American Mainstream," in *The American Party Systems*, ed. William N. Chambers and Walter D. Burnham (New York: Oxford University Press, 1967), 5.

12. Anthony Downs, *An Economic Theory of Democracy* (New York: Harper and Row, 1957), 25.

13. Dan Nimmo and Thomas D. Ungs, *American Political Patterns*, 3d ed. (Boston: Little, Brown, 1973), 275.

14. Joseph M. Hazlett II, *The Libertarian Party and Other Minor Political Parties in the United States* (Jefferson, N.C.: McFarland, 1992) 14.

15. J. David Gillespie, *Politics at the Periphery: Third Parties in Two-Party America* (Columbia: University of South Carolina Press, 1993) 15.

16. Nelson W. Polsby, "Third Parties, from TR to Trump," *Wall Street Journal*, October 22, 1999.

17. Norman Zucker, *The American Party Process* (New York: Dodd, Mead, 1968) 67.

18. For an examination of these and other third parties, see William B. Hesseltine's *Rise and Fall of Third Parties: From Anti-Masonry to Wallace* (Gloucester, Mass: Peter Smith, 1957), and *Third Party Movements in the United States* (New York: Van Nostrand, 1962).

19. For an overview of the significance of these third parties, see Gillespie, *Politics at the Periphery.*

20. William Goodman, *The Two-Party System in the Unites States* (New York: Van Nostrand, 1956), 49.

21. Schattschneider, *Party Government,* 63.

22. Gillespie, *Politics at the Periphery,* 14.

23. Hesseltine, *The Rise and Fall of Third Parties,* 9–10.

24. Hazlett, *Libertarian Party,* 15.

25. Ibid., 28.

26. Clinton Rossiter, *Parties and Politics in America,* (Ithaca, N.Y.: Cornell University Press, 1960), 61–62.

27. Charles Merriam and Harold Foote Gosnell, *The American Party System: An Introduction to the Study of Political parties in the United States* (New York: Macmillan, 1949), 59.

28. Ibid., 4.

29. Judson L. James, *American Political Parties in Transition* (New York: Harper and Row, 1974), 57.

30. V.O. Key, *Politics, Parties, and Pressure Groups,* 5th ed. (New York: Crowell, 1964), chapter 10.

31. Kevin Phillips, "The Unexpected Guest," *Los Angeles Times,* September 19, 1999.

32. Ibid.

33. Daniel Mazmanian, *Third Parties in Presidential Elections* (Washington, D. C.: Brookings Institution, 1974), 27.

34. Frederick E. Hayes, *Third Party Movements since the Civil War; with Special Reference to Iowa: A Study in Social Politics* (New York: Russell and Russell, 1966), 156.

35. Steven J. Rosenstone, Ray L. Behr, and Edward H. Lazarus, *Third Parties in America,* 2d ed. (Princeton, N.J.: Princeton University Press, 1996), 134.

36. For an examination of the theory of relative deprivation, see Ted Gurr, *Why Men Rebel* (Princeton: Princeton University Press, 1970), and James C. Davis, "Toward a Theory of Revolution," *American Sociological Review* 27 (February): 5–19.

37. Rosenstone et.al. *Third Parties in America,* 119–121.

38. Rhodes Cook, "Political Barometers: The Third Parties," *Perspective,* December 2, 1989.

39. Rossiter, *Parties and Politics in America,* 4–5.

40. Hugh A. Bone, *American Politics and the Party System* (New York: McGraw Hill Book Co., 1971), 87.

41. For an overview of these parties, see Gillespie, *Politics at the Periphery,* chapter five.

42. David Levy, "Economics for the Next Century? The New Party's Economic Policy," *Dollars and Sense,* January/February 1996.

43. Mark Paul, "Seducing the Left: The Third Party That Wants You," *Mother Jones,* May 1980, 62. For a comprehensive examination of the development of the Libertarian Party, see Hazlett, *The Libertarian Party.*

44. Gordon S. Black and Benjamin D. Black, *The Politics of Discontent: How a New Party Can Make Democracy Work Again* (New York: John Wiley, 1994), 27.

45. Kay Lawson, "The Case for a Multiparty System," in *Multiparty Politics in America:*

*People, Passions, and Power*, ed. Paul S. Herrnson and John C. Green (New York: Rowman and Littlefield Publishers, 1997), 59.

46. Rossiter, *Parties and Politics in America*, 3.

47. Black and Black, *The Politics of Discontent*, 57.

48. Key, *Politics, Parties, and Pressure Groups*, 207–208; John A. Crittenden, *Parties and Elections in the United States* (Englewood Cliffs, N.J.: Prentice-Hall, 1982), 19.

49. James, *American Political Parties in Transition*, 57.

50. Key, *Politics, Parties, and Pressure Groups*, chapter 10.

51. Mazmanian, *Third Parties in Presidential Elections*, 3.

52. In developing working definitions for these three terms or concepts, I have quoted from *Webster's Ninth New Collegiate Dictionary*, s.v. tyrannical, totalitarian, and dictatorship.

53. I use the works of C. Wright Mills (*The Power Elite* [New York: Oxford University Press, 1956] and William G. Domhoff (*Who Rules America?* [Englewood Cliffs, N.J.: Prentice-Hall, 1967; *Who Rules America Now?* [New York: Simon and Schuster, 1983], among others, to buttress my thesis.

54. Schattschneider, *Party Government*, 62.

55. For an abbreviated critique of both the political and economic aspects of liberal capitalism, see Armando Navarro, *The Cristal Experiment: The Struggle for Chicano Community Control* (Madison. University of Wisconsin Press, 1998), epilogue. For a more extensive examination that is critical of liberal capitalism and its impact on the nation's two-party system, see Howard L. Reiter, *Parties and Elections in Corporate America* (New York: St. Martin's, 1987).

56. Cited in William Ebenstein, *Today's Isms: Communism, Fascism, Capitalism, Socialism* (Englewood Cliffs, N.J.: Prentice-Hall, 1973), 145–146.

57. Ladd, *The American Polity*, 57–58.

58. For an overview of capitalism, see Reo M. Christenson, et. al., *Ideologies and Modern Politics* (New York: Dodd, Mead, 1975), 215–216.

59. Reiter, *Parties and Elections*, 12.

60. Quoted in Gillespie, *Politics at the Periphery*, 283.

61. Quoted in Janet A. Flammang et.al. *American Politics in a Changing World* (Pacific Grove, Calif.: Brooks/Cole, 1990), 206.

62. "Raza Unida Party Is Growing Fast: Colorado," *Regeneracion*.7, 4 (1970), 8–9.

63. Michael Parenti, *Democracy for the Few*, 6th ed. (New York: St. Martin Press, 1995), 181.

64. Rena Pederson, "Issues Wait while Both Parties March toward Centrism," *Dalles Morning News*, April 5, 1998.

65. Phillips, "The Unexpected Guest."

66. For an overview of Bradley's political views, see Ronald Brownstein, "Bradley Record: Tangled Trail of 'Solo Operator,'" *Los Angeles Times*, September 12, 1999.

67. Gabriel A. Almond and G. Bingham Powell, Jr., *Comparative Politics: A Developmental Approach* (Boston: Little, Brown, 1966), 23.

68. Gillespie, *Politics at the Periphery*, 29.

69. Christopher P. Gilbert, David A. M. Peterson, Timothy R. Johnson, and Paul A. Djupe, *Religious Institutions and Minor Parties in the United States* (Westport, Conn.: Praeger, 1999), 15.

70. Ladd, *The American Polity*, 64.

71. Richard Winger, "The Importance of Ballot Access," *Long Term View*, Massachusetts School of Law, Andover, Mass., Spring 1994, 40–45.

72. Rosenstone et.al., *Third Parties in America*, 16.

73. For this view, see "Proportional Representation Flunks," *New York Times*, April 24, 1993.

74. Hesseltine, *Rise and Fall of Third Parties*, 100.

75. James W. Harris, "Third Parties Out," *Nation*, November 12, 1990.

76. Bill Stall, "Perot's Bid to Create Third Party Is Given Good Odds," *Los Angeles Times*, September 30, 1997. Data derived from Ballot Access News, Associated Press.

77. Parenti, *Democracy for the Few*, 184.

78. Ibid.

79. Rosenstone et. al., *Third Parties in America*, 21.

80. Richard Winger, "Institutional Obstacles to a Multiparty System," *Multiparty Politics in America: People, Passions, and Power*, ed. Paul S. Herrnson and John C. Green (New York: Rowman and Littlefield Publishers, 1997), 169.

81. Lewis Lipsitz and David M. Speak, *American Democracy*, 2nd ed., (New York: St. Martin's Press, 1989), 257.

82. Rosenstone, et. al., *Third Parties in America*, 25–26.

83. Paul S. Herrnson, "Two-party Dominance and Minor Party Forays in American Politics," *Multiparty Politics in America: People, Passions, and Power*, ed. Paul S. Herrnson and John C. Green (New York: Rowman and Littlefield Publishers, 1997), 25.

84. Laurie Kellman, "Reform Party to Move Headquarters to Florida," *Press-Enterprise*, December 27, 1999.

85. Richard Walton, "The Two-Party Monopoly," *Nation*, August 30–September 6, 1980, 177.

86. James P. Pinkerton, "If Nothing Else, Perot May Give an Alternative," *Los Angeles Times*, September 28, 1995.

87. Allan C. Miller, "Record Shots of Corporate Cash Enrich Parties," *Los Angeles Times*, September 22, 1996.

88. David G. Savage and Janet Hook, "Justices Lift Restriction on Political Parties' Spending," *Los Angeles Times*, 1996.

89. David G. Savage, "High Court Limits Third-Party Rights," *Los Angeles Times*, April 29, 1997.

90. George Will, "Resolved: Third Candidates Should Debate," *Press Enterprise*, September 19, 1999.

91. Gillespie, *Politics at the Periphery*, 33–34.

92. David Savage, "Third Party Candidates Dealt Court Blow," *Los Angeles Times*, May 19, 1998.

93. Rosenstone et. al., *Third Parties in America*, 35.

94. Ernest Evans, "Covering Third Parties," *Christian Science Monitor*, October 20, 1988, 14.

95. Quoted in Rosenstone et. al., *Third Parties in America*, 35.

## Chapter One

1. I use the term "Chicano" to describe Méxicanos born in the United States. As was the case with my previous two books, "Chicano" here is used interchangeably with "Méxicano." Although somewhat common in the barrios, the term "Chicano" became popular during the era of the Chicano Movement. No consensus exists among scholars or activists as to its origin and definition. When activists in the late 1960s and early 1970s appropriated it and gave it a nationalistic and political connotation, it came into popular use as a definition for Méxicanos born in the United States who were active and committed to change. To some

activists, "Chicano" became the truncated version of "Méxicano." The term became the basis of Chicanismo, a quasi–ideology that was predicated on a form of nationalism grounded on the Méxicano experience in the Southwest and México.

2. Integral to this book is the proposition that internal colonialism is a viable theoretical framework that explains the poverty and social problems of, and the racism directed toward, Mexicanos. For an in-depth examination of internal colonialism along these lines, see Robert Blauner, *Racial Oppression in America* (New York: Harper and Row, 1972); Mario Barrera, Carlos Muñoz, and Carlos Ornelas, "The Barrio as an Internal Colony," *Urban Affairs Annual Reviews* 6 (1972): 465–498; Rodolfo Acuña, *Occupied America: The Chicano Struggle for Liberation* (New York: Canfield, 1972); Tomas Almaguer, "Toward the Study of Chicano Colonialism," *Aztlán: Chicano Journal of the Social Sciences and the Arts* (spring 1971): 7–21; Joan W. Moore, "Colonialism: The Case of the Mexican Americans," *Social Problems* (Spring 1970): 463–472; and Alfredo Mirande, *The Chicano Experience: An Alternative Perspective* (Notre Dame, Ind.: University of Notre Dame Press, 1985).

3. The term "Aztlán" is defined by some scholars and activists as the place of origin of the Aztecs, which was said to be somewhere within the five southwestern states: California, Arizona, New Mexico, Colorado, and Texas. In this work, Aztlán will denote all the land—some one million square miles—that was lost by Mexico as a result of the annexation of Texas and the U.S. war on Mexico (1846–1848).

4. For a general reference on the Chicano Movement, see Armando Navarro, *Mexican American Youth Organization: Avant-Garde of the Chicano Movement in Texas* (Austin: University of Texas Press, 1995); Carlos Muñoz, *Youth, Identity, Power: The Chicano Movement* (New York: Verso, 1989); and F. Arturo Rosales, *Chicano! The History of the Mexican American Civil Rights Movement* (Houston, Tex.: Arte Publico, 1996). I argue that the Chicano Movement was a result of relative deprivation—unmet rising expectations, especially among youth—and of multiple external and internal antagonisms that fostered a propitious "climate of change," all of which allowed it to become the first successful social movement in the U.S. Méxicano community.

5. Few works have been written that focus entirely on the phenomenon of the Chicano Movement. One such work is Rosales, *Chicano!* Contemporary works that focus on various aspects of the movement include: Ignacio Garciá, *Chicanismo: The Forging of a Militant Ethos among Mexican Americans* (Tucson: University of Arizona Press, 1997); Gutiérrez, *Making of a Chicano Militant*; Muñoz, *Youth, Identity, Power*; Navarro, *Mexican American Youth Organization*; and Armando Navarro, *The Cristal Experiment: A Chicano Struggle in Community Control* (Madison: University of Wisconsin Press, 1998). In addition, several Chicano historians have written works that examine the era of the Chicano Movement. See Acuña, *Occupied America*; John R. Chavez, *The Lost Land: The Chicano Image of the Southwest* (Albuquerque: University of New Mexico Press, 1984); Matt S. Meier and Feliciano Ribera, *Mexican Americans/American Mexicans: From Conquistadores to Chicanos* (New York: Hill and Wang, 1993); and Juan Gomez Quiñonez, *Chicano Politics: Reality and Promise, 1940–1990* (Albuquerque: University of New Mexico Press, 1990).

6. On these leaders, see Peter Nobokov, *Tijerina and the Court House Raid* (Albuquerque: University of New Mexico Press, 1969); Richard Griswold Del Castillo and Richard A. Garcia, *Cesar Chavez: A Triumph of Spirit* (Oklahoma City: University of Oklahoma Press, 1995); and Ernesto B. Vigil, *The Crusade for Justice: Chicano Militancy and the Government's War on Dissent* (Madison: University of Wisconsin Press, 1999).

7. For a brief historical overview of the oppressive conditions most Méxicanos in Texas faced, particularly in Crystal City, and of the PASO/Teamster, as well as biographical

information on Jose Angel Gutiérrez, see Jose Angel Gutiérrez, *The Making of a Chicano Militant: Lessons from Cristal* (Madison: University of Wisconsin Press, 1998), 15–44, and Navarro, *The Cristal Experiment*, 17–51. The biographical material that follows draws on Gutiérrez's book and my interviews with him.

8. Much of the examination of MAYO and RUP's development up to 1972 is taken from Navarro, *Mexican American Youth Organization*. For a more thorough examination, please refer to that volume. For an autobiographical perspective of MAYO, see Gutiérrez, *Making of a Chicano Militant*, 101–141.

9. To the Méxicano, the word "gringo" had a negative connotation. It was used to describe a White person who was racist and bigoted, and who generally perceived Méxicanos as inferior. Conversely, an "Anglo" or white was a person who tended to be more supportive of Méxicanos. See Navarro, *The Cristal Experiment*, 381, for a more detailed definition.

10. Ignacio Garciá, *United We Win: The Rise and Fall of the Raza Unida Party* (Tucson: Mexican American Studies and Research Center, 1989), 15.

11. José Angel Gutiérrez, interview by the author, May 16, 1973.

12. José Angel Gutiérrez, "Notes from José Angel Gutiérrez: Presently in Self–Imposed Exile," typescript, January 1969, 2, author's files.

13. Ignacio Garciá, interview by the author, April 18, 1997.

14. Navarro, *Mexican American Youth Organization*, 86.

15. See ibid., 115–148, for a comprehensive examination of MAYO's educational change struggle, particularly case studies on the Edcouch–Elsa, Kingsville, and Cristal school walkouts.

16. Garciá, *United We Win*, 20.

17. For a comprehensive examination of both groups, see Navarro, *Mexican American Youth Organization*, 153–160, and Garciá, *United We Win*, 22–23.

18. Navarro, *Mexican American Youth Organization*, 155–156. Luz Gutiérrez, interview by the author, May 9, 1973.

19. Quoted in Garciá, *United We Win*, 22.

20. For a comprehensive review of MAYO's social change activities and agenda, see *Mexican American Youth Organization*, 149–181.

21. José Angel Gutiérrez, interview by the author, September 13, 1997.

22. Pete Tijerina to José Angel Gutiérrez, letter, April 9, 1969.

23. *San Antonio News*, April 11, 1969.

24. "Race Hate," *Congressional Record*, April 3, 1969, 8590. Quoted in Garciá, *United We Win*, 27.

25. Mario Compean, interview by the author, May 5, 1997.

26. Ibid.

27. J. A. Gutiérrez interview.

28. José Angel Gutiérrez, "La Raza and Political Action" (position paper), typescript, n.d., author's files.

29. J. A. Gutiérrez interview, May 16, 1973.

30. Mario Compean, interview by the author, April 15, 1997.

31. For a more extensive examination of MAYO's involvement in this election, see Navarro, *Mexican American Youth Organization*, 186–190.

32. Compean interview.

33. Garciá, *United We Win*, 40.

34. Ibid.

35. J. A. Gutiérrez interview.

36. Alberto Luera, interview by the author, April 4, 1973.

37. José Angel Gutiérrez, "Méxicanos Need To Control Their Own Destinies," in *La Causa Politica: A Chicano Politics Reader,* ed. F. Chris Garcia (Notre Dame, Ind.: University of Notre Dame Press, 1974), 229.

38. For a comprehensive examination of the Winter Garden Project, see Navarro, *Mexican American Youth Organization,* 190–214. Compean interview, April 15, 1997.

39. For an excellent overview of the history of the Cristal school walkout, see John Staples Shockley, *Chicano Revolt in a Texas Town* (Notre Dame, Ind.: University of Notre Dame Press, 1974), 120–138; Navarro, *Mexican American Youth Organization,* 132–148; Garciá, *United We Win,* 41–50; Navarro, *The Cristal Experiment,* 61; Gutiérrez, *Making of a Chicano Militant,* 142–176.

40. Severita Lara, interview by the author, September 20, 1994.

41. Shockley, *Chicano Revolt,* 120.

42. Lara interview.

43. José Angel Gutiérrez, interview by the author, February 25, 1995.

44. Gutiérrez, *Making of a Chicano Militant,* 141.

45. Shockley, *Chicano Revolt,* 128.

47. MAYO press release, December 31, 1969.

48. Luz Gutiérrez, interview by the author, May 5, 1997.

49. Ignacio Garcia, "Mexican American Youth Organization: Precursor of Change in Texas" (Tucson, Ariz.: Mexican American Studies and Research Center, 1987), 26.

50. Viviana Santiago, interview by the author, September 17, 1994.

51. Albert Luera, interview by the author, September 17, 1994.

52. José Angel Gutiérrez, interview by the author, May 24, 1973.

53. Garciá, "Mexican American Youth Organization," 24.

54. L. Gutiérrez interview.

55. Luera interview.

56. Shockley, *Chicano Revolt,* 156.

57. J. A. Gutiérrez interview.

58. Ibid., September 13, 1997

59. "Raza Unida Party Formed," *Zavala County (Tex.) Sentinel,* January 29, 1970.

60. "Third Party Formed in Crystal City during Brown Power Political Drive," *Laredo (Tex.) Times,* January 25, 1970.

61. J. A. Gutiérrez interview.

62. For a comprehensive analysis of the Winter Garden revolt, see Navarro, *Mexican American Youth Organization,* 217–225, and *The Cristal Experiment,* 55–85; and Gutiérrez, *Making of a Chicano Militant,* 183–214.

63. Shockley, *Chicano Revolt,* 145–146.

64. For a comprehensive socioeconomic and demographic profile of the three targeted counties, see Navarro, *Mexican American Youth Organization,* 190–197.

65. Viviana Santiago Cavada, interview by the author, June 23, 1997.

66. "MAYO Requests Election Observers," *San Antonio Light,* March 13, 1970.

67. J. A. Gutiérrez interview, September 13, 1997.

68. Shockley, *Chicano Revolt,* 146–147.

69. José Angel Gutiérrez, telephone interview by the author, March 3, 1998.

70. For a much more comprehensive examination of the campaigns, see Navarro, *The Cristal Experiment,* 65–72.

71. Santiago interview, June 28, 1997.

72. Ibid.

73. J. A. Gutiérrez interview, September 13, 1997.

74. L. Gutiérrez interview.

75. Ibid., and Santiago interview, June 23, 1997.

76. "Gutiérrez: Loss Won't Hinder Raza," *San Antonio Express,* October 12, 1970.

77. Navarro, *The Cristal Experiment,* 81.

78. Garciá, *United We Win,* 64.

79. Paul McKnight, "Report from Crystal City: How They Stole La Raza Unida Party's Vote," *The Militant,* November 20, 1970.

80. "Raza Unida Petition Is Denied," *Zavala County Sentinel,* October 1, 1970; *San Antonio Express,* October 9, 1970.

81. *San Antonio Express,* October 9, 12, 1970.

82. Shockley, *Chicano Revolt,* 159.

83. Mcknight, "Report from Crystal City."

84. Luz Gutiérrez interview, May 9, 1973.

85. For an extensive and comprehensive examination of the methods used in fostering the grass-roots mobilization, see Gutiérrez, *Making of a Chicano Militant.*

86. McKnight, "Report from Crystal City."

87. "Incumbents Win Zavala Major Races," *San Antonio Express,* November 5, 1970.

## Chapter Two

1. Mario Compean, interview by the author, May 5, 1997.

2. Luz Gutiérrez, interview by the author, May 5, 1997.

3. Armando Gutiérrez, interview by the author, July 23, 1997.

4. Antonio Camejo and Tank Barrera, "Raza Unida Goes Statewide," *The Militant,* November 12, 1971.

5. Carlos Guerra, interview by the author, September 14, 1997.

6. Compean interview.

7. Alberto Luera, interview by the author, March 2, 1993.

8. Compean interview.

9. Luera interview.

10. Carlos Guerra interview, September 16,1997.

11. José Angel Gutiérrez, interview by the author, May 9, 1973.

12. "Statewide Status Proposal Approved by Raza Unida," *Corpus Christi Caller-Times,* October 31, 1971.

13. A. Gutiérrez interview.

14. Camejo and Barrera, "Raza Unida Goes Statewide."

15. Martha Cotera, interview by the author, September 11, 1997.

16. Ibid.

17. José Angel Gutiérrez, interview by the author, September 13, 1997.

18. "Raza Unida To Widen Effort," *San Antonio Express,* October 31, 1971.

19. Armando Navarro, *Mexican American Youth Organization: Avant-Garde of the Chicano Movement in Texas* (Austin: University of Texas Press, 1995, 233.

20. Ignacio Garciá, *United We Win: The Rise and Fall of the Raza Unida Party,* (Tucson: Mexican American Studies and Research Center, 1989), 74.

21. Guerra interview.

22. Garciá, *United We Win*, 79.

23. Luera interview, September 17,1994.

24. José Angel Gutiérrez, *The Making of a Chicano Militant: Lessons from Cristal* (Madison: University of Wisconsin Press, 1999), 219.

25. Guerra interview.

26. Cotera interview.

27. Ramsey Muñiz, interview by the author, May 15, 1973.

28. Antonio Camejo, "Texas Raza Unida Maps Statewide Election Campaign" *The Militant,* June 23, 1972.

29. "La Convencion," *Raza Unida Party Newsletter,* June 1972.

30. "Raza Unida Party Needs Your Help," *San Antonio Express,* June 23, 1972.

31. Luera interview.

32. For a thorough account of the incident, see Gutiérrez, *Making of a Chicano Militant,* 219–221.

33. Harry Ring, "San Juan, Texas, Chicanos Win Gains with Raza Unida Administration," *The Militant,* December 10, 1971; Antonio Camejo, "Raza Unida Party Wins Texas Elections," *The Militant,* May 26, 1972.

34. L. Gutiérrez interview.

35. A. Gutiérrez interview.

36. Ignacio Garciá, interview by the author, April 18,1997.

37. L. Gutiérrez interview.

38. Garciá, *United We Win*, 78.

39. "Muñiz Pleased: Gutiérrez Tapped To Lead Campaign," *Corpus Christi Caller-Times,* August 26, 1972.

40. See Navarro, *Mexican American Youth Organization,* for a further analysis on its decline, particularly chapter 7.

41. Guerra interview.

42. Maria Elena Martinez, interview by the author, September 15, 1997.

43. Camejo, "Texas Raza Unida Party."

44. Richard Beene, "Raza Unida Wants Ballot Spot Assured," *Corpus Christi Caller-Times,* September 8, 1972.

45. Garciá, *United We Win*, 119–120.

46. Ibid.

47. "Unions To Back All Candidates of Raza Unida," *San Antonio News,* November 1, 1972.

48. Jim Davis, "Muniz Showing Puts Raza Unida on Map," *Corpus Christi Caller-Times,* November 9, 1972.

49. Guerra interview.

50. J. A. Gutiérrez interview, September 18, 1997.

51. "Ya Basta," *Texas Observer,* August 25, 1972.

52. For an examination of the controversy behind this issue, see Armando Navarro, *The Cristal Experiment: A Chicano Struggle for Community Control* (Madison: University of Wisconsin Press, 1998), 298–300; and Garciá, *United We Win*, 123–125.

53. Harry Ring, "Raza Unida Organizes Throughout Texas," *The Militant,* November 10, 1972.

54. Frank Del Olmo, "Chicanos Called Key in Texas Governor Race," *Los Angeles Times,* October 3, 1972.

55. "GOP Sets New Gains in Texas," *San Antonio Express*, November 12, 1972.

56. "We'll Be Back, Says Raza Leader," *San Antonio Express*, November 11, 1972.

57. "GOP Sets New Gains."

58. "Raza Unida Party Loses Major Races, Claims Start Made," *Houston Post*, November 11, 1972.

59. Garciá, *United We Win*, 165–166.

60. J. A. Gutiérrez, interview, September 13, 1997.

61. Dave McNeely, "Weaknesses Cited," *Dallas Morning News*, May 5, 1973.

62. Nelson Blackstock, "Raza Unida Party Wins Seats in Texas Elections," *The Militant*, May 18, 1973.

63. Nelson Blackstock, "Texas Raza Unida Party Looks toward 1974 State Elections," *The Militant*, October 26, 1973.

65. Harry Ring, "Texas Raza Unida Party Plans Big '74 Campaign," *The Militant*, December 28, 1973

65. Ibid.

66. Evey Chapa, "Mujeres por La Raza Unida," *Carocol*, October 1974.

67. Jean Savage, "1974 Texas Raza Unida Campaign Opens," *The Militant*, February 15, 1974.

68. Compean interview.

69. Cotera interview.

70. A. Gutiérrez interview.

71. Guerra interview.

72. Kathie Miller, "Diluting Raza's Image As Chicano Party On," *Fort Worth Star Telegram*, April 28, 1974.

73. Guerra interview.

74. Compean interview.

75. Cotera interview.

76. Lupe Youngblood, interview by the author, September 16, 1997.

77. Ibid.

78. Ibid.

79. Ibid.

80. Garciá, *United We Win*, 179.

81. Youngblood interview.

82. Guerra interview.

83. Nelson Blackstock, "Texas Raza Unida Gears Up Fall Campaign," *The Militant*, October 25, 1974

84. Garciá, *United We Win*, 186.

85. Martinez interview.

86. *The Militant*, October 25, 1974.

87. Ibid.

88. Ibid.

89. Ibid.

90. Harry Ring, "Union Support Is Step Forward for Texas Raza Unida Party," *The Militant*, November 8, 1974.

91. "La Raza Unida," *Texas Observer*, November 29, 1974.

92. Garciá, *United We Win*, 189.

93. For a much more thorough examination of RUP's unprecedented county victory, see Navarro, *The Cristal Experiment*, 134–139.

94. Leodoro Martinez, interview by the author, September 15, 1997.

95. Ciro D. Rodriguez, interview by the author, April 12, 1997.

96. Quoted in *Texas Observer*, November 29, 1974.

97. Ibid.


## Chapter Three

1. In *The Cristal Experiment: A Chicano Struggle for Community Control*, (Madison: University of Wisconsin Press, 1998), I posit the argument that the Chicano Movement was moribund by 1975. In addition, in "The Post-Mortem Politics of the Chicano Movement, 1975–1996" (*Perspectives in Mexican American Studies*, vol. 6 [1997]:52–79), I make an extensive argument that the Chicano Movement declined because the epoch of protest that had been a product of various social protest movements ended.

2. Armando Navarro, *Mexican American Youth Organization: Avant Garde of the Chicano Movement in Texas* (Austin: University of Texas Press, 1995), 241–242.

3. Albert Luera, interview by the author, September 17, 1994.

4. Luz Gutiérrez, interview by the author, May 5, 1997.

5. For an extensive analysis of this social movement paradigm, see Navarro, "Post-Mortem Politics." I make this same argument in *The Cristal Experiment*, chapter 6.

6. Armando Gutiérrez, interview by the author, July 22, 1997.

7. Ignacio Garciá, *United We Win: The Rise and Fall of the Raza Unida Party* (Tucson, Ariz.: Mexican American Studies and Research Center, 1989), 197.

8. Richard Santillan, "The Politcs of Cultural Nationalism: El Partido de la Raza Unida in Southern California" (Ph.D. diss., Claremont Graduate University, Claremont, Calif., 1978), 112.

9. Mario Compean, interview by the author, May 11, 1997.

10. Harry Ring, "Texas Raza Unida Leaders Discuss Issues Facing the Party," *The Militant*, December 13, 1974.

11. Jesus "Chuy" Rameriz, interview by the author, September 16, 1997.

12. Ring, "Texas Raza Unida Leaders."

13. "La Raza Unida," *Texas Observer*, November 29, 1974.

14. Carlos Guerra, interview by the author, September 16, 1997.

15. Martha Cotera, interview by the author, September 11, 1997.

16. Lupe Youngblood, interview by the author, September 16, 1997.

17. Ibid.

18. Harry Ring, "Armando Gutiérrez Looks at Issues Facing Raza Unida in Texas," *The Militant*, June 11, 1976

19. Barry Boesch, "Party Is (Pick One) 1. Sitting This Election Out 2. Dying," *Corpus Christi Caller-Times*, September 5, 1976.

20. "Party Recovers Right to Primary," *Daily Texan*, January 30, 1976.

21. Quoted in Michael V. Miller, "Chicano Community Control in South Texas: Problems and Prospects," *Journal of Ethnic Studies*, vol. 3, no. 3 (Fall 1975): 8.

22. Carlos Guerra interview, September 14, 1997.

23. Miller, "Chicano Community Control."

24. For a broader explanation of this transition, see Navarro, "Post-Mortem Politics," 52–79.

25. For a comprehensive examination of Cuidadanos Unidos's development into a political machine, particularly Cristal's local politics from 1970 to 1980 and peaceful revolution, see Navarro, *The Cristal Experiment*, 86–116.

26. Youngblood interview.

27. Ibid.

28. For a comprehensive examination of the various aspects of the delegation's trip to Cuba, see Navarro, *The Cristal Experiment*, 163–166, and chapter 11 of this book.

29. "Raza Unida Wants To Create Little Cuba in South Texas," *Alice (Tex.) Echo News*, May 15, 1975.

30. José Mata, interview by the author, September 20, 1994.

31. Sherrill Smith, interview by the author, September 23, 1994.

32. For a comprehensive examination of the events that led up to the political rupture and the rupture itself, see Navarro, *The Cristal Experiment*, chapter 6.

33. Each one of these issues is well documented and examined in ibid., chapter 7.

34. José Angel Gutiérrez, interview by the author, September 14, 1997.

35. Navarro, *The Cristal Experiment*, chapter 6.

36. Tatcho Mindiola, "Partido de la Raza Unida," *La Voz de Texas*, February 6, 1976.

37. "Judge Rules Out Raza Unida Fees," *Dallas Morning News*, January 31, 1976.

38. Boesch, "Party Is (Pick One)."

39. Louis Proyect, "Texas Chicanos Score Gains in April Elections," *The Militant*, May 2, 1975.

40. Jim Wood, "Split Makeup of Boards Stalemates Government," *Corpus Christi Caller-Times*, June 28, 1975.

41. "Was the Election Stolen," *The Militant*, May 14, 1976.

42. Youngblood interview.

43. Harry Ring, "RUP Takes Texas Town," *The Militant*, May 14, 1976.

44. Ibid.

45. Leodoro Martinez, interview by the author, September 15, 1997.

46. Ring, "RUP Takes Texas Town."

47. Martinez interview.

48. Harry Ring, "La Raza Unida: Texas Leaders Discuss State of the Party," *The Militant*, July 16, 1976.

49. Pedro Vasquez, "RUP Activist Wins San Antonio Seat," *The Militant*, April 23, 1976.

50. "Keep on Keeping on: La Raza Unida," *Texas Observer*, October 29, 1976.

51. Harry Ring, "Texas Convention Decides, " *The Militant*, October 1, 1976.

52. Lubbock group interviews (Bidal Agueo, Juan Travez, Jesse Rangel, Alberto Ariel, Elisio Solis), September 17, 1997. Two other local RUP leaders were also part of the three-hour interview, but their names were not audible on the tape.

53. Steven Wattenmaker, "Texas," *The Militant*, November 26, 1976.

54. Evan Moore, "The Muñiz Mystery: Downfall from Destiny," *Houston Chronicle*, July 10, 1994.

55. Ibid.

56. Pat Teague, "Muñiz, Brother in Jail," *San Antonio Express*, August 2, 1976.

57. Moore, "The Muñiz Mystery."

58. Garciá, *United We Win*, 199–202.

59. Ibid.

60. Armando Gutiérrez, interview by the author, July 23, 1997.

61. Mario Compean, interview by the author, May 5, 1997.

62. Maria Elena Martinez, interview by the author, September 11, 1997.

63. Youngblood interview.

64. Rameriz interview.

65. Luera interview.

66. Garciá, *United We Win*, 197.

67. Lita Cavazos and David Diaz, "La Raza Unida Attacks 'Little Cuba' Remarks," *Daily Texan*, September 20, 1976.

68. "Making Room for Raza Unida," *Austin American—Statesman*, October 14, 1977.

69. Larry McDonald, letter, *Congressional Record*, June 18, 1976.

70. Garciá, *United We Win*, 201.

71. "La Raza Faces Problems with Survival, 'Radical' Image," *Daily Texan*, October 29, 1976.

72. "Marcha Encontra Briscoe," *La Voz de Texas*, November 26, 1976.

73. Garciá, *United We Win*, 202.

74. Harry Ring, "Gutiérrez: They're out To Destroy Us," *The Militant*, January 28, 1977.

75. For a comprehensive examination of the politics behind the defunding of RUP's cooperative farm in Cristal, see Navarro, *The Cristal Experiment*.

76. Ring, "Gutiérrez."

77. "RUP Holds State Meeting," *El Editor*, December 15–21, 1977.

78. Compean interview.

79. Garciá, *United We Win*, 220.

80. Ibid. 220–221.

81. Compean interview, May 5, 1997.

82. Shauna Hill, "Raza Unida Candidate Gives Top Qualification," *Texas Tech University Daily*, September 12, 1978.

83. Ibid.

84. Guerra interview.

85. L. Gutiérrez interview.

86. Compean interview.

87. "A Choice, Not an Echo," *Texas Observer*, October 6, 1978; Raza Unida Party press release, February 7, 1978.

88. Ibid.

89. Hill, "Raza Unida Candidate."

90. Martinez interview.

91. Ignacio Garciá, interview by the author, April 17, 1997.

92. Lubbock group interviews.

93. Guillermo Garcia, "Raza Unida Candidates Pleased with Spoiler Role," *Austin American—Statesman*, November 9, 1978.

94. Dave Montgomery, "Chicano Margin Helps Hill Upset," *Dallas Times Herald*, November 1978.

95. Garcia, "Raza Unida Candidates."

96. Ibid.

97. Garciá interview, April 18, 1997.

98. Garciá, *United We Win*, 219.

99. Compean interview.

101. For a more thorough examination of Gutiérrez's loss of power, exile, and resignation as county judge of Zavala County, see Navarro, *The Cristal Experiment*, chapters 13 and 14.

102. For an extensive examination of Cristal's politics from 1978 to early 1981, see Navarro, *The Cristal Experiment*, chapter 11.

103. Martinez interview.


## Chapter Four

1. Much of the biographical data is taken from a case study: Ernesto Vigil, *The Crusade for Justice* (Madison: University of Wisconsin Press, 1999), 5–53. Vigil devotes one chapter of his study to profiling Gonzales. Also see Stan Steiner, *La Raza: The Mexican Americans* (New York: Harper and Row, 1970), 378–392; Elizabeth Sutherland Martinez and Enriqueta Longeaux y Vasquez, *Viva La Raza: The Struggle of the Mexican American People* (Garden City, N.Y.: Doubleday, 1974), 230–261; and Tony Castro, *Chicano Power: The Emergence of Mexican America* (New York: Saturday Review Press, 1974), 129–147.

2. Martinez and Vasquez, *Viva La Raza*, 231.

3. Steiner, *La Raza*, 378–379.

4. Martinez and Vasquez, *Viva La Raza*, 232.

5. Vigil, *Crusade for Justice*, 11.

6. Ibid., 9.

7. Ibid., 28–29.

8. Jack Gookie, "Gonzales Views His Poverty Role," *Rocky Mountain News*, September 29, 1965.

9. Rodolfo Acuña, *Occupied America: A History of Chicanos*, 3d ed. (New York: Harper and Row, 1988), 331.

10. Richard Tucker, "La Raza Seeking Legal Status for Party," *Rocky Mountain News*, October 18, 1970.

11. Armando Rendon, *Chicano Manifesto: The History and Aspirations of the Second Largest Minority in America* (New York: Collier, 1971), 123.

12. Vigil, *Crusade for Justice*, 36–37.

13. Ibid., 38.

14. According to Martinez and Vasquez, *Viva La Raza*, 234, a split occurred over parliamentary procedures, specifically over how to run the meetings.

15. Juan Gómez Quiñonez, *Chicano Politics: Reality and Promise, 1940–1990* (Albuquerque: University of New Mexico Press, 1990), 113.

16. Ignacio Garciá, *Chicanismo: The Forging of a Militant Ethos among Mexican Americans* (Tucson: University of Arizona Press, 1997), 34.

17. Ibid.

18. Ernesto Vigil, interview by the author, April 18, 1997.

19. Vigil, *Crusade for Justice*, 40.

20. Steiner, *La Raza*, 383–384.

21. Ernesto Vigil, lecture on CJ and RUP in Colorado for the four-part documentary *Chicano*, Austin, Texas, September 12, 1994.

22. Ibid., 44–50.

23. Martinez and Vasquez, *Viva La Raza*, 247.

24. For a comprehensive overview, see Vigil, *Crusade for Justice*, 42–46.

25. Ibid., 78.

26. Ibid., 101.

27. Ibid., 110.

28. Matt S. Meir and Feliciano Rivera, *The Chicanos: A History of Mexican Americans* (New York: Hill and Wang, 1972), 275.

29. Sue Lindsay, "Grand Jury Probes Old Civil Rights Group," *Rocky Mountain News,* December 26, 1991.

30. Maria Subia, interview by the author, July 23, 1997.

31. Ibid.

32. Martinez and Vasquez, *Viva La Raza*, 250–251.

33. Ibid., 251.

34. Luis Valdez and Stan Steiner, eds., *Aztlán: An Anthology of Mexican American Literature* (New York: Vintage, 1972), 402–406.

35. Garciá, *Chicanismo*, 96.

36. Carlos Muñoz, *Youth, Identity, Power: The Chicano Movement* (New York: Verso, 1989), 75.

37. Al Gurule, interview by the author, July 23, 1997.

38. F. Arturo Rosales, *Chicano! The History of the Mexican American Civil Rights Movement* (Houston, Tex.: Arte Publico, 1996), 181.

49. For an overview of both "El Plan de Santa Barbara" and Movimiento Estudiantil Chicano de Aztlán, see Navarro, *Mexican American Youth Organization*, 68–79.

40. For details on both events, see Vigil, *Crusade for Justice*, 184–190.

41. Miguel Padilla, "Chicano Conference Calls for Party," *The Militant*, April 10, 1970.

42. "El Plan Espiritual de Aztlán," in *Aztlán: An Anthology of Mexican American Literature,* ed. Luis Valdez and Stan Steiner (New York: Vintage, 1972), 402–406.

43. Gurule interview.

44. Rosales, *Chicano!* 229.

45. Derrick Morrison, "Chicanos Form Colorado Party: 'La Raza Unida,'" *The Militant,* April 10, 1970.

46. "Chicano Leaders Leave Colorado Democrats," *The Militant*, April 10, 1970.

47. Vigil interview.

48. Nita Gonzales, interview by the author, July 26, 1997.

49. Gonzales interview, July 23, 1997.

50. Joséph Sanchez, "La Raza Candidates Concerned with 'Needs of People,'" *Denver Post,* May 17, 1970.

51. Vigil, *Crusade for Justice*, 230.

52. "Raza Unida Party Is Growing Fast," *El Grito Del Norte*, May 19, 1970.

53. Sanchez, "La Raza Candidates."

54. Ibid.

55. Gurule interview.

56. Vigil interview.

57. Vigil, *Crusade for Justice*, 264.

58. Gómez Quiñonez, *Chicano Politics*, 127.

59. Sal Carpio, interview by the author, July 25, 1997.

60. George Lane, "La Raza Unida Party Goals Announced," *Denver Post*, September 10, 1970.

61. Richard Santillan, "The Politics of Cultural Nationalism: El Partido de la Raza Unida in Southern California, 1969–1978" (Ph.D. diss., Claremont Graduate University, Claremont, Calif., 1978).

62. "Challenge of La Raza," *Denver Post*, September 29, 1970.

63. Bill Logan, "Challenge of La Raza Slate Ballot Listing Denied," *Rocky Mountain News*, September 29, 1970.

64. Richard Tucker, "La Raza Seeking Legal Status for Party," *Rocky Mountain News*, October 18, 1970.

65. Joan Moore and Harry Pachon, *Hispanics in the United States* (Englewood Cliffs, N.J.: Prentice-Hall, 1985), 58.

66. Vigil interview.

67. Carpio interview.

68. Vigil interview.

69. Rosales, *Chicano!* 230.

70. Zoe Von Ende, "Big Goal Is Unifying Chicanos," *Denver Post*, July 27, 1970.

71. Vigil interview.

72. Richard Tucker, "La Raza Unida Party Claims GOP, Dems Frightened," *Rocky Mountain News*, September 30, 1970.

73. Vigil interview.

74. Vigil, *Crusade for Justice*, 316.

75. "La Raza Unida Starts Project for Migrants," *Denver Post*, October 17, 1970.

76. "La Raza Fails in 10 Pct. Try," *Denver Post*, November 4, 1970.

77. Ibid.

78. Antonio Camejo, "Col. Raza Unida Spokesman: The People Are Starting To Move Collectively," *The Militant*, December 4, 1970.

79. Ibid.

80. Ron Margolis, "Denver Raza Headquarters Raided; Candidates Score Significant Vote," *The Militant*, November 13, 1970.

81. Gonzales interview.

82. "La Raza Official Is in Mayor's Race," *Rocky Mountain News*, March 9, 1971.

83. Rosales, *Chicano!* 231.

84. "Chicanos Told To Seek Allies in Cuba, Mexico," *Post Colorado Springs*, November 29, 1971.

85. "La Raza Unida Party's National and International Conference," *Albuquerque El Gallo*, vol. 5, no. 4 (n.d.).

86. Fred Brown, "La Raza Meet Held Pivotal," *Denver Post*, November 28, 1971.

87. Gonzales interview.

88. Vigil, *Crusade for Justice*, 277.

89. George Lane, "La Raza Unida Details Party's Election Plans," *Denver Post*, April 19, 1972.

90. Al Baldivia, "Colorado," *The Militant*, June 16, 1972.

91. Santillan, "Politics of Cultural Nationalism," 123.

92. "Raza Unida Holds News Conference," *Albuquerque El Gallo*, June 1972.

93. Antonio Camejo, "Raza Unida Party Discusses Campaign," *The Militant*, June 30, 1972.

94. "Battle of La Raza: Police Terrorism in Denver," *Albuquerque El Gallo*, August 1972.

95. Vigil interview.

96. Al Baldivia, "Colorado Raza Unida Fields Slate," *The Militant*, September 8, 1972.

97. Ibid.

98. "La Raza Unida Session Ends; Denverite Slain," *Post Colorado Springs,* September 25, 1972.

99. José Calderon, interview by the author, October 20, 1997.

100. "Friends Laud Falcon's Role as Humanitarian," *Denver Post*, September 2, 1972.

101. Frank Moya, "3000 Arrive for La Raza's 1st Convention," *Rocky Mountain News,* September 2, 1972.

102. "Raza Unida Delegate Murdered in N.M.," *Albuquerque El Gallo*, September 1972

103. Al Baldivia and Roy Gonzales, "Denver Chicano March," *The Militant*, October 6, 1972.

104. "Ballot Protest Ruling Expected on Monday," *Denver Post,* October 29, 1972.

105. John White, "Court Considering La Raza Vote Case," *Denver Post,* October 30, 1972.

106. George Lane, "La Raza Pledges Fight f or 'Candidates Rights,'" *Denver Post*, November 3, 1972.

107. Voting results data taken from several articles in *Denver Post*, November 8, 1972.

108. Lyle Fulks, "Col. Raza Unida Makes Good Showing," *The Militant*, November 24, 1972.

109. Carpio interview.

110. "Denver Police Attack Chicanos, Kill One Activist, Wound Others," *Albuquerque El Gallo*, April 1973.

111. Vigil interview.

112. "Angela Davis Supports Denver Raza," *Albuquerque El Gallo,* May 1973.

113. "El Grito de Denver: Free All Political Prisoners," *Albuquerque El Gallo*, June 1973.

114. "Police Harassment Using 'Gestapo' Tactics," *Albuquerque El Gallo*, July 1973.

115. "Not Guilty," *Albuquerque El Gallo*, August 1973.

116. Gonzales interview.

117. Vigil interview.

118. Santillan, "Politics of Cultural Nationalism," 125–126.

119. Ibid.

120. Gonzales interview, August 24, 1997.

121. "La Raza Unida Party 1973 State Convention," *Albuquerque El Gallo*, July 1973.

122. "5-State La Raza Conference Seeks Party Revolution Role," *Denver Post*, August 21, 1973.

123. "La Raza Unida Party's National and International Conference," *Albuquerque El Gallo*, August 1973.

124. Gonzales interview, July 24, 1997.

125. Vigil interview.

126. "La Raza Unida Convention Ends with Solidarity Vows," *Rocky Mountain News*, August 21, 1973.

127. "5-State La Raza Conference."

128. Carpio interview, July 23, 1997.

129. George Lane, "La Raza Makes Plans for '74 Election Drive," *Denver Post*, November 29, 1973.

130. Peter Seidman, "Weld County, Colo., Raza Unida Party Confronts Democrats and Republicans," *The Militant*, December 28, 1973.

131. "Chicano Community Activists in the State of Colorado Continue To Be Special Targets of Police Repression," *Albuquerque El Gallo*, April 1974.

132. Miguel Pendas, "Colo. Raza Unida Party Nominates Candidates," *The Militant*, May 3, 1974.

133. Vigil, *Crusade for Justice*.

134. Peter Seidman, "5,000 Chicanos in Denver Protest Repression," *The Militant*, October 4, 1974.

135. Vigil interview.

136. Ibid.

137. "Corky Falsely Arrested," *Albuquerque El Gallo*, July 1975.

138. Miguel Pendas, "Col. Cops Take Aim at Escuela Tlatelolco," *The Militant*, April 18, 1975.

139. Calderon interview.

140. Pendas, "Col. Cops Take Aim."

141. Carpio interview.

142. Olga Rodriguez, "Colorado Conference Debates Strategy for Independent Chicano Political Action Today," *The Militant*, February 20, 1976.

143. Eddie Montour, interview by the author, July 23, 1997.

144. Ibid.

145. "La Raza Unida Statement: Political Party's 1976 Workshop," *Albuquerque El Gallo*, February 1976.

146. Montour interview.

147. Jack Marsh, "Denver Chicano Leader Convicted in Frame-up," *The Militant*, February 13, 1976.

148. Gonzales Denies Plotting Murders of Police," *Albuquerque El Gallo*, July 1976.

149. Montour interview.

150. Vigil interview; and Harry Ring, "Crusade Members Assault Socialists in Denver," *The Militant*, October 15, 1976.

151. Montour interview.

## Chapter Five

1. For an examination of the epoch of protest, see Terry H. Anderson, *The Movement and the Sixties: Protest in America from Greensboro to Wounded Knee* (New York: Oxford University Press, 1995).

2. Armando Navarro, *Mexican American Youth Organization: The Avant-Garde of the Chicano Movement in Texas* (Austin: University of Texas Press, 1995), 1–8. In addition, for an excellent historical overview of the Chicano Movement, see F. Arturo Rosales, *Chicano! The History of the Mexican Civil Rights Movement* (Houston: Arte Publico, 1996). For cursory historical examinations of the Chicano Movement, see Rodolfo Acuña, *Occupied America: A History of Chicanos*, 3d. ed. (New York: Harper and Row, 1988), and Juan Gómez Quiñonez, *Chicano Politics: Reality and Promise, 1940–1990* (Albuquerque: University of New Mexico Press, 1990).

3. For a comprehensive examination of Chicanismo, see Ignacio Garciá, *Chicanismo: The Forging of a Militant Ethos among Mexican Americans* (Tucson: University of Arizona Press, 1997).

4. Armando Navarro, *The Cristal Experiment: The Chicano Struggle for Community Control* (Madison: University of Wisconsin Press, 1998); see the epilogue for an analysis of internal colonialism. In addition, refer to Carlos Munoz, Mario Barrera, and Charles Ornelas, "The

Barrio as an Internal Colony," in *La Causa Politica: A Chicano Reader*, ed. F. Chris Garcia (Notre Dame, Ind.: University of Notre Dame Press, 1974), 281–301.

5. Joan Moore and Harry Pachon, *Mexican Americans* (Englewood Cliffs, N.J.: Prentice-Hall, 1976), 55; Gómez Quiñonez, *Chicano Politics*, 108.

6. Joan Moore and Harry Pachon, *Hispanics in the United States* (Englewood Cliffs, N.J.: Prentice-Hall, 1985), 58.

7. Woody Diaz and Michael Maggi, "Raza Unida Candidate Runs Calif. Write-in," *The Militant*, November 17, 1972, 9. Albert Juarex, "The Emergence of El Partido De La Raza Unida: California's New Chicano Partido," in *La Causa Politica: A Chicano Politics Reader*, ed. F. Chris Garcia (Notre Dame, Ind.: University of Notre Dame Press, 1974), 307.

8. Richard Santillan, "The Latino Community in State and Congressional Redistricting, 1961–1985," in *Latinos and the Political System*, ed. F. Chris Garcia (Notre Dame, Ind.: University of Notre Dame Press, 1988), 328–348.

9. Richard Santillan, "El Partido de la Raza Unida: Revolt in the Barrios," *Regeneracíon*, vol. 2 (1972): 9.

10. For a demographic, social, educational, economic, and political profile of the Méxicano community at that time, see Joan W. Moore, *Mexican Americans*, 2d. ed. (Englewood Cliffs, N.J.: Prentice-Hall, 1976).

11. Miguel Tirado, "Mexican American Community Political Organization, 'The Key to Chicano Political Power,'" in *Aztlán: Chicano Journal of the Social Sciences and the Arts*, vol. 1, no. 1 (Spring 1970): 53–78.

12. Richard Santillan, *La Raza Unida* (Los Angeles: Tlaquilo, 1973), 36.

13. Richard Santillan, "The Politics of Cultural Nationalism: El Partido de la Raza Unida in Southern California, 1969–1978" (Ph.D. diss., Claremont Graduate University, Claremont, Calif., 1978), 149.

14. For an extensive examination of the formation of RUP in Texas, see Navarro, *Mexican American Youth Organization* and *The Cristal Experiment*.

15. At that time, Cucamonga was an unincorporated farming community located in San Bernardino County approximately forty miles south of Los Angeles and twenty-five miles north of San Bernardino. According to the U.S. Bureau of the Census, in 1970 its population was 5, 796, of which approximately 40 percent were Méxicano and the rest white. According to Donald Clucas, in *Light over the Mountain: A History of the Rancho Cucamonga Area* (Upland, Calif.: Family Publications, 1979, 7–8), the name "Cucamonga" denotes "a sandy place or place of many waters." Cucamonga had two school districts: the Cucamonga School District, in which 60 percent of the students were Méxicano, two of the administrators were Méxicano, and most of the teachers were white; and the Cucamonga Central School District, in which the overwhelming majority of students, teachers, and administrators was white. "Experiment" in this context refers to the organizing activities, issues, and projects that emanated from the struggle for community control and social change between 1968 and 1972, first in the communities of Cucamonga and Upland, then by 1970 in Ontario, Montclair, and Claremont. With the emergence of RUP in late 1970, the experiment was expanded to include the whole of San Bernardino and Riverside Counties.

16. "Community control" denotes the people's direct participation in the decision-making process for public policies. It emerged out of the various struggles of the epoch of protest that sought to "democratize" local government by having the people more directly involved in it. For a comprehensive examination, see Navarro, *The Cristal Experiment*, 3–13.

17. MAPA, minutes, March 12, 1968.

18. Both Arthur and I were professional musicians—I played trumpet and he played the conga drums. At the time I was a sophomore at a nearby community college, Chaffey College.

19. The analysis that follows is a product both of my research in primary and secondary sources, and of my observations as an active participant.

20. For a comprehensive analysis of internal colonialism, see Navarro, *The Cristal Experiment*, 352–353.

21. Armando Navarro, "Educational Change through Political Action," in *Mexican Americans and Educational Change*, ed. Alfredo Castañeda, Manuel Rameriz III, Carlos Cortés, and Mario Barrera (Riverside, Calif.: Mexican American Studies Program and Project Follow Through, 1971), 105–139.

22. For an examination of research conducted using the reputation method, see Willis D. Hawley and Frederick M. Wirt, eds., *The Search for Community Power* (Englewood Cliffs, N.J.: Prentice-Hall, 1968), 41–92.

23. The chapter's leadership, beyond the elected officers and committee chairpersons, included others whose number varied—at the apogee of the experiment this core numbered twenty-five. Women constituted about a third of the leadership.

24. MAPA, minutes, March 21, 1968.

25. "M.A.P.A., Mexican American Political Association," pamphlet, 1969.

26. Arnold Urtiaga, interview by the author, April 11, 1998. Urtiaga became one of the main leaders of MAPA in Cucamonga. He was one of three Méxicanos to get elected in the takeover of 1969.

27. Armando Navarro, "Cucamonga: Historical and Cultural Influences Leading to the Birth of a Political Organization" (senior thesis, Claremont Men's College, May 1, 1970).

28. Arthur "Turi" Ayala, interview by the author, April 25, 1998.

29. MAPA, minutes, June 24, 1968.

30. Ayala interview, April 30, 1998.

31. Navarro, *Cucamonga*, 47.

32. MAPA, minutes, September 5, 1968.

33. Navarro, "Educational Change through Political Action," 105.

34. MAPA, minutes, November 18, 1968; December 16, 1968.

35. Urtiaga interview.

36. Alfonso Navarro, interview by the author, May 3, 1998.

37. Ibid., 116.

38. "The Chicano Tradition: A Christmas 'Posada,'" *Daily Report*, December 25, 1968.

49. David Ortega, interview by the author, April 18, 1998.

40. Navarro, *Cucamonga*, 54.

41. Urtiaga interview.

42. Ibid., 50.

43. Ayala interview.

44. MAPA, minutes, February 26, 1969.

45. Ayala interview.

46. Navarro, "Educational Change through Political Action," 120–121.

47. "Cucamonga School District Candidates," *Daily Report*, April 11, 1969.

48. Urtiaga interview.

49. Navarro, "Educational Change through Political Action," 119–120.

50. MAPA, minutes, March 26, 1969.

51. Ayala interview.

52. "Incumbents Win and Lose in Area School Elections," *Daily Report*, April 16, 1969.

53. For a thorough examination of the Cristal takeover, see Navarro, *The Cristal Experiment,* chapter 1.

54. Cucamonga School District Board, minutes, August 28, 1969.

55. I was reelected chair; Ruben Andrade, vice-chair; Emilio Arroyo, vice-chair; Carmen Betancourt, secretary; Stella Perez, corresponding secretary; Alfonso Navarro, treasurer. The city chairs were Felix Martel, Cucamonga; Edward Guerra, Ontario; and Irma Welsh, Upland. Chairing the standing committees were Roberto Perez, Dee Small, Rogelio Granados, Ozzie Murrujo, David Hernandez, David Ortega, Manuel Contreras, Roger Lopez, José Bencomo, Roberto Gil, Leo Juarez, Arturo Ayala, Jr., Manuel Luna, and Gilbert Arias. Although most of the leaders were men, women played a significant and vital secondary leadership role; they included Veronica Young, Rita Hernandez, Rose Guerra, Rose Ann Gonzales, Maria Navarro, Isabel Contreras, Lydia Jimenez, and Millie Andrade. "West End MAPA Organizational Chart," n.d., author's files.

56. The demands called for the hiring of more Méxicano teachers, administrators, and staff commensurate with the district's ethnic and racial makeup; retirement of teachers and administrators past the age of sixty-five; ongoing evaluation of teachers and administrators; expansion of the district's bilingual/bicultural program; determination of why the district was not using Title VII funds for its bilingual/bicultural program; establishment of reading and tutorial programs; and the activation of the Title I parent-advisory committee (Cucamonga School District Board, minutes, January 13, 1970).

57. Navarro, *Cucamonga,* 67.

58. "Cucamonga School Boss Fired, Hired," *Daily Report*, May 1970.

59. Cucamonga School District Board, minutes, May 12, 1970.

60. "La Raza Unida Conference," *Daily Report*, April 7, 1971.

61. Raza Unida Party minutes for San Bernardino/Riverside Counties, January 9, 1971.

62. Santillan, *La Raza Unida* , 105.

63. Ibid., 105–106.

64. I formulated the trinity Concept for Community Development in response to the Chicano Movement's lack of ideology or comprehensive strategy for change. For the particulars of the model, see Armando Navarro, "The Development of a New Concept," *Agenda: A Journal of Hispanic Issues,* vol. 10, no. 5 (September/October 1980).

65. Others from throughout the two counties in leadership roles included: David Serena from the Coachella Valley; Rafael Cardosa and Ricardo Martinez, both from Redlands; David Serrano and Paul Bocanegra, San Bernardino; Jose Soriano, Fontana; Virginia Duran, Rialto; Israel Arriaga and Vicente Rodriguez, Riverside; and in the West End of San Bernardino County, Rogelio Granados, Arnold Urtiaga, David Hernandez, Mike Espinoza, and most of the West End MAPA chapter leadership previously mentioned in the text. RUP Central Coordinating Committee Meeting, minutes, May 13, 1972.

66. RUP Central Coordinating Council, minutes, May 20, 1972.

67. During this time I was in graduate school and working on my Ph.D., raising a family, and playing in an orchestra on weekends. I spent an average of twenty hours per week working on RUP-related activities.

68. Virginia Duran from Rialto and, from the West End of San Bernardino County, Rita Hernandez, Dee Small, Irma Welch stood out for their leadership abilities. Armando Navarro, "The Formation of a New Entity: La Raza Unida," typescript, March 26, 1971, author's files.

69. The discussion of RUP's ideology that follows is drawn from ibid.

70. Among those I met with were Gilbert Perez, Manuel Bocanegra, and José Hernandez.

71. Jorge Avila, "The Ontario School Walkouts," typescript, Spring 1997, author's files. This in-depth case study was completed as a course requirement.

72. Letter from Christian Majority to Armando Navarro, November 17, 1971.

73. The demands included: hiring Chicano teachers and administrators; establishing cultural centers in each high school; Chicano Study courses in the curriculum; teacher cultural awareness in-service training; establishing a fifteen-person community committee to monitor implementation of demands. Many front-page articles appeared in local newspapers.

74. See numerous articles and editorials in the two largest local newspapers, *Daily Report* and *Progress Bulletin*.

75. Armando Navarro, "La Raza Unida: Central Coordinating Committee Guidelines" (position paper), typescript, 1971.

76. Mark Johnson, "5 New Homes Give Breath to Barrio Rebirth," *Daily Report*, August 24, 1971.

77. Alfonso Navarro, interview by the author, May 4, 1998. Alfonso is my older brother. He was the primary organizing force in the building of the seven homes.

78. Vicente Rodriguez, interview by the author, May 4, 1998.

79. David Ortega interview.

80. Luna, handwritten document, mid-1971, author's files.

81. Gustavo Ramos, interview by the author, April 17, 1998.

82. "Ontario Candidates," *Daily Report*, April 9, 1972.

83. Sara Ramos, interview by the author, April 17, 1998.

84. Ramos interview, April 10, 1998.

85. Mark Johnson, "West End Chicano Leader Honored," *Daily Report*, February 28, 1972.

86. Diaz and Maggi, "Raza Unida Candidate."

87. "Elections Bring out Brown Vote," *Daily Report*, April 16, 1973.

88. Urtiaga interview, April 18, 1998.

89. In 1974 I took a position at the University of Utah in the Department of Political Science, where I spent two and a half years. While there I assisted in various organizing efforts. In December 1976, I returned to Upland, California, where I, with the assistance of four organizers I had trained in Utah, started a major organizing effort that lasted from 1977 to 1992. In 1992 I took a position as an assistant professor in ethnic studies at the University of California, Riverside. By December 1999 I had been promoted to full professor and chair of the Department of Ethnic Studies.

## Chapter Six

1. Alberto Juarez, "The Emergence of El Partido de la Raza Unida: A California New Chicano Party," in *La Causa Politica: A Chicano Politics Reader*, ed. F. Chris Garcia (Notre Dame, Ind.: University of Notre Dame Press, 1974), 304–305.

2. Ibid.

3. For a comprehensive examination of internal colonialism and the Chicano see: Mario Barrera, Carlos Muñoz, and Carlos Ornelas, "The Barrios As an Internal Colony," in *La Causa Politica: A Chicano Politics Reader*, ed. F. Chris Garcia (Notre Dame, Ind.: University of Notre Dame Press, 974), 282.

4. Richard Santillan, "The Politics of Cultural Nationalism: El Partido de la Raza Unida in Southern California" (Ph.D. diss., Claremont Graduate University, Claremont, Calif., 1978), 145–146.

5. Fernando Guerrero, "N. Calif. Raza Unida Party Conference Held," *The Militant*, December 25, 1970.

6. Ibid.

7. Ibid.

8. Santillan, "Politics of Cultural Nationalism," 151

9. Richard Santillan, interview by the author, August 6, 1997.

10. Baxter Smith, "L.A. Raza Unida Party Holds Convention," *The Militant*, March 12, 1971.

11. Richard Santillan, *La Raza Unida* (Los Angeles: Tlaquilo, 1973), 56.

12. "La Raza Unida: Organize New Political Party," *Belvedere Citizen, May* 20, 1971.

13. Santillan, "Politics of Cultural Nationalism," 153.

14. Herman Baca, interview by the author, May 31, 1997.

15. Froben Lozada, "Calif. MAPA Leader Calls for Support to Raza Unida Party," *The Militant*, February 19, 1971.

16. Ignacio Garciá, *United We Win: The Rise and Fall of La Raza Unida Party* (Tucson, Ariz.: Mexican-American Studies and Research Center, 1989), 100.

17. Ibid.

18. Bert Corona, *MAPA and La Raza Unida Party: A Program for Chicano Political Action for the 1970s* (National City, Calif.: RUP, 1971).

19. Santillan, "Politics of Cultural Nationalism," 153.

20. Santillan interview.

21. Garciá, *United We Win*, 145.

22. Raul Ruiz, interview by the author, May 3, 1997.

23. Xenaro Ayala, interview by the author, August 8, 1997.

24. Cireño Rodriguez, interview by the author, April 19, 1997.

25. Gilbert Lopez, "La Raza Unida Party Attempts To Qualify through the Courts," *La Raza Magazine*, September 1973, 4.

26. "California Election Codes: Deterrent to La Raza Unida," *La Raza Magazine*, 7.

27. Andres Torres, interview by the author, November 15, 1997.

28. Olga Rodriguez, "Raza Unida Makes Good Showing in LA," *The Militant*, November 5, 1971.

29. Santillan, "Politics of Cultural Nationalism," 203.

30. Ruiz interview.

31. Ibid.

32. Ibid.

33. "Unidos Venceremos: Ruiz 48th Assembly District," leaflet, n.d., author's files.

34. Quoted in Santillan, "Politics of Cultural Nationalism," 205.

35. Olga Rodriguez, "Raza Unida Confronts Muskie in L.A. Barrio," *The Militant*, November 19, 1971.

36. Raul Ruiz, "El Partido de La Raza Unida," editorial, *La Raza Magazine*, January 1972, 3–5.

37. Rodriguez, "Raza Unida Makes Good Showing."

38. Ruiz interview.

49. Santillan interview.

40. Mariana Hernandez, "L.A. Raza Unida Party Rallies Support for Nov. 16 Elections," *The Militant*, November 12, 1971.

41. Rodriguez, "Raza Unida Makes Good Showing."

42. Rodriguez, "Raza Unida Confronts Muskie.

43. Olga Rodriguez, "Raza Unida Builds Strong Campaign in L.A.," *The Militant*, October 22, 1971.

44. Rodriguez, "Raza Unida Confronts Muskie."

45. Ibid.

46. Frank Del Olmo, "Chicano Party Says It Defeated Alatorre in 48th District," *Los Angeles Times*, November 20, 1971.

47. Ibid.

48. Juan Gómez Quiñonez, *Chicano Politics: Reality and Promise* (Albuquerque: University of New Mexico Press, 1990), 136.

49. Santillan, *La Raza Unida*, 86.

50. Del Olmo, "Chicano Party Says."

51. Santillan, *La Raza Unida*, 87.

52. Herman Baca, interview by the author, June 11, 1998.

53. Santillan, "Politics of Cultural Nationalism," 160.

54. "La Raza Unida Party Registration Statistics," RUP report, August 13, 1973, author's files.

55. Santillan, "Politics of Cultural Nationalism," 161.

56. Larry Martinez to Vicente Gonzales, letter, January 13, 1972, author's files.

57. "La Raza Unida State-wide Conference, San José, California," political workshop document, April 1972, author's files.

58. Ibid.

59. Ibid.

60. Ibid.

61. "Victory in San José!" *San Diego County: La Raza Unida Party Newsletter*, May 1972.

62. Elias Castillo, "First National Meeting: U.S. Chicano Caucus Opens Today in S.J.," *The Mercury*, April 21, 1972.

63. Communiqué, n.d., author's files.

64. Baca interview, May 31, 1997.

65. Elias Castillo, "Protester Group Claims Victory: Chicano Caucus Shuns GOP, Demos," *San José Mercury*, April 24, 1972.

66. "National Political Caucus," RUP press release, April 23, 1972, author's files.

67. Castillo, "Protestor Group Claims Victory."

68. Ibid.

69. "Radical Leftists Infiltrate La Raza, Organizer Charges," *San José Mercury*, April 22, 1972.

70. "Chicano Caucus Ends in Furor," *San José Mercury*, April 24, 1972.

71. "Agenda Session for State Convention," State RUP, minutes, June 3, 1972.

72. Antonio Camejo, "California Raza Unida Party: Activists Discuss Problems of Building a Chicano Party," *The Militant*, July 21, 1972.

73. Ibid.

74. Ibid.

75. Ruiz interview.

76. Gilbert Blanco, "On Organizing the Partido," *La Raza Magazine*, September 1972, 8.

77. "L.R.U.P. State Convention," *San Diego County La Raza Unida Party Newsletter*, August 1972.

78. Ruiz interview.

79. Los Angeles RUP Central Committee, minutes, July 29, 1972

80. La Raza Unida Party Organizing Committees: Southern Region, "On the Status of the Raza Unida Party in Califas, Aztlán: A Position Paper," August 21, 1972.

81. The politics of RUP's national convention at El Paso, Texas, are examined comprehensively in Chapter Nine. See also Garciá, *United We Win*, 103–116.

82. Santillan, "Politics of Cultural Nationalism," 210–212.

83. Ibid.

84. Gilbert Lopez, "Some Aspects of Political Development," typescript, 1973, 39.

85. Santillan interview.

86. Ayala interview.

87. Fred Aguilar, interview by the author, May 17, 1997.

88. Ruiz interview.

89. Lopez, "Some Aspects of Political Development," 44.

90. Ibid.

91. Santillan, "Politics of Cultural Nationalism," 214.

92. Ibid., 215–216.

93. Ruiz interview.

94. "Raza Unida Party Registration Statistics."

## Chapter Seven

1. The clashing of ideologies and their content are examined in detail in the Epilogue.

2. For an excellent book that examines the various aspects of Chicanismo, or cultural nationalism, see Ignacio Garciá, *Chicanismo: The Forging of a Militant Ethos* (Tucson: University of Arizona Press, 1997).

3. For illustrations or excerpts of the various RUP platforms, see Richard Santillan, *La Raza Unida* (Los Angeles: Tlaquilo, 1973), 52–57.

4. Armando Navarro, speech at RUP State Conference, Chaffey College, Cucamonga, April 17, 1971 (audio tape recording), author's files.

5. "Why La Raza Unida?" *San Diego County La Raza Unida Party Newsletter*, May 1972.

6. "The Alternative La Raza Unida," *La Raza Magazine*, vol. 1., no. 7: 115

7. Los Angeles RUP Central Committee, minutes, January 15, 1972.

8. Santillan, *La Raza Unida*, 51–52.

9. Ibid., 53.

10. RUP State Central Committee, minutes, April 7, June 30, October 6, 1973; January 14, March 30, August 16, 1974; September 20, 1975.

11. Ibid, September 20, 1975.

12. Herman Baca, interview by the author, May 31, 1997.

13. Richard Santillan, "The Politics of Cultural Nationalism: El Partido de la Raza Unida in Southern California" (Ph.D. diss., Claremont Graduate University, 1978), 187–188.

14. Xenaro Ayala, interview by the author, August 8, 1997, and Andres Torres, interview by the author, November 15, 1997.

15. Miguel Pendas, "Raza Unida Party Aids Striking Rubber Workers," *The Militant*, June 8, 1973.

16. Ibid.

17. Santillan, "Politics of Cultural Nationalism,"180.

18. Raza Unida Party State Convention Resolutions, August 10, 11, 12, 1973.

19. Baca interview.

20. RUP State Central Committee Report on RUP Number Registered, August 13, 1973.

21. Gilbert Lopez, "La Raza Unida Party Attempts To Qualify through the Courts," *La Raza Magazine*, September 1973.

22. Santillan, "Politics of Cultural Nationalism," 258.

23. Miguel Pendas, "Calif. Raza Unida Party To Enter Governor's Race," *The Militant*, September 21, 1973

24. Committee for Democratic Election Laws, press release, February 1, 1974. Also quoted in Santillan, "Politics of Cultural Nationalism," 185.

25. Cited in Joan Moore and Harry Pachon, *Hispanics in the United States* (Englewood Cliffs, N.J.: Prentice-Hall, 1985), 185.

26. Miguel Pendas, "Raza Unida in S. Calif. Race," *The Militant*, January 26, 1973.

27. Torres interview.

28. Miguel Pendas, "So. Calif. Campaign Won New Support for RUP," *The Militant*, March 16, 1973.

29. Kenneth Reich, "Robbins Election Expenditure Sets Record," *Los Angeles Times,* May 5, 1973.

30. Torres interview.

31. Fred Aguilar, interview by the author, May 17, 1997.

32. "Feb.13 Voten por Ernie Macias Porras, City Council Puente," campaign tabloid, 1973, author's files.

33. Aguilar interview.

34. Ibid.

35. For an examination of the 1961 and 1963 incorporation efforts, see Howard Schuman, "The Incorporation of East Los Angeles as a Separate City: Problems and Prospects" (master's thesis, University of Southern California, 1965).

36. Ridgely Cummings, "County Given ELA Cityhood Report," *Belevedere (Calif.) Citizen*, May 20,1971.

37. La Raza Unida Party Incorporation Committee, "Attention: Why We Need Incorporation," flyer, 1974.

38. Rodolfo Acuña, *Occupied America: A History of Chicanos* (Cambridge, Mass.: Harper and Row, 1988), 368.

39. For a thorough examination of the 1973–1974 East Los Angeles incorporation issue, see Jorge Garcia, "Forjando Ciudad: The Development of a Chicano Political Community in East Los Angeles" (Ph.D. diss., University of California, Riverside, 1986). Santillan, in "Politics of Cultural Nationalism," examines the various aspects of the politics, issues, and problems encountered in the unsuccessful incorporation endeavor; see particularly pages 220–244.

40. Santillan, "Politics of Cultural Nationalism," 221.

41. Garcia, "Forjando Ciudad," 248.

42. Waunetah Goins, "The Incorporation of East Los Angeles and La Raza Unida Party," typescript, 1998, author's files.

43. RUP Fact Sheet, n.d., author's files.

44. Miguel Pendas, "Why East Los Angeles Incorporation Drive Failed," *The Militant*, December 6, 1974.

45. Goins, "Incorporation of East Los Angeles."

46. Garcia, "Forjando Ciudad," 249.

47. Frank Del Olmo, "Defeat of East L.A. Laid to Fear of Property Tax," *Los Angeles Times*, November 9, 1974.

48. Garcia, "Forjando Ciudad," 263–264.

49. Ruiz interview, May 3, 1997.

50. Pendas, "Why East Los Angeles."

51. For a thorough examination of the various reasons for the measures' defeat, see Santillan, "Politcs of Cultural Nationalism," 237–244.

52. Juan Gómez Quiñonez, *Chicano Politics: Reality and Promise* (Albuquerque: University of New Mexico Press, 1990), 137.

53. Ruiz interview.

54. For an extensive examination of post-1975 Chicano politics, particularly the emergence of the "Viva Yo" generation, see Armando Navarro, "The Post-Mortem Politics of the Chicano Movement, 1975–1996," *Perspectives in Mexican American Studies*, vol. 6 (1997), and Garciá, *Chicanismo*.

55. Ruiz interview.

56. RUP State Central Committee, minutes, May 22, 1976.

57. Aguilar interview.

58. Ayala interview.

59. RUP State Central Committee, minutes, September 25, 1978.

60. Ibid., Chapter Dues Report, October 19, 1981.

61. Ayala interview.

62. Aguilar interview.

63. Richard Santillan, interview by the author, August 8, 1997.

64. Torres interview.

65. Miguel Pendas, "San Fernando City Council Race: Raza Unida Party Challenges Democrats," *The Militant*, March 5, 1976.

66. Ayala interview.

67. Miguel Pendas, "Raza Unida in California," *The Militant*, May 28, 1976.

68. Steve Warshell, "Raza Unida Parties Assess Nov. 2 Voting: California," *The Militant*, November 26, 1976. See also Santillan, "Politics of Cultural Nationalism," 245–246.

69. RUP San Fernando, minutes, n.d., author's files.

70. John Simmons, "Hispanic Candidate Aims To Beat Brown," *San Fernando Valley Sun and the Breeze*, August 1978.

71. RUP State Central Committee, minutes, n.d.

72. Aguilar interview, July 16, 1998.

73. Eugene Hernandez, "Importance of Political Elections to La Raza Unida" (position paper), typescript, n.d., author's files.

## Chapter Eight

1. The following are major works on the historical experience of the Méxicano in New Mexico, most by Méxicano historians: Juan Gómez Quiñonez, *Roots of Chicano Politics, 1600–1940* (Albuquerque: University of New Mexico Press, 1994), and *Chicano Politics: Reality and Promise, 1940–1990* (Albuquerque: University of New Mexico Press, 1990); Carey McWilliams, *North from Mexico* (New York: Greenwood, 1968); Rodolfo Acuña, *Occupied America: A History of Chicanos,* 3d. ed. (Cambridge, Mass.: Harper and Row, 1988); Matt S. Meier and Feliciano Ribera *Mexican Americans/American Mexicans: From Conquistadores to Chicanos* (New York: Hill and Wang, 1993); and John R. Chavez, *The Lost Land: The Chicano Image of the Southwest* (Albuquerque: University of New Mexico Press, 1984).

2. McWilliams, *North from Mexico,* 52.

3. George I. Sanchez, *Forgotten People: A Study of New Mexicans* (Albuquerque: University of New Mexico Press, 1940), 30.

4. Carey McWilliams, *Brothers under the Skin* (Boston: Little, Brown, 1943), 128.

5. Ibid.

6. Gómez Quiñonez, *Roots of Chicano Politics,* 257–258.

7. Acuña, *Occupied America,* 60–61. The "new Mexican experience" refers to that of post-1848 New Mexico.

8. Gómez Quiñonez, *Roots of Chicano Politics,* 278–279.

9. Acuña, *Occupied America,* 71–74.

10. For a comprehensive examination of the developments of Las Gorras Blancas and of the PPU, see Robert Johnson Rosenbaum, "Méxicano versus Americano: A Study of Hispanic-American Resistance to Anglo-American Control in New Mexico Territory, 1870–1900" (Ph.D. diss., University of Texas at Austin, 1972).

11. Gómez Quiñonez, *Roots of Chicano Politics,* 280.

12. Juan José Peña, interview by the author, July 22, 1997.

13. Gómez Quiñonez, *Roots of Chicano Politics,* 281.

14. Rosenbaum, *Méxicano versus Americano,* 223.

15. Acuña, *Occupied America,* 73.

16. Ibid., 74.

17. Jack E. Holmes, *Politics in New Mexico* (Albuquerque: University of New Mexico Press, 1967), 12.

18. Meier and Ribera, *Mexican Americans/American Mexicans,* 100.

19. Holmes, *Politics in New Mexico,* 12.

20. Ibid., 17.

21. Gómez Quiñonez, *Chicano Politics,* 45–48.

22. Ibid.

23. Quoted in Ernest B. Fincher, *The Mexican American: Spanish-Americans as a Political Factor in New Mexico, 1912–1950* (New York: Arno, 1974), 3.

24. Sanchez, *The Forgotten People,* 13.

25. For an examination on the development of the Alianza and its leader, Tijerina, see: Peter Nabokov, *Tijerina and the Court House Raid* (Albuquerque: University of New Mexico Press, 1969), and Richard Gardner, *Grito! Reies Lopez Tijerina and the New Mexico Land Grant War of 1967* (Indianapolis: Bobbs-Merrill, 1970).

26. For a historical overview of the Tijerina and the Alianza, see Armando Navarro, *Mexican American Youth Organization: Avant–Garde of the Chicano Movement in Texas* (Austin: University of Texas Press, 1995), 23–28. For a more extensive examination, see Nabokov, *Tijerina and the Courthouse Raid.*

27. For an overview analysis of the Partido Constitucional del Pueblo, see Maurillo Vigil, *Chicano Politics* (Washington, D.C.: University Press of America, 1977), 210–219.

28. Ibid., 215.

29. Ibid., 216.

30. Gómez Quiñonez, *Chicano Politics,* 117.

31. Vigil, *Chicano Politics,* 218–219.

32. Navarro, *Mexican American Youth Movement,* 27–28.

33. Ibid.

34. Juan José Peña, "The Chicano Movement in New Mexico," typescript, n.d., author's files.

35. Joan Moore and Harry Pachon, *Hispanics in the United States* (Englewood Cliffs, N.J.: Prentice-Hall, 1985), 185.

36. Acuña, *Occupied America,* 368.

37. Peña interview.

38. Harry Ring, "Raza Unida Party in New Mexico: Evolution of a Chicano Leader," *The Militant,* October 22, 1976.

39. Peña interview, July 30, 1998.

40. Peña, "Chicano Movement in New Mexico."

41. Ibid.

42. Santillan, "Politics of Cultural Nationalism."

43. Levi Winters, "Raza Unida Party Formed in New Mexico," *The Militant,* August 4, 1972.

44. Richard Winger, "New Mexico," *Ballot Access News,* n.d.

45. Winters, "Raza Unida Party Formed."

46. Peña interview.

47. Peña interview, August 12, 1998.

48. *Raza Unida Party Newsletter: San Miguel County,* March 23, 1974, 2.

49. Peña interview, July 30, 1998.

50. For a comprehensive case study of MAYO see Navarro, *Mexican American Youth Organization.*

51. Peña interview.

52. Santillan, "Politics of Cultural Nationalism," 128.

53. *Las Vegas Daily Optic,* August 3, 1972.

54. Ibid.

55. Juan José Peña, "Raza Unida de Nuevo Mexico: A Manual and Political Program," typescript, n.d., author's files.

56. Peña interview.

57. Peña, "Raza Unida de Nuevo Mexico."

58. Ibid.

59. Harry Ring, "Raza Unida Party in New Mexico: A Talk with Juan José Peña," *The Militant,* October 1976.

60. Peña interview, July 22, 1997.

61. Ibid., 58.

62. Peña, *The Chicano Movement in New Mexico*, 60.

63. Vigil, *Chicano Politics*, 230.

64. Peña, "Raza Unida de Nuevo Mexico."

65. Peña interview, July 30, 1998.

66. Vigil, *Chicano Politics*, 231–232.

67. Peña interview, July 22, 1997.

68. Peña, *Chicano Movement in New Mexico*, 68, and Peña interview, July 22, 1997.

69. Richard Everett, "Area Raza Unida Party a Dynamic Force," *Santa Fe New Mexican*, August 12, 1973.

70. Mike Collins and Connie Allen, "Chicano Students Arrested in N. Mex.," *The Militant*, October 12, 1973.

71. Peña interview, July 30, 1998.

72. Ibid.

73. Antonio DeVargas, interview by the author, July 23, 1997.

74. Richard Rosenstock, "Death of a System"(typescript, 1978, author's files), examines the politics of Rio Arriba County from 1975 to 1978. It focuses on the Naranjo machine and its decline as well as on RUP as its biggest political adversary.

75. Ibid., 3.

76. For a thorough examination of the ongoing conflict between RUP and the Naranjo political machine, see Rosenstock, "Death of a System."

77. Arnold Weissberg, "Raza Unida in New Mexico: Sheriff's Reign of Terror," *The Militant*, September 3, 1976.

78. Richard Rosenstock, interview by the author, August 18, 1998.

79. Peña, *Chicano Movement in New Mexico*, 73–74.

80. Raza Unida Party, "The Pueblo Slate: The Candidates, the Platform," February 1974. Quoted in Vigil, *Chicano Politics*, 246.

81. Peña, *Chicano Movement in New Mexico*, 61.

82. *Raza Unida Party Newsletter: County of San Miguel*, March 23, 1974.

83. Vigil, *Chicano Politics*, 233.

84. Santillan, "Politics of Cultural Nationalism," 129.

85. Moore and Pachon, *Hispanics in the United States*, 185.

86. Winger, "New Mexico."

87. "La Raza Holds Convention," *Santa Fe New Mexican*, April 29, 1976.

88. Ibid., September 17, 1976.

89. Ibid.

90. Ibid.

91. Office of the Secretary of State, "Canvass Returns of General Election Held on November 2, 1976—State of New Mexico," n.d.

92. Steve Warshall, "Raza Unida Parties Assess Nov. 2 Voting," *The Militant*, November 29, 1976.

93. Peña, *Chicano Movement in New Mexico*, 61.

94. Peña interview, July 22, 1997.

95. Arturo Rameriz, "NM Raza Unida Names U.S. Senate Candidate," *The Militant*, May 14, 1976; Arnold Weissberg, "Raza Unida in New Mexico: Land for Those Who Work It," *The Militant*, September 10, 1976; Arnold Weissberg, "Raza Unida in New Mexico: A Dynamic

Chicano Party," *The Militant*, September 17, 1996; Ring, "Talk with Juan José Peña"; Ring, "Evolution of a Chicano Leader."

96. DeVargas interview.

97. Juan José Peña, "The Partido de la Raza Unida de Nuevo Mexico: The Socialist Workers Party Question," bulletin no. 4, May 1979, author's files.

98. Ibid. Peña produced several bulletins for the purpose of generating discussion within RUP. They did not necessarily represent the views of the rest of RUP's leaders or members.

99. Juan José Peña, "The Chicano Movement, the Southwest, and the Role of the National and State Partido de La Raza Unida in the Southwest: An Economic, Historic, Social and Political Profile from 1890 to the Early 2000's," bulletin no. 1, May 1977, author's files.

100. Gómez Quiñonez, *Roots of Chicano Politics*, 152.

101. Santillan, "Politics of Cultural Nationalism," 130–131.

102. For a theoretical examination of radical pedagogy, see **Pablo Friere,** *Pedagogy of the Oppressed* (New York: Seabury, 1973).

103. Juan José Peña, "Partido de la Raza Unida de Nuevo Mexico on the Question of Christian Theology," bulletin no. 6, 1979.

104. Peña, "Socialist Workers Party Question."

105. Peña interview.

106. Rosenstock interview.

107. DeVargas interview.

108. Rebecca Hill, interview by the author, August 28, 1998.

109. Ibid.

110. Acuña, *Occupied America*, 368.

111. Peña interview, August 5, 1998.

112. Peña, "Chicano Movement in New Mexico," 108.

113. DeVargas interview.

114. Ibid.

115. Ibid.

116. Peña interview, July 22, 1997.

117. Rosenstock interview.

118. Isabel Blea, interview by the author, August 17, 1998.

119. Cindy McCarver, "New Mexico Raza Unida Announces 1978 Slate," *The Militant*, July 15, 1977; Harry Ring, "N.M. Raza Unida Candidate: I Like Telling People What I Think," *The Militant*, September 2, 1977; Nei Burns, "New Mexico Conference Set," *The Militant*, September 23, 1977.

120. Raza Unida Party, "Raza Unida de Nuevo Mexico: A Manual and Political Program," n.d. (estimate 1977), author's files.

121. Peña interview; Blea interview; Hill interview.

122. Blea interview.

123. Peña interview.

124. Ring, "N.M. Raza Unida Candidate."

125. Office of the Secretary of State, "Canvass of Returns of General Election Held on November 7, 1978—State of New Mexico," n.d., author's files.

126. Blea interview.

127. Peña interview, August 5, 1998.

128. Office of the Secretary of State, "Canvass of Returns."

129. *Rio Grande Sun*, October 30, 1980.

130. Ibid., November 6, 1980.

131. Peña interview.

132. DeVargas interview.

133. Peña interview, July 22, 1997.

## Chapter Nine

1. For a historical analysis that buttresses this argument see Rodolfo Acuña, *Occupied America: A History of Chicanos*, 3d. ed. (Cambridge, Mass.: Harper and Row, 1988); Juan Gómez Quiñonez, *Chicano Politics: Reality and Promise, 1940–1990* (Albuquerque: University of New Mexico Press, 1990); Matt S. Meier and Feliciano Ribera, *Mexican Americans/American Mexicans: From Conquistadores to Chicanos* (New York: Hill and Wang, 1993); John R. Chavez, *The Lost Land: The Chicano Image of the Southwest* (Albuquerque: University of New Mexico Press, 1984); and Carey McWilliams, *North from Mexico* (New York: Greenwood, 1968).

2. David E. Camacho, "La Raza: U.S. Citizens of Mexican Descent in Arizona," in *Politics and Public Policy in Arizona*, ed. Zachary A. Smith (Westport: Praeger, 1993), 142.

3. David J. Weber, *Foreigners in Their Native Land: Historical Roots of the Mexican Americans* (Albuquerque: University of New Mexico Press, 1973), 144.

4. Raul Grijalva, interview by the author, August 21, 1998.

5. Weber, *Foreigners in Their Native Land*, 144.

6. McWilliams, *North from Mexico*, 129.

7. Camacho, "La Raza," 148.

8. For an examination of the Alianza and other mutualista organizations, see José Hernandez, *Mutual Aid for Survival: The Case of the Mexican American* (Melbourne, Fla.: Krieger, 1983).

9. Camacho, "La Raza," 149.

10. Weber, *Foreigners in Their Native Land*, 145.

11. McWilliams, *North from Mexico*, 52.

12. Raymond Johnson Flores, "The Socio-Economic Status Trends of the Mexican People Residing in Arizona" (master's thesis, Arizona State University, 1951).

13. Camacho, "La Raza," 150.

14. Leo Grebler, Joan W. Moore, and Ralph Guzman, *The Mexican American People: The Nation's Second Largest Minority* (New York: Free Press, 1970), 106.

15. See Armando Navarro, "The Evolution of Chicano Politics," *Aztlan: Chicano Journal of the Social Sciences and the Arts*, vol. 5, nos. 1 and 2 (Spring and Fall 1974): 71; and John Martinez, "Leadership and Politics," in *La Raza: Forgotten Americans*, ed. Julian Samora (Notre Dame: University of Notre Dame Press, 1966), 54–55.

16. Gómez Quiñonez, *Chicano Politics*, 70.

17. Maurillo Vigil, *Chicano Politics* (Washington, D.C.: University Press of America, 1977), 205.

18. Joan Moore and Harry Pachon, *Mexican Americans* (Englewood Cliffs, N.J.: Prentice-Hall, 1976), 156.

19. Grijalva interview.

20. Salamon Baldenegro, interview by the author, July 20, 1997.

21. Grijalva interview.

22. F. Arturo Rosales, *Chicano! The History of the Mexican American Civil Rights Movement* (Houston, Tex.: Arte Publico, 1996), 211. Outside of a brief mention by Rosales, very little has been published on the politics of the Chicano Movement in Arizona; much more research needs to be done on its history there. The Movement there also contributed significantly to the dynamism of that era.

23. Baldenegro interview, August 11, 1998.

24. Ibid.

25. For a further examination of MASO's activities, see Rosales, *Chicano!* 212–213.

26. Baldenegro interview.

27. Grijalva interview.

28. Initially it was called the Mexican American Liberation Committee. But, according to historian Lupe Castillo, who was a member, the name was subsequently changed to the Chicano Liberation Committee.

29. Baldenegro interview.

30. Grijalva interview.

31. Frank de la Cruz, interview by the author, August 29, 1998.

32. Rosales, *Chicano!* 211.

33. Lupe Castillo, interview by the author, October 15, 1998.

34. Ibid.

35. Baldenegro interview.

36. Castillo interview.

37. Ibid.

38. De la Cruz interview.

39. Rosales, *Chicano!* 211.

40. Grijalva interview.

41. Castillo interview.

42. Ibid.

43. Baldenegro interview.

44. De la Cruz interview.

45. "A Reprehensible Threat," *Arizona Daily Star,* August 13, 1970.

46. De la Cruz interview.

47. Ibid.

48. Baldenegro interview.

49. De la Cruz interview.

50. Baldenegro interview.

51. "Coalition Protests El Rio Park Snub," *Tucson Daily Citizen,* January 27, 1971.

52. Baldenegro interview, August 11, 1998.

53. Grijalva interview.

54. De la Cruz interview.

55. Grijalva interview.

56. Baldenegro interview, July 20, 1997.

57. Ibid.

58. Grijalva interview.

59. "Chicanos Planning New Party," *Tucson Daily Citizen*, February 23, 1971.

60. Ibid.

61. See "Tucson Chicanos Plan Own Political Party," *Arizona Daily Star*, February 23, 1971, and "Chicanos Planning New Party."

62. "New Political Movements," *Arizona Daily Star*, March 1, 1971.

63. Greg Nickel, "Arizona Raza Unida Party Formed," *The Militant*, March 12, 1971.

64. Ibid.

65. Adolfo Quesada, "La Raza Unida Organized, To Buck Democrats, GOP," *Tucson Daily Citizen*, March 1, 1971.

66. Raza Unida Party, "Report on RUP Conference," n.d., Salamon Baldenegro personal archives.

67. De la Cruz interview.

68. Castillo interview.

69. Baldenegro interview.

70. Grijalva interview.

71. Quesada, "La Raza Unida Organized.".

72. De la Cruz interview.

73. Grijalva interview.

74. Cecilia Baldenegro, interview by the author, July 20, 1997.

75. De la Cruz interview.

76. Castillo interview.

77. Ibid.

78. Ibid.

79. Grijalva interview.

80. *Tucson Daily Citizen*, "200 Join in Chicano Moratorium: Draft Offices Were Picketed," March 25, 1971.

81. Ibid.

82. "La Raza Unida Plans Meeting," *American Daily Star*, March 19, 1971.

83. "To Replace Ruck: Baldenegro Seeks Council Election," *Tucson Daily Citizen*, March 31, 1971.

84. Ibid.

85. Ibid.

86. John Rawlinson, "Record Vote Seen in Mayor-Council Election," *Arizona Daily Star*, October 31, 1971.

87. De la Cruz interview.

88. Raza Unida Party, "Baldenegro—Councilman Ward 1," campaign literature.

89. Grijalva interview.

90. S. Baldenegro interview.

91. John Rawlinson, "Candidates Agree on One Issue: Improvement of Zoo," *Arizona Daily Star*, October 31, 1971.

92. Ibid.

93. S. Baldenegro interview.

94. Rosales, *Chicano!* 231.

95. John Rawlinson, "GOP Keeps Majority, Murphy Upsets Corbett: Romero, Kennedy, Mcloughlin Win," *Arizona Daily Star*, November 1, 1971.

96. De la Cruz interview.

97. "Politics in Arizona," *Arizona Daily Star*, October 25, 1971.

98. S. Baldenegro interview.

99. Grijalva interview.

100. De la Cruz interview.

101. Grijalva interview.

102. José Galvez, "Share Same Goals," *Arizona Daily Star*, May 28, 1972.

103. Castillo interview.

104. De la Cruz interview.

105. Castillo interview.

106. De la Cruz interview.

107. Castillo interview.

108. S. Baldenegro interview, August 11, 1998.

109. Phil Hamilton, "Demos Make Clean Sweep in South Tucson Voting," *Tucson Daily Citizen*, May 30, 1973.

110. De la Cruz interview.

111. C. Baldenegro interview.

112. Castillo interview.

113. Grijalva interview.

114. "La Raza Unida Seeks Funds for Pre–School," *Arizona Daily Star*, June 19, 1973.

115. C. Baldenegro interview.

116. Ibid.

117. Ibid.

118. Ibid.

119. C. Baldenegro interview.

120. Castillo interview.

## Chapter Ten

1. This chapter provides only some important highlights of RUP's organizing efforts in the Midwest; much more research needs to be done.

2. Ricardo Parra, interview by the author, October 10, 1998

3. Ibid.

4. Leo Grebler, Joan W. Moore, and Ralph Guzman, *The Mexican American People: The Nation's Second Largest Minority* (New York: Free Press, 1970), 83. For a historical overview of Méxicano population growth that includes the Midwest, see Matt S. Meier and Feliciano Ribera, *Mexican Americans/American Mexicans: From Conquistadores to Chicanos* (New York: Hill and Wang, 1993), 118–130.

5. Joan Moore and Harry Pachon, *Mexican Americans* (Englewood Cliffs, N.J.: Prentice-Hall, 1976), 112.

6. Ibid., 56.

7. Ibid.

8. Pat Velasquez, interview by the author, October 9, 1998.

9. Ernesto Chacon, interview by the author, October 13, 1998.

10. Richard Santillan, interview by the author, August 25, 1998.

11. Chacon interview.

12. Raza Unida Party Convention, press release, September 4, 1972.

13. Richard Santillan, *La Raza Unida* (Los Angeles: Tlaquilo, 1973), 145.

14. Ignacio Garciá, *United We Win: The Rise and Fall of the Raza Unida Party* (Tucson: Mexican American Studies Center, 1989), 140.

15. "La Raza Unida de Ohio," Raza Unida Party newsletter, June 1972.

16. Parra interview.

17. José Juarez, interview by the author, October 12, 1998.

18. Ricardo Parra, "Mid–West Chicano Organizations: Past, Present, and Possibilities," typescript, Midwest Council of La Raza, University of Notre Dame, Notre Dame, Indiana, March 28, 1974.

19. Olga Villa Parra, interview by the author, October 10, 1998

20. Parra, "Midwest Chicano Organizations," 15.

21. Villa Parra interview.

22. Juarez interview.

23. Villa Parra interview.

24. Parra interview.

25. Moore and Pachon, *The Mexican American People,* 112.

26. Parra interview.

27. Juarez interview.

28. Tony DeLeon, "Chicano Candidate Wins Place on Illinois Ballot," *The Militant,* June 1, 1973.

29. Velasquez interview.

30. Eugenio Lara to Rudy Collum, letter, July 12, 1972.

31. Chacon interview.

32. "La Raza Unida Expands, Opens Office in Jefferson," *The Jefferson,* August 25, 1975.

33. Chacon interview.

34. "La Raza Unida Expands."

35. William G. Murphy, "A Comparison of the Raza Unida Party in Utah and the Raza of Utah," typescript, August 1976, author's files.

36. Ibid.

37. Ibid.

38. Chacon interview

39. Ibid.

40. Ino Alvarez, "Raza Unida Party: El Partido in the Mid-West, Progress Report," April 7, 1973, author's files.

41. Velasquez interview.

42. Chacon interview.

43. Villa Parra interview.

44. Juan José Peña, interview by the author, August 13, 1998.

45. Velasquez interview.

46. Parra, "Mid-West Chicano Organizations."

47. Angel Moreno to José Angel Gutiérrez, letter, November 14, 1973.

48. Chacon interview.

49. Villa Parra interview.

50. Juarez interview.

51. Velasquez interview.
52. Juarez interview.


## Chapter Eleven

1. See former Crusade for Justice leader Ernesto Vigil, *The Crusade for Justice: Chicano Militancy and the Government's War on Dissent* (Madison: University of Wisconsin Press, 1999), a case study of the Crusade for Justice from its inception in 1966 to its demise by the early 1980s.

2. Ignacio Garciá, *United We Win: The Rise and Fall of the Raza Unida Party* (Tucson: Mexican American Research Center, 1989), 96.

3. For a more thorough examination of this debate between these two Texas leaders, see Armando Navarro, *Mexican American Youth Organization: Avant-Garde of the Chicano Movement in Texas* (Austin: University of Texas Press, 1995), 229–230.

4. Garciá, *United We Win*, 102.

5. F. Arturo Rosales, *Chicano! The History of the Mexican American Civil Rights Movement* (Houston: Arte Publico, 1996), 238.

6. Ibid., 91.

7. Rosales, *Chicano!* 238.

8. José Angel Gutiérrez, interviews by the author, September 12–13, 1997.

9. Ibid.

10. Garciá, *United We Win*, 103.

11. My report of what transpired between June and September vis-à-vis the Gutiérrez and Gonzales power struggle is open to interpretation and based only on my sources. Without the opportunity to interview Gonzales, I have based much of my analysis on interviews with Gutiérrez himself and other RUP leaders who were supporters of either Gutiérrez or Gonzales.

12. Gutiérrez interviews.

13. "Raza Unida Holds News Conference," *Albuquerque El Gallo*, June 1972.

14. Gutiérrez interviews.

15. Antonio Camejo, "Raza Unida Party Says No to McGovern and Nixon," *The Militant*, September 22, 1972.

16. José Angel Gutiérrez to President Richard Nixon, letter, July 7, 1972, author's files.

17. Ibid.

18. Nita Gonzales, interview by the author, July 27, 1997.

19. "Gonzales: No Compromise to Any Other Party or Any Other Candidate," *The Militant*, October 13, 1972.

20. Rosales, *Chicano!* 238.

21. Gutiérrez interviews.

22. José Angel Gutiérrez to Democrat presidential candidate George McGovern, letter, August 19,1972.

23. Ibid.

24. Garciá, *United We Win*, 104.

25. Gutiérrez interviews.

26. Garciá, *United We Win*, 104.

27. Gutiérrez interviews.

28. Gonzales interview, July 25, 1997.

29. Sal Carpio, interview by the author, July 24, 1997.

30. Reies Lopez Tijerina to Gutiérrez, letter, August 8, 1972.

31. I was a participant and observer at the convention and headed a small delegation of RUP activists from San Bernardino and Riverside Counties, California.

32. Raza Unida Party, "La Raza Unida Calls National Convention," press release, n.d. (probably late August).

33. Ernesto Vigil, interviews by the author, April 17–18, 1997. See also "Chicanos Ask Probe of Death," *Milwaukee Journal,* September 1, 1972.

34. Raza Unida Party, "Telegram from La Raza Unida Convention," August 30, 1972.

35. Tony Castro, "Delegate Slaying Mars Convention of La Raza Unida," *Washington Post,* September 1, 1972.

36. Vigil interviews.

37. Raza Unida Party Colorado delegation, "Statement on the Death of Ricardo Falcon," August 31, 1972.

38. Garciá, *United We Win,* 106.

39. Raza Unida Party, Colorado delegation, National Convention Headquarters, telegram, August 31, 1972, author's files.

40. George McGovern to José Angel Gutiérrez and RUP, telegram, RUP National Convention Headquarters, August 31, 1972, author's files.

41. Roberto Mondragon to RUP, telegram, RUP National Convention Headquarters, August 31, 1972, author's files.

42. Tony Castro, "Chicano Party Elects Texan as Chairman," *Washington Post,* September 5, 1972.

43. Rosales, *Chicanos!* 239.

44. Garciá, *United We Win,* 106.

45. Many of these observations about RUP's national convention are the result of my involvement and presence as a participant-observer.

46. Carlos Guerra, interview by the author, September 16, 1997.

47. Camejo, "Raza Unida Party Says No."

48. Rogelio Grandos, interview by the author, August 17, 1975.

49. Gutiérrez interviews.

50. Rual Ruiz, interview by the author, May 3, 1997.

51. Raza Unida Party, "Convention Schedule," August 8, 1972.

52. MEChA, "La Raza Unida Convention, El Paso, Texas," report, n.d., author's files.

53. Gutiérrez interviews.

54. Garciá, *United We Win,* 109.

55. Tony Castro, *Chicano Power; The Emergence of Mexican America* (New York: Saturday Review Press, 1974), 179.

56. "Raza Unida Party Declines To Back Either Major Party," *Corpus Christi Caller-Times,* September 3, 1972.

57. Castro, "Delegate Slaying."

58. Fred Aguilar, interview by the author, May 17, 1997.

59. Garciá, *United We Win,* 113.

60. Ibid., 112–113.

61. "La Raza Unida Session Ends; Denverite Slain," *Denver Post,* September 5, 1972.

62. Castro, "Delegate Slaying."

63. Camejo, "Raza Unida Party Says No."

64. Castro, "Chicano Party Elects Texan."

65. MEChA, "Raza Unida Party Convention, El Paso, Texas," report, n.d., author's files.

66. "La Raza Unida Session Ends."

67. Raza Unida Party, "National RUP Results," n.d., author's files.

68. MEChA, "Raza Unida Party Convention."

69. Castro, "Delegate Slaying."

70. Rosales, *Chicano!* 241.

71. Castro, *Chicano Power*, 172–174.

72. Gutiérrez interviews.

73. "La Raza Unida Starts Out as Political Neutral," *Milwaukee Journal*, September 5, 1972.

74. Rosales, *Chicano!* 241; and Garciá, *United We Win*, 116.

75. "Congreso for Land and Culture," *Grito Del Norte* November 1972.

76. Rosales, *Chicano!* 242.

77. "Congreso for Land and Culture."

78. Peña, *Chicano Movement in New México*, 65.

79. Richard Garcia, "New México Meeting Backs Raza Unida," *The Militant*, November 17, 1972.

80. Juan José Peña, interview by the author, July 22, 1997

81. "Congreso for Land and Culture."

82. "Colorado's La Raza Unida Party Position Statement," *Albuquerque El Gallo*, November–December 1973.

83. Vigil interviews.

84. For an examination of how the two major party national committees are structured and operated, see Frank J. Sorauf, *Party Politics in America* (Boston: Little, Brown, 1968).

85. Gutiérrez interview, September 1, 1998.

86. Ignacio Garciá, interview by the author, September 1, 1998.

87. "El Gallo Informs the People on La Raza Unida Party," *Albuquerque El Gallo*, n.d. (vol. 6, no. 5).

88. José Calderon, interview by the author, October 20, 1997.

89. Vigil interviews.

90. Raza Unida Party Congreso Meeting, minutes, November 25, 1972.

91. In this section I examine the salient issues that permeated the politics of self-destruction within the context of the Congreso, rather than every Congreso meeting. Much more research needs to be done in this area. Very little has been written on the developments that occurred within the Congreso and how they affected RUP's ultimate decline.

92. "Ballot Protest Ruling Expected on Monday," *Denver Post*, October 29, 1972.

93. Vigil interviews.

94. "Colorado's La Raza Unida Party."

95. Gutiérrez interviews.

96. Raza Unida Party Congreso Meeting, minutes, November 26, 1972.

97. Ibid., November 27,1972.

98. Gutiérrez interview, September 1, 1998.

99. Tito Lucero to all Congreso representatives, letter, December 28, 1972.

100. "Colorado's La Raza Unida Party."

101. "José Angel Gutiérrez at the Houston Convention," *Caracol* 1, no. 3 (November 1974).
102. José Angel Gutiérrez, "Congreso De Aztlán," Fall 1977.
103. Gutiérrez interview.
104. Peña interview, September 3, 1998.
105. Ibid.
106. Congreso de Aztlán workshop, minutes, January 18, 19, 20, 1974.
107. National Chicano Forum Steering Committee, letter, n.d. (March 1976).
108. Harry Ring, "400 Attend National Chicano Forum in Utah," *The Militant,* June 18, 1976.
109. "Support Grows for Antideportation Actions," *The Militant,* June 10, 1977.
110. Gutiérrez's letter, "Call for Action," was published in its entirety in *The Militant,* "A Call for Action," June 10, 1977.
111. The conference will be dealt with in greater length in subsequent chapters. Reports of the number of conference attendees differ from article to article. This figure was taken from political scientist Mario Barrera, "Factionalism Splits Chicano Movement," source unknown, November 16–22, 1977.
112. Ibid.
113. José G. Perez, "Chicanos Unite To Fight Carter's Deportation Scheme," *The Militant,* November 11, 1977.
114. "In the summer of 1977, Carter unveiled his plan to control the border. The Carter Plan . . . offered amnesty for the undocumented workers and their families entering the country before January 1970; those arriving after January 1970 would assume a temporary nondeportable worker's status; it fined employers for hiring undocumented workers, allocating more funds for border guards and foreign aid and loans to Mexico." Rodolfo Acuña, *Occupied America: A History of Chicanos,* 3. ed. (Cambridge, Mass.: Harper and Row, 1988), 36.
115. Perez, "Chicanos Unite To Fight."
116. From José Angel Gutiérrez to Maria Elena Martinez, letter, January 17, 1979.
117. Gutiérrez interview.
118. Aguilar interview.
119. For a comprehensive analysis of the political rupture that occurred within RUP in Cristal in 1975 and after, see Armando Navarro, *The Cristal Experiment: The Chicano Struggle for Community Control* (Madison: University of Wisconsin Press, 1998), 158–343.
120. Vigil interviews.
121. M. Romero, 1980 RUP National Convention Report, June 20–22, 1980.
122. Ibid.
123. This section provides a brief analysis and examination of RUP's involvement in the international political arena. Much more research needs to be done in order to give a fair and comprehensive appraisal of RUP's involvement in foreign affairs.
124. Gutiérrez interview.
125. For an extensive analysis of efforts by Méxicanos in the United States to bridge or create what I call an *acercamiento* with Mexico, see: Tatcho Mindiola and Max Martinez, eds., "Introduction to Chicano-Méxicano Relations," in *Chicano-Méxicano Relations* (Houston: Mexican American Studies Program, 1986), 1–34; and Maria Rosa Garcia-Acevedo, "Return to Aztlán: México's Policies toward Chicanas/os," in *Chicanas/Chicanos at the Crossroads: Social, Economic, and Political Change,* ed. David R. Maciel and Isidrio D. Ortiz (Tucson: University of Arizona Press, 1996), 130–155.
126. Peña interview, July 22, 1997

127. For a thorough examination of the first takeover or "revolt," see Navarro, *The Cristal Experiment*, 17–51.

128. Gutiérrez interview.

129. Ibid.

130. Mindiola and Martinez, "Chicano-Méxicano Relations," 4–5.

131. Ibid., 265.

132. Garcia-Acevedo, "Return to Aztlán," 135.

133. Gutiérrez interview.

134. Ibid.

135. Ibid.

136. Navarro, *The Cristal Experiment*, 163–166

137. Aguilar interview.

138. Gutiérrez interview.

139. Ibid.

140. Garcia-Acevedo, "Return to Aztlán," 135–136.

141. Andres Torres, interview by the author, November 15, 1997.

142. Gutiérrez interview.

143. Ibid.

144. Navarro, *The Cristal Experiment*, 212.

145. Andres Torres, interview by the author, November 15, 1997.

146. Peña interview.

147. Aguilar interview.

148. Peña interview.

149. Ibid.

150. Aguilar interview.

151. The delegation was led by RUP national chair Juan José Peña from New México. It included eight others: Larry and Rebecca Hill and Fred Saint John, New México; Frank Schafer Corona, Washington D.C.; Danny Ozuna, Tony Gonzales, and Miguel Perez, California; and Eddie Canales, Texas.

152. Ibid.

153. Rebecca Hill, interview by the author, August 28, 1998.

154. Ibid.

155. Peña interview.

156. Garciá interview, April 14, 1999.

157. Peña interview.

158. Ibid.

159. Ibid.

## Chapter Twelve

1. Cireño Rodriguez, interview by the author, April 10, 1997.

2. For an in-depth examination of Chicanismo, see: Ignacio Garciá, *Chicanismo: The Forging of a Militant Ethos among Mexican Americans* (Tucson: University of Arizona Press, 1997).

3. Eddie Montour, interview by the author, July 23, 1997.

4. Herman Baca, interview by the author, May 31, 1997.

5. Ignacio Garciá, interview by the author, April 18,1997.

6. On Chicanismo and its impact on the Chicano Movement, see Garciá, *Chicanismo*.

7. Ernesto Vigil, interview by the author, April 18, 1997.

8. José Angel Gutiérrez, "Méxicanos Need To Control Their Own Destinies," in *Pain and Promise: The Chicano Today*, ed. Edward Simmen (New York: New American Library, 1972), 249–257. This section of the book also offers an overview of what Gutiérrez meant by control.

9. Fred Aguilar, interview by the author, May 17, 1997.

10. Raul Ruiz, interview by the author, May 3, 1997.

11. Mario Compean, interview by the author, May 5, 1997.

12. Garciá interview.

13. Rodriguez interview, April 19, 1997.

14. Marta Cotera, interview by the author, September 11, 1997.

15. Maria Elena Martinez, interview by the author, September 11, 1997.

16. For Gonzales's analysis of the importance of nationalism as a key to unity, see Rodolfo Gonzales, "Chicano Nationalism: The Key to Unity for La Raza," in *A Documentary History of the Mexican Americans*, ed. Wayne Moquin and Charles Van Doren (New York: Bantam, 1971), 488–493.

17. Lita Gonzales, interview by the author, July 24, 1997.

18. Compean interview.

19. Richard Santillan, interview by the author, August 6, 1997.

20. Juan José Peña, interview by the author, August 22, 1997.

21. Baca interview.

22. Xenaro Ayala, interview by the author, August 9, 1997.

23. Ruiz interview.

24. Raza Unida Party, "Raza Unida de Nuevo México: A Manual and Political Program," typescript, 1976.

25. Vigil interview.

26. Carlos Guerra, interview by the author, September 16, 1997.

27. Baca interview..

28. Enrique Cardiel, interview by the author, July 22, 1997.

29. Ayala interview.

30. Ibid.

31. Cardiel interview.

32. Ayala interview.

33. Congreso del Partido Nacional de La Raza Unida, "Re-Emergence of El Partido Nacional de la Raza Unida," August 13–15, 1993.

34. The various exogenous and endogenous antagonisms to be examined represent what I consider the most salient related to third parties; there are, however, others that need to be examined. For other factors that impacted RUP's development, particularly in Texas, refer to Armando Navarro, *The Cristal Experiment: The Chicano Struggle for Community Control* (Madison: University of Wisconsin Press, 1998), 344–374.

35. Compean interview.

36. Montour interview.

37. Andres Torres, interview by the author, November 15, 1997.

38. J. David Gillispie, *Politics at the Periphery* (Columbia: University of South Carolina Press, 1993), 24.

39. Richard Santillan, "The Politics of Cultural Nationalism: El Partido de la Raza Unida in Southern California (1969–1978)" (Ph.D. diss., Claremont Graduate University, Claremont, Calif., 1978), 271–272.

40. Ibid.

41. Ernesto Vigil, in *The Crusade for Justice: Chicano Militancy and the Government's War on Dissent* (Madison: University of Wisconsin Press, 1999), provides a well-documented scholarly study on the government's infiltration, disruption, and destabilization of the Crusade for Justice—the mother organization of RUP in Colorado.

42. For a broader examination of the this argument, see Navarro, *The Cristal Experiment*.

43. For an in-depth analysis of the "Viva Yo" generation, see Armando Navarro, "The Post-Mortem Politics of the Chicano Movement, 1975–1996," *Perspectives in Mexican American Studies*, vol. 6 (1997).

44. "Hispanic" denotes a lineage or cultural heritage and roots exclusive to Spain. In the political context of the late 1970s and 1980s, the term was used erroneously by governmental agencies, corporations, and some moderate-to-conservative groups to describe all persons with origins in Latin America or Spain; its incorrectness stems from the fact that the cultural roots of most people from Latin America lie both in Spain and in Latin America itself.

## Epilogue

1. David Montejano examines the argument that the United States is declining in his anthology *Chicano Politics and Society in the Late Twentieth Century* (Austin: University of Texas Press, 1999), 239–241.

2. For an overview analysis on the status of Latinos in the United States, see Tad Szulc, "An American Experience: The Fastest-Growing Minority in America," *Parade Magazine*, January 3, 1999, 4–6.

3. "Intelligence for Hispanic Marketing," *Hispanic Confidential*, April 1, 1996.

4. "Latino Population Up in Every State Since 90," *Hispanic Link Weekly Report*, September 14, 1998.

5. Jason Margolis, "State's White Majority Is in Minority," *San Francisco Examiner*, February 12, 1999.

6. For an overview of the projected demographic profile of the Latino community, see Armando Navarro, *The Cristal Experiment: The Struggle for Chicano Community Control* (Madison. University of Wisconsin Press, 1998), epilogue.

7. Ricardo Alonzo—Zaldivar, "Big Apple Takes on a Flavor of Mexico, *Los Angeles Times*, February 19, 1999.

8. Brook Larmer, "Latin USA, How Young Hispanics Are Changing America," *Newsweek*, July 12, 1999.

9. Nancy Cleeland, "Unionizing Is Catch–22 for Illegal Immigrants," *Los Angeles Times*, January 16, 2000

10. Szulc, "An American Experience," 6.

11. "California: Loving It, Leaving It," *The Press Enterprise*, December 28, 1994.

12. Kitty Calavita, "Immigration: Why Revive an Inhumane Program?" *Los Angeles Times*, July 18, 1999.

13. Nancy Cleeland, "Immigration Policies Threaten U.S. Growth, " *Los Angeles Times,* April 11, 1999.

14. "Mexico's Workers' Patience Wears Thin," *The Press Enterprise,* January 2, 2000.

15. For a brilliant exposé of the brutal realities of the U.S. global domination argument, see Michael Parenti, *Against Empire* (San Francisco: City Lights, 1995).

16. There are several works on the ill-effects produced by globalization, including Jeremy Brecher and Tim Costello, *Global Village or Global Pillage: Economic Reconstruction from the Bottom Up* (Boston: South End, 1994).

17. For a scholar that propounds such a view, see Paul Kennedy, *Preparing for the Twenty-First Century* (New York: Vintage, 1994).

18. In my forthcoming book entitled *What Needs to Be Done: The Building of a New Movement* I will examine in great detail all aspects of the crises that will pervade the twenty-first century. In addition, I will delineate a course of ideological, organizational, and strategic options that Méxicanos and Latinos need to consider for extricating themselves from the morass of the crisis the liberal capitalist system has fostered.

19. Dave Lesher and Dan Morain, "Davis Asks Court To Mediate on Prop. 187," *Los Angeles Times,* April 16, 1999.

20. Patrick J. McDonnell, "Prop.187 Talks Offered Davis Few Choices," *Los Angeles Times,* July 30, 1999.

21. "Prop. 187 Backers Plan New Campaign," *The Press Enterprise,* January 5, 2000.

22. Tim Goden, "Judge Chops Prop. 209," *The Press Enterprise,* December 24, 1996.

23. For a much more comprehensive examination of this argument, see Navarro, *The Cristal Experiment,* epilogue.

24. Steve Scott, "Competing for the New Majority Vote," *California Journal,* January 2000, 20.

25. NALEO, National Roster of Latino Elected Officials, 1990, 1997.

26. Scott, "Competing for the New Majority Vote,"18.

27. James P. Pinkerton, "The Future Is Neither Quotas nor Separatism," *Los Angeles Times,* March 2, 1997.

28. Peter Mass, "Built Moderate and Rising Fast in California," *U.S. News and World Report,* March 17, 1997, 28.

29. Scott, "Competing for the New Majority," 21.

30. For details on these issues, see Nicholas Riccardi, "Molina Accuses Supervisors of Racism in Debate over Hospital," *Los Angeles Times,* April 14, 1999; Dan Morain, "Bustamante to Try to Block Prop. 187 Mediation Request," *Los Angeles Times,* April 22, 1999; Antonio R. Villaraigosa, "End the Politics of Vitriol and Division over Immigration," *Los Angeles Times,* April 18, 1999.

31. Elisabeth Jensen, Gregg Braxton, and Dana Calvo, "NBC, NAACP, in Pact to Boost Minorities in TV," *Los Angeles Times,* January 6, 2000; Dana Calve and Gregg Braxton, "NBC–NAACP Diversity Plan Irks Coalition," *Los Angeles Times,* January 7, 2000.

32. José Angel Gutiérrez, interview by the author, January 13, 2000.

33. Maribel Hasting, "Se Reduce el Indece de la Pobreza de los Latinos," *La Opinion,* October 1, 1999.

34. Tony Pugh, "Poverty Falls in U.S. but Not in California," *The Press Enterprise,* October1, 1999

35. "By the Numbers: Hispanics in California," *California Journal,* January 2000, 38–39.

36. Marx Arax, Mary Curtis, and Soraya Sashadder Nelson, "California's Income Gap Grows amid Prosperity," *Los Angeles Times,* January 9, 2000.

37. Oswaldo Zavala, "Study: Two-thirds of Latino Students Not Prepared to Go to College," *Hispanic Link,* December 20, 1999.

38. "The Status of Latinos in California Report," *William C. Velásquez Institute,* July 1999.

39. Bob Egelko, "UC Berkeley Suit over Rrejection of Minority Applicants," *The Press Enterprise,* February 3, 1999.

40. Gutiérrez interview.

41. Kenneth R. Weiss, "UC Regents OK Plan to Admit Top 4%," *Los Angeles Times,* March 20, 1999.

42. Emily Bazar, "Fewer Minorities Apply to Medical Schools," *The Press Enterprise,* March 23, 1999.

43. Green Lining Institute Report on the U.C. System

44. *The Press Enterprise,* "Poll Boosts Third Party," April 13, 1995.

45. Steve Scott, "The No-Party System," *California Journal,* December 1999.

46. Sam Delson, "Growing Number of Voters Ditching Traditional Parties," *The Press Enterprise,* May 10, 1999.

47. Matt Bai and David Brauer, "Jesse Ventura's 'Body' Politics," *Newsweek,* November 16, 1998.

48. Jenifer Warren and Maria L. LaGanga, "Upset Puts Green Party on the Map," *Los Angeles Times,* April 1, 1999.

49. Richard L. Berke, "Vote Turnout Lowest since '42, Study Says," *The Press Enterprise,* May 10, 1999.

50. Miguel Bustillo, "GOP Survey Offers Hope for Gaining Latino Voters," *Los Angeles Times,* January 14, 2000.

51. Berke, "Vote Trnout Lowest."

52. Ruben Navarrette, "Immigration Lessons of a 6-Year-Old," *Los Angeles Times,* January 16, 2000.

53. James L Wood and Maurice Jackson, *Social Movements: Development, Participation, and Dynamics* (Belmont, Calif.: Wadsworth, 1982), 3.

54. Norman I. Fainstein and Susan S. Fainstein, *Urban Political Movements: The Search for Power by Minority Groups in American Cities* (Englewood Cliffs, N. J.: Prentice- Hall, 1974), 249.

55. This book in progress is my fourth of a four part "cuadrilogy." The "seminal" work is in three parts. Part 1 will provide a historical examination of the evolution of Latino politics in general and Méxicano politics in particular from 1846 to 2000. Part 2 provides a present and future demographic, political, economic, social, educational, and cultural profile and analysis of Latinos. And Part 3 provides four strategic options and the tactical aspects of implementing each proposed option in response to the question, What Needs to Be Done?

56. Armando Navarro, "The Post Mortem Politics of the Chicano Movement: 1975–1996," *Perspectives in Mexican American Studies,* vol. 6 (1997).

# Index

*Throughout this index tables are indicated by the page number followed by (t).*

*continued*

*continued*

*continued*

as organizer, 233–34; platform, 241; Ruiz as chairman, 238, 241, 242; Socialist Workers' Party (SWP), 238; state delegations, 239(t); and Tijerina, 184, 240; triggers polarization in California, 153; urban expansion approved, 42; voting results, 242. *See also* Gutiérrez-Gonzales power struggle

national RUP convention (1980), Albuquerque, 253–54

nationalism, cultural (*see* cultural nationalism)

Navarro, Alfonso, 128

Navarro, Armando: accused in incident, 122; author, ix; at California conference (1970), 123–24; CFR state director, 170; chairman of MAPA chapter, 112; Chicano of the Year (1972), 131; co-chair of National Chicano Forum, 226; death threat, 127; demands superintendent's resignation, 120; in early organizational meetings, 111; opposes Gonzales, 151; part of delegation to Mexico (1976), 72; plans National Chicano Forum, 249; recommendations for future, 297–300; resigns as RUP chairperson, 131–32; rift with Luna (1971), 129

NBC (National Broadcasting Company), 290–91

Nebraska, LRU case study, 224

Neighborhood Youth Corps, 82

New Guard, 66, 74

New Hispano Party, 82

New Mexico Raza Unida Party (RUP): advocacy agenda, 1977–1981, 196–98; anti-Republicanism, 175; ballot-access laws, 198; and bilingualism, 177; Chicano Associated Student Organization (CASO), 181; Chicano Movement (CM), 173, 178, 179–80; Chicanos United for Justice (CUJ), 188; constitutional convention (1910), 176–77; convention, statewide, 192–93; counties organizing RUP, 181, 185; Crusade for Justice influences politics, 179–80; De Vargas, Antonio, sole candidate, 199; demise of, 200–201; East Las Vegas issues, 187; eclectic ideology of, 1971–1981, 194–96; electoral agenda (1974–1976), 191–93; electoral agenda (1977–1981), 198–200; endorses SWP candidate for governor, 193; first statewide convention (1972), 182–83; Las Gorras Blancas (the White Caps), 174–75; legacy of, 200; Marxist (Maoist) ideology, 191–95; and MAYO, 182; overview, 173–79; Partido Socialista de los Trabajadores (Socialist Workers Party), 198; Peña resigns as national chairperson, 200; platform (1972), 184; police brutality in Albuquerque, 180; political climate, 1965–1972,

179–80; and PPU, 174–175; Pueblo Unido (People United), 192; radical image of, 196; reasons for demise, 200–201; Rio Arriba County, 198, 200; Rio Arriba history, 189–90; rise of, 1971–1972, 180–85; San Miguel County RUP chapter, 187–88, 197; and SLP, 181, 194; social change advocate (1973–1976), 185–88, 191–93; State Central Committee, 182; and SWP, 193, 195; United Mexican American Students (UMAS), 180; Violence Committee, 187–88; violence erupts, 188

new movement proposal, 283–300

New Party, 4, 48, 296

Nimmo, Dan, 3

Nixon administration, 129

Nixon, Richard, 234, 236, 239, 242

North American Free Trade Agreement, 286

Oakland, California, 135

"obituary" for RUP, 57. *See also* politics of self-destruction

Obledo, Mario, 236

Ochoa, Ralph, 141

October League, 264

Oficina de la Gente, 37

Ojeda, David, 33

Oliva, Tom, 144

Olmeda, Cruz, 246

Oñate, Juan, 173

Ontario, California, 119, 121, 130, 166, 251

Operation Clean-Up (1968), 114

Operation Gate Keeper, 288

opposition to RUP, 41

options, future. *See* future options for Latinos and Méxicanos

organizing efforts, early, 262

organizing strategy for RUP lacking, 280–81

Ornelas, Carlos, 135

Orozco, E. C., 153

Ortega, Joaquin, 177

Ortiz, Desiderio, 239(t)

Ortiz, Juan, 34

Paiz, Patrico, 188

Palacios, Diana, 29

Palestinian Liberation Organization (PLO), 196, 256

Parenti, Michael, 12

Parra, Olga Villa, 222, 227

Parra, Ricardo, 222, 227, 239(t)

partido, forming a new Méxicano, 296–98